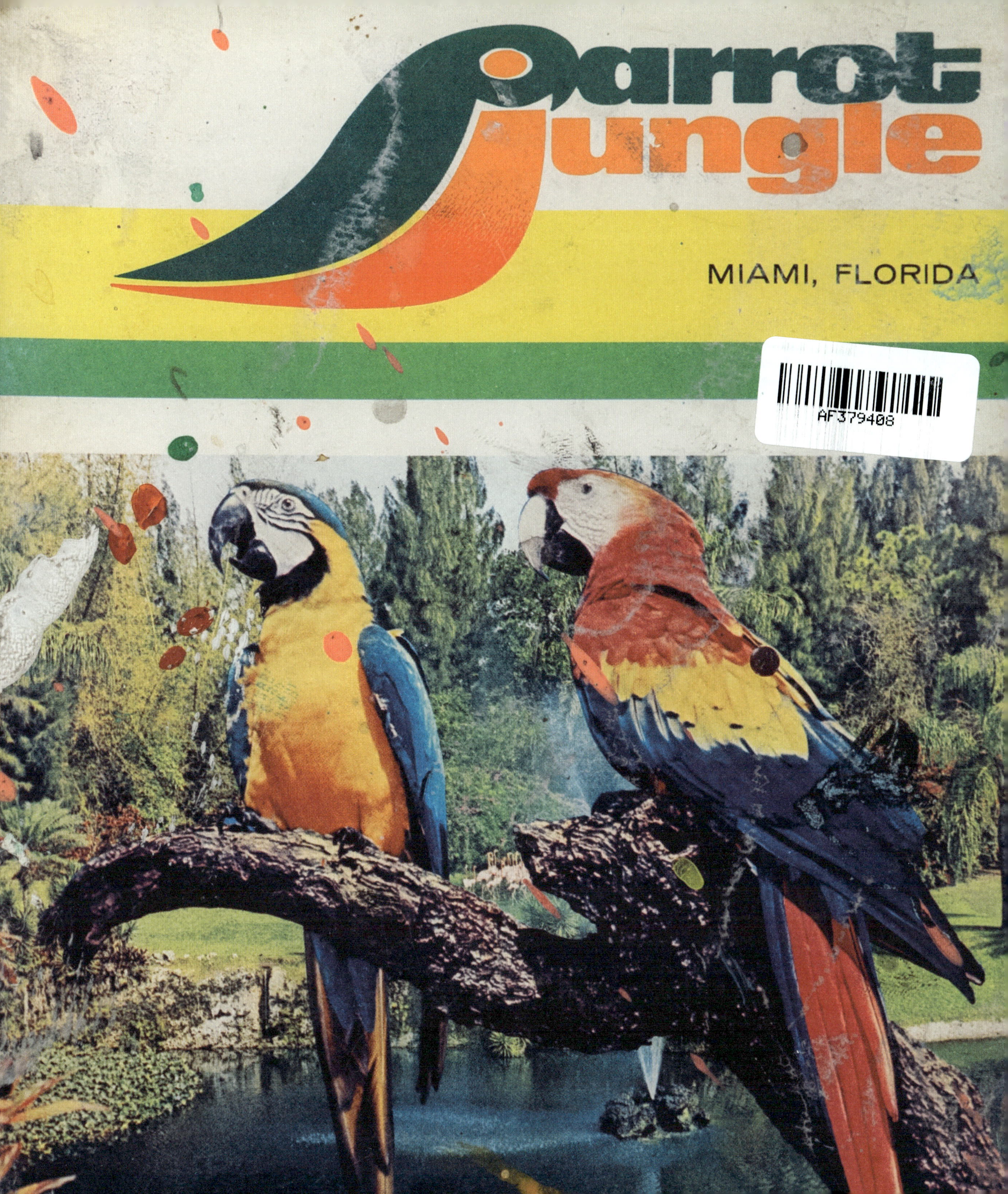

parrot jungle
MIAMI, FLORIDA
AF379408

Walasse Ting

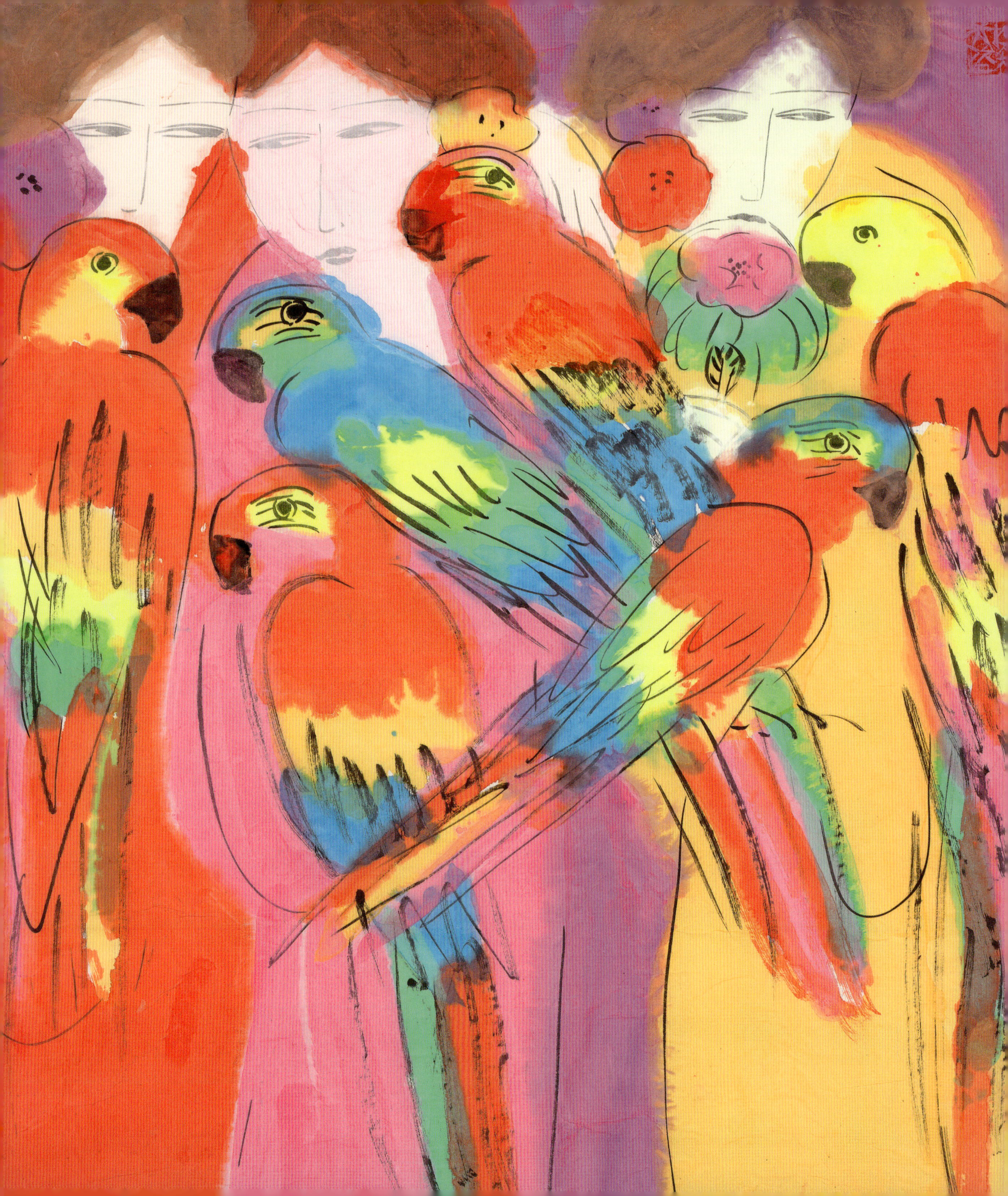

Walasse Ting
Parrot Jungle

edited by
Ariella Wolens

introduction by
Bonnie Clearwater

additional texts by
Pierre Alechinsky, Xiao (Amanda) Ju,
and Mia Ting

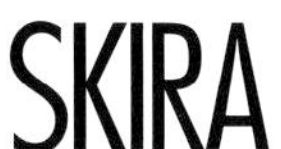 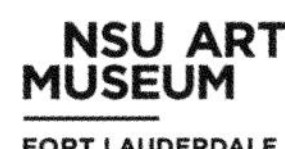 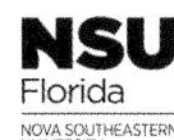

Walasse Ting
Parrot Jungle

NSU Art Museum Fort Lauderdale
November 9, 2023 – March 12, 2024
Curated by Ariella Wolens
Bryant-Taylor Curator

Walasse Ting: Parrot Jungle is sponsored by those who wish to remain anonymous,
Stephen & Joan Marks, Barron Family Foundation, Imperfect Family Foundation,
Funding Arts Broward, Inc., Sam Francis Foundation in honor of Francis' 100th birthday,
Marlène Brody, Marion Lefebre & Robert S. Pynoos, Wenise Wong & Eric Barron.

Major support for NSU Art Museum Fort Lauderdale is provided by the David
and Francie Horvitz Family Foundation Endowment, the City of Fort Lauderdale,
Wege Foundation, Community Foundation of Broward, Lillian S. Wells Foundation,
the Broward County Cultural Division, the Cultural Council, and the Broward County
Board of County Commissioners, and the State of Florida through the Division
of Arts and Culture and the National Endowment for the Arts.

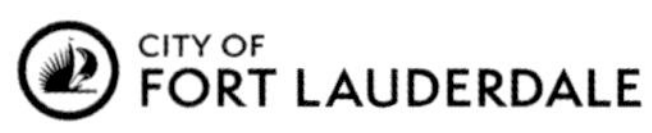
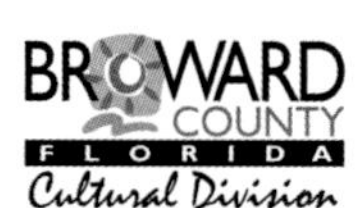
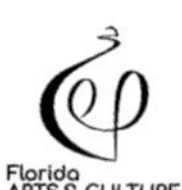
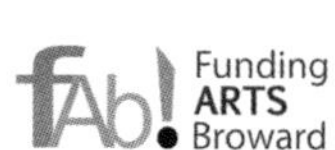
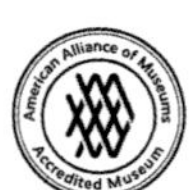

Contents

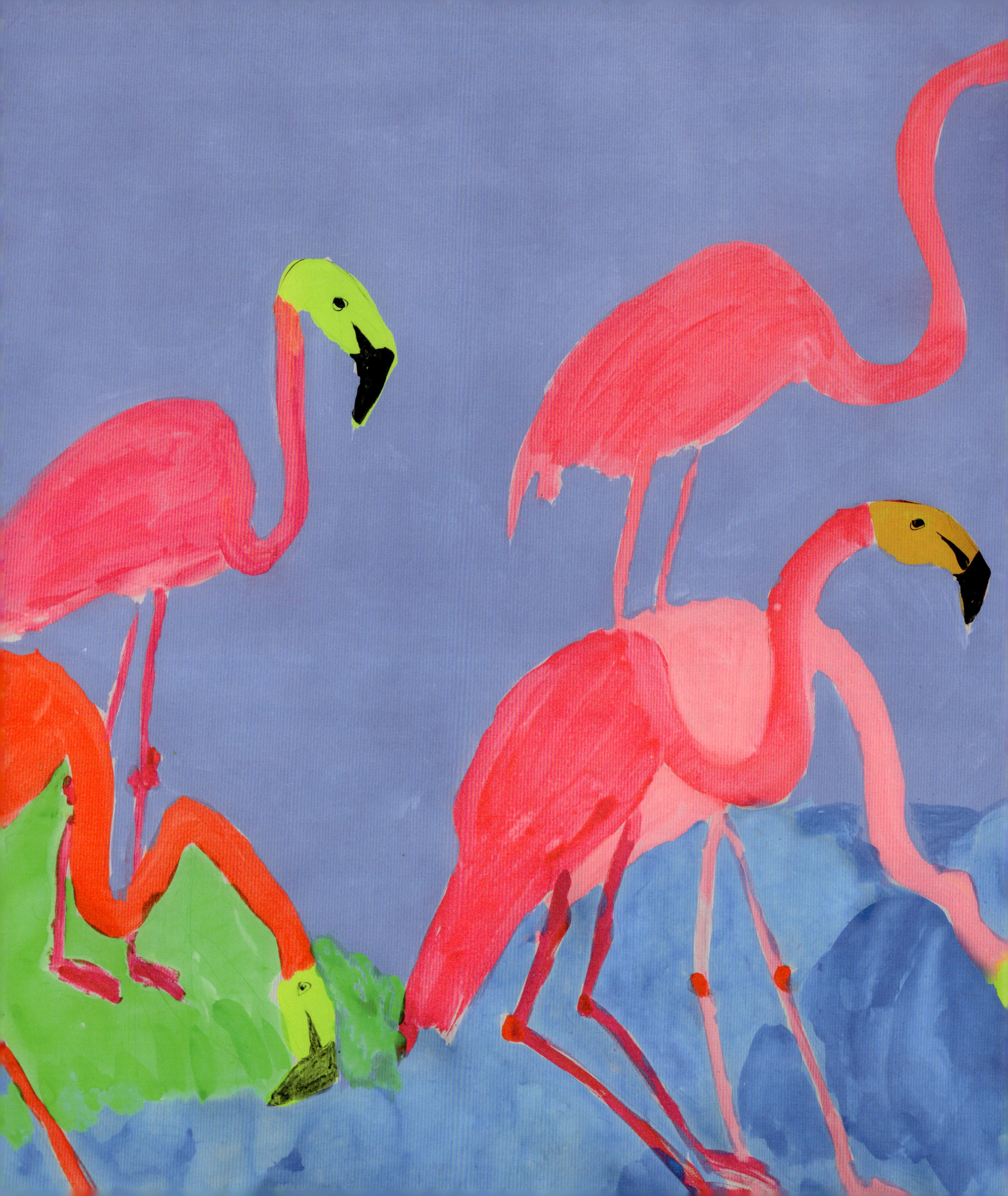

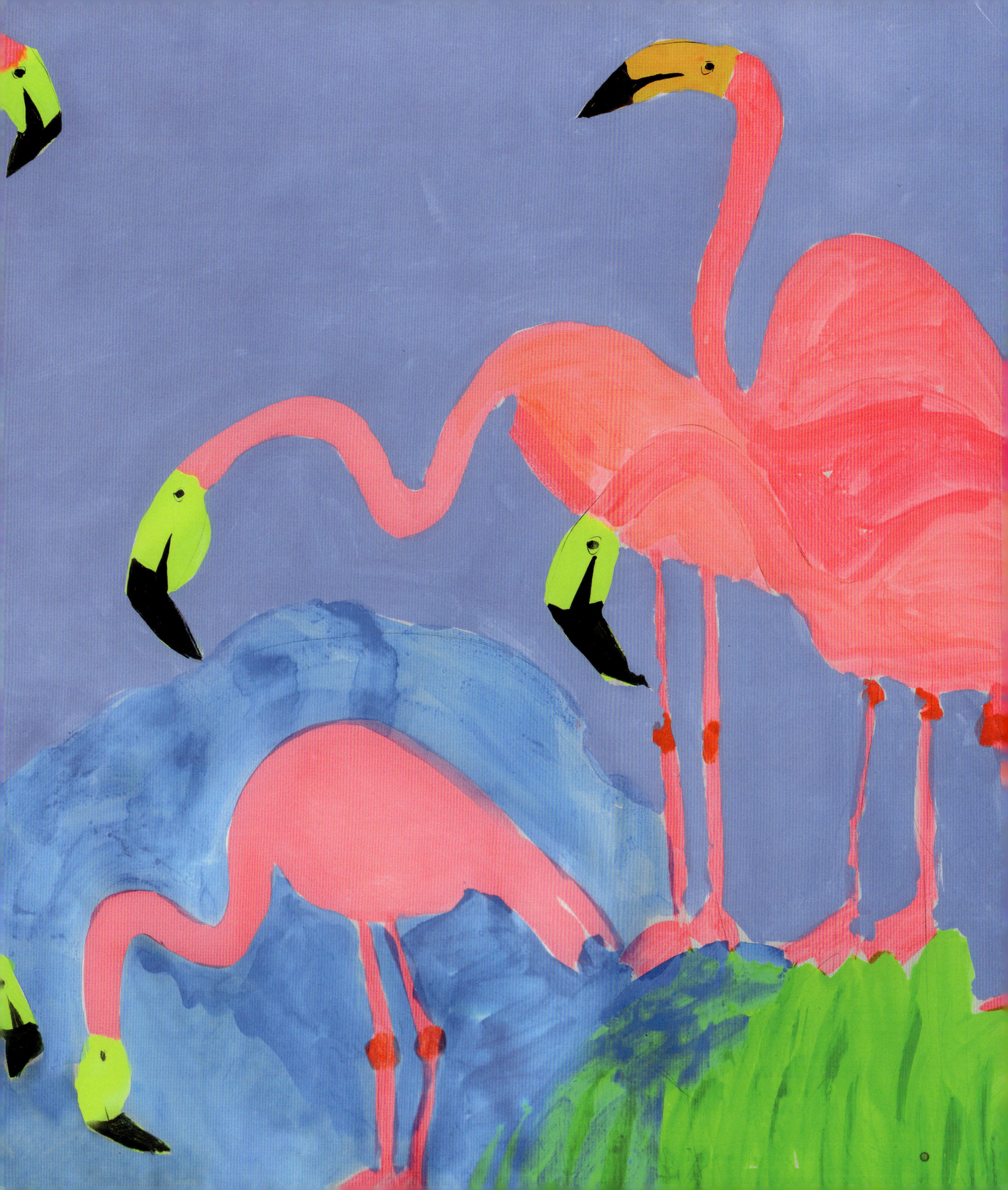

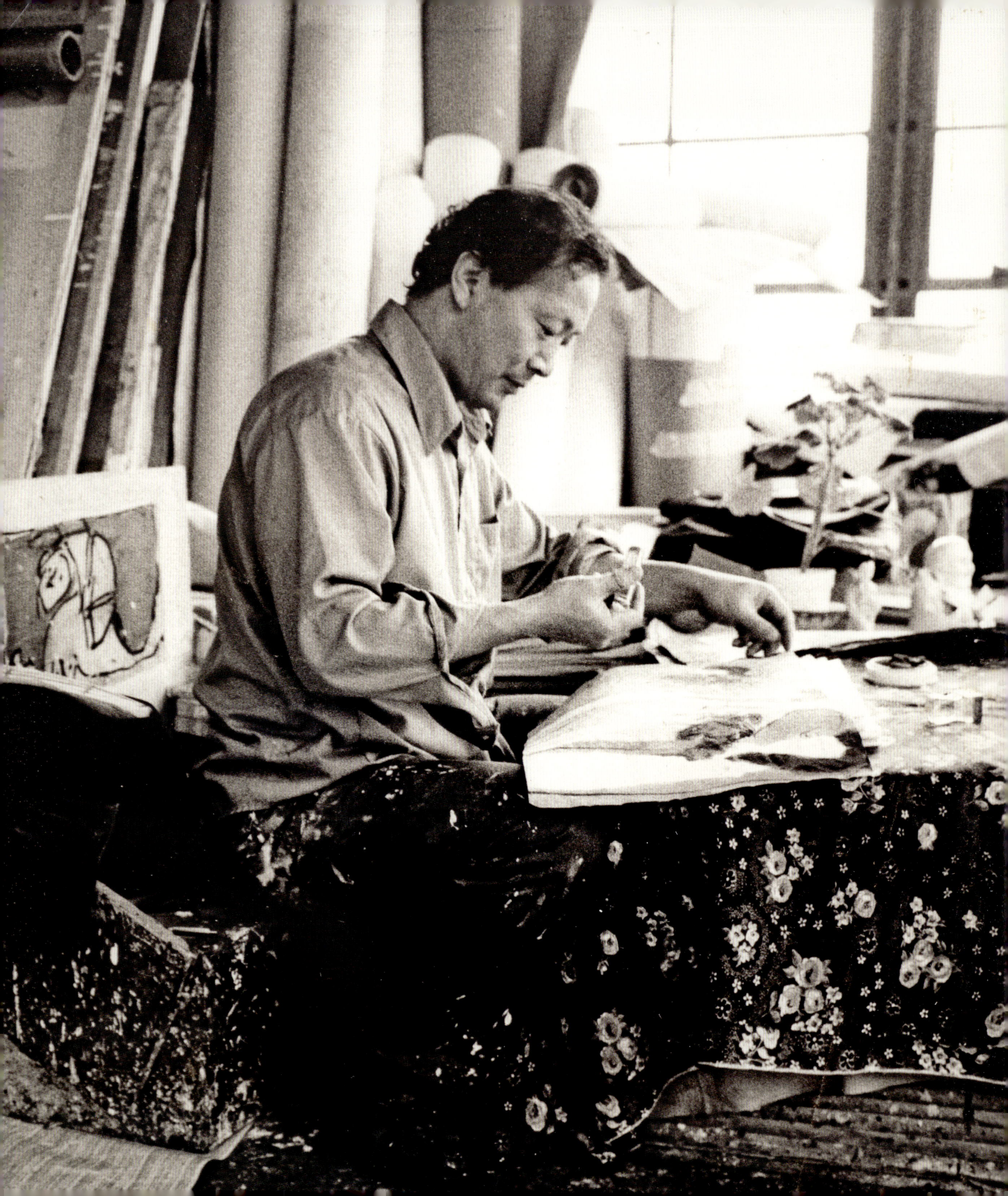

Introduction

NSU Art Museum Fort Lauderdale is proud to organize and present the first American museum retrospective of Walasse Ting. Born in Wuxi, China, in 1928, Ting achieved prominence as a fiercely independent artist in each of the art worlds he orbited: Hong Kong, Paris, New York, and the Netherlands. Essentially self-taught in the Chinese tradition of calligraphic brushwork, the European avant-garde, American Abstract Expressionism and Pop Art, the gregarious Ting was a natural bridge between various factions of artists, while never aligning with any one group. Although he achieved notoriety for his neon-hued paintings of spritely nudes, luscious flowers and a menagerie of animals and birds, his most well-known achievement was the publication of the artist book *1¢ Life* (1964). This book was a labor of love that compiled 62 original lithographs of 27 mid-century artists with Ting's poetry. All pages are loose and removable. It represented a snapshot of New York's multifaceted art of the time and of the artist friends Ting accumulated across continents. The European artists he befriended in Paris: Pierre Alechinsky, Karel Appel and Asger Jorn—were spiritually linked with American abstract painters Sam Francis and Joan Mitchell, Pop artists Roy Lichtenstein, Claes Oldenburg, Andy Warhol, and Tom Wesselmann, and Fluxus artists Allan Kaprow and Öyvind Fahlström. And then there were the artists like Ting, who could not be easily categorized: Robert Indiana, Alfred Jensen, Alfred Leslie, and the Austrian-born Kiki (Kiki O.K.) Kogelnik, who also found a place in *1¢ Life*. Produced with the support of his close friend Sam Francis and the maverick Detroit collector Florence Barron, published by Eberhard W. Kornfeld, Bern, Switzerland, and printed by Maurice Beaudet, this magnum opus made its museum debut at the Museum of Modern Art in New York in the exhibition *Contemporary Painters and Sculptors as Printmakers* (1964).

The artist who placed himself at the center of the New York art world in 1964 with the publication of *1¢ Life* and who garnered critical recognition, major gallery representation, and inclusion in significant museum exhibitions including *Fresh Air School*: *Exhibition of Paintings*: *Sam Francis*, *Joan Mitchell*, *Walasse Ting*, Museum of Art, Carnegie Institute (1972–73); whose work was collected by museums around the world; and who counted a Guggenheim Memorial Fellowship (1970) among his honors, seemed to slip out of the annals of Western art history. Claiming no affiliation with any one art faction or any one nation, Ting was an outlier who was difficult to pin down. Other factors contributed to Ting's apparent obscurity: at the height of his American success, his New York gallery Lefebre closed following the death of its founder John Lefebre in 1986, and to this day he is without New York gallery representation. The gallery's closing was a significant loss as, despite Ting's steadfast disassociation with any one art movement, his work was optimally contextualized in a gallery that successfully marketed and placed works from its uniquely focused stable of artists, including Pol Bury, Reinhoud and Carl-Henning Pedersen, in private collections, museum exhibitions and collections. Ting spent his last decades shuttling between America, Asia, and the Netherlands. Moreover, he painted nudes, animals and still lifes with vibrant and lush pinks, blues, greens and yellows at a time when figurative art and delectability was derided by the New York art world establishment. Most regrettably, a debilitating brain hemorrhage cut short his career.

And yet, Ting, the artist who followed his own path in his art and poetry, was hiding in plain sight all along. The recent revival of interest in his work is spontaneous and organic. Despite lacking gallery representation in New York, Ting was a sensation in Hong Kong, represented and promoted by Alisan Fine Arts since the 1980s, and Europe, where he showed with Galerie Birch in Copenhagen and Gallery Delaive in Amsterdam. His work was reverently collected by private collectors and museums, including major institutions such as the Carnegie Museum of Art, Pittsburgh; Guggenheim Museum, New York; the Metropolitan Museum of Art, New York; the Norton Simon Museum in Pasadena, and the Stedelijk Museum, Amsterdam, among others. Posthumous retrospectives were held at the Taipei Fine Arts Museum (2010) and the Musée Cernuschi, Paris (2016), both with accompanying monographs.

Ting's close friendship with artists and his artist-book compendium *1¢ Life* perpetuated his reputation and has sparked recent exhibitions. Notably, his correspondence with his long-time friend Sam Francis, now preserved at the Getty Research Institute, Los Angeles, was the subject of an article by John Seed, "DEAR Big SAM, The Letters of Walasse Ting to Sam Francis Tell the Story of Their Friendship Over Time" (*Arts of Asia*, 2018), which in turn sparked the exhibition of the work of Francis and Ting in *Celebrating a Friendship* at Alisan Fine Arts, Hong Kong (2021). In the course of organizing this retrospective, the museum's curatorial staff discovered that New York University's Grey Art Gallery will be including Ting's work in the exhibition, *American in Paris: Artists Working in Postwar France, 1946–1962*, and The Norton Simon Museum in Pasadena, California, is currently showcasing his work in their permanent collection galleries.

How did NSU Art Museum Fort Lauderdale come to organize Ting's first retrospective in an American museum? As home to the largest collection of work by Cobra artists in an U.S. institution, NSU Art Museum has made the research and exhibition of this post-war European art movement a major focus. Cobra, an international, interdisciplinary and collective art movement dating from 1948 to 1951, is an acronym for the three capital cities from which its founding members originated: Copenhagen, Brussels and Amsterdam. The museum's Cobra collection of over 1,700 works exists thanks to a phenomenal gift of Miami Beach collectors Meyer and Golda Marks in 1978. The keen eye and determination of these avid collectors formed a historically significant and comprehensive collection of Cobra art and archival materials. The museum's Bryant-Taylor Curator Ariella Wolens, who holds a specialty in Cobra art, was introduced to the resplendent art of Walasse Ting by Pierre Alechinsky while conducting research for the museum's exhibition *Confrontation: Pierre Alechinsky and Keith Haring* (2022). Ting acquainted Alechinsky with the practice of East Asian calligraphy, and the duo collaborated on several works (their so-called four-handed paintings), of which two are in the museum's collection; the museum also owns Ting's *1¢ Life* (all gifted by

Meyer and Golda Marks). With the museum's focus on furthering the research of Cobra's extension into contemporary art, Ariella Wolens embarked on the organization of this major retrospective and accompanying book with great admiration for the artist and his place in art history, and respect for the museum's dedication to the work of Cobra artists and their circle. Many thanks go to her for bringing this artist into sharper focus.

Ting's daughter Mia and son Jesse are exceptional keepers of their father's flame. Their love for their unconventional father and deep knowledge of his work was indispensable to organizing this retrospective and book. Mia's preface situates her father in South Florida, where he luxuriated in the region's tropical milieu during family treks to visit his retired in-laws there. His paintings of Florida's exotic birds and resplendent flowers gave him a fitting excuse to let loose with hot hued flourishes. Mia and Jesse's incomparable cooperation greatly contributed to the success of this project and we thank them for all their support and participation. We are so honored as well to include Alechinsky's tribute to his dear friend and collaborator in this publication. We are thankful to him for bringing his fraternal light to Ting's work.

The support for this project also extends to Cobra collectors Meyer and Golda Marks' next generation. Their daughter Linda Nathan Marks along with Berenice Fisher, and their son Stephen Marks and wife Joan have devoted considerable resources and time to furthering the preservation, research and exhibition of their parents' treasured collection, for which we are forever grateful.

Ting's friendships and associations were so far ranging that at times there was no more than a one degree of separation between us and his supporters. I was elated to discover that Florence Barron was an early and influential patron of Ting's as it reunited me with her son Guy Barron and his wife Nora, who not only loaned work to the exhibition but also supported the exhibition through the Barron Family Foundation, with additional support from their son Eric Barron and his wife Wenise Wong. I was also delighted to discover Ting's close friendship with Roy Lichtenstein, which prompted my reconnection with my colleague Jack Cowart, Director of the Roy Lichtenstein Foundation, who responded favorably to this project and Dorothy Lichtenstein, who enthusiastically recommended a grant from the Imperfect Family Foundation. The longtime friendship between Ting and Sam Francis also garnered a generous grant from the artist's foundation to mark Francis' 100th birthday, with the encouragement of Executive Director/President Debra Burchett-Lere and Associate Director Beth Ann Whittaker-Williams. The early major support provided by an anonymous donor long associated with NSU Art Museum made it possible to move forward with this exhibition and book as did Funding Arts Broward's commitment, along with Marlène Brody, Marion Lefebre and Robert S. Pynoos. We thank all of these contributors for supporting this retrospective and publication. Deep appreciation also goes to Nancy Bryant and Jerry Taylor for endowing the Bryant-Taylor Curator through the Jerry Taylor and Nancy Bryant Foundation.

The global appreciation of Ting's work meant gathering many essential works from international and American museums and private collections. We thank these lenders for their generosity in sharing Ting's work in this retrospective: Guy and Nora Barron, Marlène Brody, the Guggenheim Museum, Museum Jorn and the Stedelijk Museum.

I am thankful to NSU Art Museum's curatorial staff for providing exceptional support for the research assistance, coordination, and realization of the exhibition and book: Oliver Loaiza, Caroline McNabb, Jordyn Newsome, Chuck Ross, Rebecca Vaughn, and our team of art preparators. Thanks also goes to David Guidi for preparing the visuals for this book. Appreciation is also extended to Skira for editing, designing and publishing this book.

Thanks also go to the Board of Governors of NSU Art Museum, chaired by Michelle Howland, for their generous support of the museum and our exhibition and education programs.

Bonnie Clearwater
Director and Chief Curator
NSU Art Museum Fort Lauderdale

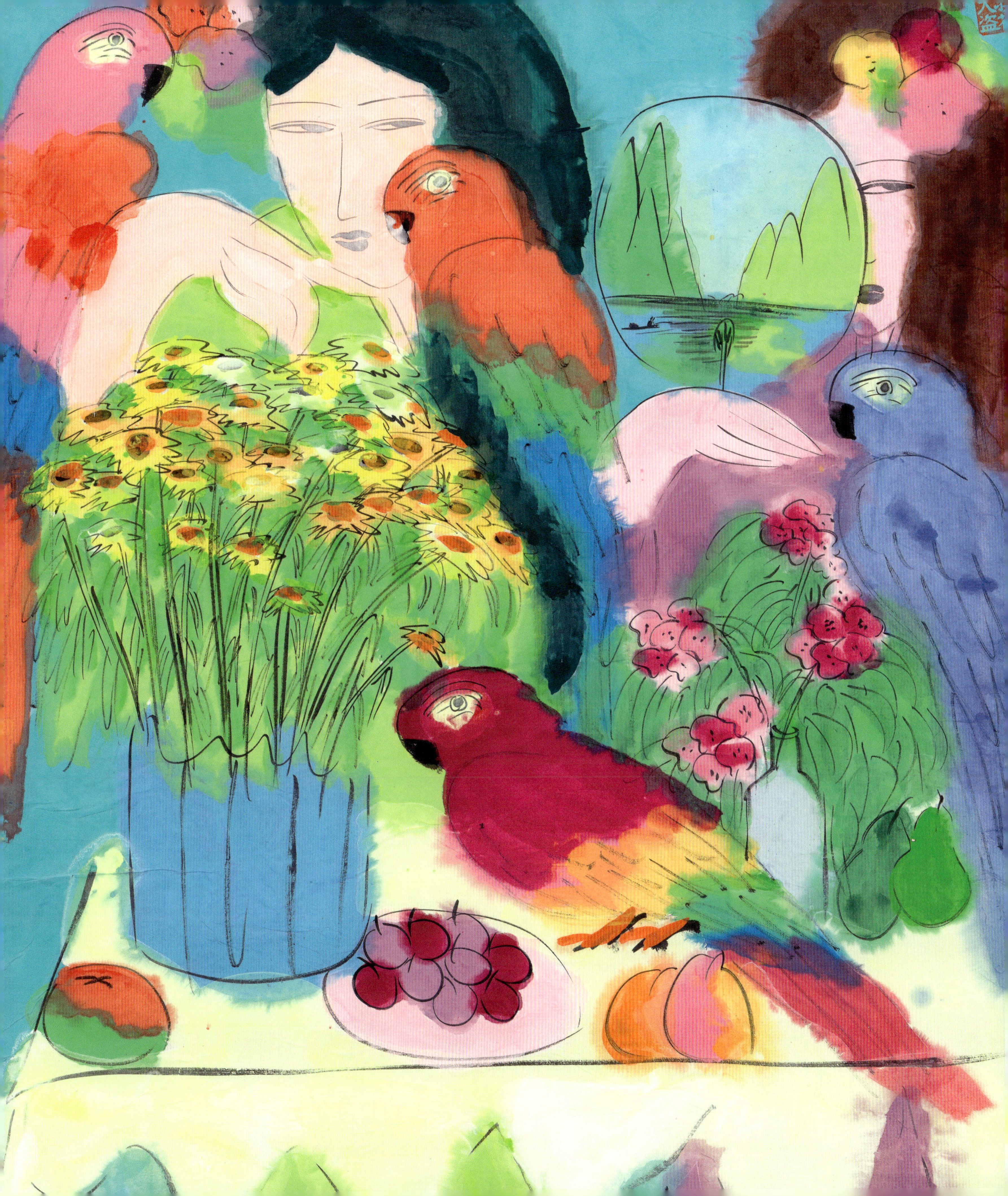

Preface

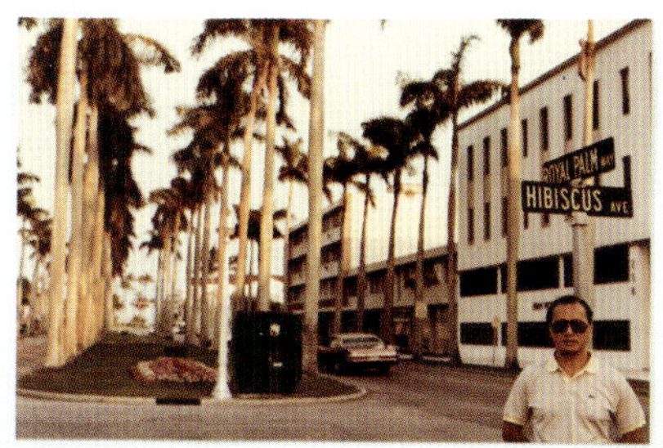

fig. 1. Walasse Ting in West Palm Beach, c. 1980

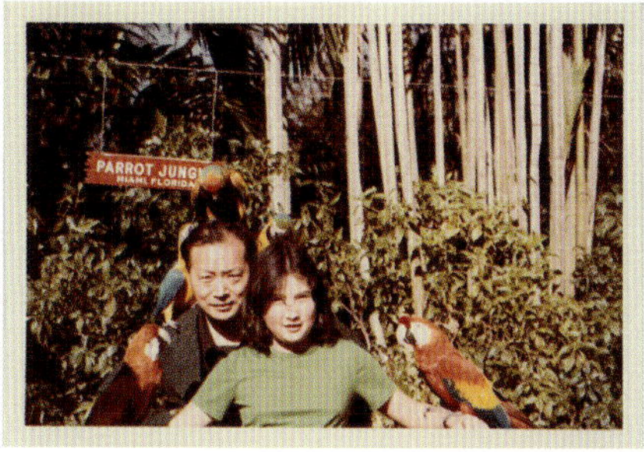

fig. 2. Mia and Walasse Ting at Parrot Jungle, Pinecrest Gardens, Pinecrest, Florida, February 1977

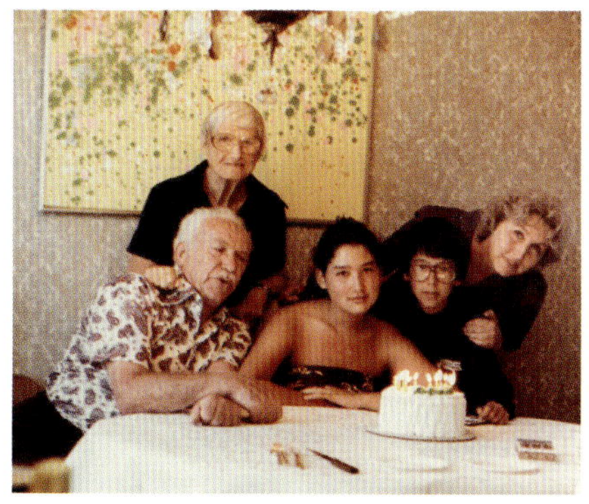

fig. 3. Mia Ting's maternal grandparents Al and Rose Lipton, Mia, Jesse and Natalie Ting, in front of a Walasse Ting painting, Century Village, West Palm Beach, c.1980

In 1971, when I was five years old and my brother Jesse a mere two, something terrible happened: my beloved grandparents retired and moved to Florida. West Palm Beach? Century Village? It may as well have been the moon. We would no longer have Sunday visits with my grandparents who brought whitefish, "novie," homemade potato salad and bialys from Brooklyn to Greenwich Village. And who was going to take me to Carvel?

As it turned out, Florida was NOT the moon. It was way better. Sunshine, swimming pools and beaches. Flowers and fruit everywhere.

My grandfather said that they lived in paradise. Maybe he was right?

Oddly enough, my father, Walasse Ting, loved it best of all. It was surprising. I could barely imagine my father out of New York City. No studio? No painting? No Chinatown? They all seemed like impossibilities. Especially for a man who hated the country (including our summer bungalow in Orange County) with no painting, no Chinese restaurants and plenty of mosquitos.

Every year we would look forward to our February vacation in Florida. We would pick oranges at Anthony's groves, huge honeybells dripping with juice. It was also strawberry and tomato season. While my mother and I picked fruit, my father and Jesse would have "Tomato Wars," which consisted of them throwing overripe tomatoes at each other, running through the fields. They would emerge laughing, covered in tomato pulp.

My father loved it all, the big blue sky and the bright sunshine. We would eat mangoes, papayas and other tropical fruit every day, as well as grapefruit from Grandpa's little tree. Daddy took photographs of all the flowers—oleander, bougainvillea, orange blossom and his favorite, hibiscus.

Best of all was our annual trip to Parrot Jungle. Parrots! Flamingos! Every kind of bird in every color! My father took countless photographs of all of us, separately and in groups: parrots on our arms, parrots on our heads! Our most exciting encounter was with the resplendent creatures at Flamingo Lake. While we couldn't get very close to them, my father would be snapping away at the reposing, very beautiful flamingos. Every once in a while, they would run in a thrilling group of cascading pinks and oranges.

Sometimes we would go to Miami Beach and admire the Art Deco buildings, oddly reminiscent of the architecture in Shanghai's foreign concessions. We would end a beautiful day with dinner in Miami at The Embers, where Daddy loved the spit-roasted duck.

These memories would have to sustain us until our next visit. But my father had more than memories to sustain him. Hundreds and hundreds of photographs that he would paint from. Chinese ink for the lines of the birds, mixes of bright acrylics for the color. A quick stroke of the brush and the birds and flowers would emerge. Then shades of green, blue and magenta, would take life during the cold New York winters.

My father later traveled to other tropical places across the world that also inspired him to make beautiful paintings. Wherever he was, in Florida or perhaps in the Far East, each day he picked up a wide brush full of paint; yellow perhaps. He gave life to the iris in a vase, the feathers of a parrot, the hair of a woman reclining. Each color in turn found its place, the tableau becoming more and more alive, until the final colors were added and the painting was complete.

Mia Ting
July 2023

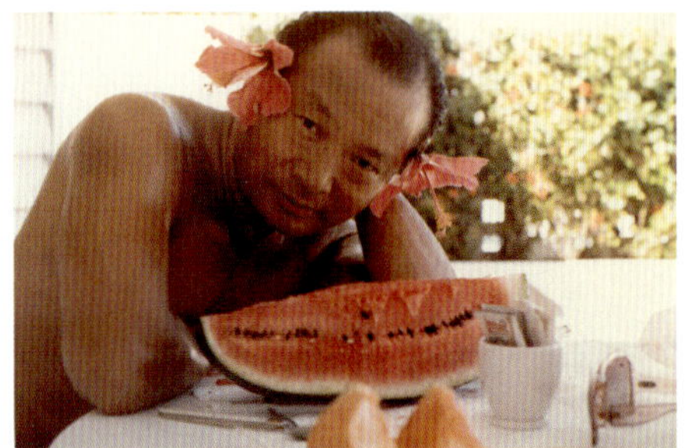

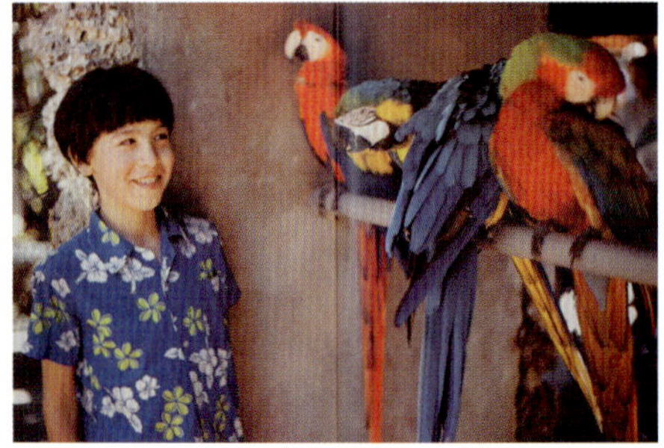

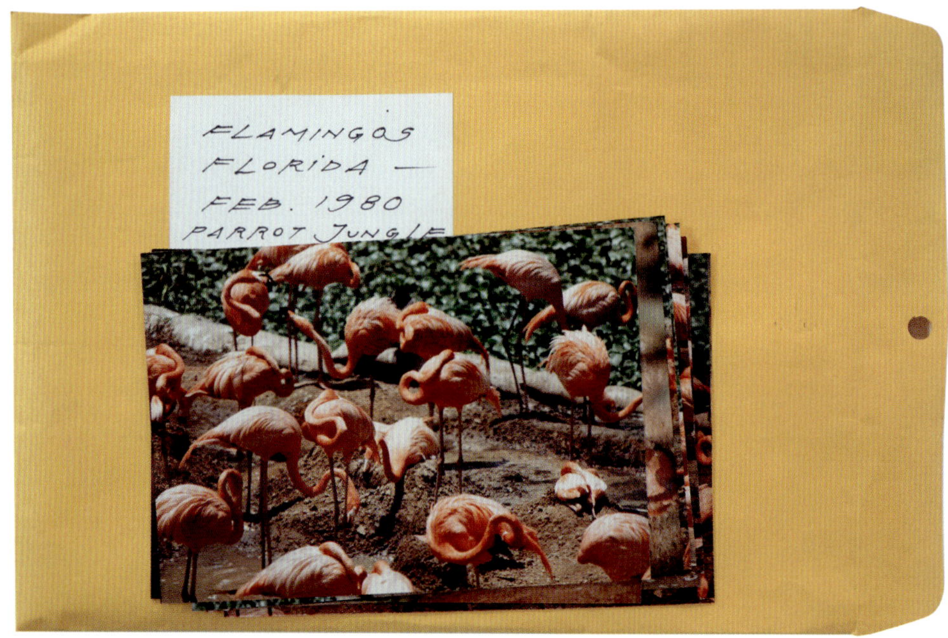

fig. 4. Walasse Ting posing with hibiscus and watermelon, West Palm Beach, c. late 1980s

fig. 5. Jesse Ting at Parrot Jungle, Pinecrest Gardens, Pinecrest, Florida, c. 1977

fig. 6. Walasse Ting's collection of Parrot Jungle flamingo photographs, February 1980

fig. 7. Walasse Ting at Parrot Jungle, February 1977

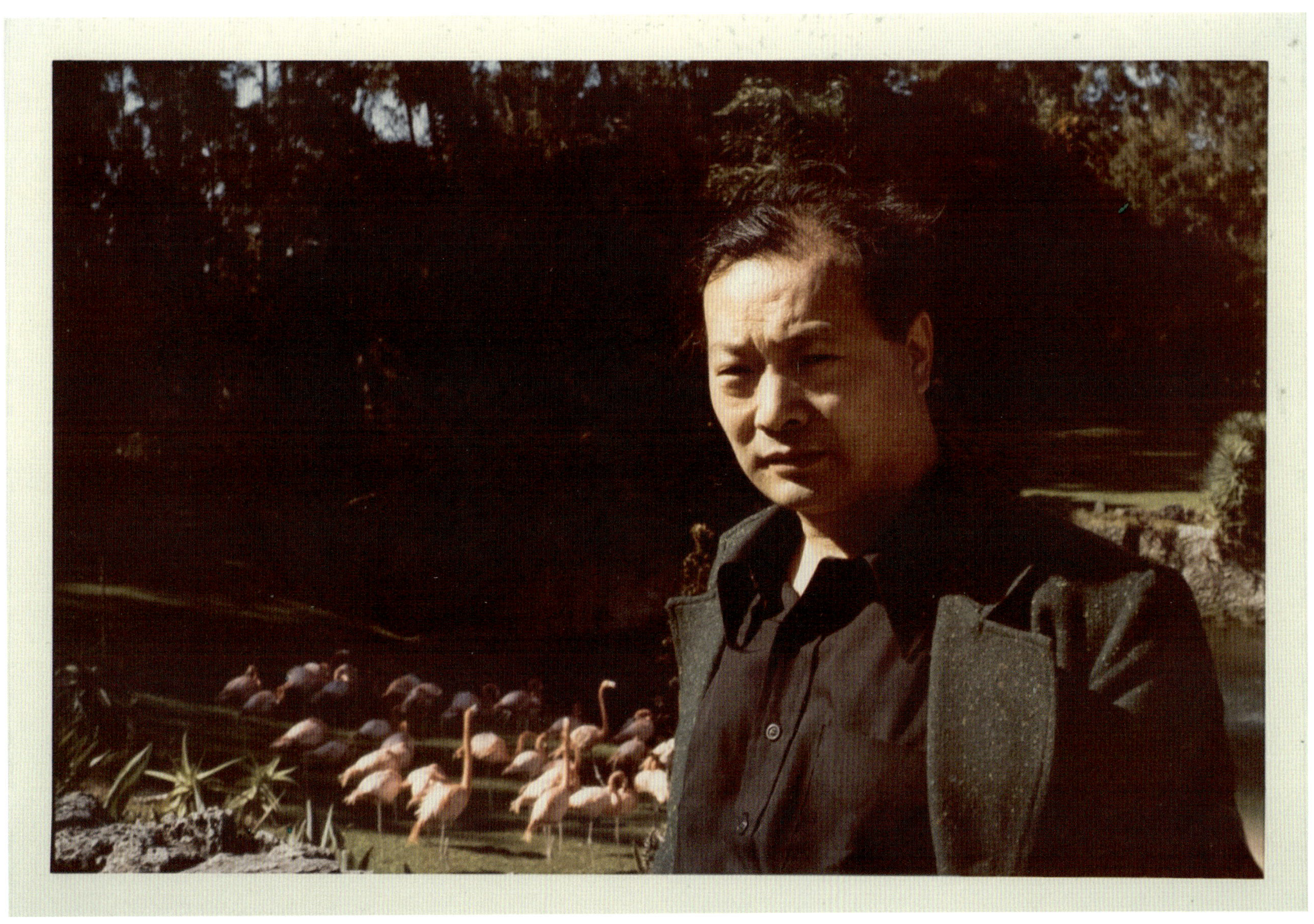

Plates

Section One

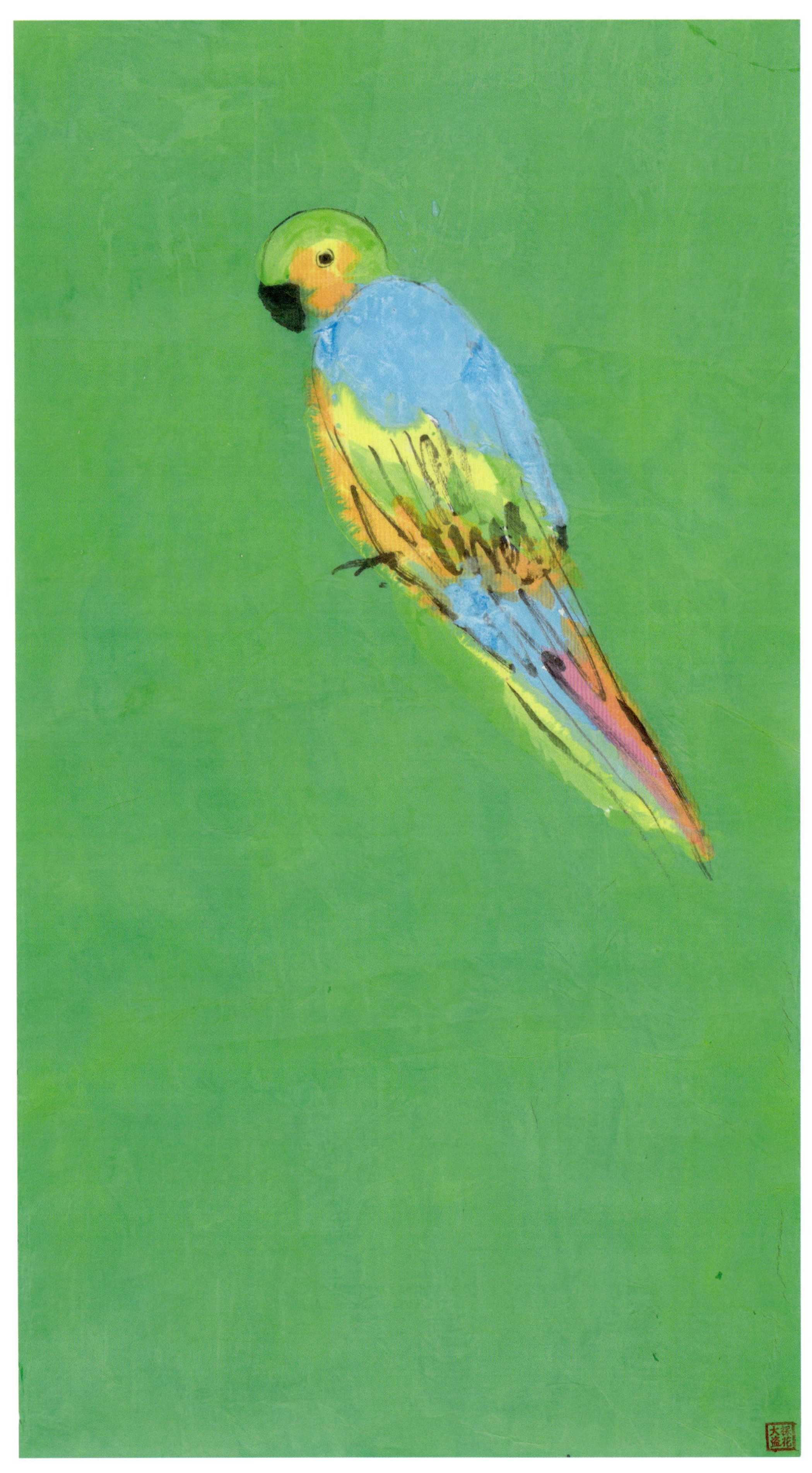

Pages 20–23
Untitled, late 1970s–early 1980s
Acrylic and Chinese ink on rice paper
70 × 38 in. / 177.8 × 96.5 cm (each)

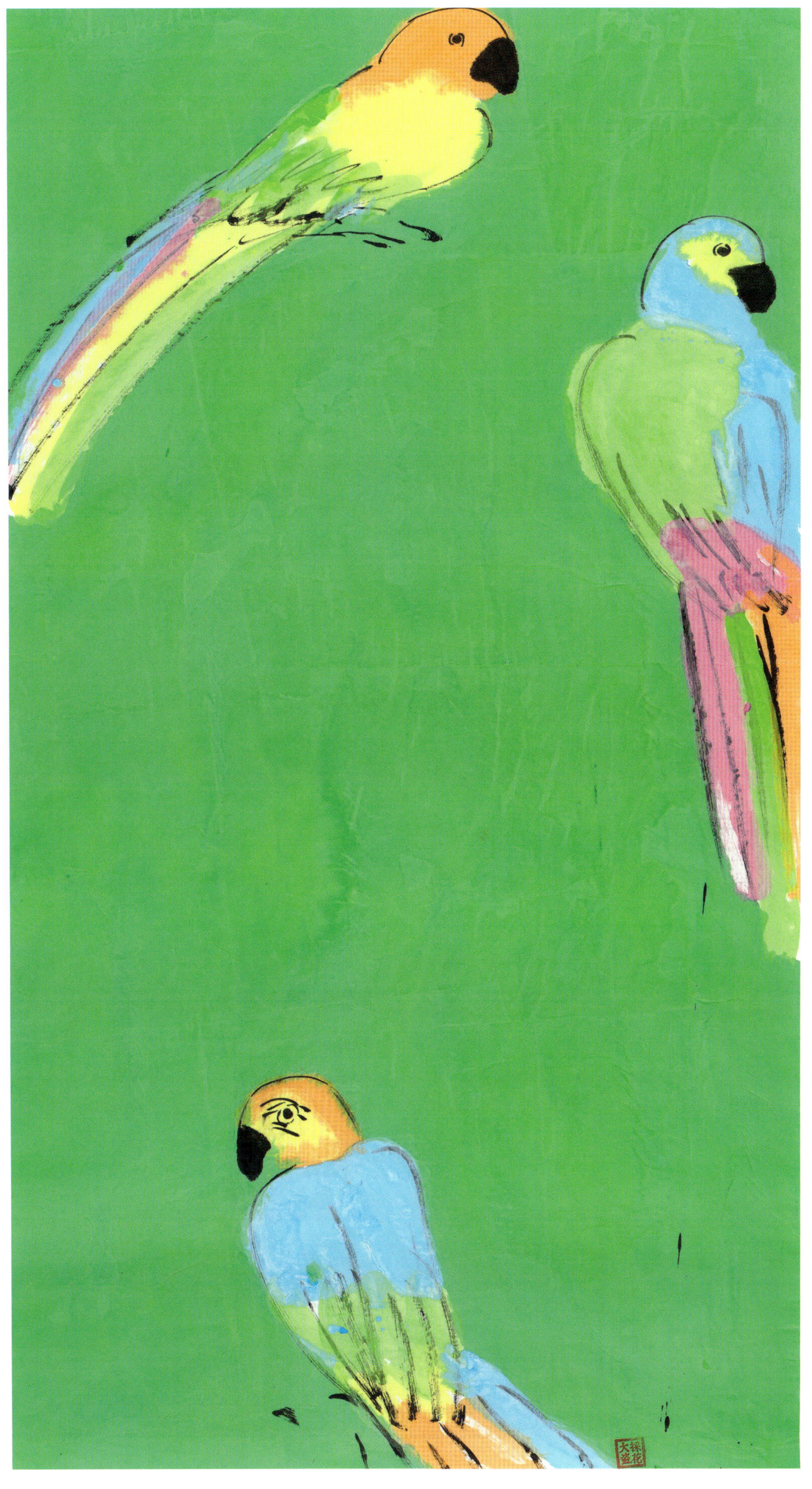

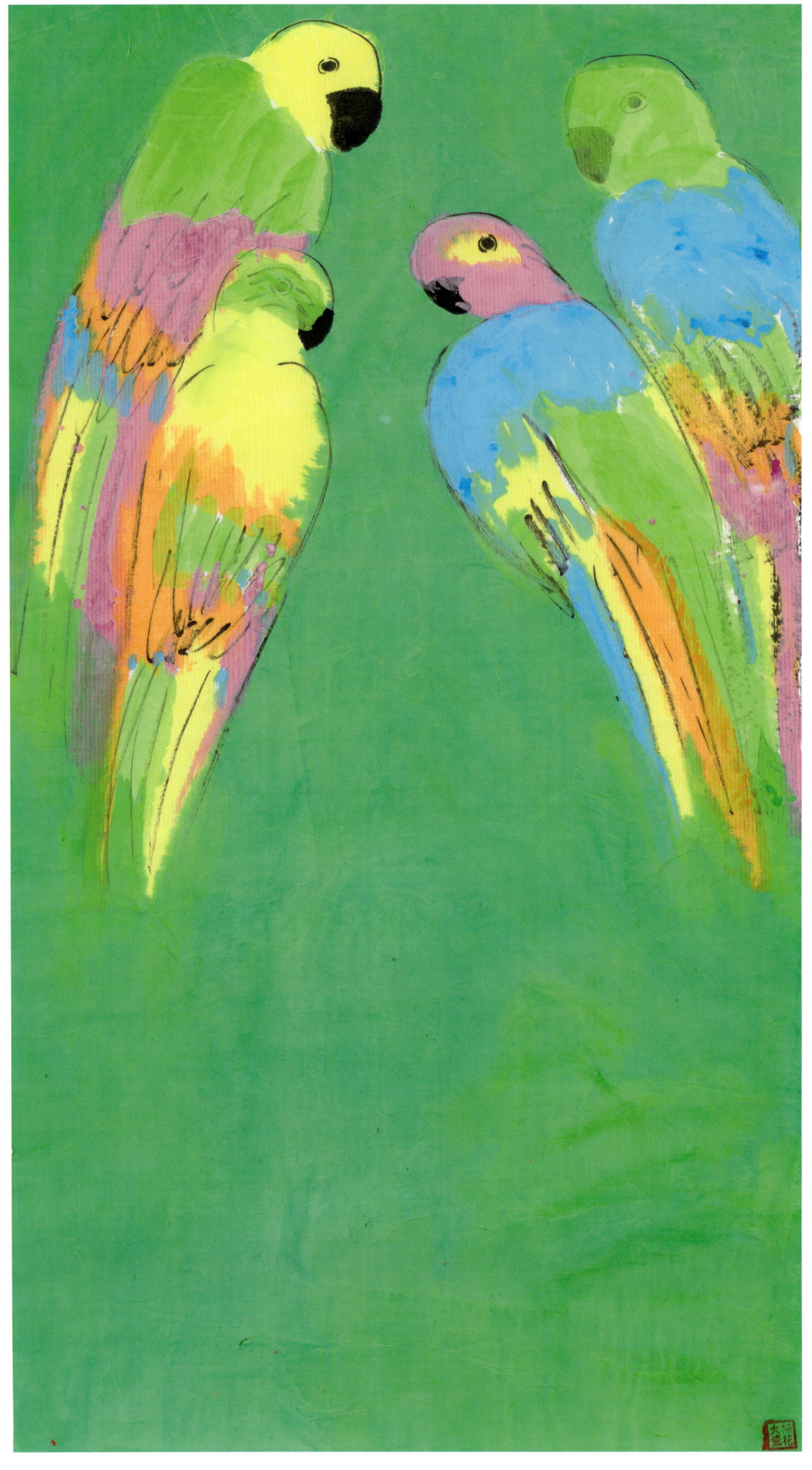

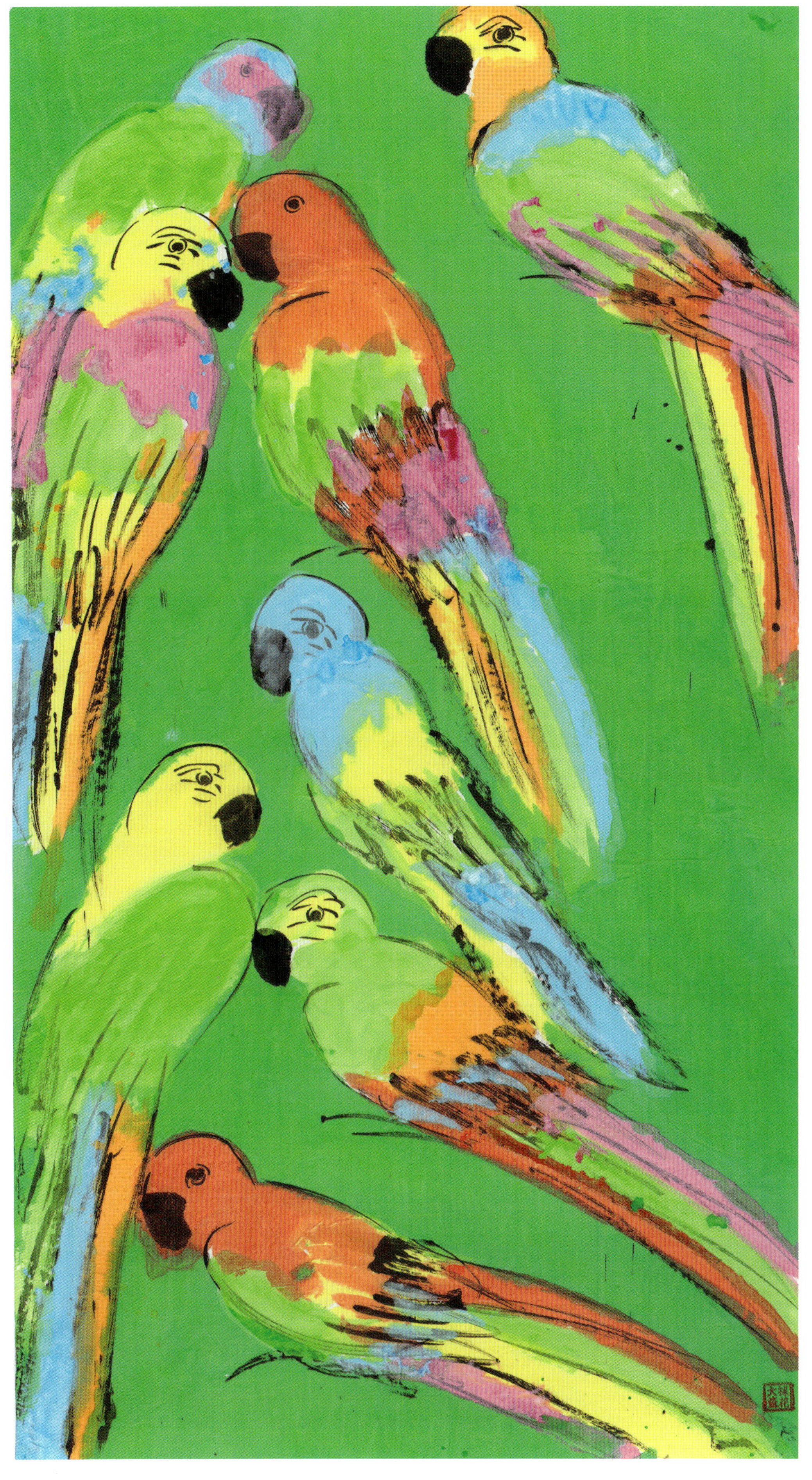

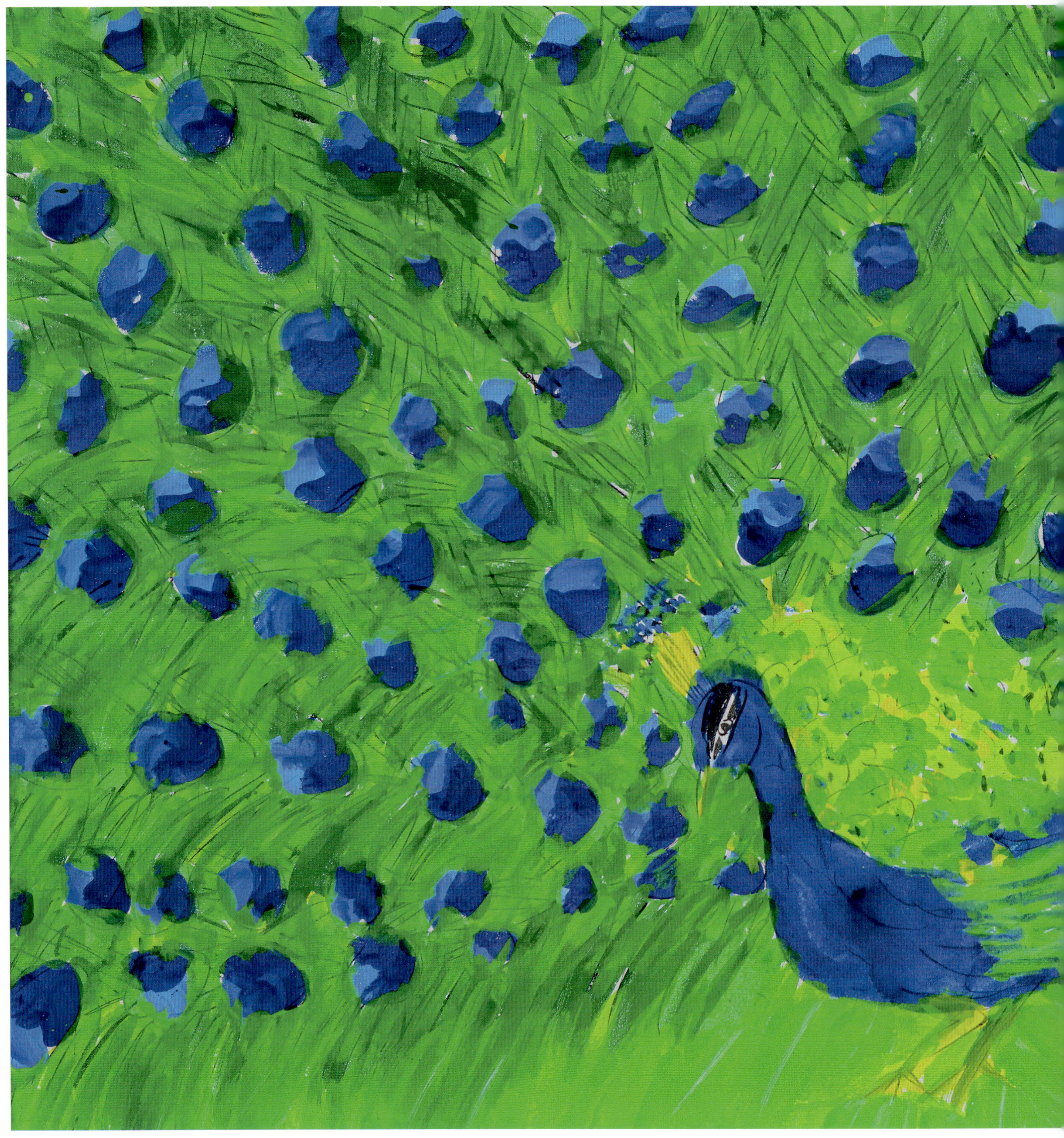

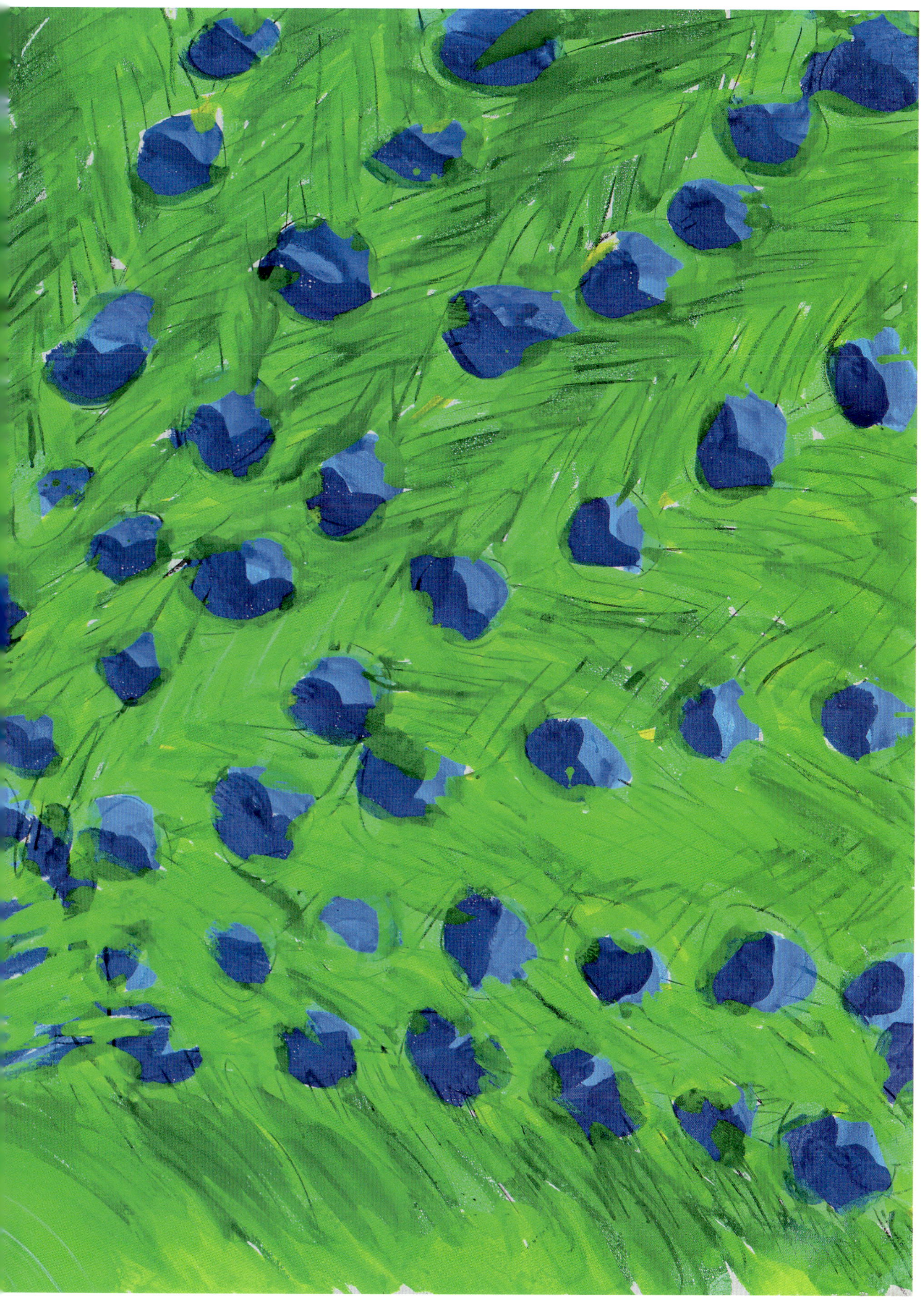

Green Peacock, January 16, 1995
Acrylic and Chinese ink on rice paper
48.1 × 85.1 in. / 122 × 216 cm
Private Collection, Amsterdam

Untitled, early 1980s
Acrylic and Chinese ink on rice paper
mounted on canvas
25 × 45 in. / 63.5 × 114.3 cm
Collection Marlène Brody

Following pages
Untitled, late 1980s–early 1990s
Acrylic and Chinese ink on rice paper
38 × 70 in. / 96.5 × 177.8 cm
Private Collection, New York

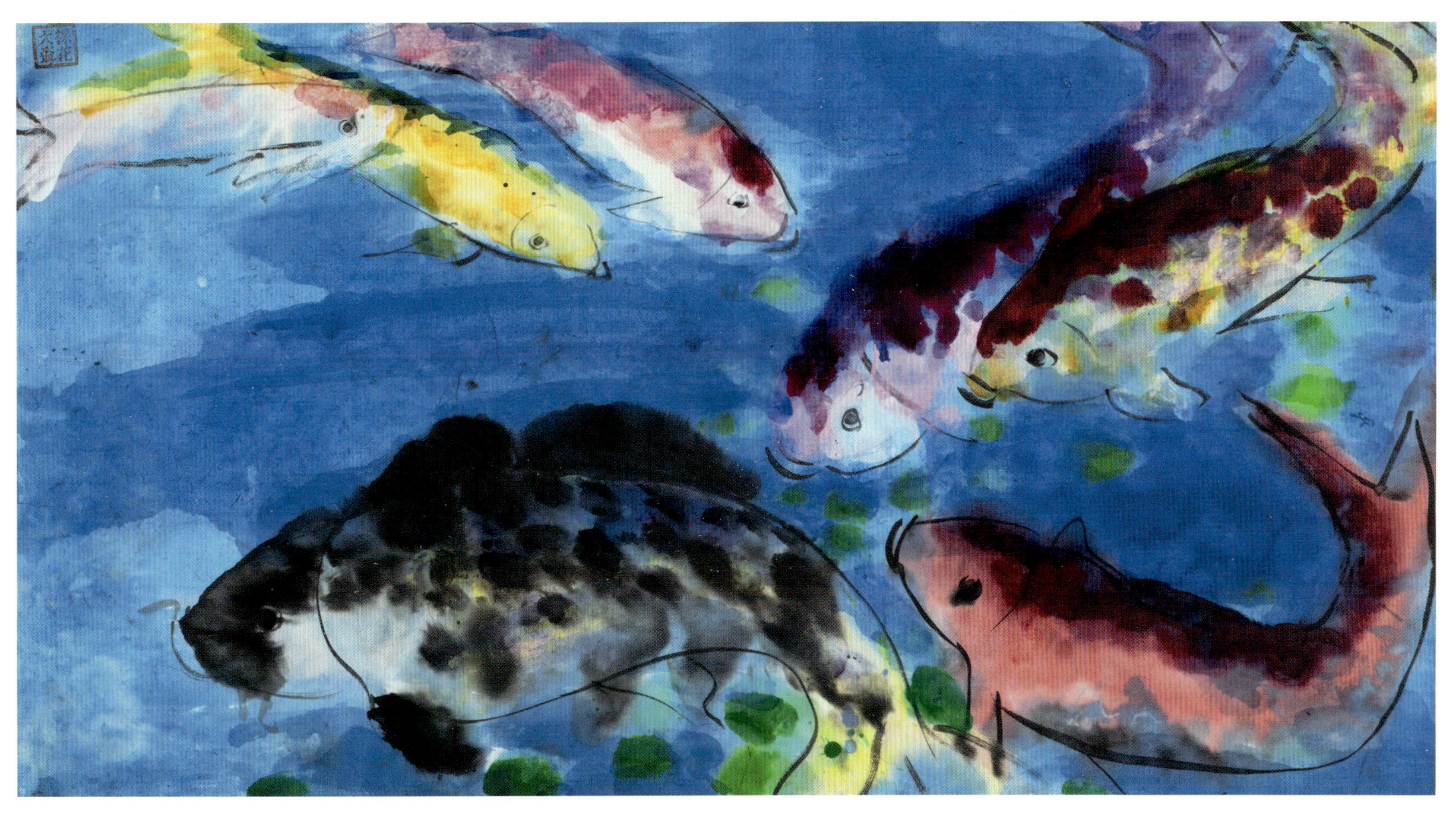

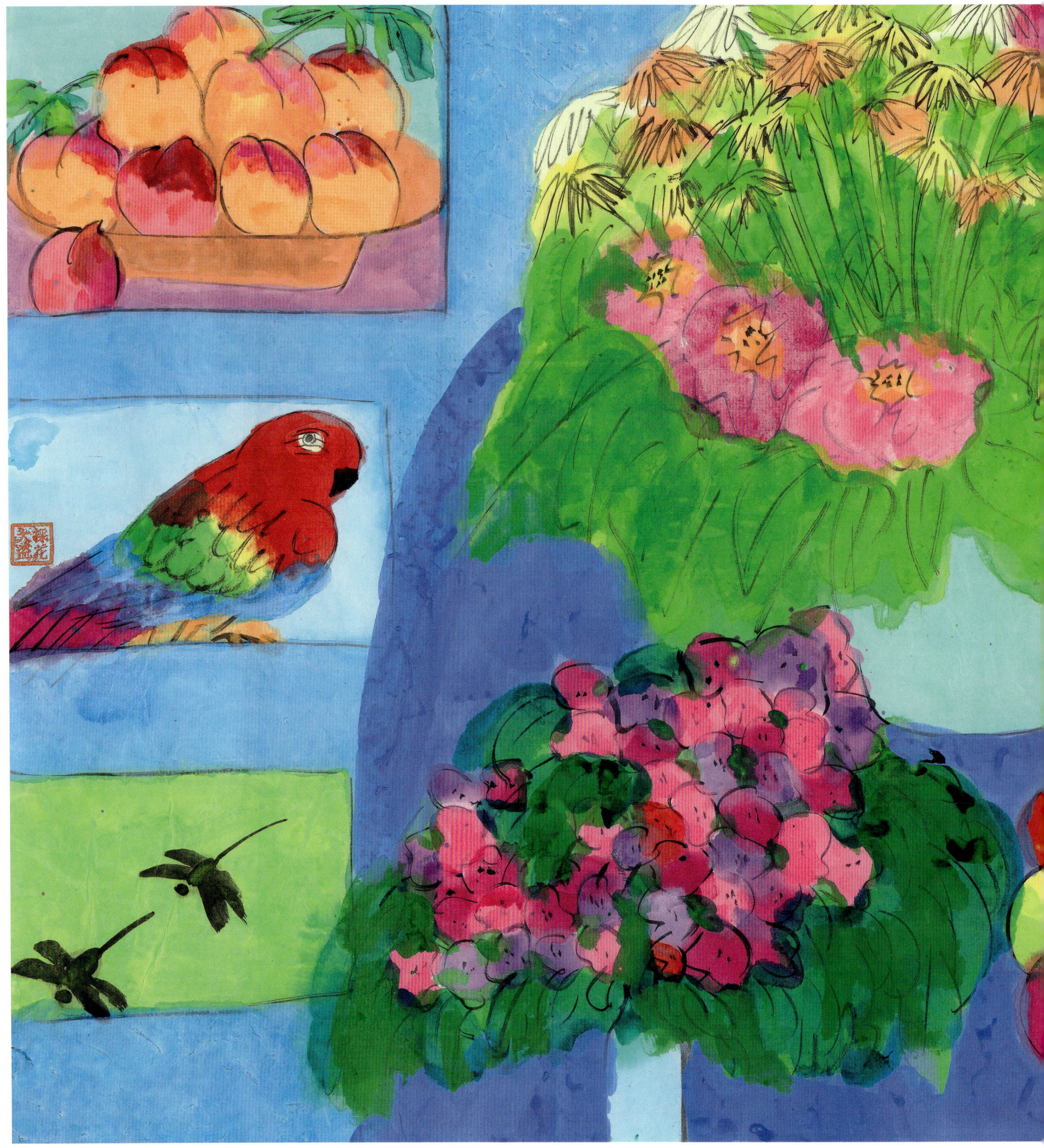

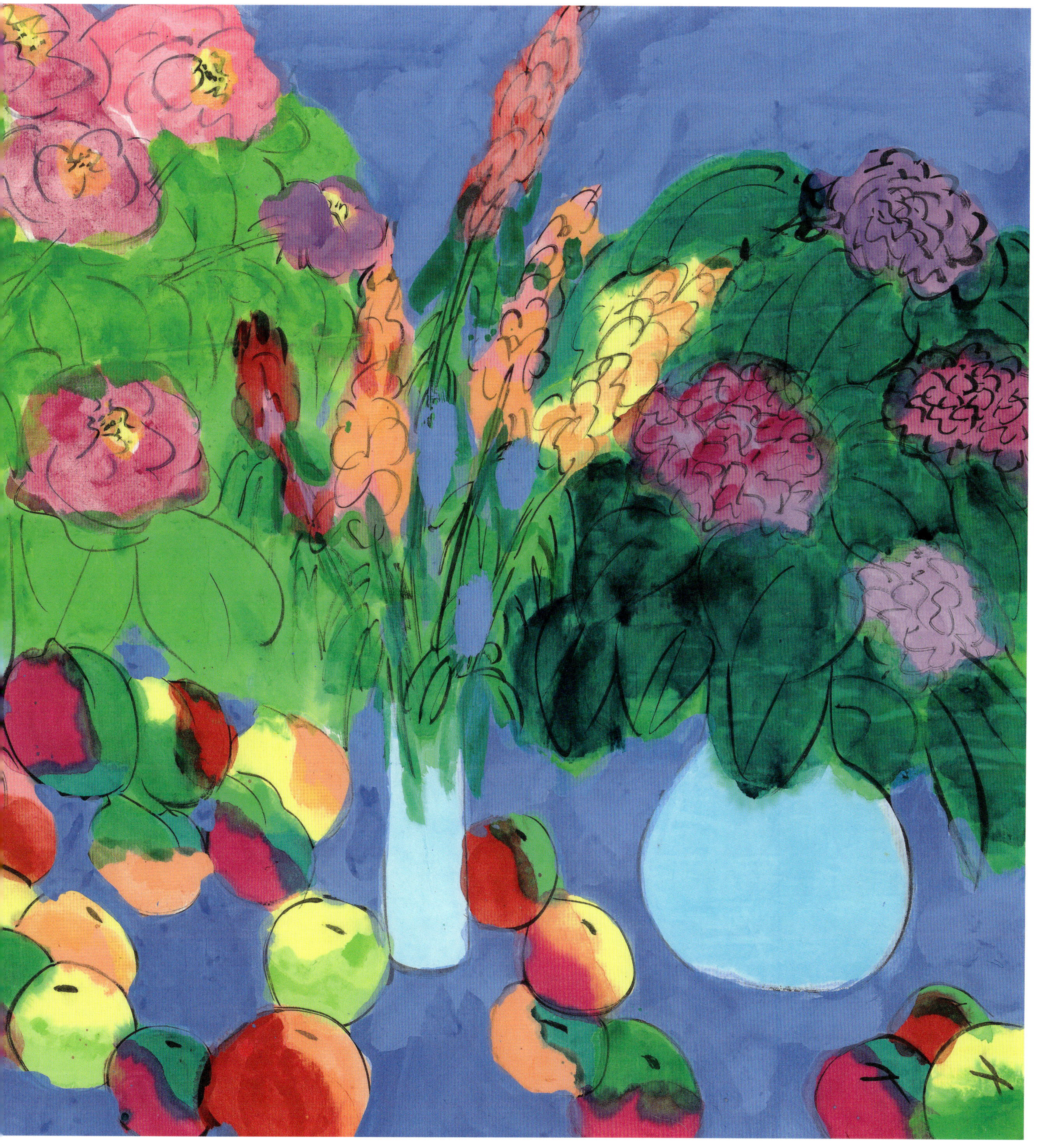

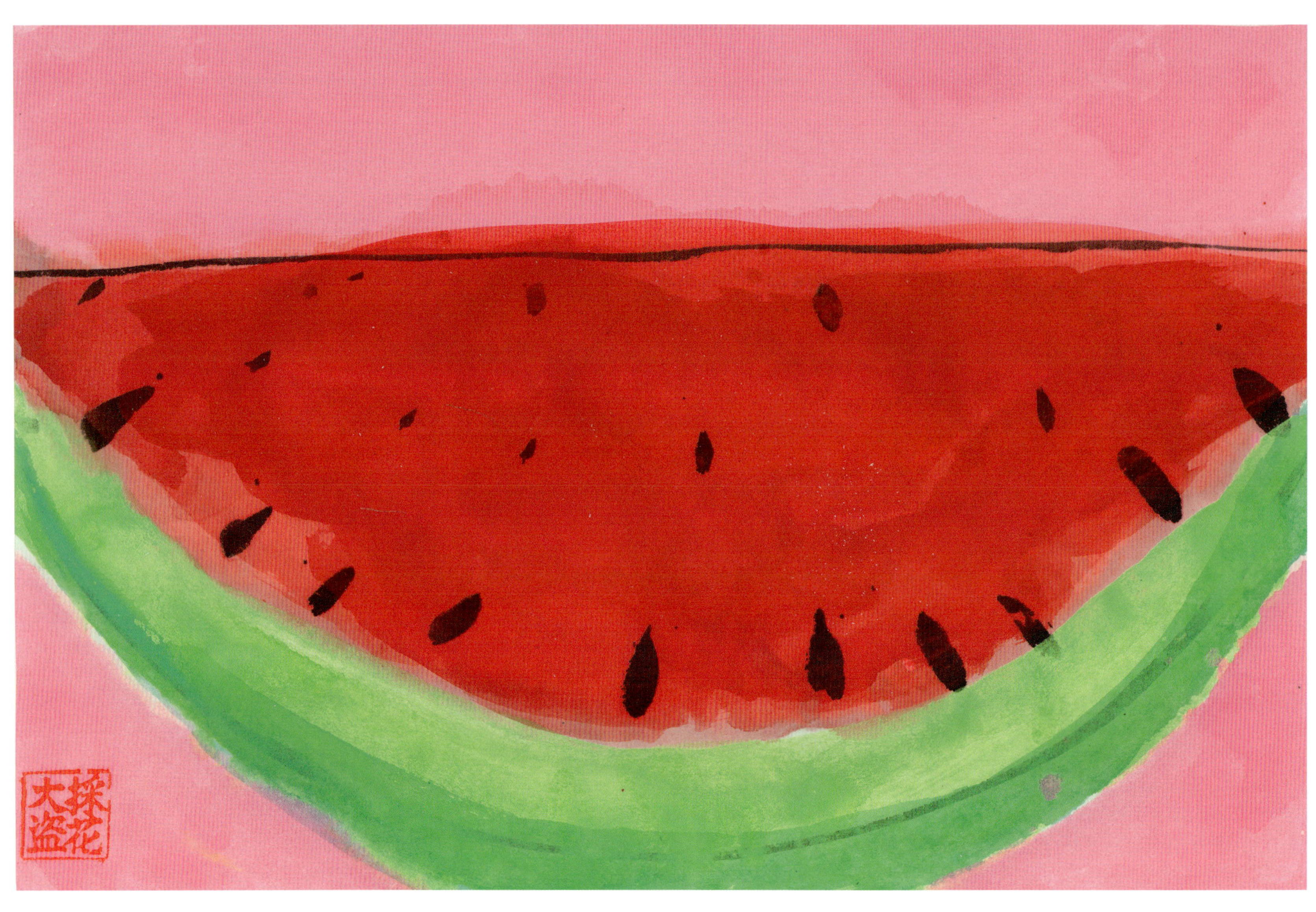

Untitled, mid-1990s
Acrylic and Chinese ink on rice paper
11.8 × 17 in. / 29.8 × 43.2 cm
Private Collection, New York

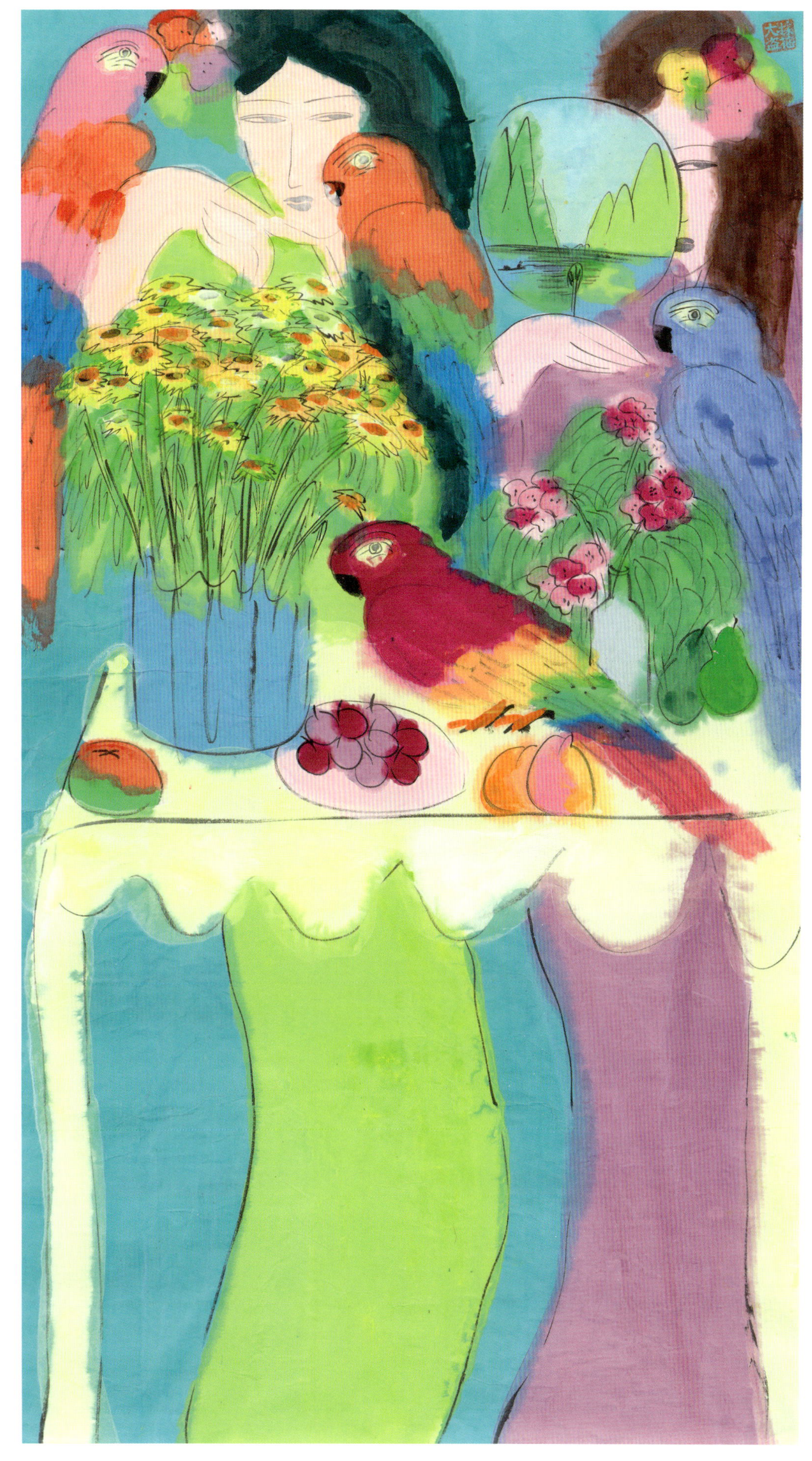

Untitled, early 1980s
Acrylic and Chinese ink on rice paper
70 × 38 in. / 177.8 × 96.5 cm
Private Collection, Hong Kong

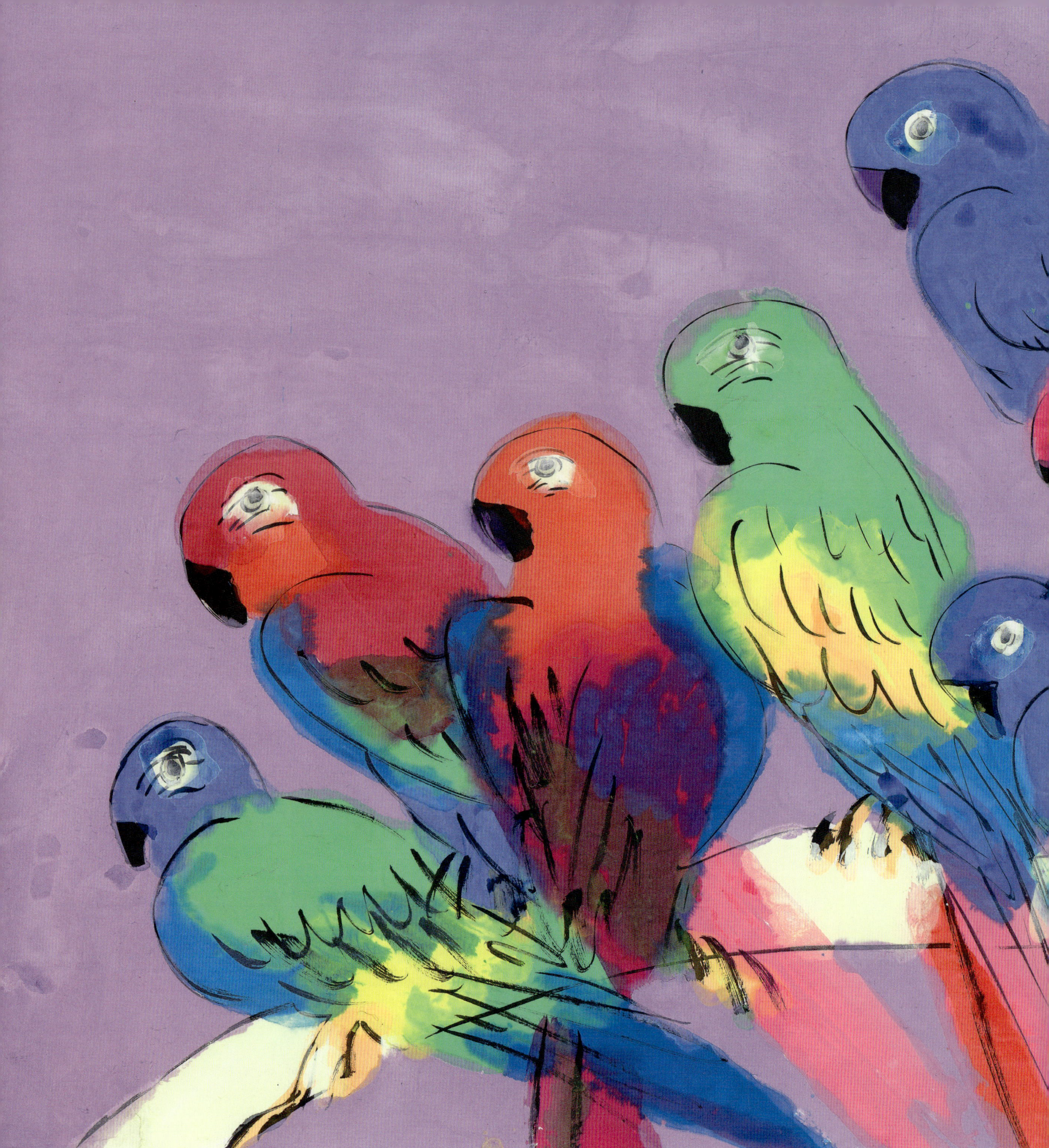

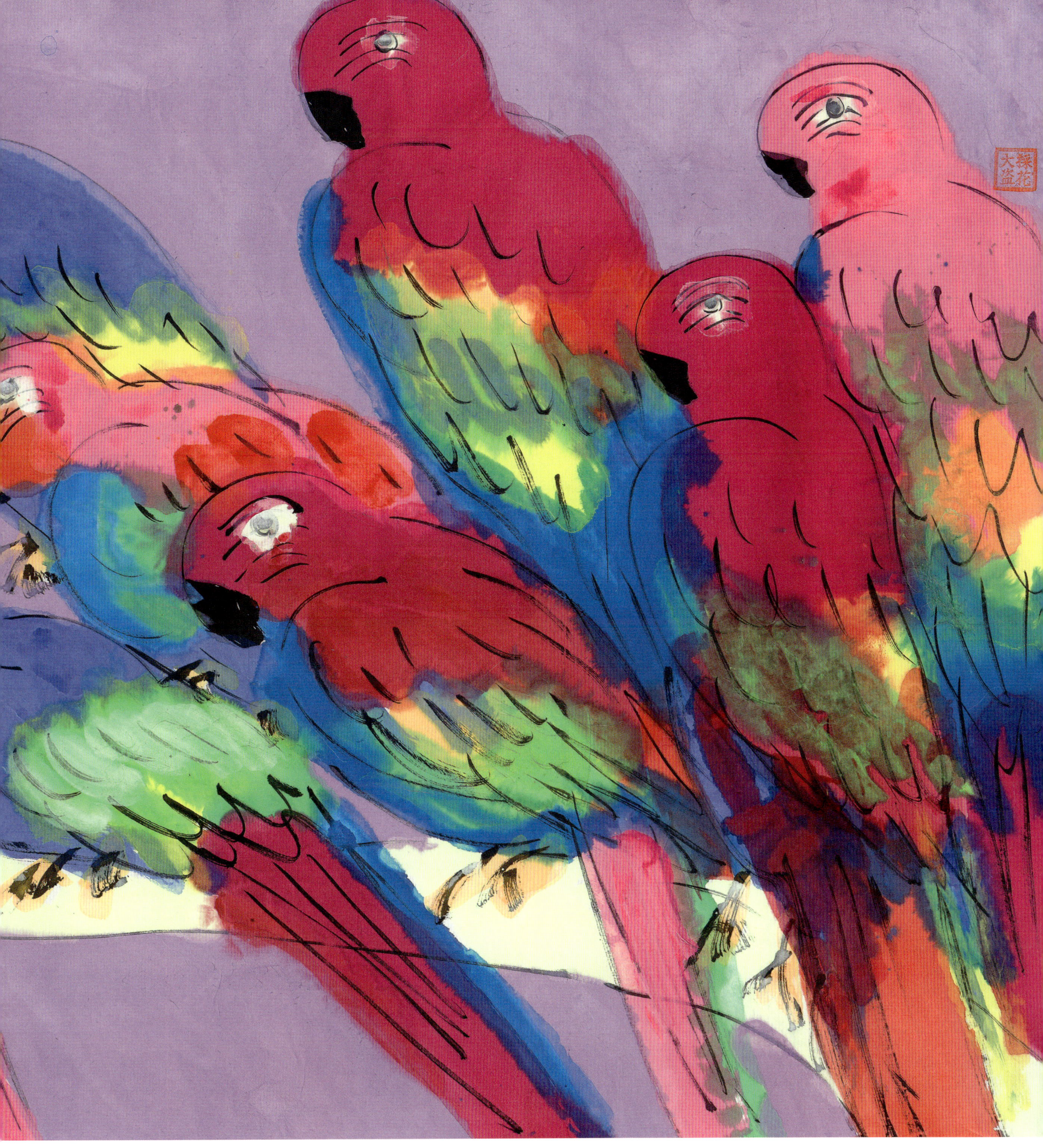

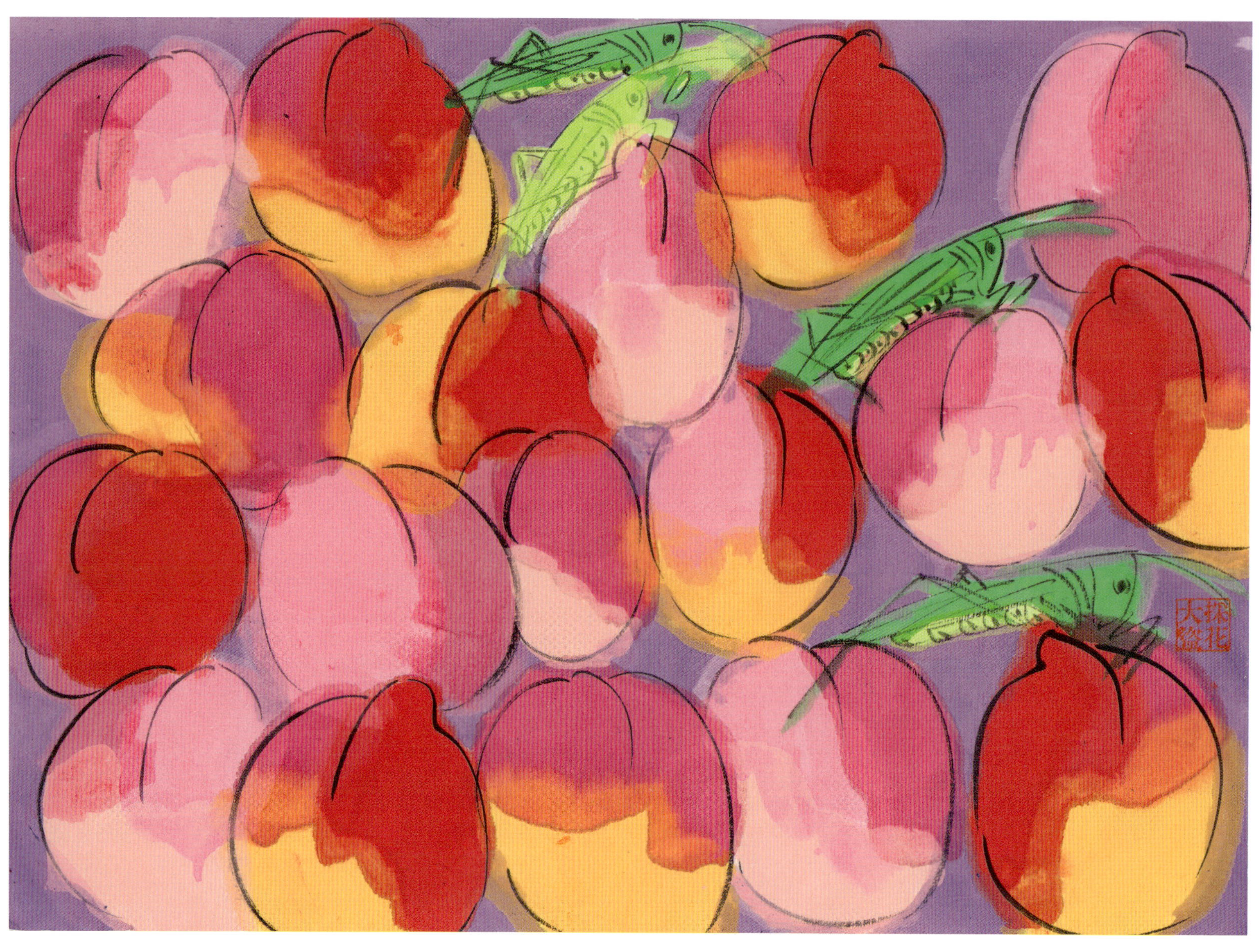

Previous pages
Untitled, mid-1980s
Acrylic and Chinese ink on rice paper
38 × 70 in. / 96.5 × 177.8 cm
Private Collection, Amsterdam

Untitled, mid-1980s
Acrylic and Chinese ink on rice paper
14 × 19 in. / 35.5 × 48.2 cm
Private Collection, New York

34

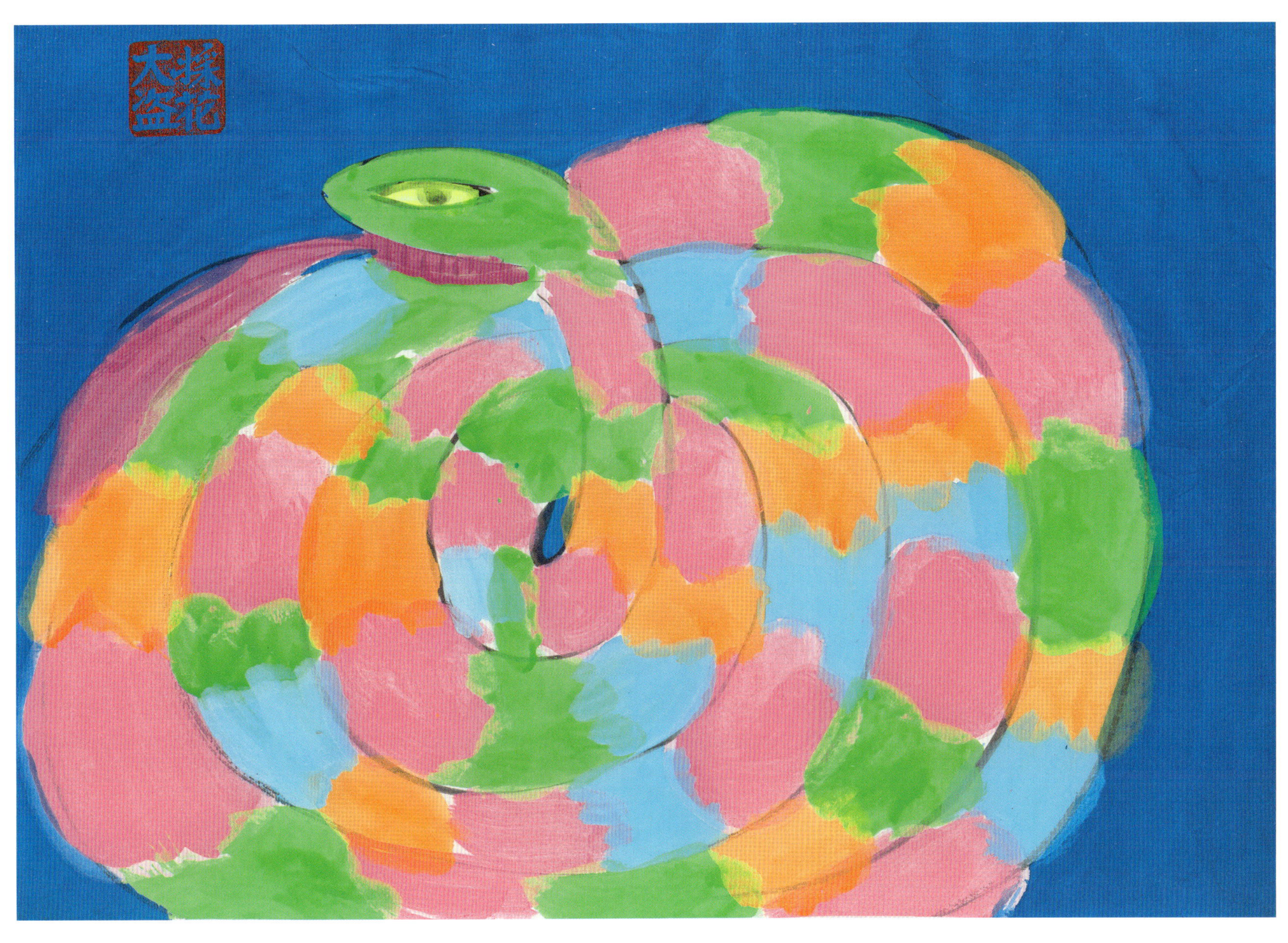

Untitled, mid-1980s
Acrylic and Chinese ink on rice paper
27.5 × 38 in. / 69.9 × 96.5 cm
Private Collection, Shanghai

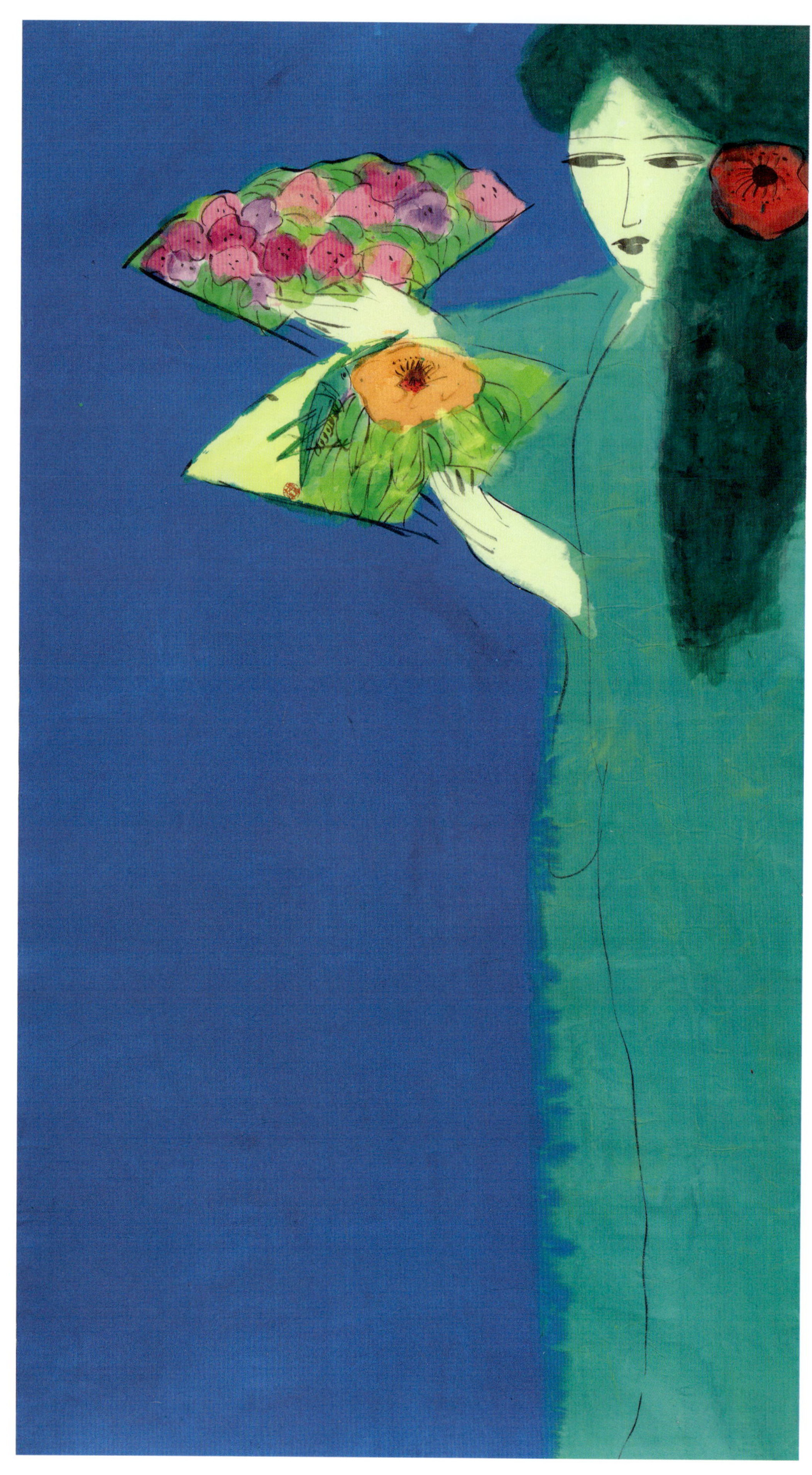

Untitled, early 1980s
Acrylic and Chinese ink on rice paper
70 × 38 in. / 177.8 × 96.5 cm
Private Collection, Amsterdam

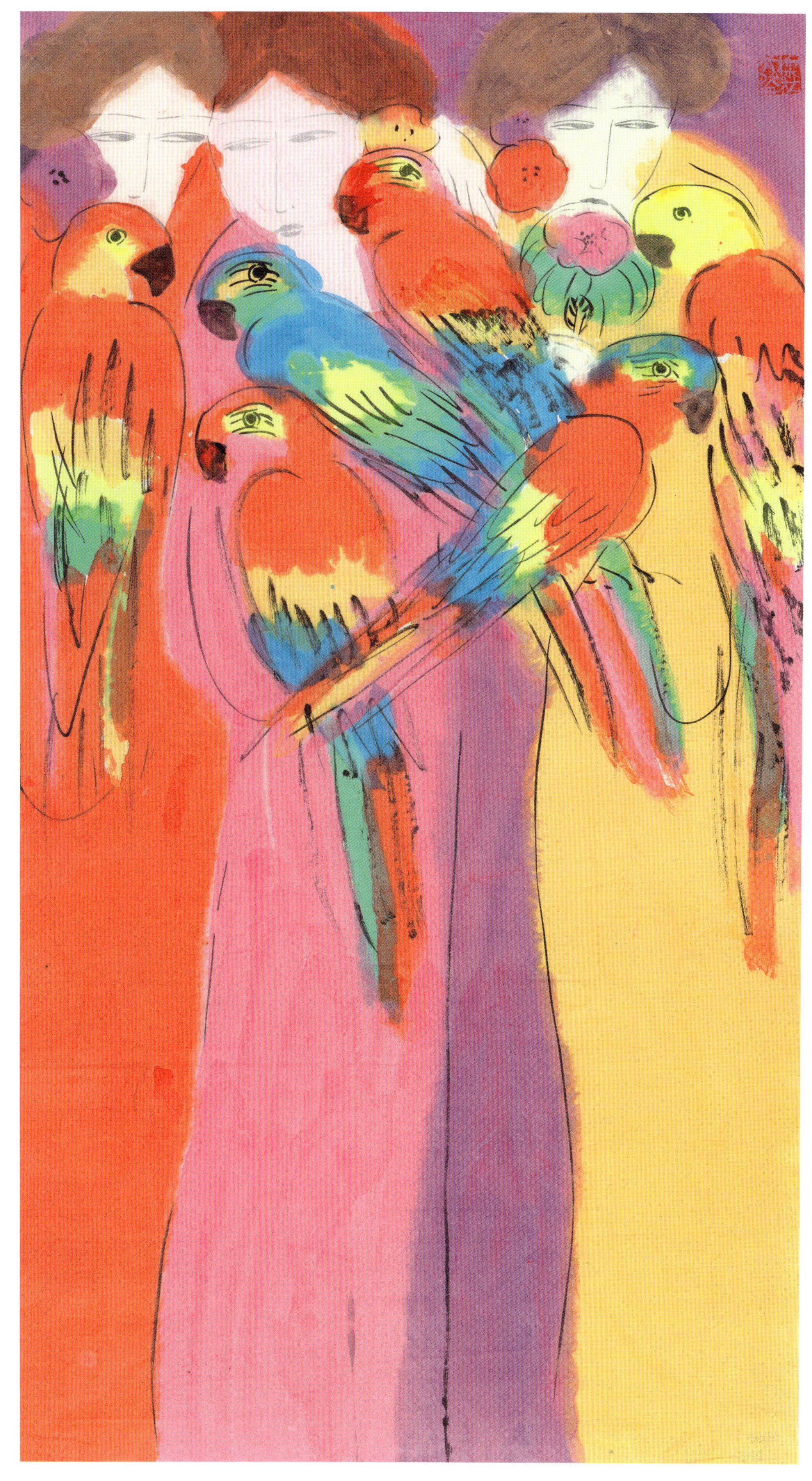

Untitled, late 1980s–early 1990s
Acrylic and Chinese ink on rice paper
70 × 38 in. / 177.8 × 96.5 cm
Private Collection, New York

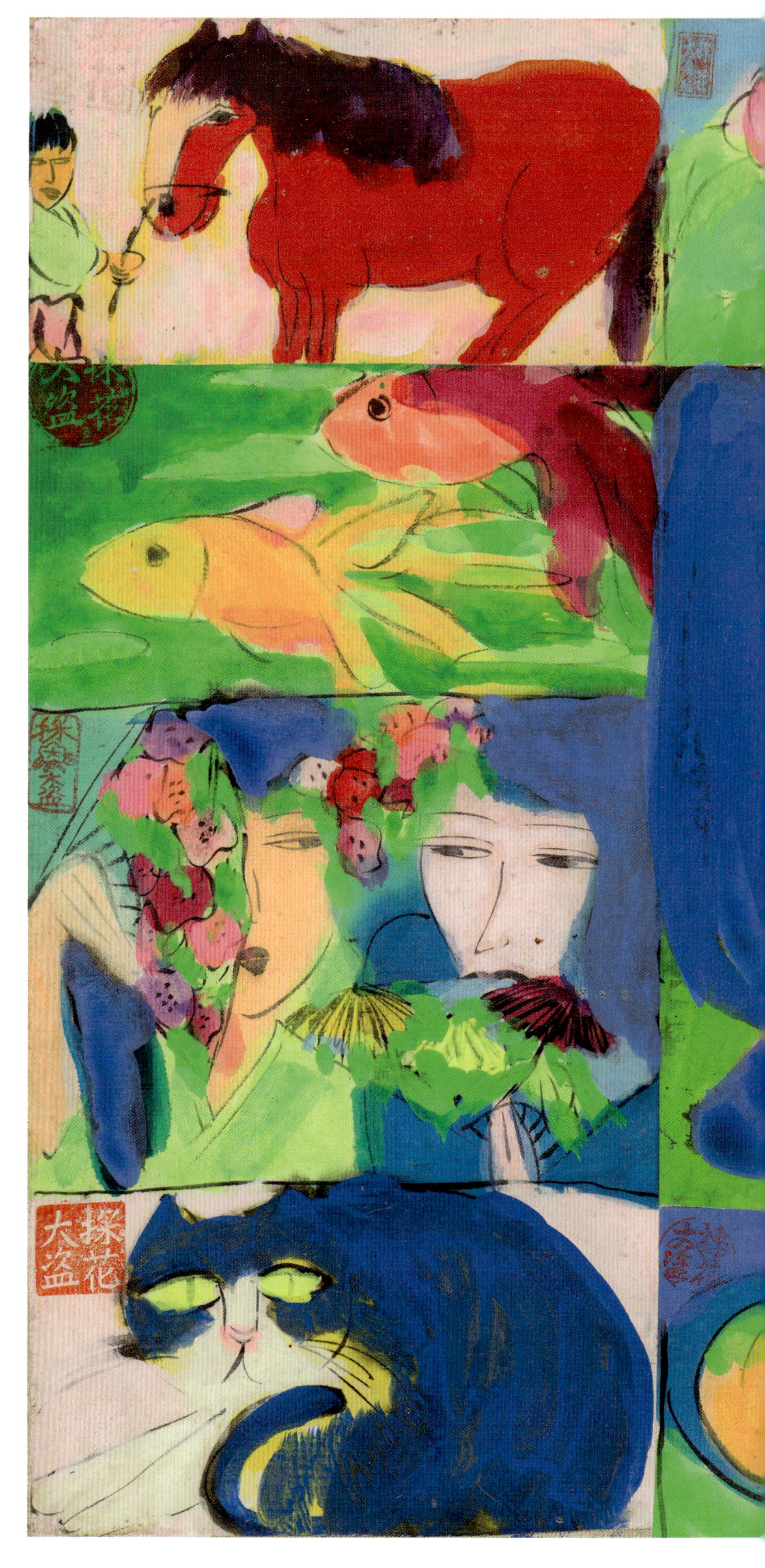

My World, 1985
Acrylic and Chinese ink on rice paper
mounted on canvas
16 × 23 in. / 40.6 × 58.4 cm

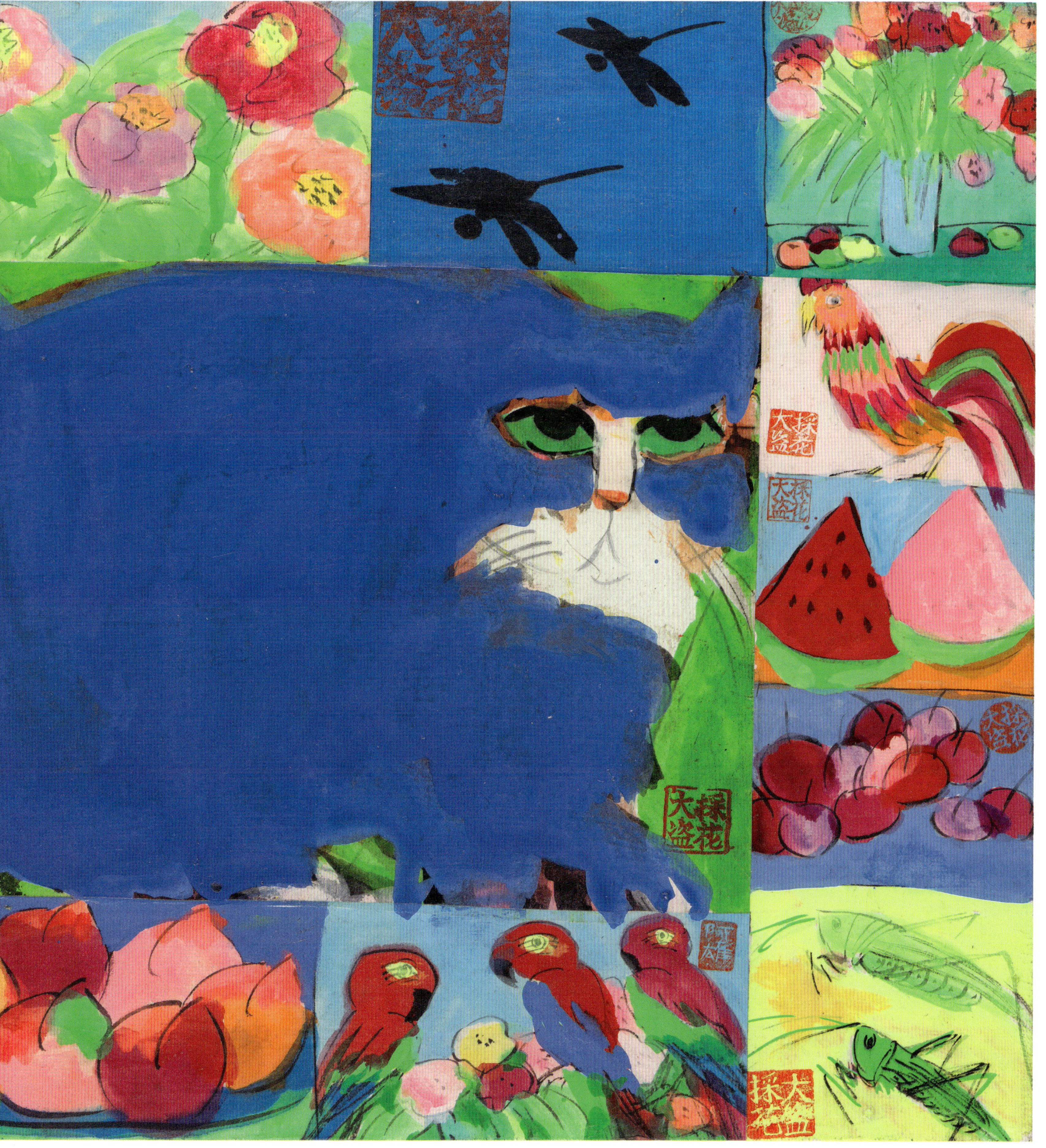

before i paint i'm man
before i paint i'm pillow
before i paint i'm summer
before i paint i'm tiger
before i paint i'm hair
before i paint i'm flower
before i paint i'm hot
before i paint i'm night
before i paint i'm earth
before i paint i'm mountain
before i paint i'm icebox
before i paint i'm tea leaf
before i paint i'm orange
before i paint i'm steel
before i paint i'm wood
before i paint i'm sour
before i paint i'm tree
before i paint i'm skyscraper
before i paint i'm mirror
before i paint i'm ice
before i paint i'm ice cream
before i paint i'm sea
before i paint i'm fire
before i paint i'm river
before i paint i'm shadow
before i paint i'm teeth
before i paint i'm chimney
before i paint i'm locomotive
before i paint i'm mad
before i paint i'm egg
before i paint i'm roast duck
before i paint i'm thousand years old
before i paint i'm here

after i paint i'm woman
after i paint i'm peacock open fan
after i paint i'm spring
after i paint i'm butterfly
after i paint i'm green grass
after i paint i'm pollen
after i paint i'm faint
after i paint i'm day
after i paint i'm sun
after i paint i'm wind
after i paint i'm stove
after i paint i'm warm tea
after i paint i'm orange juice
after i paint i'm bridge
after i paint i'm boat
after i paint i'm sweet
after i paint i'm forest
after i paint i'm wildflower
after i paint i'm sky
after i paint i'm rain
after i paint i'm cloud
after i paint i'm dew
after i paint i'm sunset
after i paint i'm waterfall
after i paint i'm morning
after i paint i'm bee
after i paint i'm smoke
after i paint i'm rainbow
after i paint i'm thunder
after i paint i'm chicken
after i paint i'm restaurant
after i paint i'm infant
after i paint i'm gone

Walasse Ting

WALASSE TING by WALASSE TING
Born in Shanghai, China, 1929
4 years old paint in sidewalk. 10 years
old draw on wall. 20 years old left
China to traveling after reading the
book of I-Ching. In 1953 arrived in
Paris. Six months later meet Pierre
Alechinsky. Six months later meet
Asger Jorn. Six months later meet
Karel Appel; drink coffee with them
in Paris-Cafe. Working all kinds of job
to making a very simple living. Living
in a six inches window room. Paint
there, eat there. In 1963 arrived in
New York City. Six months later meet
Sam Francis. Six months later meet
Tom Wesselmann. Six months later
meet Claes Oldenburg. Eat hot & sour
soup with them in Chinese restaurant.
Not working any kinds job. Sleeping
all day living in a sixty feet window
loft. Eat there, paint there. Self-
taught. Individual. Not belong to any
group.

Travel Once and All the Way

Ariella Wolens

"How can one remain Chinese after the shock of Western thought?"[1]
—Julien Alvard, 1957

The first chapter in the story of Walasse Ting's journey to Florida begins in 1946, when at the insatiable age of 18, Ting (then Ding Xiongquan, 丁雄泉) received his father's instruction to leave their Shanghai home. Following the resurgence of the Chinese Civil War in 1945, the inevitability of Communist takeover was becoming increasingly apparent, as was concern for the fledgling artist Xiongquan. By the mid-1940s Chairman Mao Zedong had already made it clear that the new China would be no place for independent thought or *l'art pour l'art*.[2] More than a freethinking artist, Xiongquan was singularly headstrong. As a child, his parents nicknamed him, 'Huài Lai Shee' (壞得很), "spoiled" in Shanghai phonetics.[3] Clearly, his defiant nature had been established at an early age. This defining characteristic would remain Ting's greatest virtue and vice throughout his life.

fig. 1. "33 times night & day and WALASSE TING by WALASSE TING," *Sam Francis, Joan Mitchell, and Walasse Ting, Fresh Air School* catalogue, 1972, n.p. Carnegie Museum of Art

fig. 2. Walasse Ting envelope posted to self, 1977

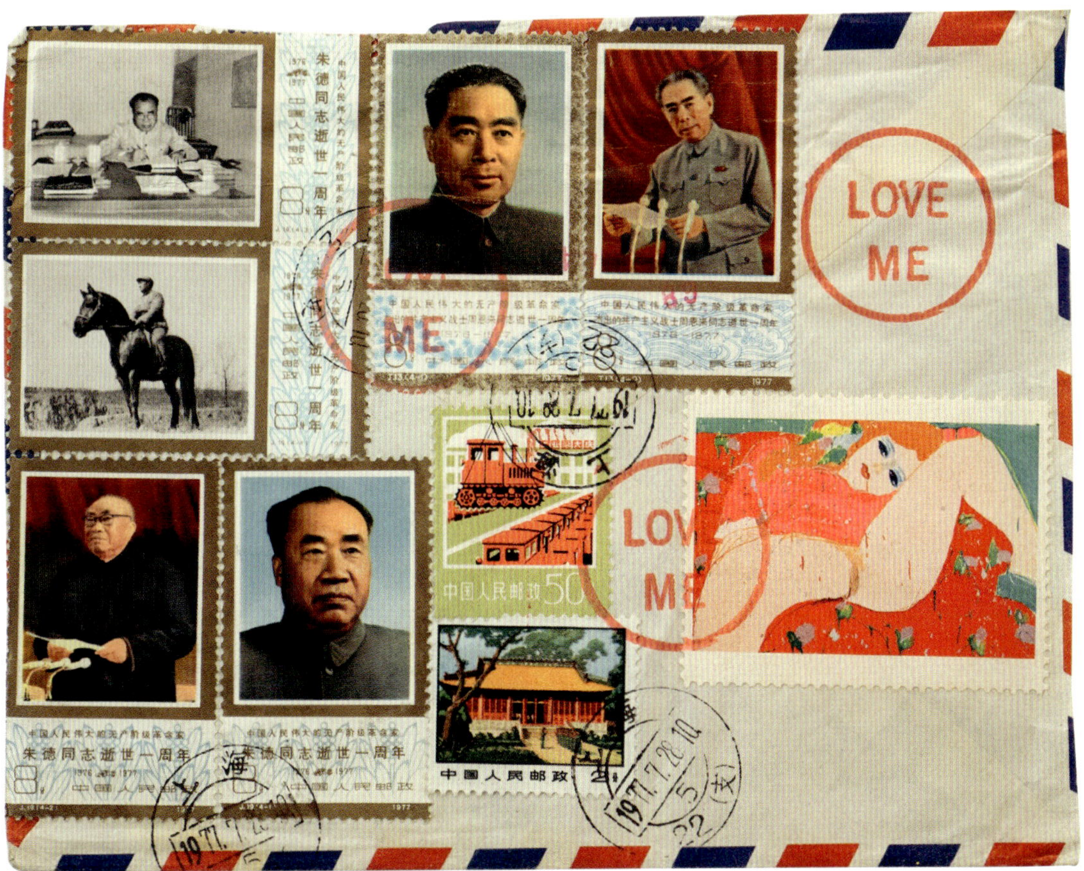

[1] Julien Alvard, *Walasse Ting: Paintings, March 12–April 6, 1957* (New York: Galerie Chalette, 1957), 2.
[2] "'There is in fact no such thing as art for art's sake'" Mao Zedong, Talks at the Yan'an Forum on Literature and Art, quoted in Qilin Fu, "The Reception of Mao's Talks at the Yan'an Forum on Literature and Art in English-language Scholarship," *CLCWeb: Comparative Literature and Culture 17.1* (2015), 3.
[3] Walasse Ting, "Tsan Hua Ta Tao is Walasse Ting / Walasse Ting is Tsan Hua Ta Tao," in *Rice Paper Painting / Peinture sur papier du riz* (Paris: Yves Rivière, 1984), 41.

For once following instruction, Ting ventured to Hong Kong, initiating his multicultural formation. A new world order was underway here, courtesy of the British, who in 1898 had "leased"[4] what was known as "The New Territories" from China for 99 years. Hong Kong's position as Asia's port of entry to the West meant the ways of the colonizers had become well known. Among the Western ideas that flowed through in this post-war period were the transgressive schemes of Modernism, which in 1950s Hong Kong, informed the makings of the New Ink Painting Movement, now defined by the work of artists such as Lui Shou-Kwan (呂壽琨), Irene Chou (周綠雲) and Wucius Wong (王無邪). Though Ting operated within the same creative milieu, his billing as a solo act had already been defined.

Ting: The Anti-Oedipus

Prior to his arrival in Hong Kong, Ting experienced a brief and disappointing stint in academic training at the Shanghai Art Academy. In keeping with his dogged individuality, the artist would later declare he was self-taught, outlining his creative formation as, "4 years old paint in sidewalk. 10 years old draw on wall."[5] Despite his lack of interest in creative instruction—of which he remarked, had the dulling rigor of medical science—[6] the auto-didact was quick to realize his interest in the happenings of the avant-garde and cultural histories stretching beyond his purview; Renaissance masters and European modernists became known to him through titles perused in Hong Kong bookstores. Sensing the appeal of broadening horizons, Ting chose as the name for his debut exhibition at Hong Kong's Hotel Cecil, *Modern Paintings of Eastern & Western Styles*.

Upon entering the exhibition, viewers were met with a salon-style arrangement of mounted handscrolls, rendered in both oil and ink: the ultimate cultural collision. A photograph of the installation shows bands of calligraphic line

fig. 3. Walasse Ting on Des Voeux Road, Hong Kong, October 1953

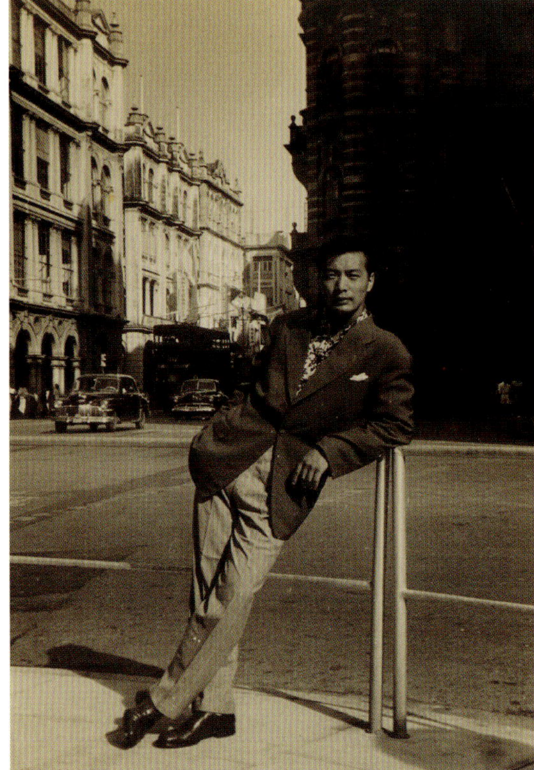

[4] Quotation marks are author's own provided for the purpose of emphasis.
[5] Walasse Ting, "WALASSE TING by WALASSE TING," in *Fresh Air School: Sam Francis, Joan Mitchell, Walasse Ting* (Pittsburgh: Carnegie Institute, 1972), n.p.
[6] "Academies something like for medical science. Medical science, there's the dead body, everybody cut. Academy, live nude in the middle, everybody draw…," Peter Downey and Jeff Lewis, "Walasse Ting on Painting, Artists, Prostitutes, Love and Life," *The Real World*, Issue 12, Summer 1979, 24.

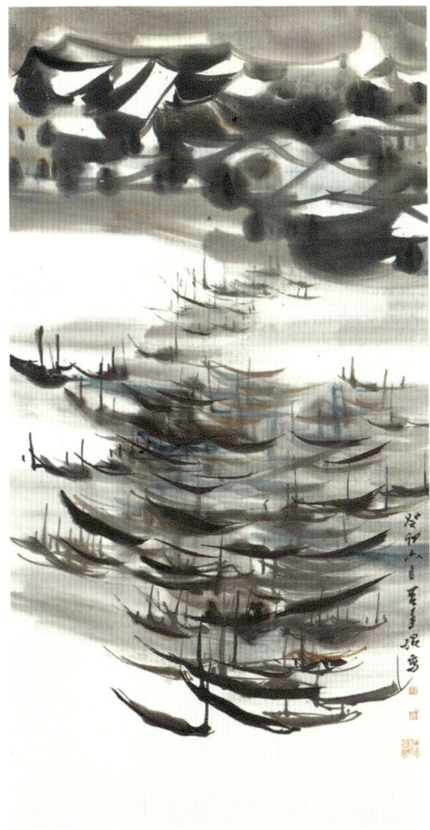

fig. 4. Lui Shou-Kwan
Fishing Port, 1963
Chinese ink and color on rice paper
36.4 × 18.5 in. / 92.5 × 47 cm
Courtesy Alisan Fine Arts

fig. 5. Walasse Ting with guests
in the main room of his exhibition,
*Walasse Ting: Modern Paintings of
Eastern & Western Styles*, Hotel Cecil,
Hong Kong, September 1952

[7] Kwo Da-Wei, *Aesthetics of Chinese
Brushwork. Chinese Brushwork in Calligraphy
and Painting: Its History, Aesthetics, and
Techniques* (Mineola NY: Dover
Publications, 2012), 63.
[8] Anja Loughhead, "Helen Frankenthaler and
the influence of Japanese art and culture,"
National Gallery of Australia, June 2, 2020,
https://nga.gov.au/stories-ideas/question-
helen-frankenthaler-and-the-influence-of-
japanese-art-and-culture/.

sprawling across picture planes; broad swoops in which Eastern script and the bold, undulating lines of the Fauves converge. In one work, Ting's linear abstractions transform into a single half-length portrait (wholly Western). The painting is countered by scenes of chariot processions, an ancient motif central to Chinese visual culture.

Despite his distaste for the academy, the works within the 1952 presentation reveal Ting's deference to ancient Chinese iconography: martial, monarchial, and mythological, as well as a traditional understanding of the fundamental essence of line. The young artist was innately adept in conveying movement with the swiftness of his brushstroke, demonstrating the Chinese quality known as Li (力): vigorous strength.[7] His fluid forms dance through large voids of negative space, an aesthetic decision rooted in Taoism.

Ting's surviving artworks from this time reveal his chromatic experimentation, with notes of colored ink seeping into the paper's weave. In considering on the significance of Ting's Hotel Cecil presentation—and the endless need to reposition the landmarks of art history—it is worth noting that Ting was playing with the tradition of *Po Mo* (潑墨) (wet on wet application of ink on rice paper) while inflecting European accents into Eastern customs, at the same time Helen Frankenthaler was similarly looking to subvert the mores of Western painting in New York. The invention of her "soak-stain" technique made a reverberating statement in an art world that would soon collide with Walasse's own. On reflection, the echoing of Asian traditions is suffused within not only Frankenthaler's work, but so much of Modernism. As succinctly stated by curator Anja Loughead, the influence of Asian art principles on the Abstract Expressionism is "entangled in the historicized trajectory of [M]odernism at large: a European and North American desire to create a visual language for the future, often stylistically motivated by other cultures around the world."[8] This craving for a new method and understanding of painting is a bellwether for the indelible impression Ting was to have on the many pioneering Western artists he intersected with in the years to come.

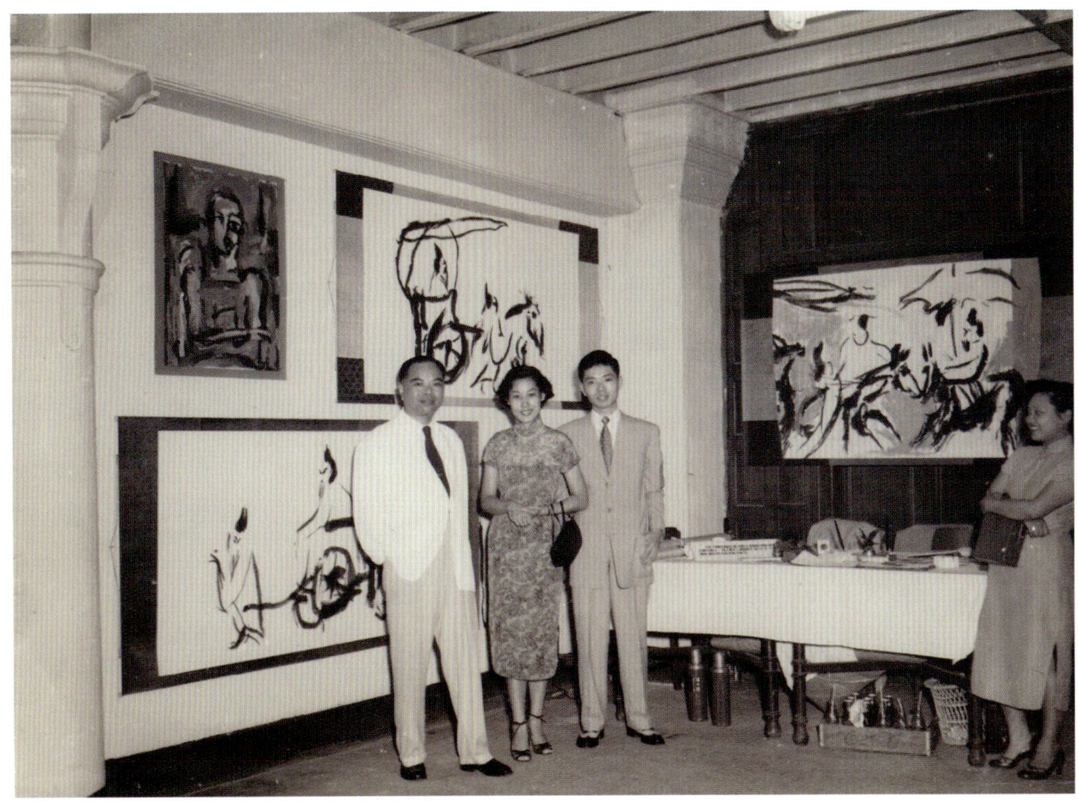

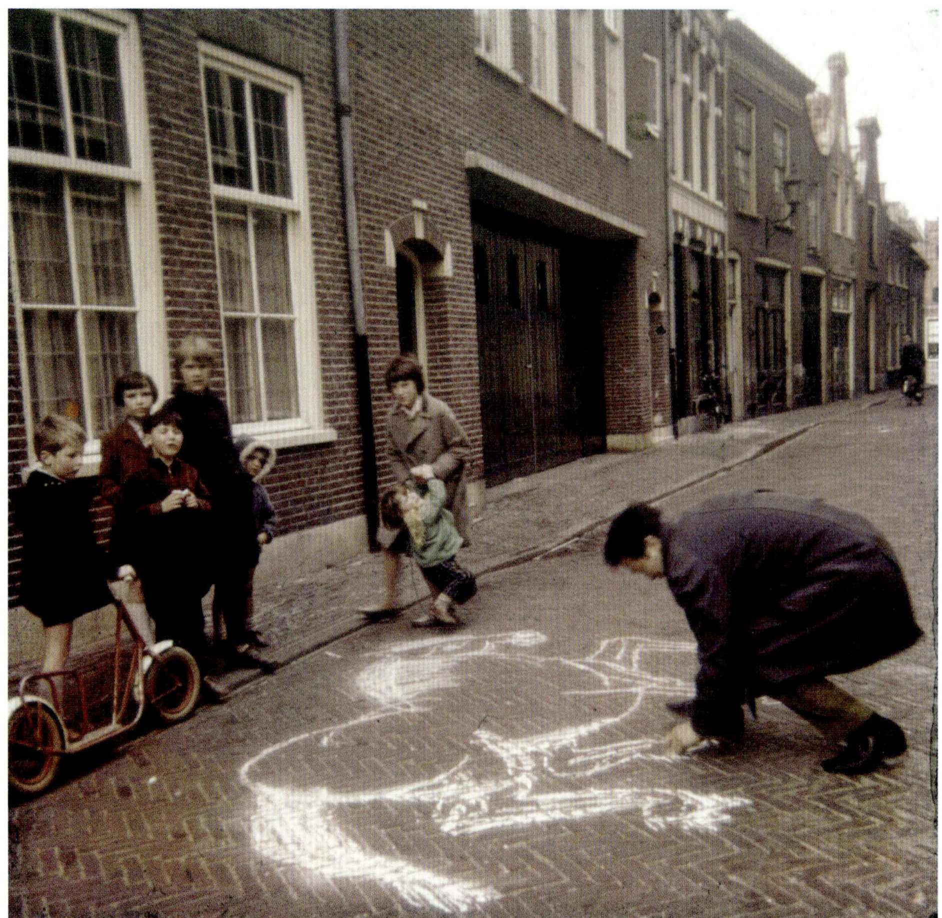

Cultural Parallax

The altern-geographic approach to East meets West Modernism within Ting's inaugural show not only marks the beginnings of the artist's creative creolization, but simultaneously, the start of his cultural alienation, an irrefutable reason behind the overdue nature of this retrospective. At the time of Ting's artistic emergence in the early 1950s, Modernism was able to be utilized in the West as a symbol of freedom of expression, a Cold War tactic through which to contrast the oppressive dictates of Socialist Realism. Through government-backed projects such as the 1946–47 traveling exhibition, *Advancing American Art*, liberal-minded creativity could be used in the West as a signal of political superiority.[9] For Ting however, his cultural meanderings held little in the way of patriotic currency for the People's Republic of China.

In 2007, art historian James Elkins proffered the darker jingoist motivations that have been—and though they have become more nuanced, often remain—the impetus for the cultivation of knowledge and artistic representation. As he writes in his introductory essay to his book, *Is Art History Global?*:

> A sense of nationalism or ethnicity have been the sometimes explicit impetus behind art historical research from its origins in [Giorgio] Vasari and [Johann Joachim] Winckelmann. The current interest in transnationality, multiculturalism, and postcolonialism has not altered that basic impetus but only obscured it by making it appear that art historians are now free to consider themes that embrace various cultures or all cultures in general.[10]

[9] See Lauren Ross, "When art fought the Cold War: A touring exhibition recreates the CIA's 1946 secret weapon that scandalized conservatives," *The Art Newspaper*, April 30, 2013, https://www.theartnewspaper.com/2013/05/01/when-art-fought-the-cold-war-a-touring-exhibition-recreates-the-cias-1946-secret-weapon-that-scandalised-conservatives.

[10] James Elkins, "Art History as Global Discipline," in *Is Art History Global?* (New York: Routledge, 2006), 9.

Ting's cultural synthesis distinguishes him as a pioneering figure whose practice specifically engages with a globalized experience, a precursor to contemporary international artists such as Etel Adnan and Gabriel Orozco. Despite our current interest in multiculturalism, historical precedents have yet to be properly confronted, at least within Western contexts. Ting's defining embrace of the foreign, from his days in Hong Kong to his years in France, America and the Netherlands, disrupted the cultural fundamentalism that is foundational to art historic discipline. Unable to be neatly categorized, his work cannot be claimed by a single nation, it refuses to stick to an essentialized narrative of linear cultural progression or a clear set of relations to other artists. Ting's obstinate refusal to be labelled marks the closing note in his biographical statement: "Individual. Not belong to any group."[11] In dissociating himself from all nuclear families, Ting rejected the Oedipal bond that would locate him within the assembly line of cultural production. This individualism comes at a cost to posterity. To be an individual relegates an artist to being a stateless citizen in the land of art history.

The Year of the Snake

Ting would attribute his next decision, to leave Asia altogether, to reading the *I-Ching*, or, *The Book of Changes*, the ancient compendium which outlines the divine significance of one's intuitive placement of linear objects.[12] In 1952, with the assurance of ancient cleromancy and his restless ambition, Ting made his way from Hong Kong to the shores of Marseilles via freighter, arriving to Paris in 1953. Although by this time, the French capital's status as the mecca of culture was waning, it remained central to Western art history, which Ting was eager to confront.

The artist's assimilation into European culture had already been in motion since his Hong Kong exhibition, at which time, he had rechristened himself "Walasse". Typically spelled Wallace, the artist's unique reconstruction of the name cleaved phonetic elements of Ting's childhood nickname, Huài Lai Shee, with a homographic homage to the French painter, Henri Matisse (who coincidentally, would die in 1954, shortly after Walasse took up the moniker…a cosmic passing of the torch perhaps?). In a 1976 letter, artist Pierre Alechinsky, describes seeing a recent print by his dear friend Ting, "a magnificent litho in black, very simple; the hand of Matisse now lives in your hand."[13] The deft, natural flow of Ting's outlines in black Chinese ink (along with his bold palette of flat, rich tones) would evoke

fig. 7. Henri Matisse
The Red Studio. Issy-les-Moulineaux, 1911
Oil on canvas
71 ¼ × 72 ¼ in. / 181 × 219.1 cm
Mrs. Simon Guggenheim Fund
The Museum of Modern Art, New York
© 2022 Succession H. Matisse / Artists
Rights Society (ARS), New York

[11] Walasse Ting, *Fresh Air School*.
[12] Ibid. For further explanation and analysis of the I Ching, see James Legge, *The I Ching, Or The Book of Changes: The Yi King* (Middletown DE: CreateSpace Independent Publishing Platform, 2008).
[13] "J'ai vu chez Arte une magnifique litho en noir, trés simple: la main de Matisse vit maintenant dans ta main." Pierre Alechinsky to Walasse Ting, March 2, 1976, The Estate of Walasse Ting Archive, New York.

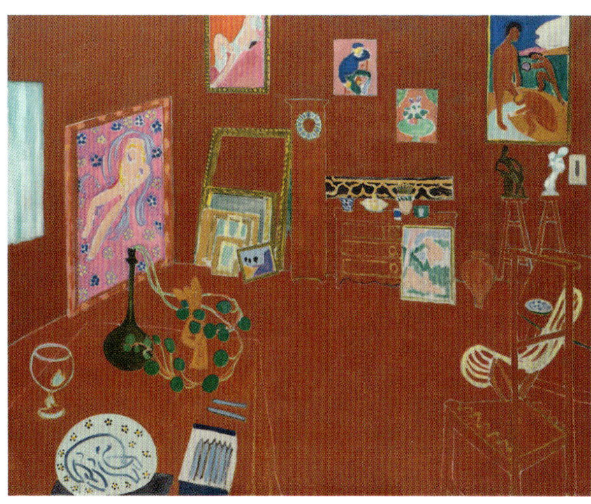

fig. 8. Walasse Ting
Pink Room, 1993
Acrylic on canvas
59.1 × 98.4 in. / 150 × 250 cm

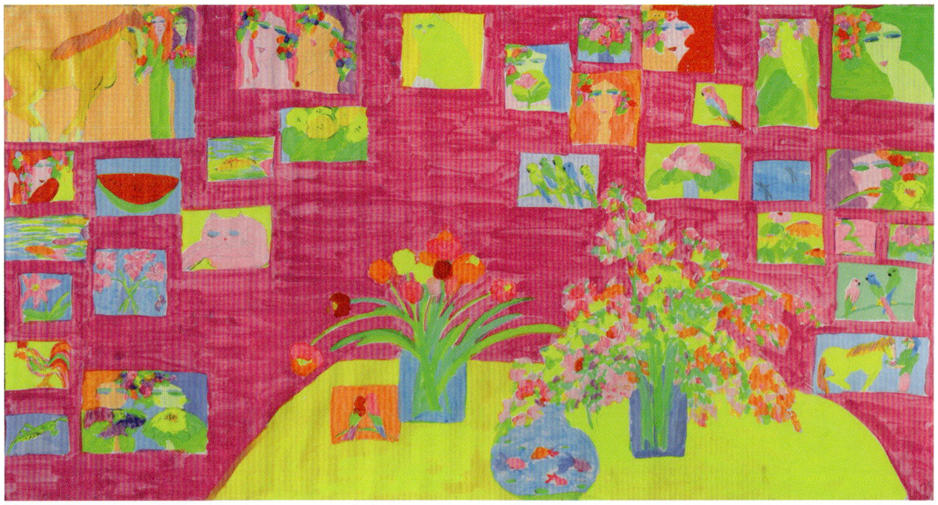

visions of Matisse's fluidity throughout Ting's career. In overtly associating himself with the great Matisse, Ting initiated his apotheosis into an artist-legend, a critical aspect of his work that forges part of his connection to Pop Art as the movement that created the art of persona.

Walasse Ting's time in Paris coincided with the sojourns of numerous young American artists he would later become close to such as Sam Francis and Roy Lichtenstein, who had come to study the traditions of academic art in situ courtesy of the GI Bill. However, despite their geographic overlap and later kinship, Walasse's most critical introductions in Paris would be with a cadre of Northern European artists, whose practices were as internationally inclined and free as his own:

> In 1953 arrived in Paris. Six months later meet Pierre Alechinsky. Six months later meet Karel Appel. Six months later meet Asger Jorn. Working all kinds of job to making a very simple living. Living in a six inches window room. Paint there. Eat there.[14]

This is the summation of Walasse's time in the French capital. Pierre Alechinsky was introduced to Walasse at his Paris debut exhibition at Galerie Facchetti in 1954, where Ting displayed his dabblings in Cubist abstraction. Alechinsky had been the youngest member of the recently disbanded artist group, Cobra; the collective had officially been active from 1948–1951, dates defined by the signing of a manifesto, *La cause était entendu* (*The Matter was Settled*), the publication of magazines *Cobra* and *Le Petit Cobra*, and the mounting of two self-organized exhibitions.

The name Cobra was a portmanteau, a combination of the founder's home cities: CO-penhagen (Asger Jorn), BR-russels (Christian Dotremont and Joseph Noiret) and A-msterdam (Karel Appel, Constant [Nieuwenhuys] and Corneille [Guillaume Cornelis van Beverloo]), all of whom, with the exception of Noiret, Walasse would collaborate with on what they called "four-handed paintings." Cobra's rejection of any kind of formalism or cultural singularity matched Ting's own ideological refute. Their break-up had been consequent to their dedication to spontaneity, along with the ailing health of two of the main organizers: Asger Jorn and Christian Dotremont, and disagreements regarding the politicization of art.[15]

[14] Walasse Ting, *Fresh Air School*.
[15] The makings of this catalogue and exhibition are indebted to NSU Art Museum Fort Lauderdale's commitment to the study and stewardship of art related to the Cobra movement. The museum holds the largest collection of work by Cobra affiliated artists in the United States, established by the donation of over 1,700 works by South Florida collectors, Golda and Meyer Marks. We are wholly grateful to the Marks family for their unwavering support of the museum and the legacy of Cobra.

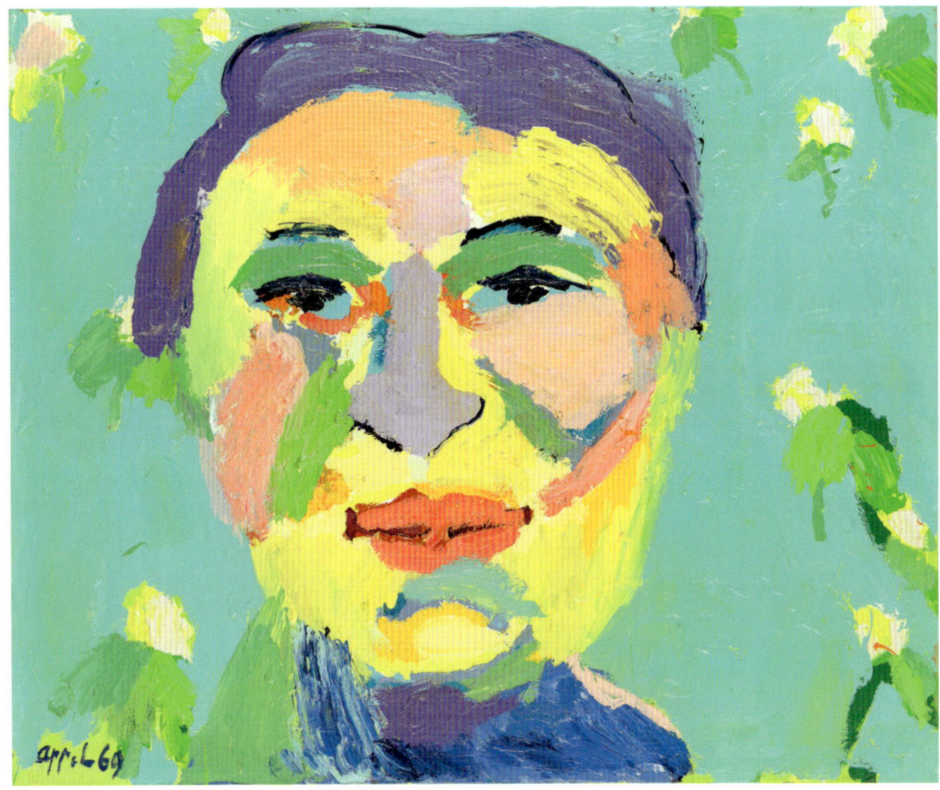

fig. 9. Karel Appel
Portret (Portrait) of Walasse Ting, 1969
Acrylic on canvas
53 × 63 in. / 134.6 × 160 cm

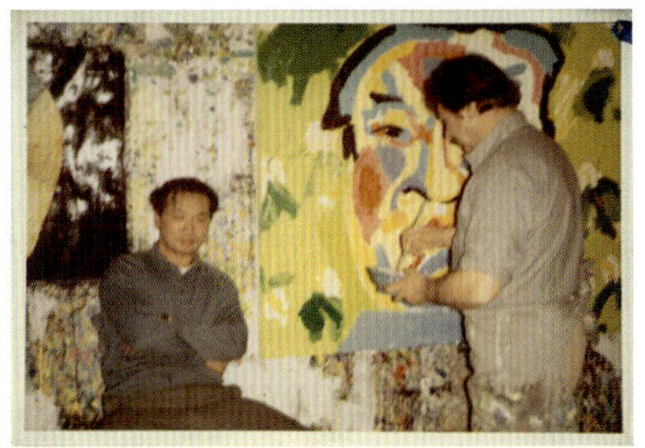

fig. 10. Walasse Ting portrait sitting
for Karel Appel, Walasse Ting studio,
January 1969

16 Pierre Alechinsky, quoted in Alfred
Frankenstein, "Cobra," in *Karel Appel*,
New York, (New York: Harry N. Abrams,
1980), 21.
17 See Asger Jorn and Walasse Ting, *La Flûte
de Jade / Jadefløjten / The Jade Flute*
(St. Gallen: Erker Verlag, 1970) and Guy
Atkins, *Asger Jorn: The Crucial Years*
(London: Lund Humphries Publishers Ltd,
Inc., 1977), 98.
18 Willemijn Stokvis, *Cobra: A History
of a European Avant-Garde Movement:
1948–1951* (Rotterdam: nai010 publishers,
2017), 323.

Nonetheless, many of the Cobra artists maintained close ties and continued working together long after their official end. An essential aspect of Cobra's particular approach to collaboration was cross-disciplinary practices; in Alechinsky's words, "Painters write, writers paint."[16] Whether Walasse's ambidexterity as a poet-painter came before or after his Cobra encounter, he spoke their same pidgin language.

"Pidgin" is a phrase frequently used by Ting and the Cobra artists to describe their common language. The word is first mentioned in association with Christian Dotremont's text, "Les grands choses" (The Big Things) in *Le Petit Cobra 2* (1949). The inherent philological dissolution within pidgin language is championed as a creative device within Ting's poetry, most significantly in *The Jade Flute* (1970), a collaborative publication by Ting and Asger Jorn. In 1940, Jorn created his first formal series of lithographs, accompanied by his own French-to-Danish translations of *The Jade Flute*, a book of poetry by ancient Chinese author, Li Po (李白) (A.D. 701–762).

In 1970, Jorn reissued the printing and invited Ting to add to the linguistic détournement. Ting made the circuitous decision that rather than basing his English translation on the Chinese original, he would approach the text by way of Jorn's Danish reworking.[17] The result is a mash-up of signs and symbols that reveals the flexibility of language and the distinct texture of the written word.

Ting's welcome into the Cobra fold provided connections that stretched beyond Paris. In 1956, the artist presented his third solo exhibition at Galerie Taptoe in Brussels. The space was host to a pseudo-Cobra revival; those invited had to be fluent in the group's stateless, native language.[18] In the exhibited works, the regimented brushwork that had kept a gentle grip on Walasse during his time in Hong Kong had been fully dropped. In lieu of these controlled lines,

Ting presented a cacophony of abstract scores and spirals. While some lines convey quick, vigorous strength, others languish in pools of viscous oil paint. Ting's traditionally Chinese, sparse approach to composition had been replaced by a horror vacui in which menacing creatures emerge from formless molds in quintessentially Cobra style.

Lao Ting

In honor of Ting's Belgian debut, Alechinsky swapped paint for pen and wrote, *Nuit et Jour (Night and Day)*. It would be the first of many texts the Cobra alum would come to write about his friend Walasse. Within a stream of oblique pronouncements, the artist writes, "a hand in the belly hides the brush, in the darkness and the very fire of our consciousness. A black hand identifies its ink mission."[19] Here, and throughout Alechinsky's writings on Ting, he describes an anthropomorphic energy within the artist's brush. The lines flow from the vital activation of the tool, rather than from thinking. This concept of painting as an unconscious revelation of form connects back to Ting's following of the *I Ching* and divination through pictures (hexagrams). Despite his irreverence, Ting's approach to painting always remained rooted in Chinese tradition. While he would continuously add elements of visual intrigue from his global ventures, his thesis on art remained connected to the ancient ideals of painting as a flow of energy, a matter of instinct over idea, and the treatment of ink and brush as not tools but participants in the spiritual act of painting. With his adept knowledge of Chinese art history and poetics, the essence of Ting's principles may have been gleaned from verses such as the following, by Tang era scholar Chang Yen-yüan (張彥遠):

> [Painting] penetrates completely the divine permutations of nature and fathoms recondite and subtle things. Its merit is equal to that of the Six Classics, and it moves side by side with the

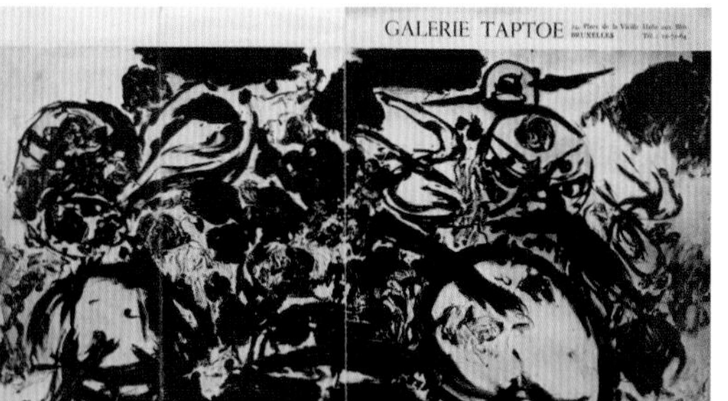

fig. 11. *Walasse Ting*, Galerie Taptoe exhibition catalog, Belgium, Brussels, 1956

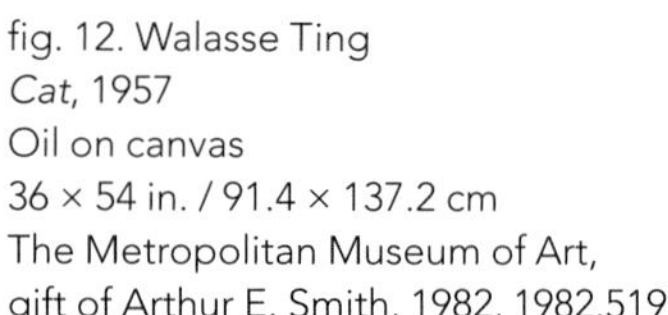

fig. 12. Walasse Ting
Cat, 1957
Oil on canvas
36 × 54 in. / 91.4 × 137.2 cm
The Metropolitan Museum of Art,
gift of Arthur E. Smith, 1982, 1982.519

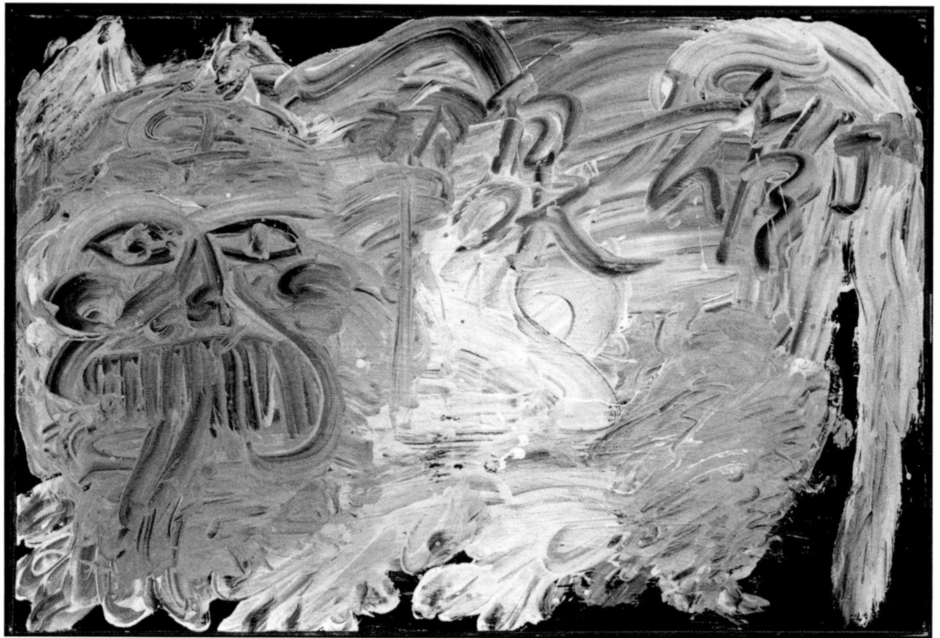

19 "une main dans le ventre cache du pinceau, dans le noir et le feu même de notre conscience. Une main noire identifiée à sa mission d'encre." Pierre Alechinsky, "Nuit et Jour," in *Walasse Ting* (Brussels: Galerie Taptoe, 1956), 2.

four seasons. It proceeds from nature itself and not from [human] intervention or transmission…Maps and pictures contain the greatest treasures of the empire, the strands and leading ropes which can regulate disorders…Without doubt [painting] is one of [the] things which may be enjoyed within the teachings of Confucianism.[20]

The resonance of these ancient words with Ting's practice demonstrates the ways in which his art was not just cross-cultural but cross-temporal, he was "30 year in face with 800 year in heart,"[21] equally concerned with the rebellious spirit of the avant-garde as with ancient principles of breath. Later, in New York, Ting's fellow Chinese artists would refer to him as Lao Ting (老丁) (Old Ting), showing their deference to "a scholarly painter of the ancient times living in modernity."[22]

Ting engaged in the many different art worlds: Chinese tradition, the European avant-garde and eventually, Action Painting and Pop, yet his work suggests an asynchronous space with its own set of relations. While the Western informed post-war movements sought notions of progress, built on the concept of a linear timeline with a contained, chain reaction of developments, the work of Ting communicates a distinctly timeless, borderless position that only increases throughout his life, particularly after discovering the technicolor world of acrylic paint and the abundance of American Capitalism. Ting's hyperconnectivity to myriad moments in time, territories, people and ideas, indicates his pioneering role as globalist artist *avant la lettre*. The dual presence of tradition and innovation, East and West, foreshadows the ways in which our universal present has led to the collapse of art history with its centralized narrative. As discussed in the writings of art historian Keith Moxey, along with critics and historians such as Arthur Danto and Hans Belting, contemporary art has disrupted the narrative of progress embodied in Modernism, and requires acknowledgement of different modes of cultural production operating in temporal frameworks outside of our own teleological canon. As Moxey writes, resurrecting the spirits of Sigfried Kracauer and Walter Benjamin:

> The [M]odernist movement in the arts has been decisively challenged and no longer serves as the motivation for most contemporary art. Beginning in the last quarter of the century, the narrative of progress ascribed to artistic production by influential critics such as Clement Greenberg has been called into question. No longer is it possible to distinguish art from nonart on the basis of whether a work seems to encourage the movement of the spirit in history, whether the medium in which it materialized is more or less aware of its essential nature. Artists and critics have tired of the idea that an avant-garde can define art's future.[23]

The multi-site formation of Ting's work requires access to an art history beyond cultural divisions and notions of progress, in the same vein as our own contemporary moment.

[20] Chang Yen-yüan, *Li-tai ming-hua chi (Records of Famous Painters of All Dynasties, LTMHC), Book 1* (A.D. 847) quoted in "On the Origins of Painting" 27, 29. Referenced in Susan Bush and Hsio-yen Shih, *Early Texts on Chinese Painting* (Hong Kong: Hong Kong University Press, 2012), 48.
[21] Walasse Ting, "My Shit and My Love," in *My Shit and My Love* (Galerie Smith: Brussels, 1961), n.p.
[22] Chihung Yang, "Two or Three Things I know about Him," in *From Heroic Expression to Resplendent Color: Walasse Ting Retrospective Exhibition* (Taipei: Taipei Fine Arts Museum, 2010), 23.
[23] Keith Moxey, *Visual Time: The Image in History* (Durham NC and London: Duke University Press, 2013), 16.

figs. 13–14. Walasse Ting
Untitled (Manet), 1956
Oil pastel on paper
8.5 × 11 in. / 21.6 × 27.94 cm (each)

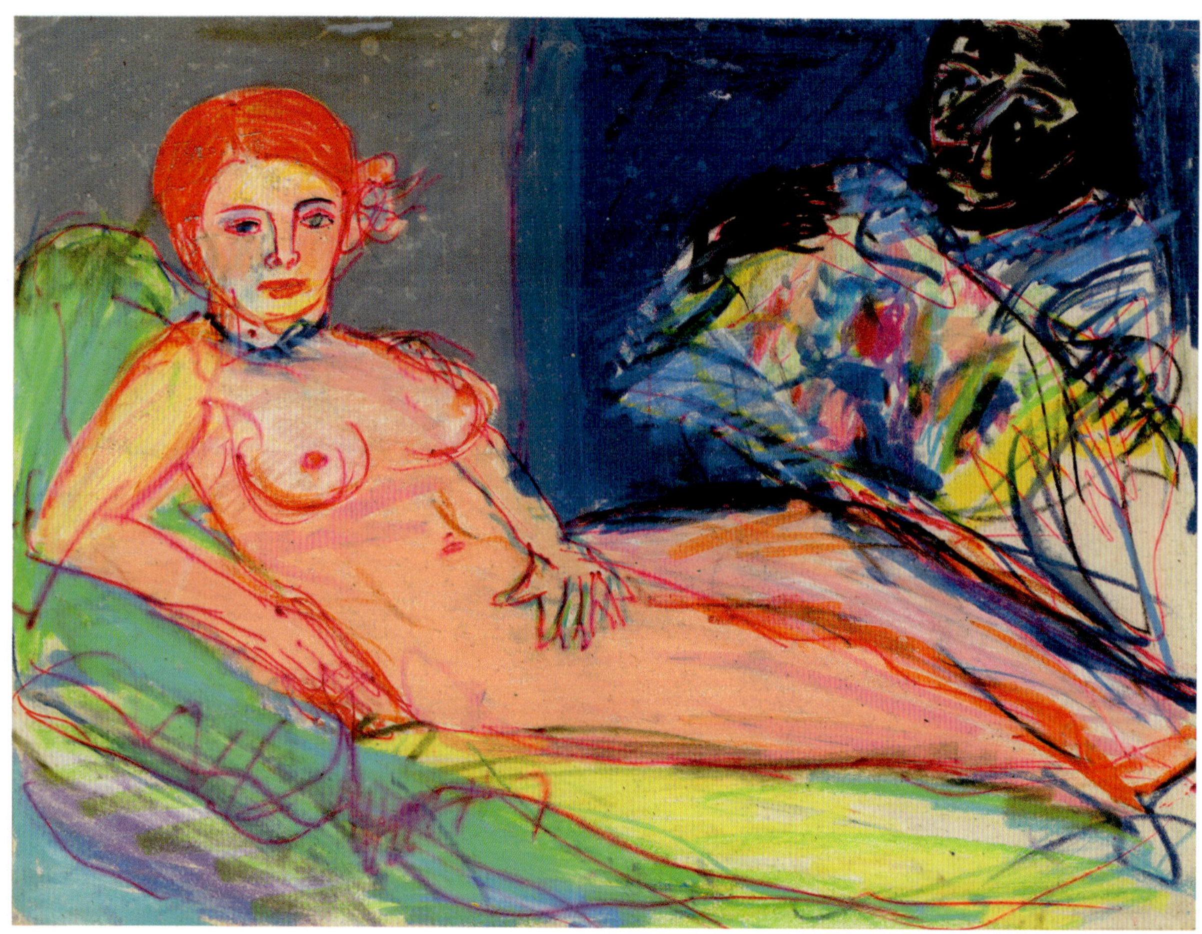

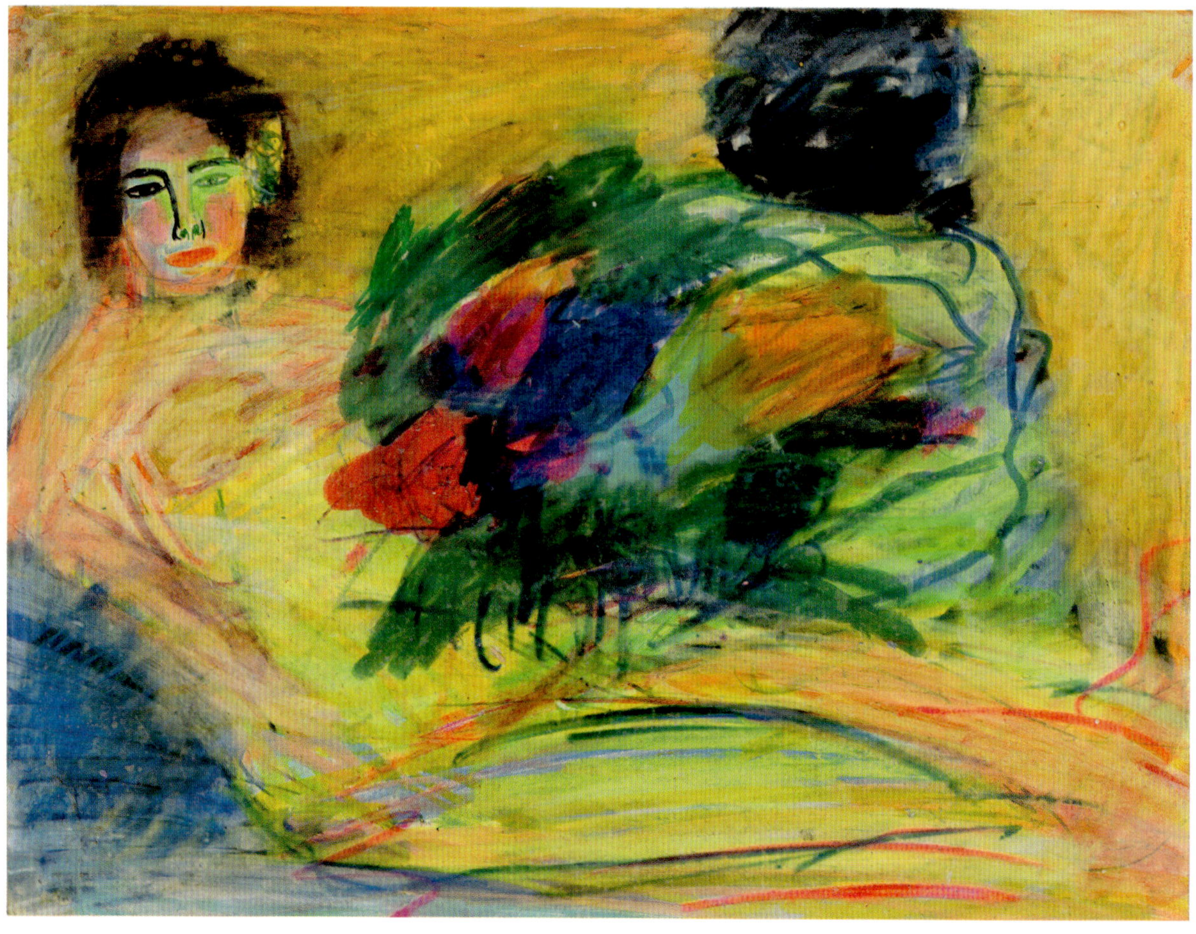

Ting: Connoisseur of Women

While Ting's social assimilation into the European art scene came via Cobra, his independent study in the language of Western art focused on a direct, primary engagement with the female nude. From his Paris days onwards, the subject would be the axis on which his art would turn.

In a series of small pastel drawings from 1956, Ting copies and progressively disfigures the odalisque icon of Modernism, Édouard Manet's *Olympia* (1863). The choice of this iconic nude as Ting's academic contender is a subject ripe for analysis. Did Ting see something of himself in Manet's embrace of this flagrant courtesan? Or even, in that immodest businesswoman *herself*?[24] Ting facetiously admits to this Jungian projection of the anima within a 1977 interview, stating "Who knows…maybe those pretty girls are me."[25] While Ting's art has run the risk of fetishizing the female form as sex object, there is not only a tenderness, but an empathic identification with the female subject in his work that requires greater consideration. In these initial grapplings with the feminine, it may be too soon to tell where Ting's portrait lies, however the yin and yang of Ting's holistic world becomes increasingly reflective in the synthesized work of his later years.

Returning to Ting's copy and subsequent defacement of *Olympia*, the artist leaves no question of his formal approach being an aesthetic impulse rather than a question of skill. In what can only be considered the starting image, what begins as a technicolor mimesis of Manet's model, Victorine Meurent's recumbent pose, sloping breasts and unapologetic gaze descends into a frenzied linear explosion by the time the eye reaches the bouquet wielding Black attendant (the model, Mlle. Laure), an erasure that follows the real-life marginalization of the Realist's favored model.[26]

In what is proposed to be Ting's sequential copy of *Olympia*, the brief former moments of delineation on both sitters are almost totally disregarded, with the slight exception of the naively rendered multi-hued face of the courtesan. The attending Laure is now cartoonishly garish in a way that foreshadows Ting's next move, that sees him swap Manet for the New York School master of the female nude, Willem de Kooning. Ting's flagrant, multi-colored nudes of the late 1950s and early 1960s embody the same kind of Ur-femininity art historian Robert Rosenblum speaks of in de Kooning's 1950s *Women* series: "we feel that the spirit of the Stone Age Venuses of Willendorf or Lespugue lies at the root of this art, as do so many of the Mesopotamian figures, with their bug-eyed stare and threatening frontality."[27] Over time, this staunch, atavistic sexuality epitomized by de Kooning would become softened for Ting, as the freshness of Florida and other idylls become the setting for the artist's mature work.

The Impudence of the Emigrant

In 1957, Walasse Ting resumed his voyage from home, heading further westward to the city of roving modernity: New York. The year was marked by the critical establishment of the second wave of the New York School, which included artists such as Allan Kaprow, Alfred Leslie, Joan Mitchell and Robert Rauschenberg,[28] all of whom would definitively become part of Ting's world by contributing to his artist anthology, *1¢ Life* (1964).

[24] This argument is an acknowledgement and proposed extension of Seymour Howard's theory of Manet's *Olympia* as the 19th-century artist's female other. See Seymour Howard, "Manet's Men's Women," *Arts Magazine* 60, no. 6 (1986), 78-80.

[25] Robert Smythe, "Eros and eggs: sensual painting goes to Market," *The Citizen* (Ottowa), December 9, 1977, 49.

[26] The illuminating narrative of Manet's frequent sitter, the Black Model, Mlle. Laure, is indebted to the scholarship of art historian Dr. Denise Murrell and her exhibition, *Posing Modernity: The Black Model from Manet and Matisse to Today / Le Modèle noir, de Géricault à Matisse*, The Wallach Art Gallery at Columbia University and the Musée d'Orsay, 2019.

[27] Robert Rosenblum, "The Fatal Women of de Kooning and Picasso," *Art News*, October 1985, 100.

[28] The periodization of second wave Abstract Expressionism was pronounced through contemporary exhibitions including the 1957 exhibition at the Jewish Museum, New York, unequivocally titled *Artists of the New York School: Second Generation*.

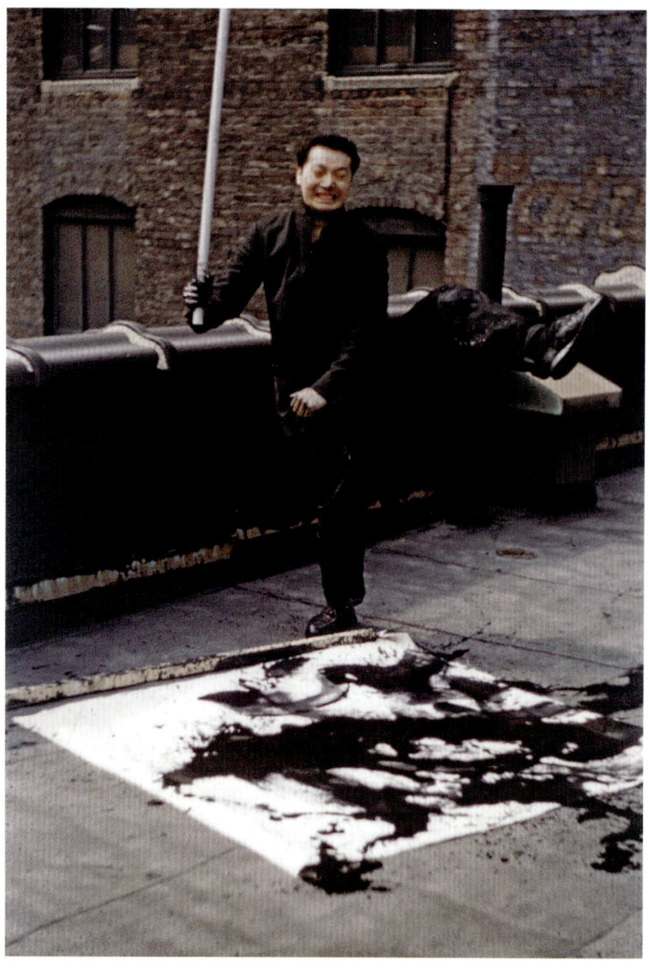

Upon relocating, it did not take long for the exuberant Ting to make
his presence known in New York circles. In 1959, he mounted an exhibition
at the historic Martha Jackson Gallery on East 69th Street. The show consisted
of a commanding series of monochromatic black-on-white action paintings,
with bold proclamations such as, *The Sex Act, Homage to the Unknown*
and *Black Cry* for titles. The painting *Fire* (1959) is exemplary of this moment
in Ting's oeuvre. The work is composed of wild ribbons of paint hitting
the surface of an unprimed canvas. The central black mass breaks into contrailed
streaks, revealing the artist's fevered movement. In following the rapid lacerations
of Ting's line, the artist seems to have transitioned from depicting warrior scenes
to enacting them with his brush. Photographs from this time seem to confirm
this, showing Ting standing proudly next to his scenes of carnage, or grimacing
while wielding some obscure object, knee bent and ready to strike with an
axe kick. The immediacy and haptic traces of the artist's brush within these works
hold their own against the era-defining paintings of Franz Kline, Robert Motherwell
and Ting's fellow Martha Jackson artist, Adolph Gottlieb; enhanced by Ting's
studied understanding of the exalting connection between mental and physical
automatism, removed from any cerebral speculation, before, during or after
painting. As written in the leaflet accompaniment to his 1959 exhibition,
"Handle the brush and forget about it and make the picture and forget about it.
Rather allow the painting come by itself than search for it. Without ideas is better
than with them."[29]

[29] Walasse Ting, *Walasse Ting: Paintings: From
the Painters Notebook, 1959* (New York:
Martha Jackson Gallery, 1959), n.p.

While Ting would never receive the same critical adulations of Kline, Motherwell et. al, from his American debut until the 1986 closure of Lefebre Gallery (Ting's U.S. representative from 1963 onwards), the artist remained a common fixture among the exhibition reviews and gallery openings of the New York art world. By the mid-1960s, mentions of Ting in *The New York Times*, *Arts News* and *The Herald Tribune* appear without introduction, typically followed by a charmed disarmament of his pure embrace of color. In the words of his frequent supporter, *Times* critic, John Canaday, "Mr. Ting has an ebullience about him that can seduce you into forgiving any excess, and he is a one-man proof that spirited triviality is a virtue in opposition to inflated efforts to be serious."[30] After 1986, when no New York gallery stepped in to take the place of gallerist John Lefebre in showcasing Ting and numerous Cobra artists, Ting took it as an opportunity to return to Asia. From then onwards, Ting's work would primarily be seen in Taipei, Shanghai, Hong Kong, while also remaining consistently present across the Cobra cities. Now almost forty years later, Ting is being resurrected in the U.S., which in our globalized present is not accidental. Finally, we have come to a point where the vagaries of his life and work, along with his refusal to theorize his work in terms that were acceptable to Western art criticism, are no longer detractions but the inherent, pioneering value of his art.

In Living Color

In the 1960s, Ting's abstractions received a color conversion that was aided by the high-viscosity paints produced by Liquitex and Lefranc Bourgeois. Unlike the turgid masses of oil paint, the advancements of acrylic provided Ting with a kaleidoscopic instrument, whose smooth application offered the kind of fluvial glide reminiscent of Chinese ink.

> Walasse Ting's new paintings are, like most of his best work, lovely and redolent of a pure, sweet joy. In line with his recent practice, each is heavily stained a single vibrant color which, like a key signature, sets the tenor of the subsequent energetic dripping and spattering of lighter and darker hues. The activity in most of these pictures is more economical than in Ting's previous shows. In general, it occupies the upper regions of the canvas, raining its incidental scintillas down and across the rest of the field like daylight fireworks. The overall effect, besides being highly decorative, is one of intense pleasure in the fact of color and the act of painting, a visual frolic disciplined by the artist's sure sense of when and where to stop.[31]

This statement by then-*New York Times* critic Peter Schjeldahl perfectly summarizes the formal characteristics and "weightless" ideals at the heart of Ting's multicolored abstractions. While drip and splatter paintings were ubiquitous in this era, in considering a work such as *Whistling All Night* (1971), we see Ting's earnest engagement with the brilliance of color in nature, the saccharine shades of flowers spreading like pollen across the picture plane.[32] This evocation of floral breeding is central to Ting's vision. While there is a freedom in the artist's appreciation of color, and the life in the brush wielding these technicolor splashes, color is entwined with the artist's language of eroticism. The excitement of pigment, even

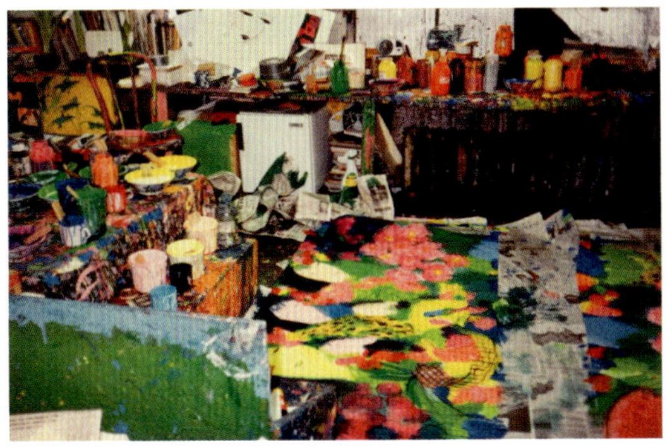

fig. 16. Walasse Ting studio, late 1980s

[30] John Canaday, "Nivola and Ting Have Gallery Exhibitions," *The New York Times*, December 31, 1966, 35.
[31] Peter Schjeldahl, "Understanding Walasse Ting," in *Walasse Ting: New Paintings* (New York: Lefebre Gallery, 1973), n.p.
[32] Pierre Alechinsky, "Walasse Ting, painter obbligato," in *Walasse Ting: Recent Paintings, Very Chinese* (New York: Lefebre Gallery, 1980), n.p.

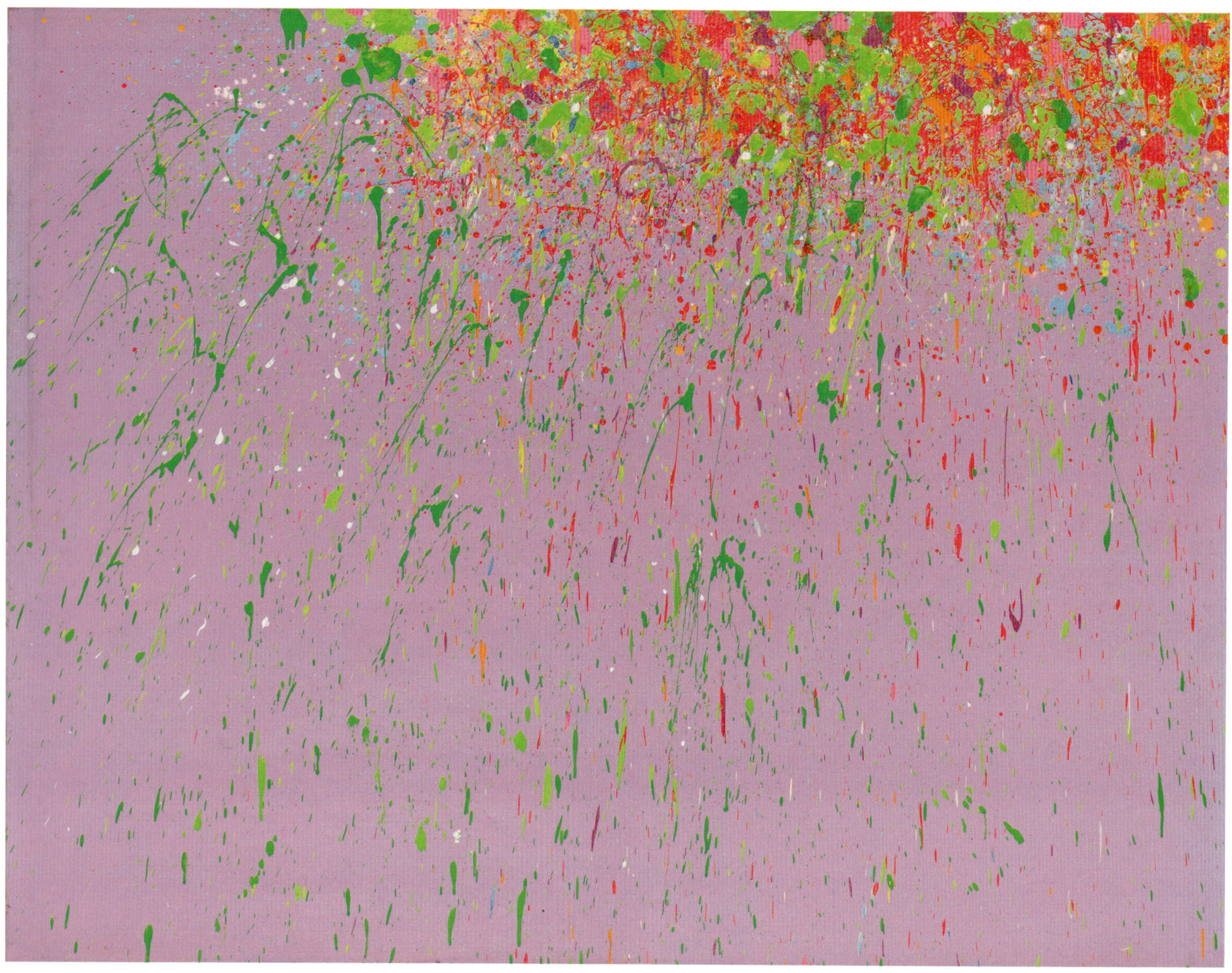

fig. 17. Walasse Ting
Whistling All Night, 1971
Acrylic on canvas
70 × 90 in. / 177.8 × 228.6 cm
Private Collection, New York

33 Walasse Ting, *Green Banana* (New York and Copenhagen: Lefebre Gallery and Rosengreen Litografi, 1971), n.p.

in the absence of figures, is charged with oracular pleasure. Indulging the eye in the joy of Ting's juicy palette almost seems like a guilty pleasure, one that he guilelessly equates with sex and masturbation. The artist frequently makes use of the classic Chinese metaphor of rain and clouds as representing intercourse: "SOMEONE MAKE LOVE / HIDE INSIDE CLOUDS / STICK RAIN DROPS / LIKE BABIES."[33] In works such as *La Naissance de Vénus* (1966), the allusion is just as overt, with Venus emerging from the spray of multicolored seeds. The central figure of the umbrella is posited as a stand in for the female model, whose body (and orifices) would be at the forefront of Ting's 1970s nudes, anthologized in his book, *Red Mouth* (1977).

In a recent series of swirling abstractions titled *SLUTS* (2023) by the Norwegian artist Bjarne Melgaard, Ting's projection of carnal joy into the realm of color and abstraction is resuscitated. Melgaard speaks of the accessible pleasures of color as equivalent to the availability of prostitutes, and the freedom with which

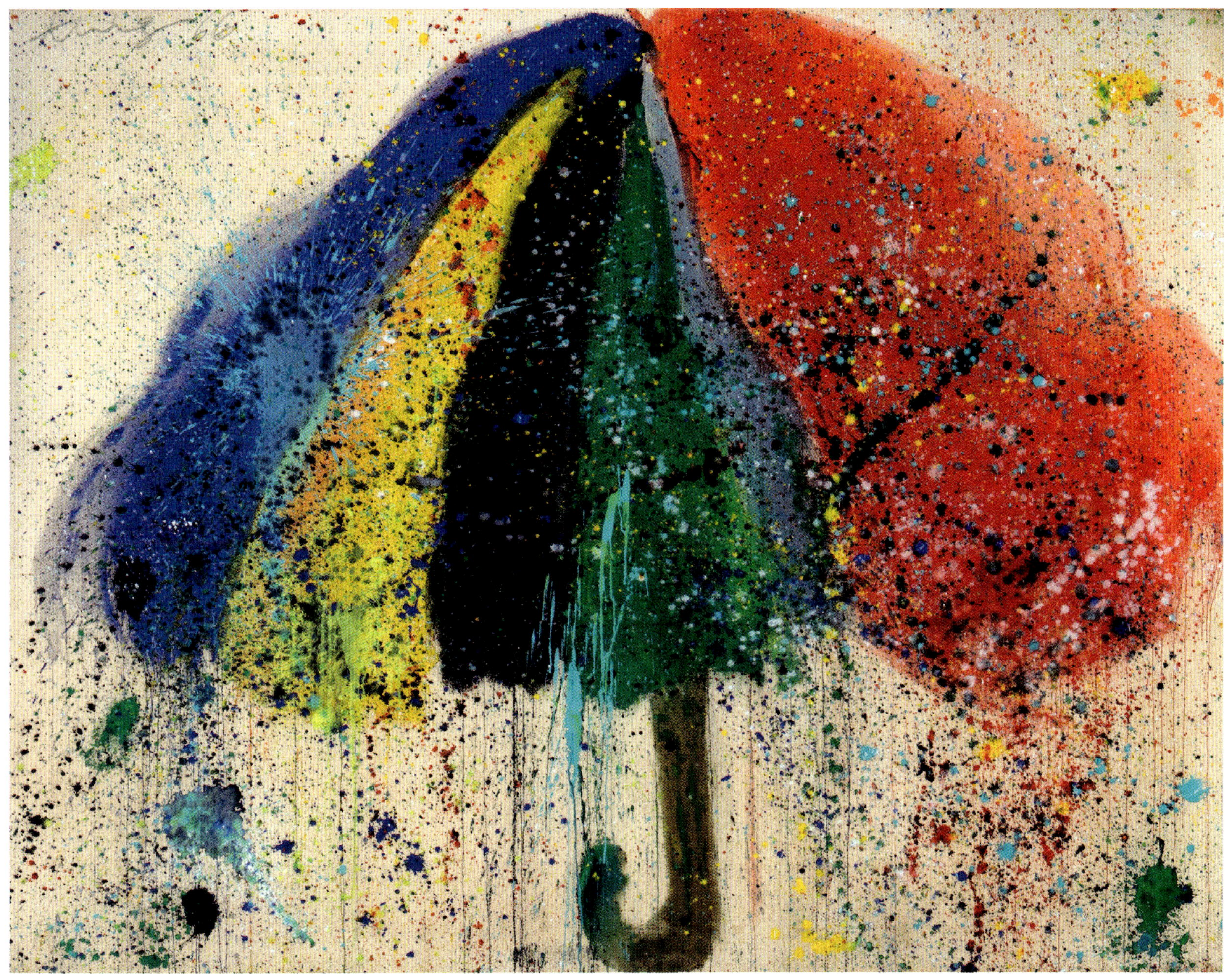

fig. 18. Walasse Ting
La Naissance de Vénus
(The Birth of Venus), 1966
Acrylic on canvas
72.1 × 90.6 in. / 183 × 230 cm
Pierre Alechinsky Archives

[34] Bjarne Melgaard, "SLUTS: BJARNE
MELGAARD 2023" artist's statement
distributed via email, March 2023.

one may come and go as mirroring an encounter with painting. In describing the intimate moments in which these works emerge, he writes:

> Color is essential here, the seductive part of taking advantage, of how color produces content. Just as much as the pure joy of feeling free to just use any color available and taking the risk that these paintings can be completely silent. Absent of any true meaning they somehow create themselves, my companions for later nights in the studio and my studies is a pleasure to paint.[34]

Like Ting, Melgaard is open to the seduction of color as something that is a part of life, equivalent to the joys of sex, that undeniably gives pleasure and feeds desire. While Melgaard finds this mirrored reality in the world of sex work, Ting finds it in the flower, and neither are willing to apologize to the cynics who deem it sybaritic or banal.

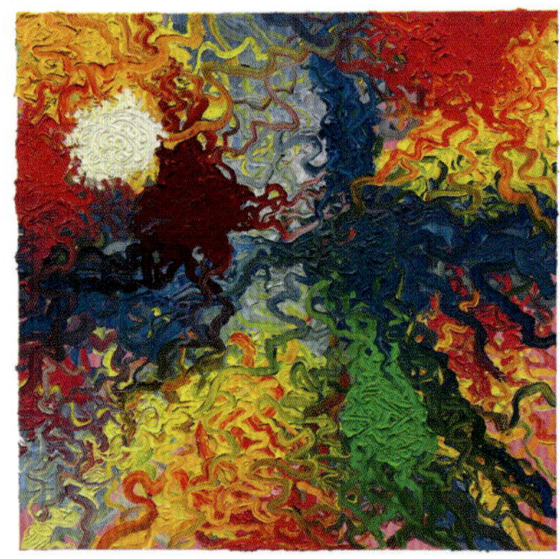

fig. 19. Bjarne Melgaard
SLUTS 12, 2023
Oil on canvas
39.4 × 39.4 in. / 100 × 100 cm
Courtesy of the artist and Thaddaeus
Ropac, London, Paris, Salzburg, Seoul

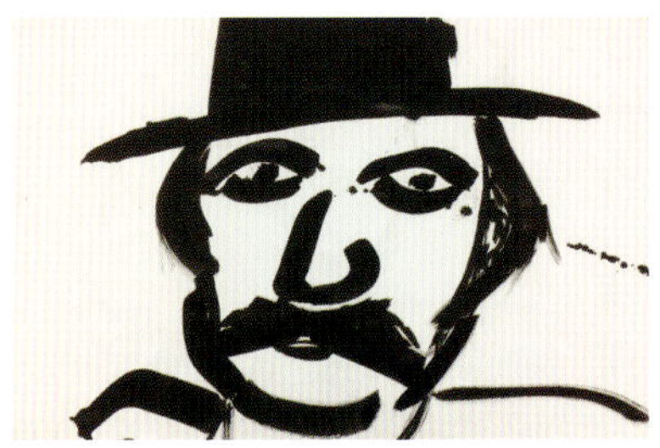

fig. 20. Sam Francis by Walasse Ting, n.d.
Sam Francis Papers, Getty Research
Institute, Los Angeles

[35] Guan Guan, "A few words about Walasse Ting" in *From Heroic Expression to Resplendent Color: Walasse Ting Retrospective Exhibition* (Taipei: Taipei Fine Arts Museum, 2010), 19.
[36] Walasse Ting, "Tsan Hua Ta Tao is Walasse Ting / Walasse Ting is Tsan Hua Ta Tao," in *Rice Paper Painting / Peinture sur papier du riz* (Paris: Yves Rivière, 1984), 41.
[37] "WALASSE TING by WALASSE TING" in *Walasse Ting: The Flower Thief* (Paris: Paris Musées, 2017), 214.
[38] Peter Downey and Jeff Lewis, "Walasse Ting on Painting, Artists, Prostitutes, Love and Life," *The Real World*, Issue 12, Summer 1979, 25.
[39] Walasse Ting, "Near 1¢ Life," *Art News* 65, No. 3 (May 1966), 38.

Love From My Pocket

While in New York, when Ting was not communing with the women inside his paintbrush, he was often playing the role of impresario, holding court in Chinatown over a banquet of "terrapins, pig knuckles, meatballs and fish" with his many artist friends.[35] His studio was an open door for every Cobra artist stopping over in New York, a regular meeting place for an expansive network: "Sometimes, Pierre Alechinsky from Paris and Sam Francis from Los Angeles come to visit me, and go out for a Chinese dinner. They all interest to look what I draw because those girls eyes full of sweet and sour soup."[36]

Ting's gregarious love for his fellow artists crystallizes in the making of *1¢ Life* (1964), the artist book which until now has remained Ting's most enduring legacy in Western art. It's a twisted irony that the artist whose defining words were, "Self-taught. Individual. Not belong to any group,"[37] is best known for this prolific act of collaboration. The list of 28 contributors reads like a rolodex of mid-century artist icons, ranging from Asger Jorn to Andy Warhol. Though seemingly incongruous (how does one get from Antonio Saura to Tom Wesselmann?), everyone is bound by their connection to Ting, the great master of ceremonies. In the same way he gathered visual threads, Ting brought people together, often around a table where he would order 30 dishes to simply be tasted, in keeping with his love of excess.

The artist book, *1¢ Life*, was birthed from Ting's imagination, and delivered by publisher Eberhard Kornfeld, the visionary Detroit based collector Florence Barron and Francis, who Ting nicknamed BIG SAM.

Sam Francis, the abstract painter who matched Ting's hedonistic love of women, food, painting and Far East philosophies, was Ting's kindred American spirit. Ting describes their visual and spiritual overlaps as crosstown traffic:

> [He] has gone from western to eastern. He studied Matisse, he studied
> Zen. I'm from east to west. I interested in Matisse, interested in west,
> so we are like a city bus, when we pass all of the streets, look at same
> kind of landscape. He mixed with the east, I mix with the west.
> He have a Japanese wife. I have an American wife. The same thing.
> So everything similar.[38]

Francis and Ting met sometime in the late 1950s, likely by way of their gallerist Martha Jackson. In the summer of 1961, Ting spoke to Francis and Kornfeld of his desire to create a book in which a many different artists would respond to his poetry by way of a lithograph.[39] The anthology drew critical attention in both America and Europe, though most critics were too consumed with the sheer heft and encyclopedic list of artist contributors to consider its contents. While its legendary status is largely due to the ways in which it is a global summation of this moment in art, it also is a definitive picture of Ting himself. The project captures the artist's sense of contradiction as both an outlier and ringleader, his cleaving of art and language, the plethora of visual information that is funneled through his practice, and his radically impractical sense of ambition.

Ting's independent work from this time is primarily identified through his intensely saturated palette, a characteristic mark of his work from

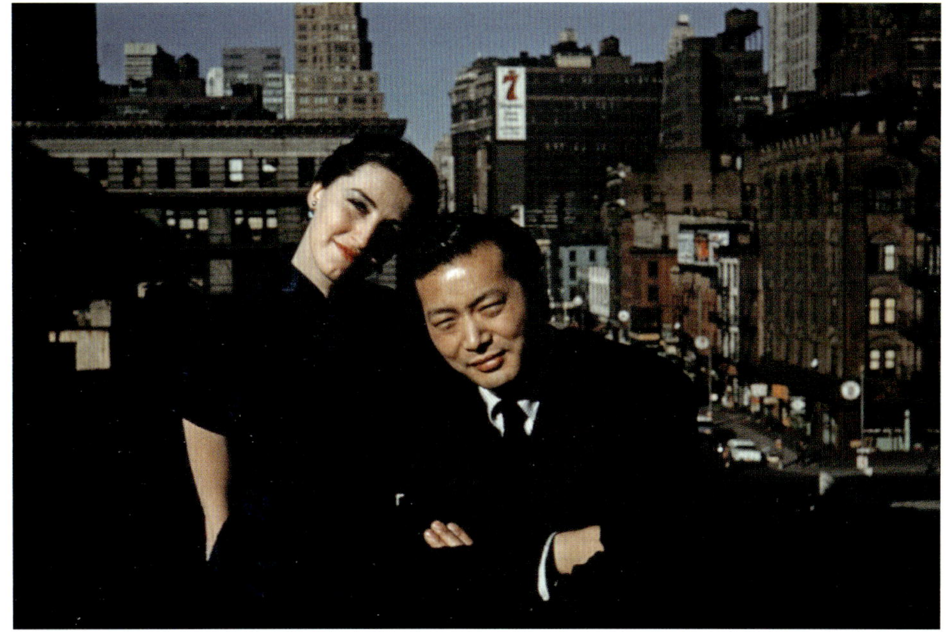

fig. 21. Walasse and Natalie Ting on the roof of his studio building, 100 West 25th Street between 6th and 7th Avenue, late 1950s

1960 onwards. Relinquishing the sacred Chinese, all-encompassing world of black ink, he embraced acrylic color paint with a zeal that "would give a computer a nervous breakdown."[40] Ting's technicolor update created an American appetite for his work, who could rationalize its aesthetic purpose as a sensory exploration of color. This was a language of expression that translated to Western critics, whom at times were confounded by Ting, and read the work as a mere sampling of styles without aesthetic proposition. Ting's delight in color was contemporaneously aligned with the Pop Art movement, and their engagement with the bold technicolor hues that were used as a tactic of seduction within mass marketing. However, beyond this surface allusion, Ting's adjacency to Pop Art is also found in the ways in which he manifested his artist persona (starting with his name) and indulged his passions with a capitalist appetite. As argued by Alison M. Gingeras, the legacy of Pop that today remains most securely intact is the commodification of the artist themselves and the transforming of the artist biography into a marketable and mythical personality that becomes a viable asset within the fame economy.[41]

On Saturdays, Ting was known to frequent the Chelsea Flea Market with Andy Warhol, the *collectioneur* and definitive master of celebrity. The artists shared a *more is more* mentality and indulged their passions for shopping without remorse. To go through Ting's archive is to fall into a wonderland of tchotchkes: jade frogs, crystal amulets and porcelain figures, an endless number of fountain pens, watches, ties, suits, brushes, inks, books, magazines, fans, postcards… The all-American surfeit provides a lens through which to read Ting's repeated forms and prolific output as the true impact of the West on this Chinese artist, who so narrowly escaped the deadly austerity of Communism.

Ting's most definitively American act took place beyond the confines of art, seeing the artist blaze the trail of self-promotion and once again, pioneer the language of our current approach to culture. In 1993, Ting released *Blue Sky*, a look book showcasing his foray into the world

[40] Walasse Ting at Lefebre Gallery exhibition review, *New York Post*, February 17, 1968, Lefebre Gallery Archives, Los Angeles.
[41] For further discussion see Alison M. Gingeras, "Andy Warhol Now," *Tate Etc.* (Issue 48, Summer 2020), https://www.tate.org.uk/tate-etc/issue-48-spring-2020., and "Lives of the Artists," *Tate Etc.* (Summer 2004), 24–32.

of fashion. The artist appears on the cover in a lavender sharkskin suit and panama hat, arms folded and looking towards the camera with allure. Inside, women, parrots, cats, crickets, fishes and flowers are the patterns that adorn the snazziest of suits, ties, dresses and t-shirts, modelled by a group of young and beautiful twenty-somethings (the artist's children and friends) in extremely 1980s poses. True to his free spirit, Ting vowed to make his way into the world of fashion on his own, independently producing his own textiles with multi-process screen printing, a mad venture for even the most dedicated entrepreneur. Ultimately, this American dream proved too rich, even for the dreamy Ting; true to his words, "1 CENT LIFE THROW AWAY SIDEWALK / MANY FOOLISH LOVE GO FROM MY POCKET."[42]

Ting's Menagerie

Following his tour through rainbow abstractions, Walasse Ting wholeheartedly returned to figuration in the 1970s. This homecoming was coupled with the discovery of a tropical haven that would serve as the setting for so many of his doe-eyed women, and now, for this retrospective. In 1962, Ting had married the American artist Natalie Lipton, a Jewish woman from Brooklyn whose parents relocated to South Florida in the early 1970s. With their two children Mia and Jesse in tow, the family made their annual visit to the American Riviera. While the *shtetl in the sun*,[43] may have seemed an ill fitted place for a Chinese artist immigrant—settled within the crazed vibrations of Manhattan—Florida held all the "fresh stimuli" Ting sought in every place he ventured.[44] Once Ting had filled his appetite for the paint-splattered females of the 1970s, the artist spent the next two decades synthesizing his creative peregrinations and firmly placing his vision within the tropical utopia we now know as Ting's World. As his daughter Mia recounts in this catalogue, the region inspired her father, and its cornucopia of exotic pleasures came together for him under the umbrella of Parrot Jungle, a bygone wildlife park that embodied the charm of Old Florida. Among the parrots, flamingos, conures and cockatoos, Ting found the perfect companions for his painted goddesses.

Ting's rice paper paintings of the 1980s and 1990s mark the fourth and final season of his life and art, with which he returned to his starting point. Across the expanses of his cultural transgressions, with Zen-like action, he comes back to ink and rice paper, closing the circle in his journey through painting.

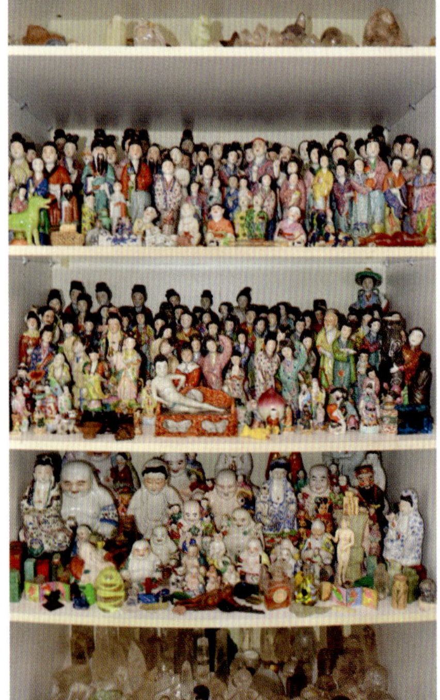

fig. 22. Walasse Ting's collection of Chinese porcelain figures

figs. 23–24. *Blue Sky* lookbook interior images, 1993

[42] Walasse Ting, "Ten Cents A Day," in *1¢ Life* (Bern: Eberhard W. Kornfeld, 1964), 34.
[43] This phrase is attributed to photographer Andy Sweet's publication of the same name, that documents the Jewish community within Miami's South Beach during the late seventies. Brett Sokol, ed., *Shtetl in the Sun: Andy Sweet's South Beach 1977-1980* (Miami: Letter16 Press, 2019).
[44] Walasse Ting, *Red Mouth Series 2 (1973–1977). Acrylic & Oil Pastel on Western Paper* (Shanghai: Longmen Art Projects, 2012), 25.

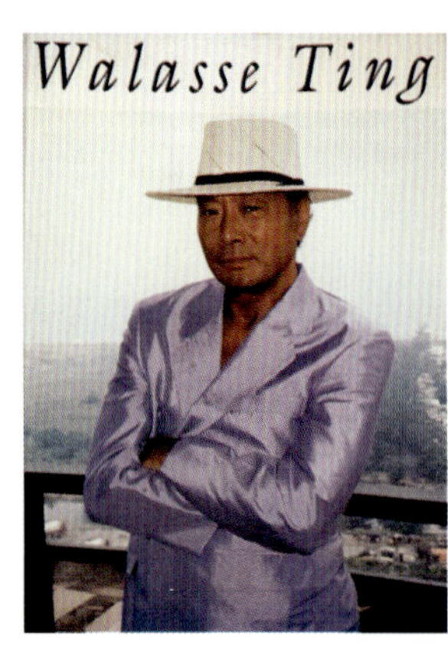

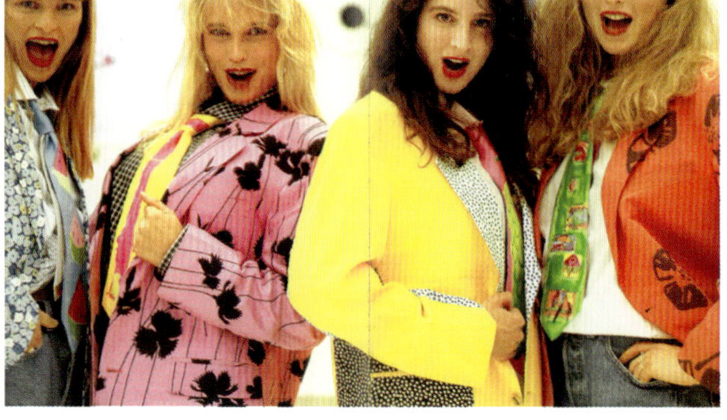

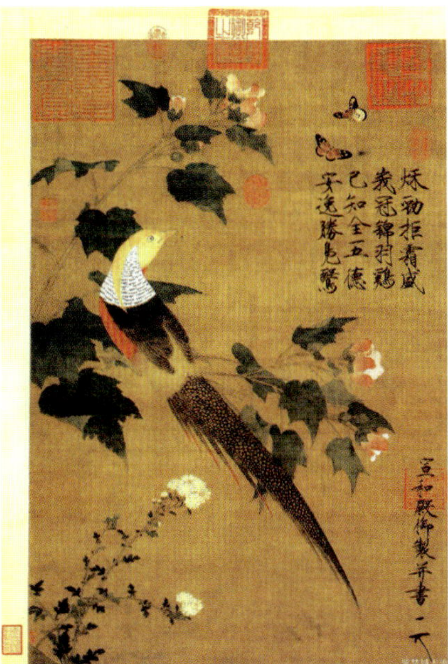

fig. 25. Zhao Ji (1082–1135)
Hibiscus and Golden Pheasant,
Song Dynasty
Ink and color on silk
32 × 21.1 in. / 81.5 × 53.6 cm
The Palace Museum, Beijing

As a timeless traveler, Ting found refuge among the creatures of Florida's Parrot Jungle. While it may be that the foreignness of the scene is what sparked his imagination, perhaps there was a sense of atavistic familiarity. In this technicolor terrarium, perhaps Ting saw the imperial gardens captured in the scrolls of Tang Dynasty, where birds and flowers are the language of harmony. Florida is a place that embodies contradiction, both wonderful and bizarre. In this wonderland at the gulf of the Western world, Ting traveled a thousand years.

Editorial notes

First: Any grammatical errors within quotes by Walasse Ting have been left unchanged for the purpose of veracity. These unedited citings are also intended to emphasize the artist's distinctly irreverent approach to cultural constructions, including but not limited to art and language.

Second: The essay title is taken from a fictive correspondence Ting wrote to himself from Ming dynasty era painter, Tang Yin (1470–1524). In a frenzied jumble of Shanghainese and Cantonese, the 15th-century master berates the young artist for his narcissism and technical inability. The imperative statement is a mistranslation by the essayist, left as an imperative in homage to the subject's application of Chinese sentence structure to English translation, an embrace of the unattainability of a perfect translation.

Third: Critical dates within Ting's biography—most significantly his birth—vary throughout records. Though it's commonly stated that the artist's birth year is 1929, his actual birthdate was October 13, 1928. When he arrived in France (leaving in 1952 and arriving in 1953), Ting made a miscalculation, attributed to the fact that in China, a baby is considered one year old at birth. Adding to the confusion, traditionally (and still for horoscopic purposes) Chinese birthdates follow the Lunar calendar. The artist's daughter, Mia Ting, notes that after this information had been published in exhibition materials, and faced with the daunting task of trying to explain Chinese chronology to a Western audience, the artist chose to leave the mistake uncorrected. Since his death, the estate has chosen to amend this factual error. Nonetheless, the revelation of this biographical secret only adds to the legend of Ting's biography, and self-mythologized persona.

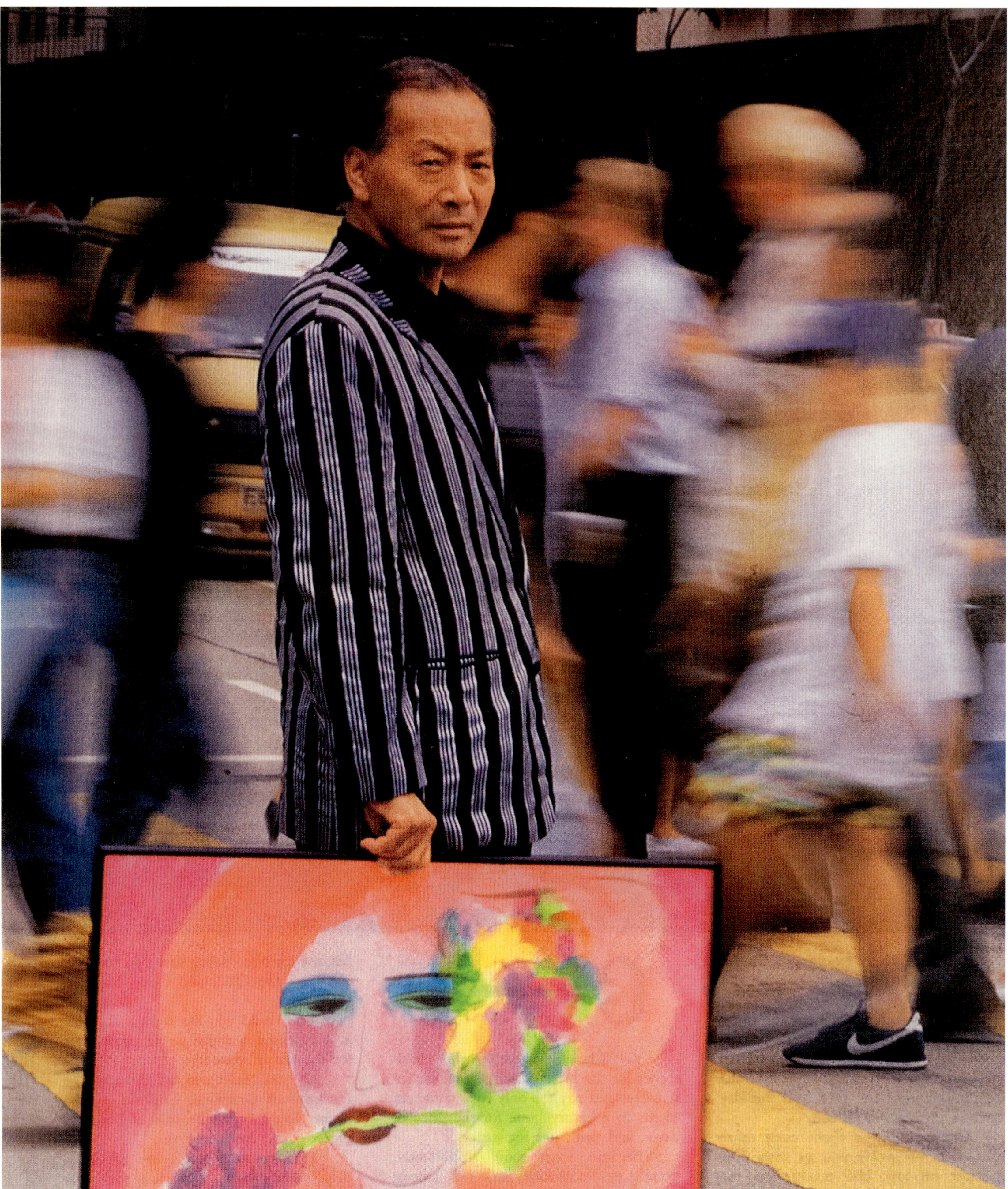

Walasse Ting photographed
for *Esquire HK*, September 1997

Plates
Section Two

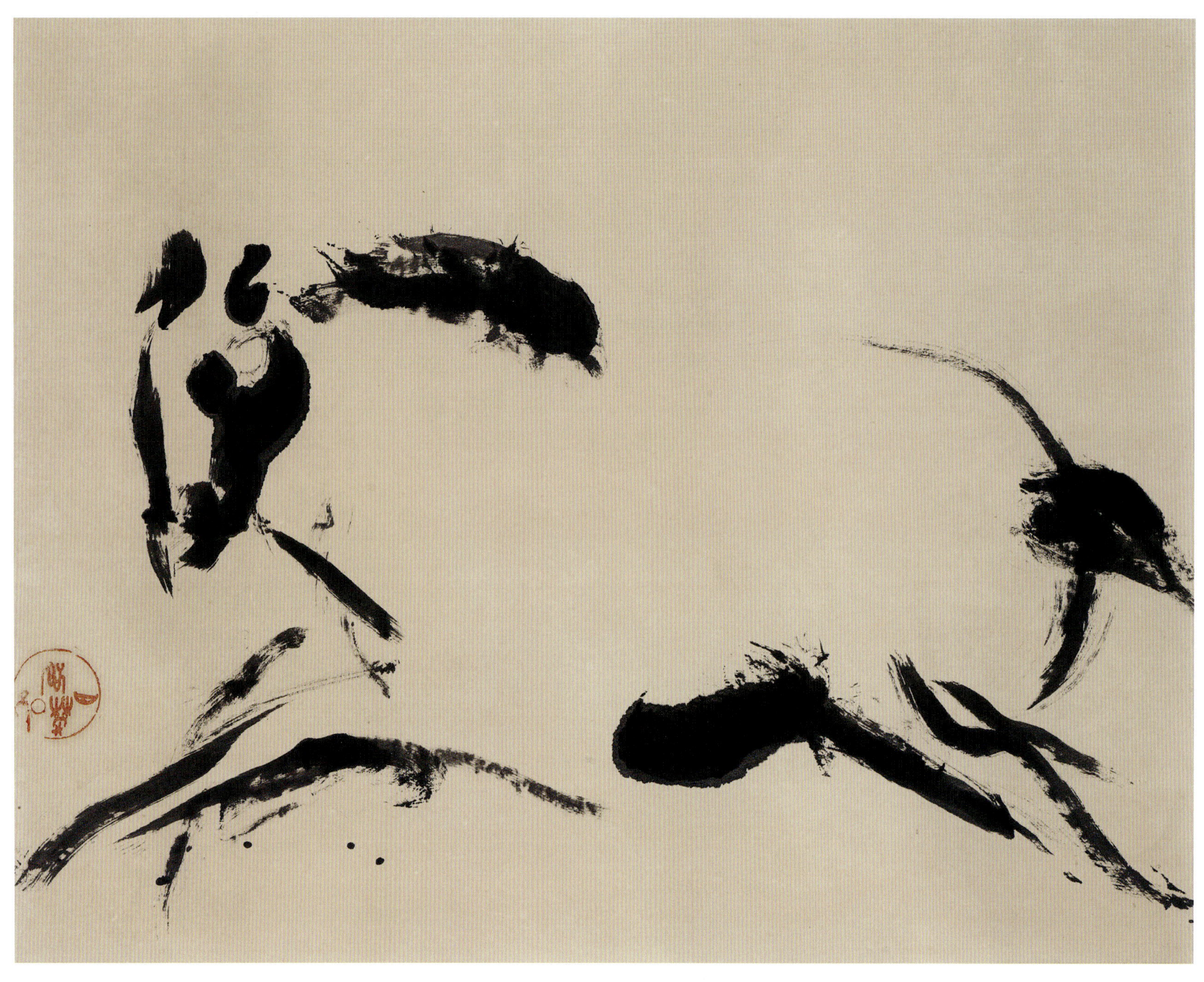

Sans titre (Cheval) (Horse), c. 1952
Ink on paper
77.5 × 96.7 in. / 196.9 × 245.6 cm
Musée Cernuschi, Asian Arts Museum
of Paris

64

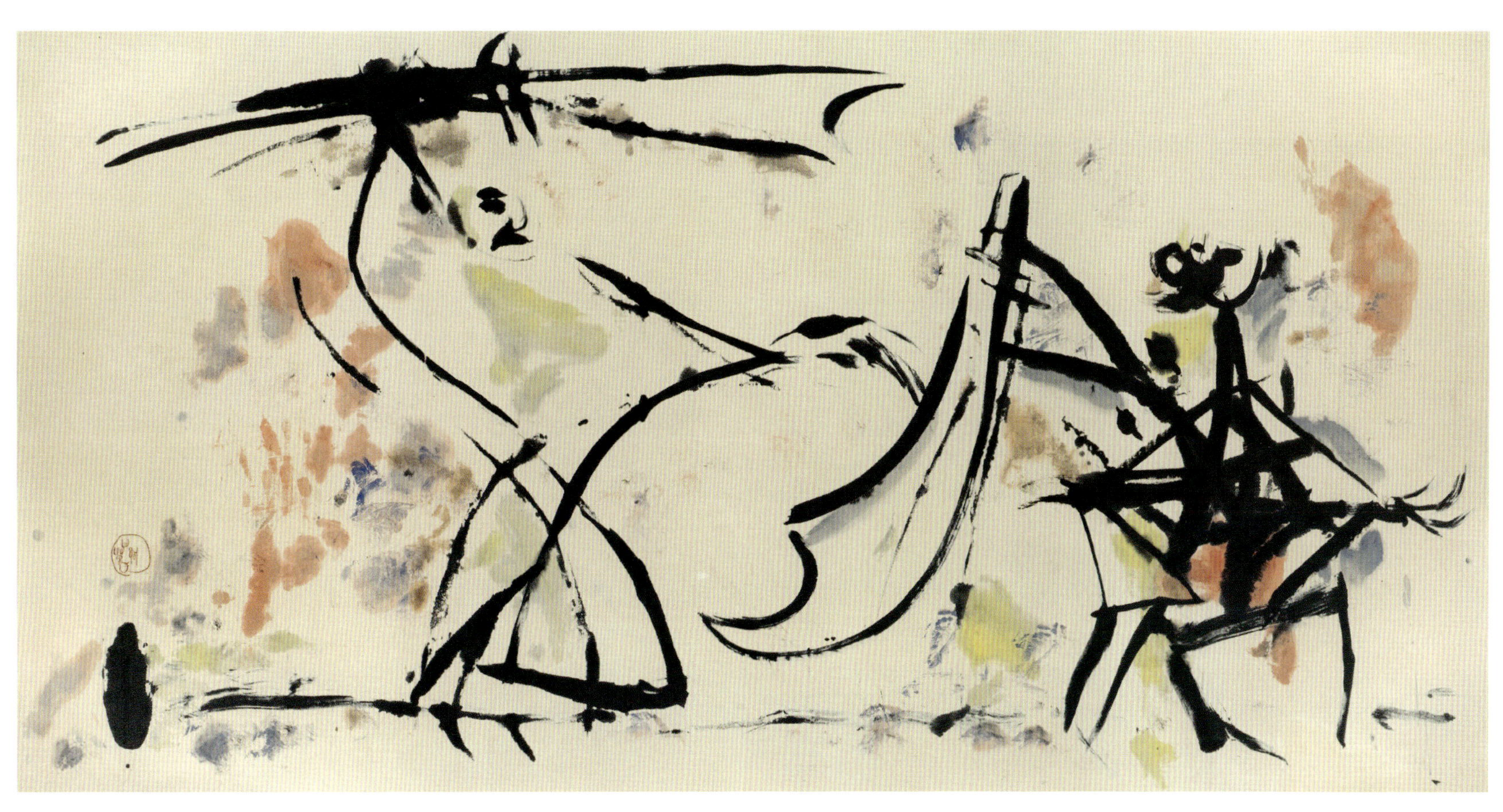

Sans titre (Combat aux grands sabres)
(Fight with Big Swords), c. 1952–54
Ink on paper
91.8 × 177.5 in. / 233.2 × 450.9 cm
Musée Cernuschi, Asian Arts Museum
of Paris

Pekin Opera, 1955
Chinese ink and oil on paper mounted
on canvas
35.1 × 39.8 in. / 89 × 101 cm

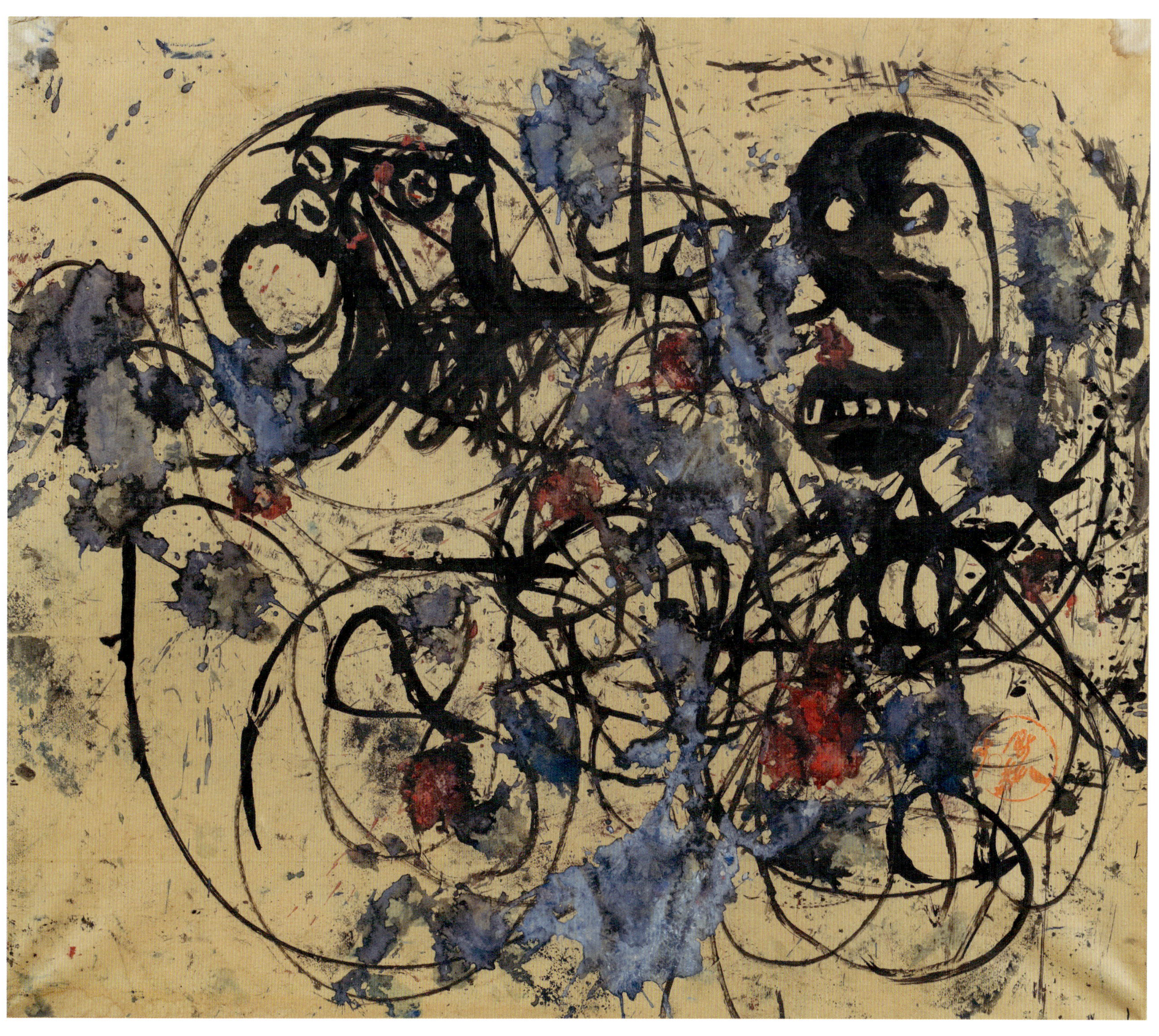

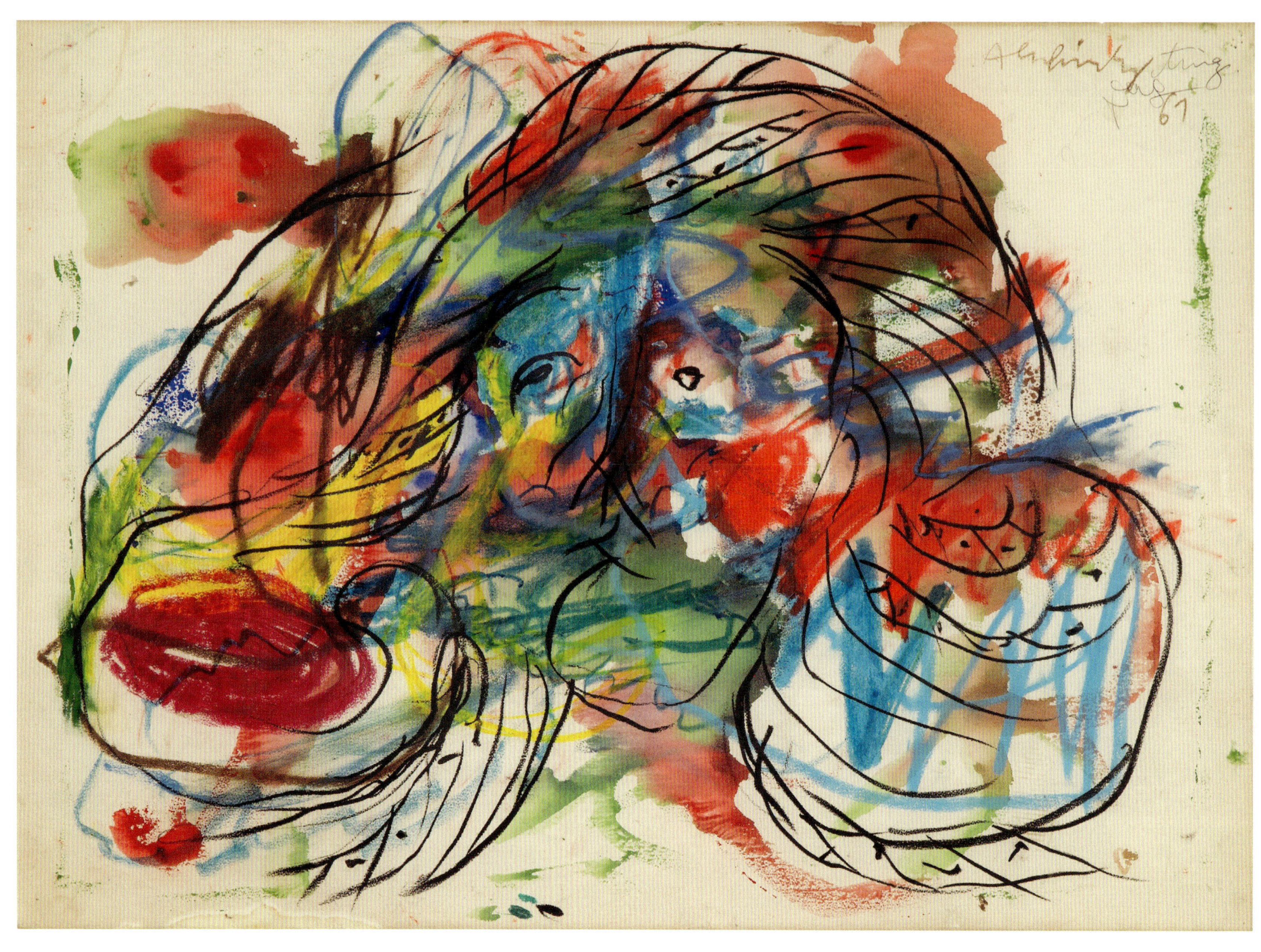

Walasse Ting, Pierre Alechinsky
Aleching, 1961
Gouache and crayon on paper
22.1 × 29.5 in. / 56 × 75 cm
Museum Jorn, Silkeborg

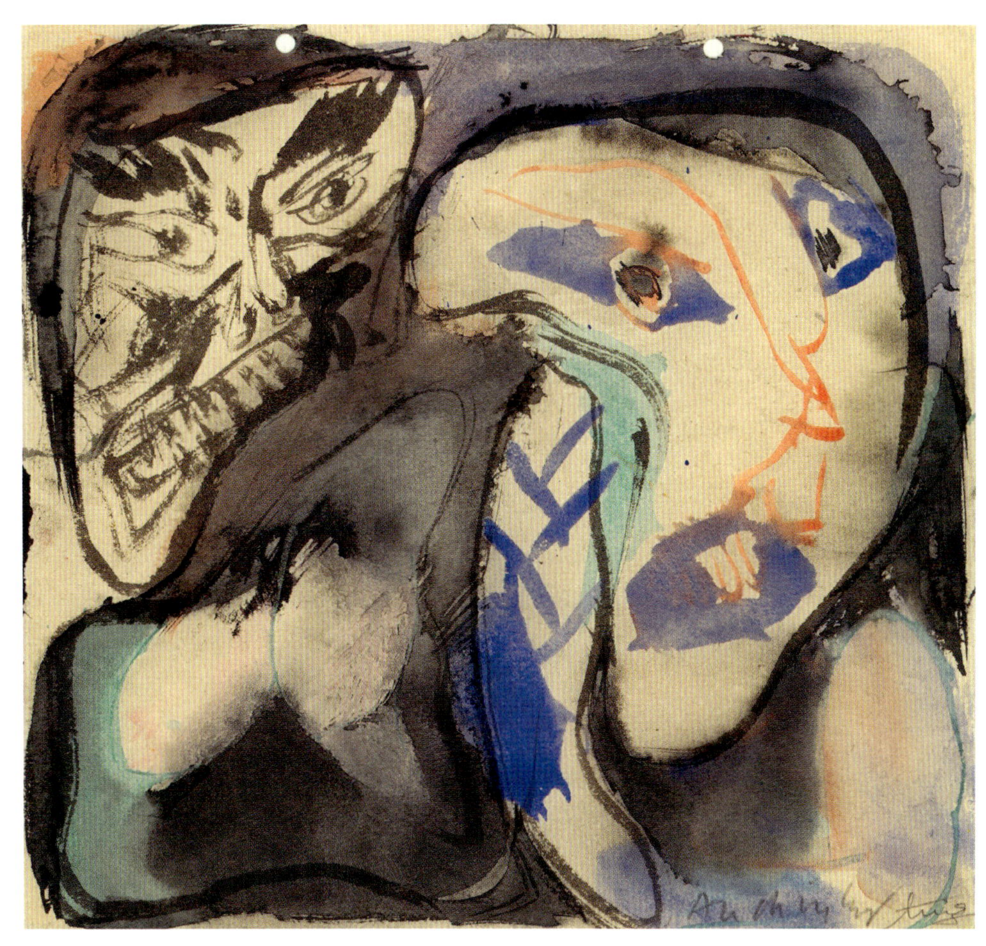

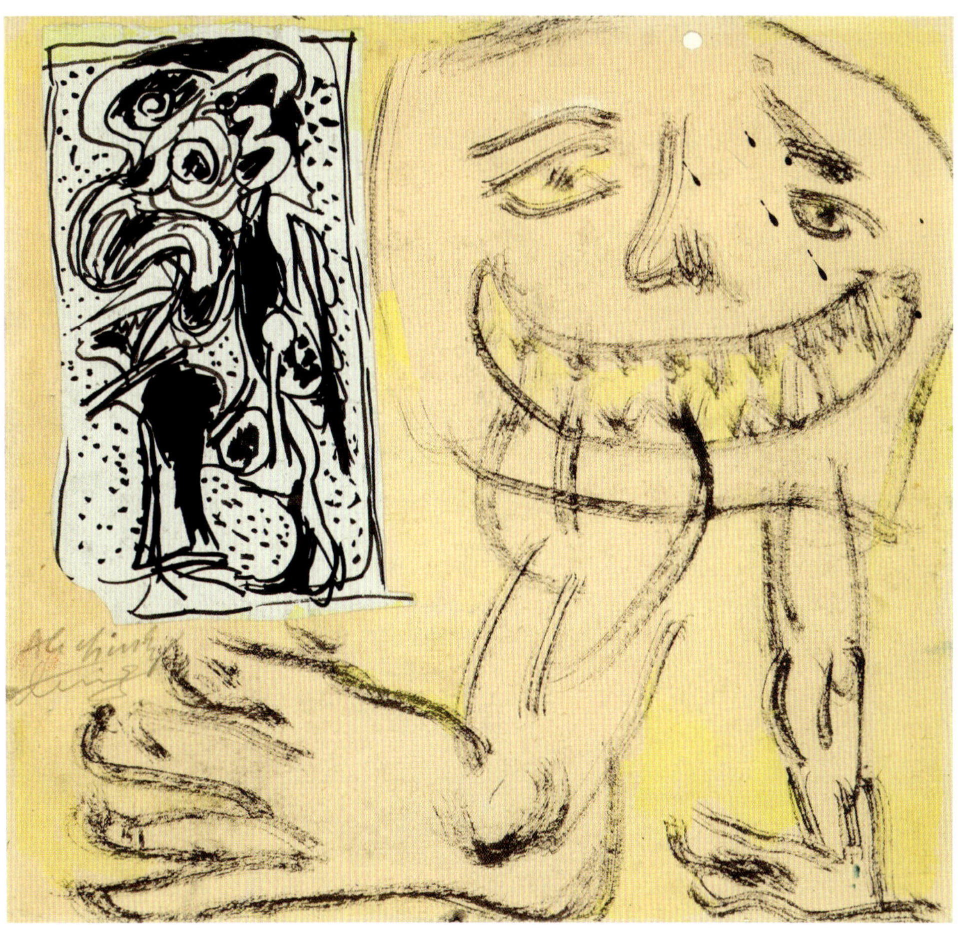

Walasse Ting, Pierre Alechinsky
Aleching, n.d.
Watercolor on paper
11.8 × 12.3 in. / 29.8 × 31.3 cm (each)
Museum Jorn, Silkeborg

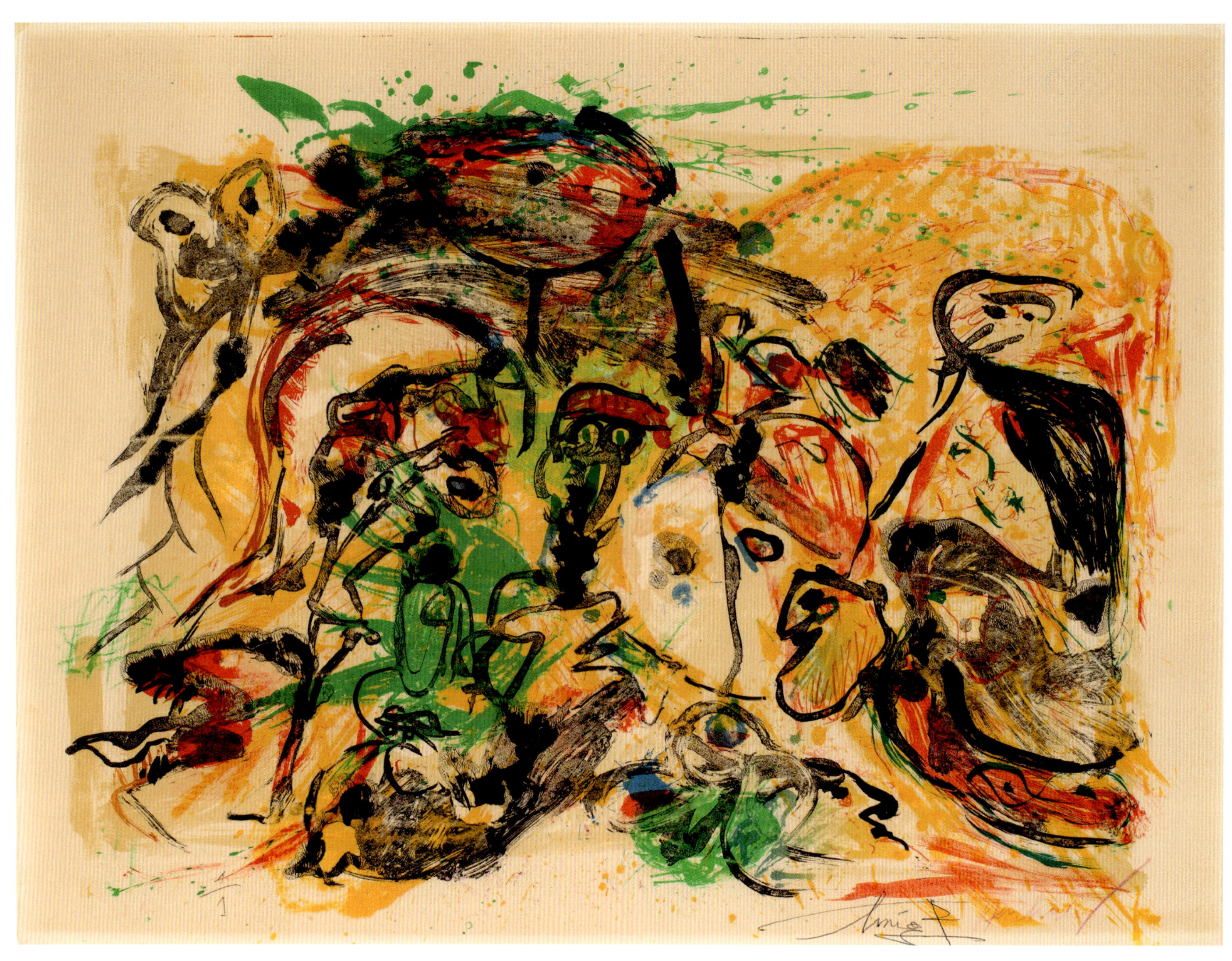

Walasse Ting, Pierre Alechinsky
Untitled, 1969
Etching and aquatint on paper
19.6 × 25.8 in. / 50.5 × 65.4 cm
NSU Art Museum Fort Lauderdale,
Cobra Collection, gift of Golda
and Meyer Marks

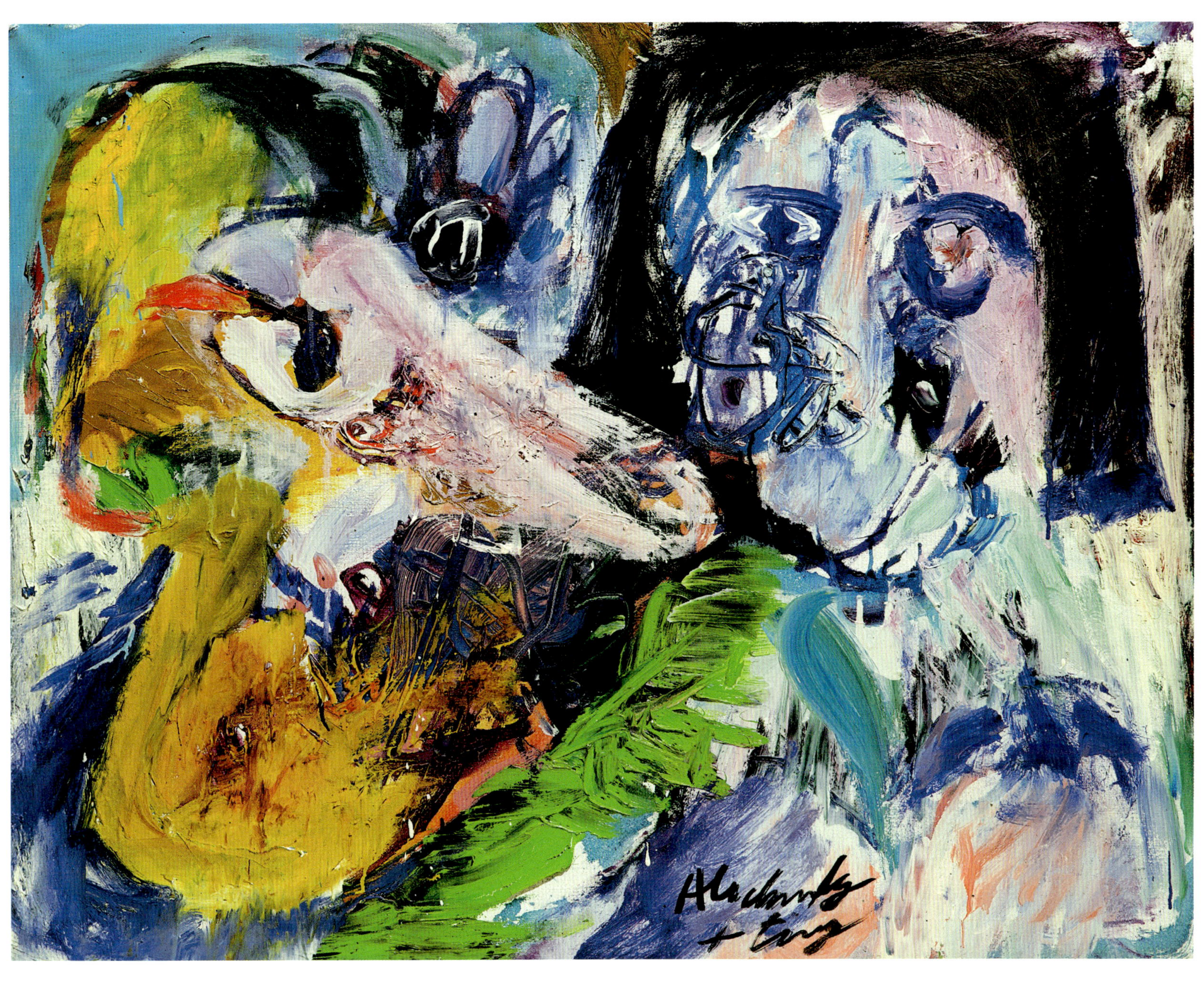

Walasse Ting, Pierre Alechinsky
Divorce Lent, 1962
Oil on canvas
31.5 × 39.4 in. / 80 × 100 cm
Museum Jorn, Silkeborg

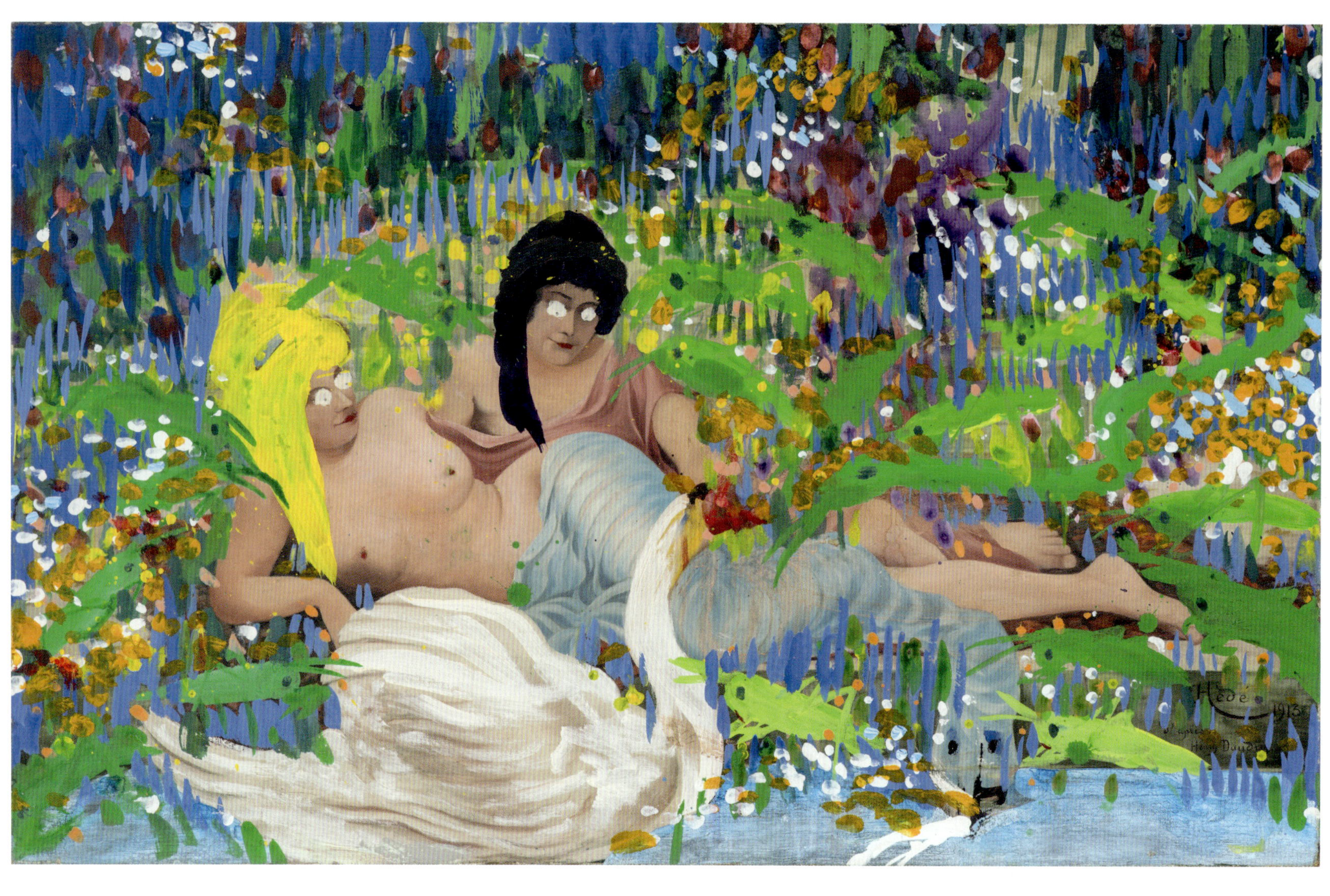

Walasse Ting, Asger Jorn
Spring Garden for Asger, 1963
Acrylic on found oil painting on canvas
25.5 × 39.5 in. / 64.7 × 100.3 cm

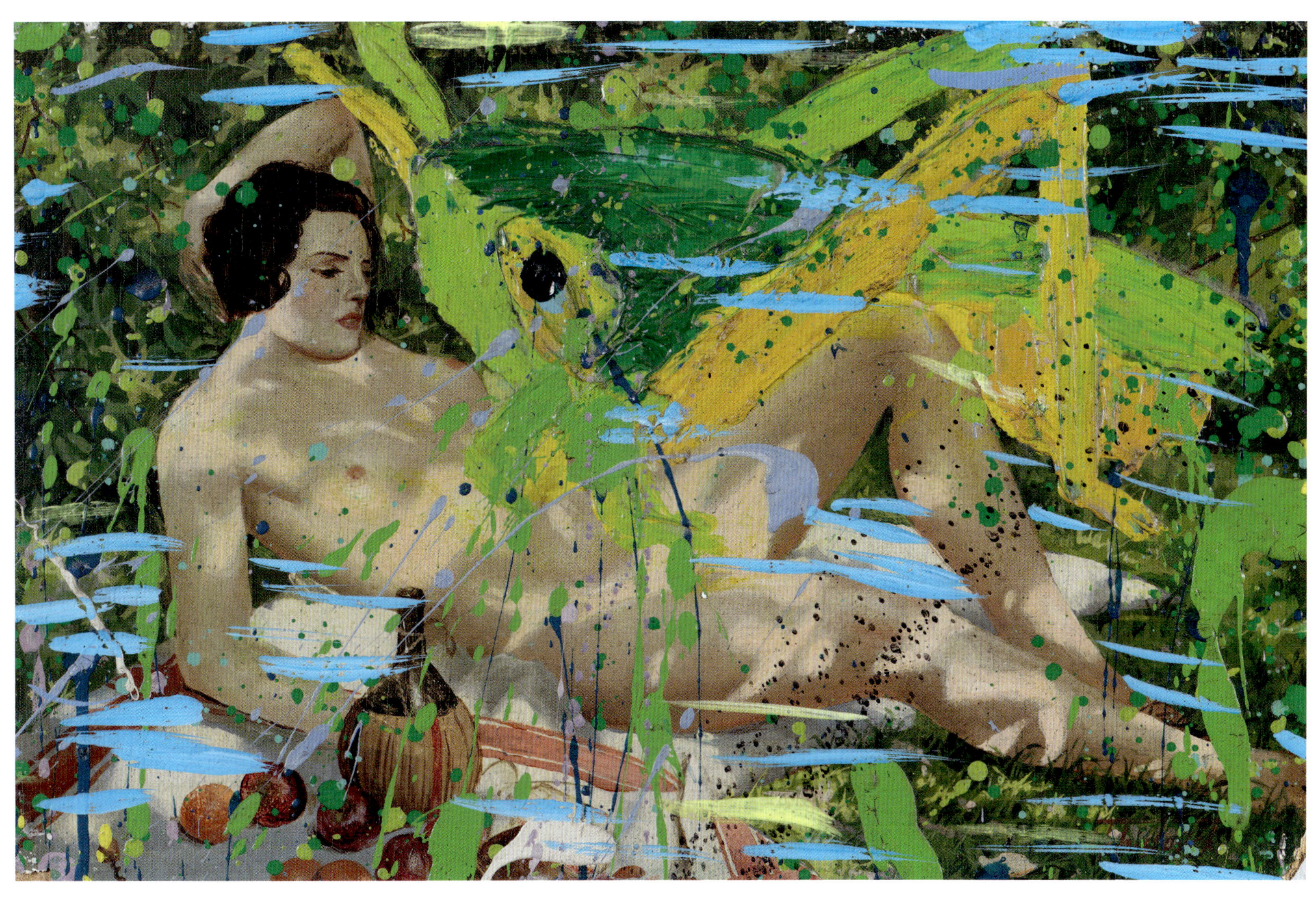

Walasse Ting, Asger Jorn
Come to Me Give to Me Baby, 1968
Acrylic on found oil painting on canvas
11 × 16 in. / 27.9 × 40.6 cm

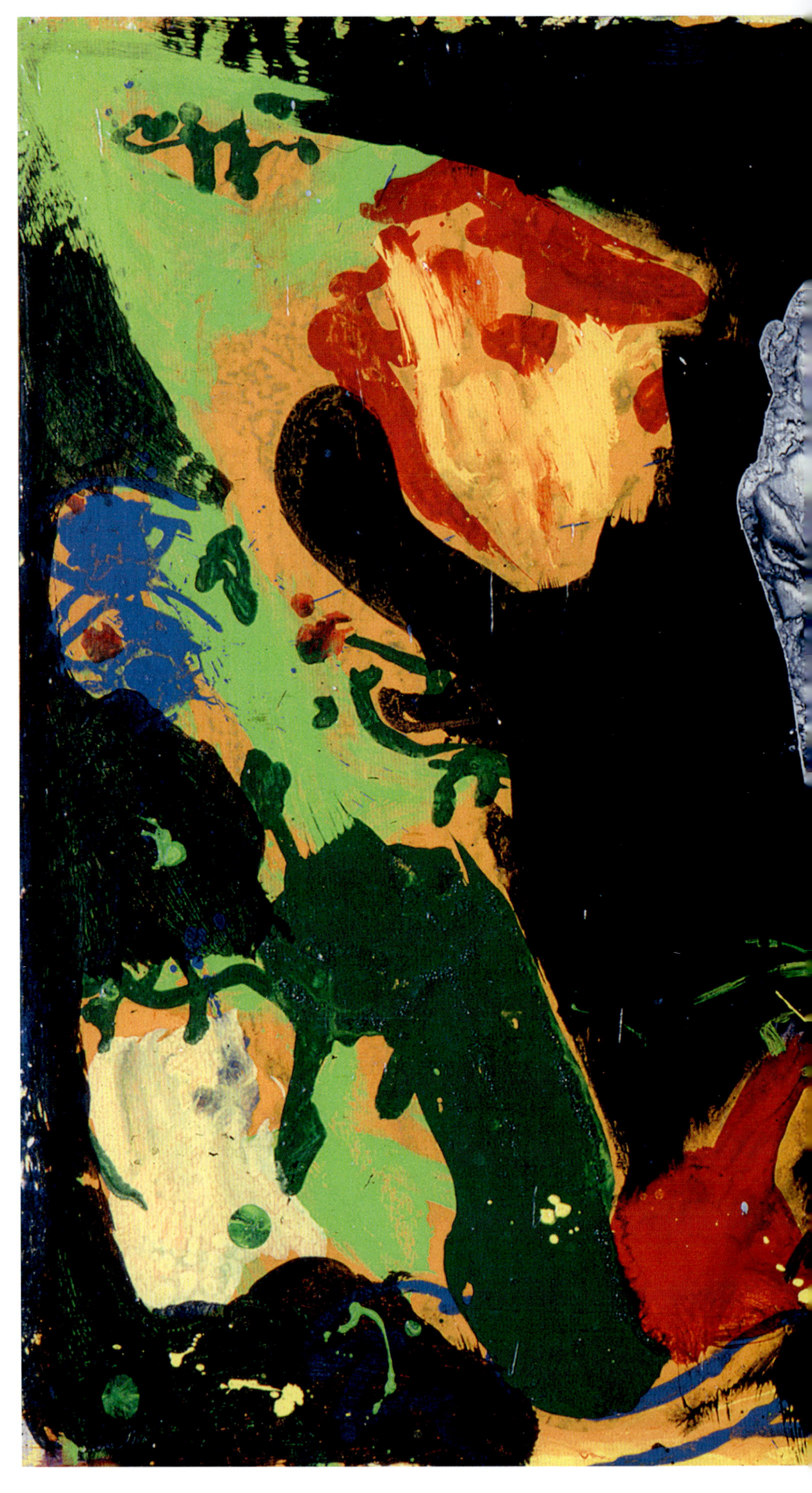

Walasse Ting, Pierre Alechinsky, Asger Jorn
Jorn's grave?, 1970–1993
Acrylic on paper mounted on canvas
25.2 × 37 in. / 64 × 94 cm
Museum Jorn, Silkeborg

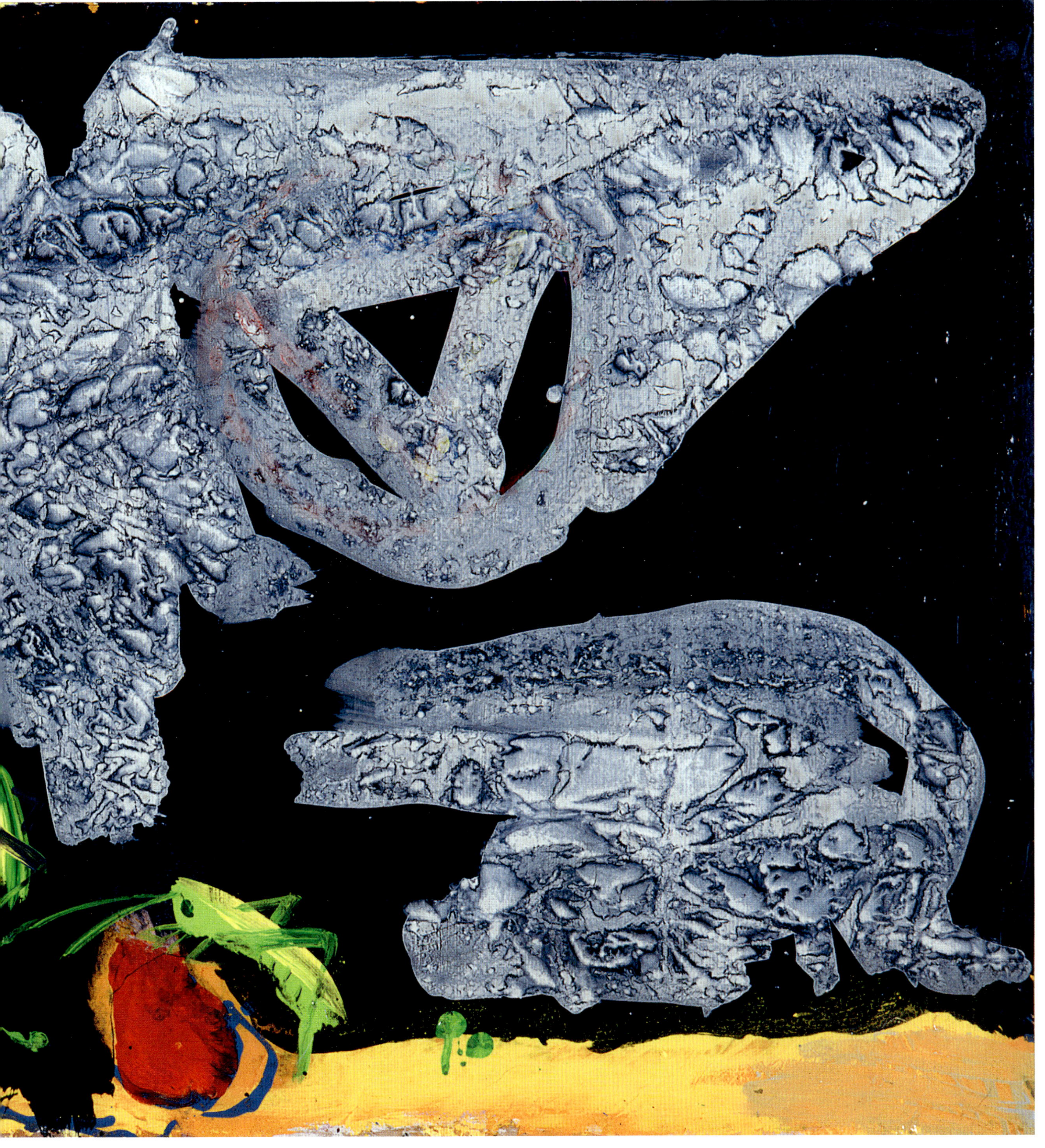

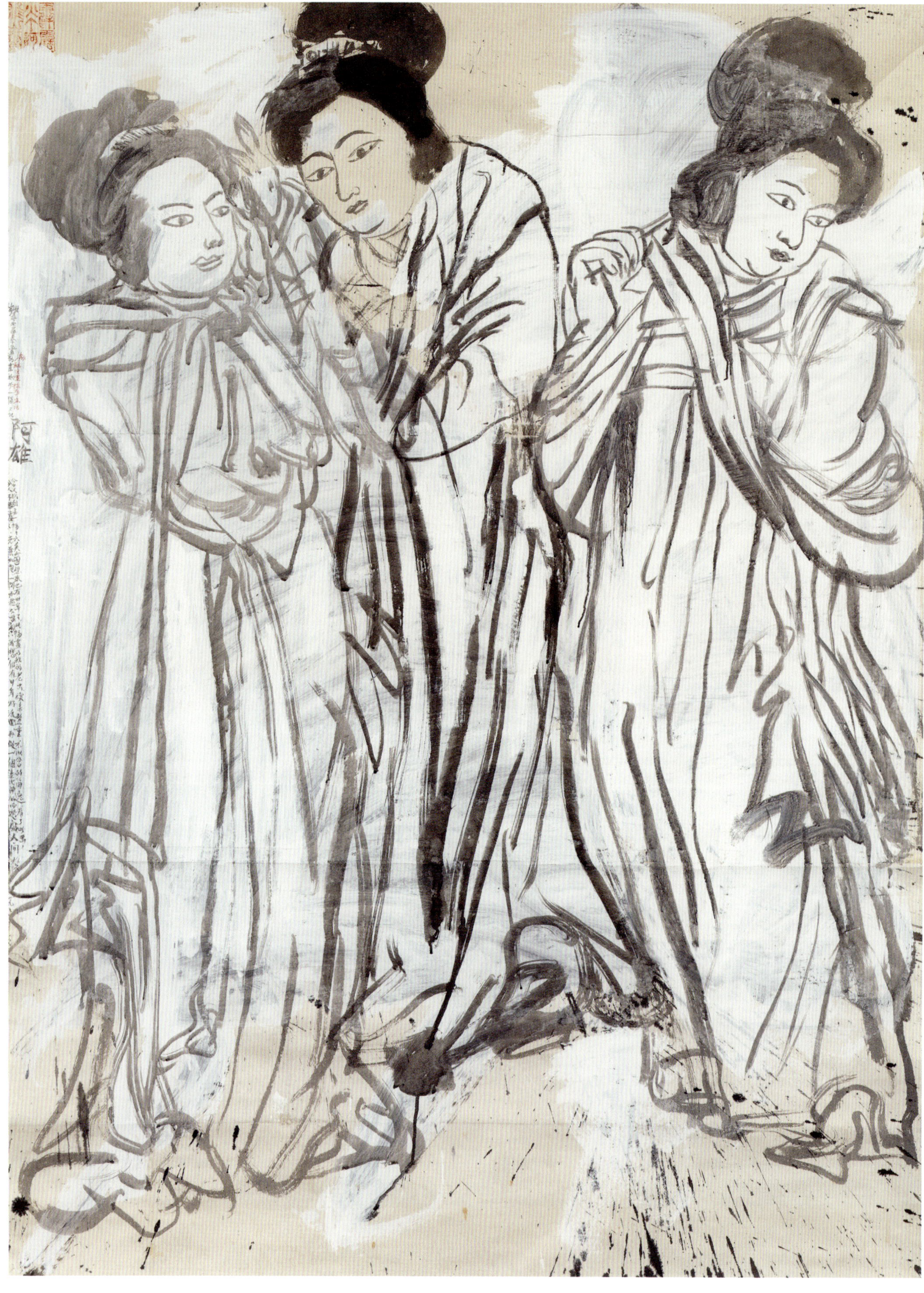

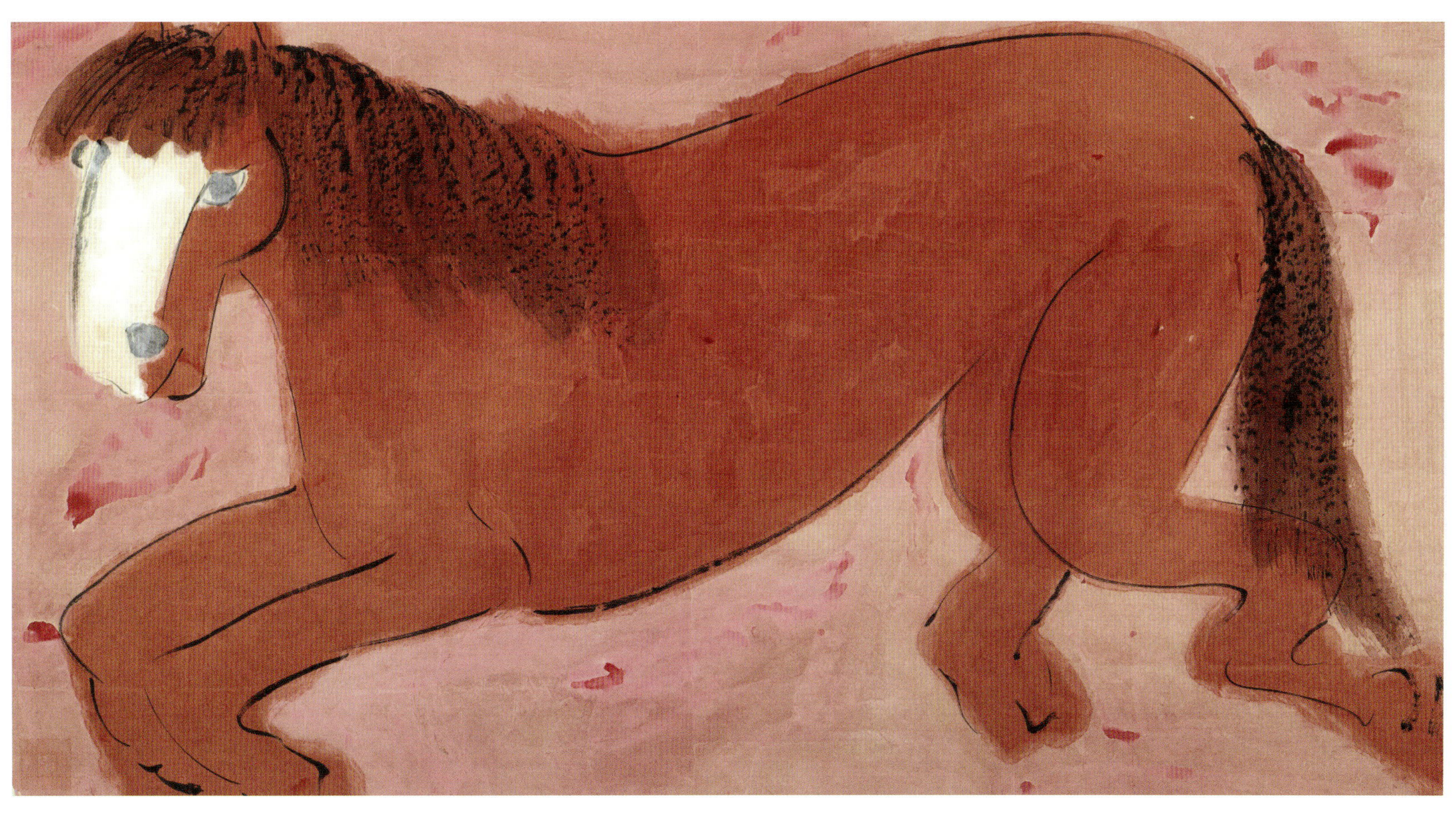

Three Tang Era Women, 1960s
Acrylic and Chinese ink mounted
on black silk and bamboo scroll
65 × 47 in. / 165.1 × 119.4 cm

The Red Horse, early 1980s
Acrylic and Chinese ink on rice paper
mounted on canvas
38 × 69 in. / 96.5 × 175.2 cm
Collection Marlène Brody

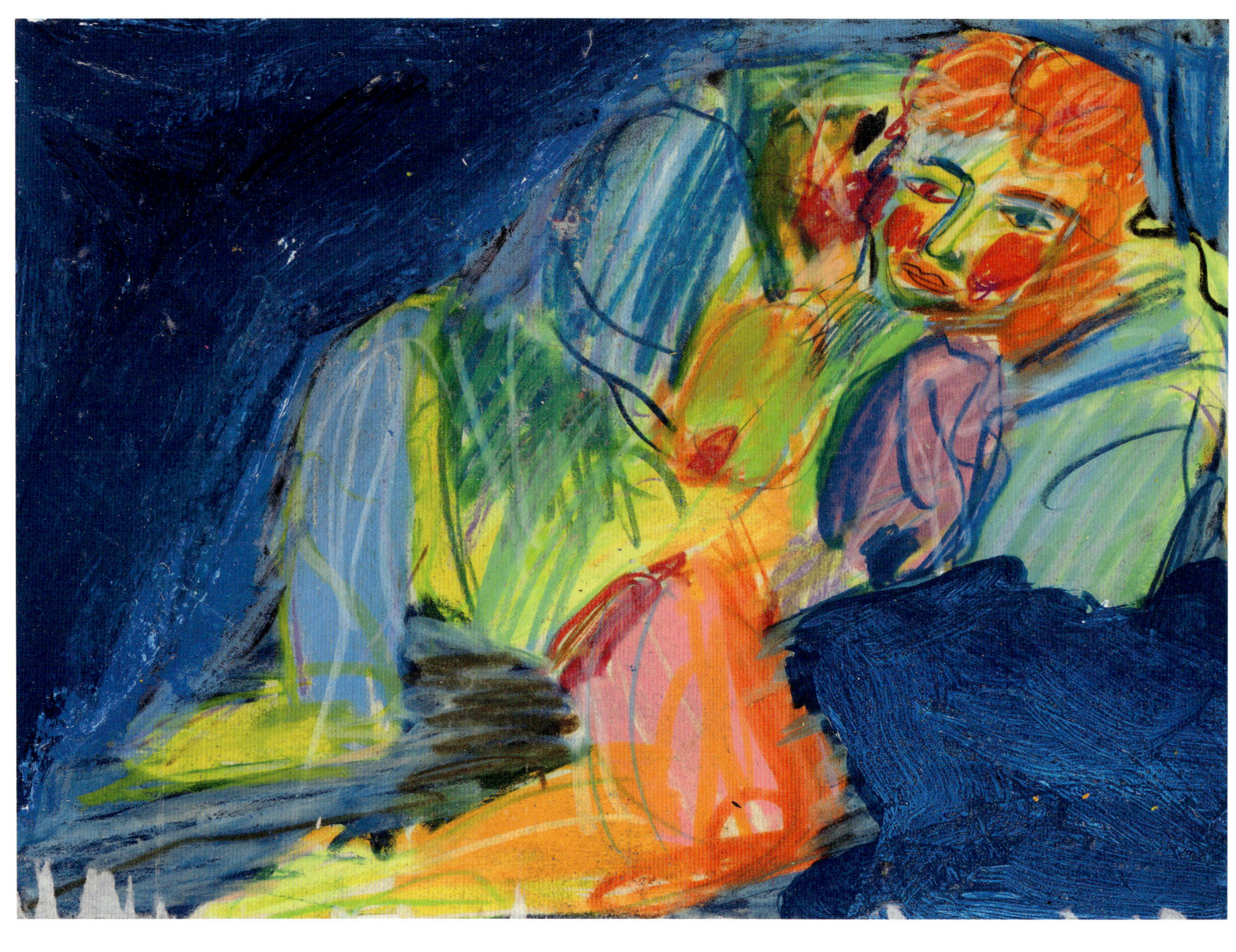

My Blue Mood, 1959
Acrylic and oil pastel on paper
12.5 × 17.5 in. / 31.8 × 44.5 cm

Baby Girl, 1953
Oil on canvas
25 × 21 in. / 63.5 × 53.3 cm

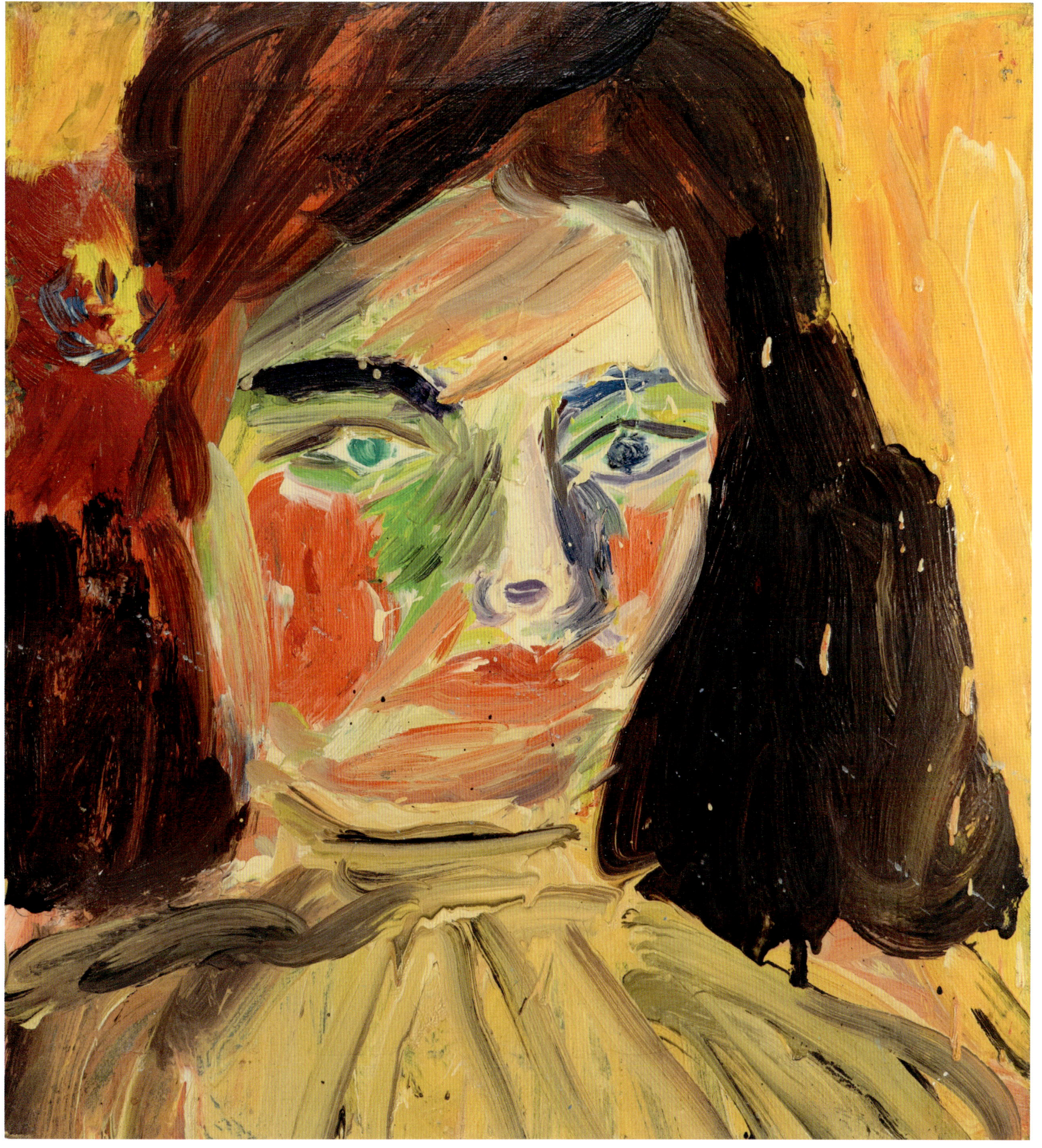

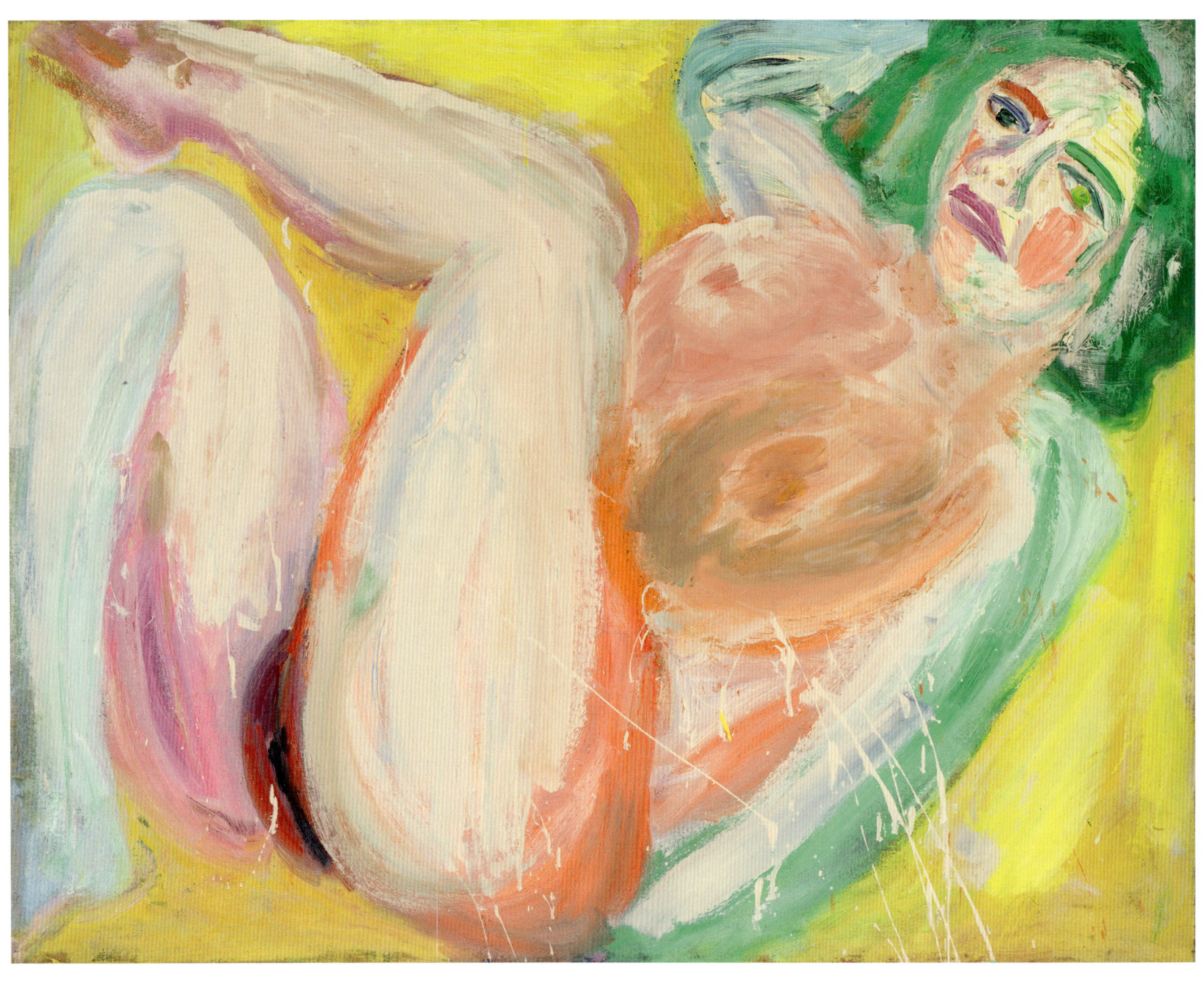

Walasse Ting
No Fuck S.V.P, 1962
Oil on canvas
48 × 60 in. / 121.9 × 152.4 cm

My Sweetheart Thinks too Much, 1962
Oil on canvas
59.8 × 32.3 in. / 152 × 82 cm
Collection Stedelijk Museum, Amsterdam

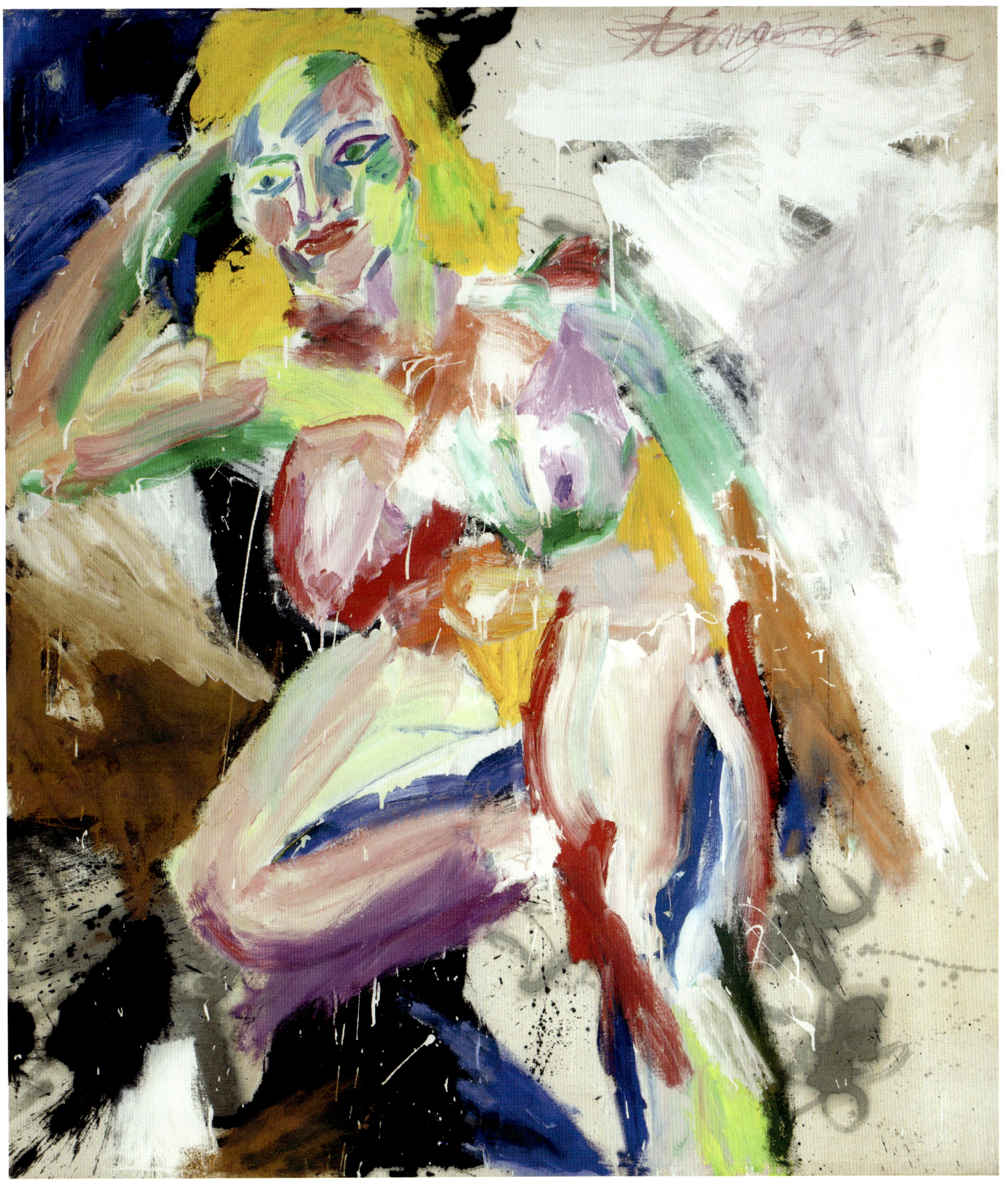

My Memory is Too Much, 1958
Oil on canvas
53.4 × 70.3 in. / 135.5 × 178.8 cm

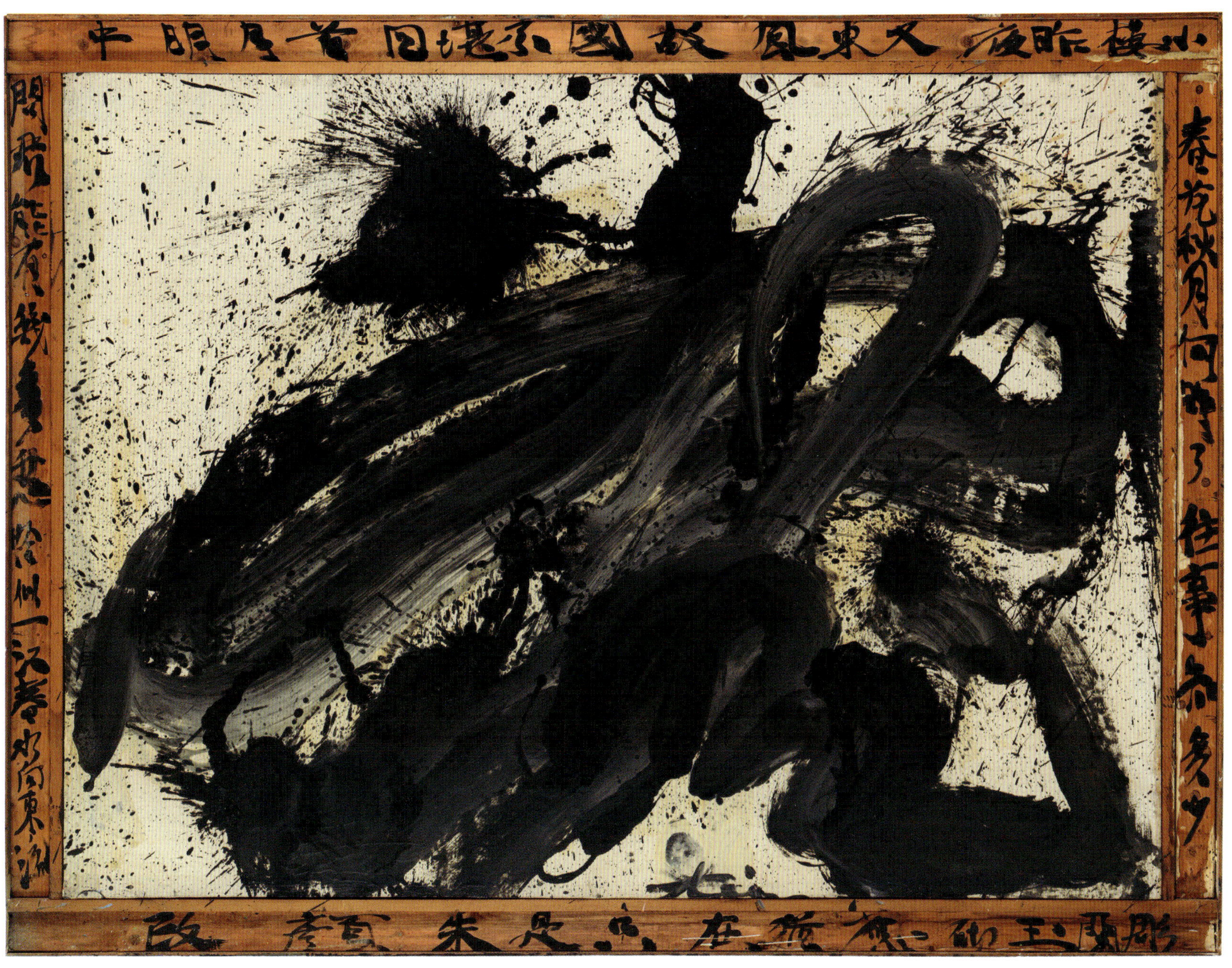

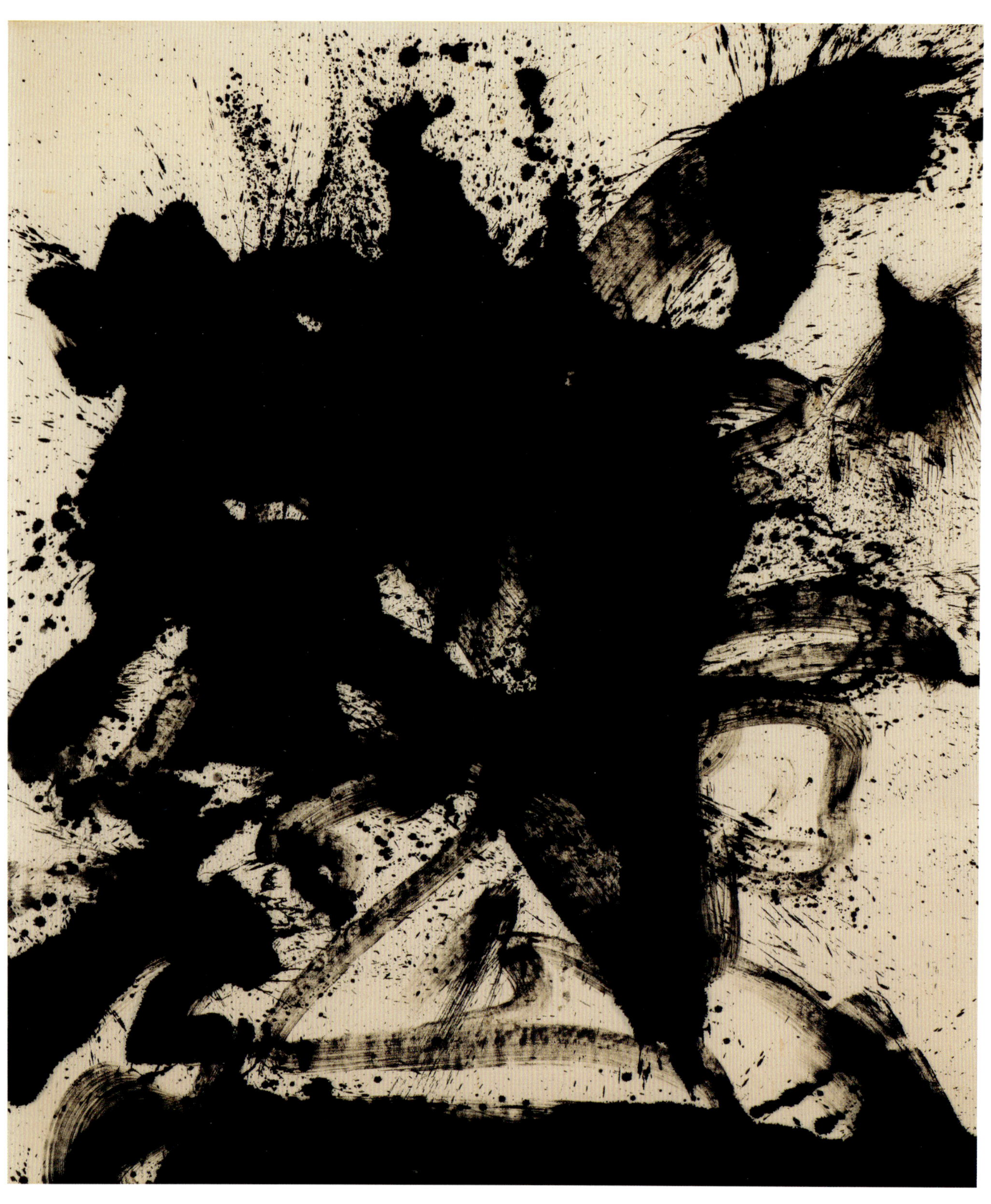

Fire, 1959
Oil on unprimed canvas
88 × 72 in. / 223.5 × 182.8 cm
Guy and Nora Barron Family

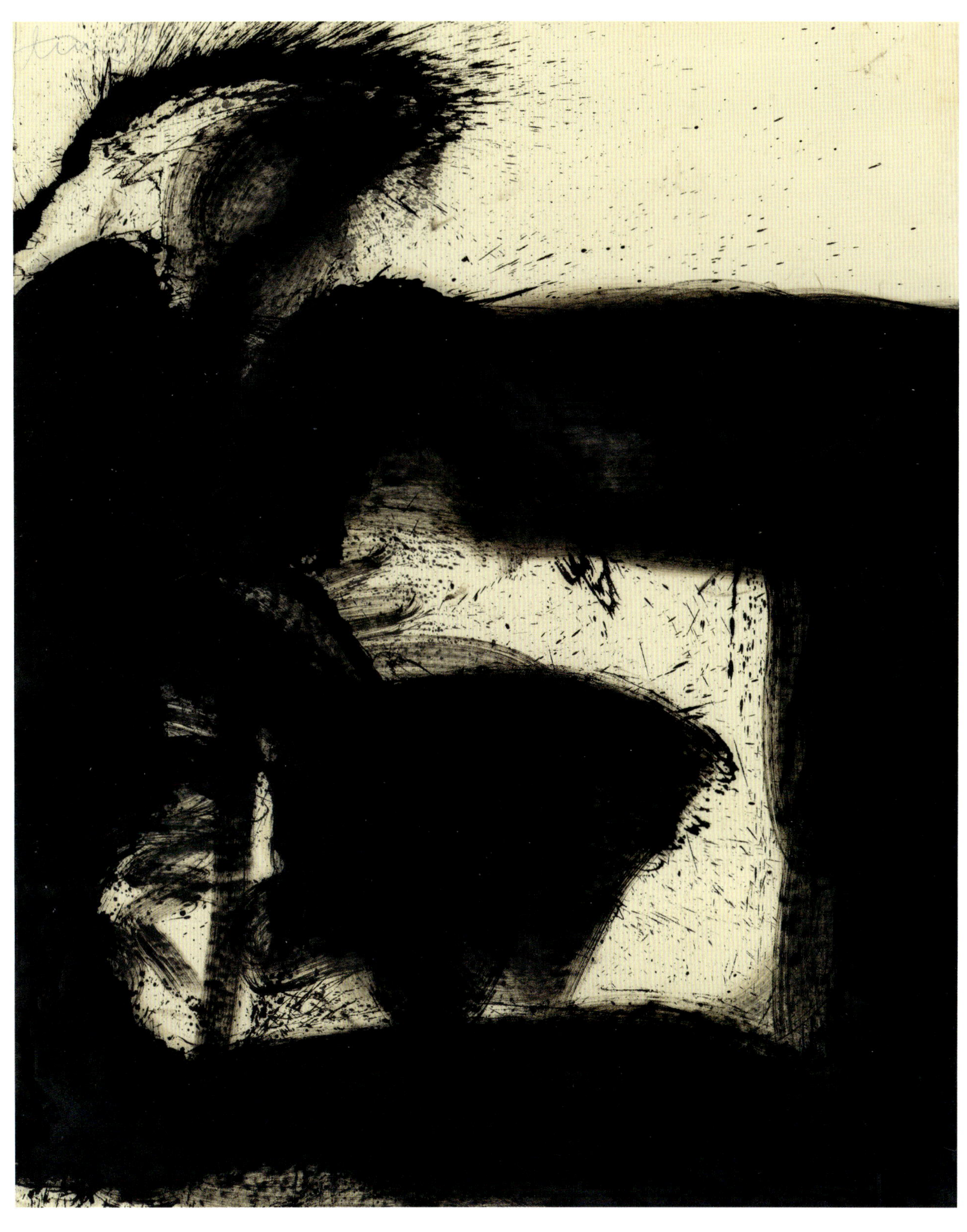

Chinese City, 1959
Oil on canvas
90.5 × 70.8 in. / 230 × 180 cm

Fresh Green Leaves, 1972
Oil on canvas
40.4 × 60.4 in. / 102.6 × 153.4 cm
Private Collection

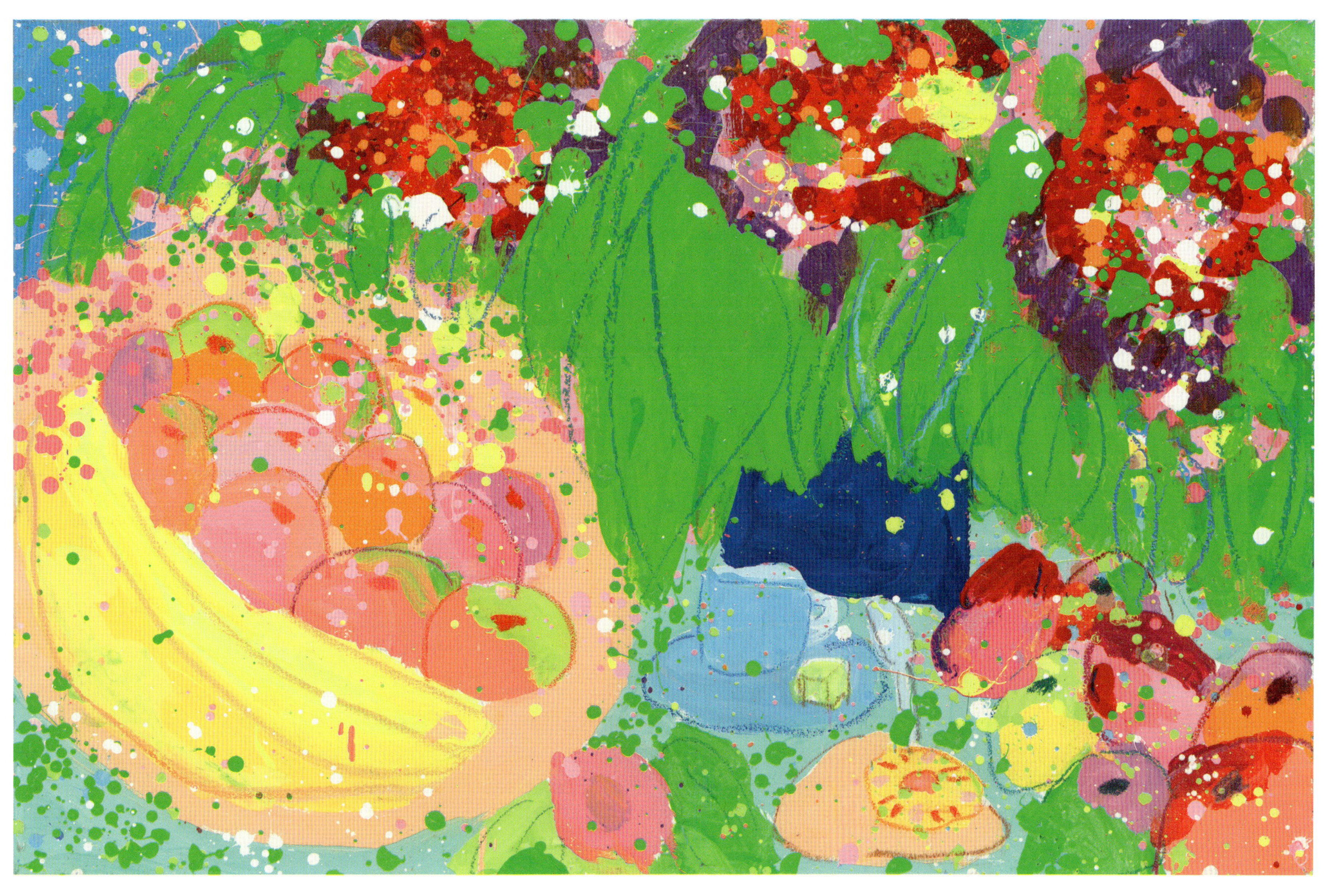

It is Warm Today, 1985
Acrylic on canvas
28 × 42 in. / 71.1 × 106.7 cm
Private Collection

Following pages
Looking for a Bee, 1968
Acrylic on canvas
80 × 140.3 in. / 203.2 × 356.2 cm
Solomon R. Guggenheim Museum,
New York
Gift of David Kluger, 1975, 69.1890

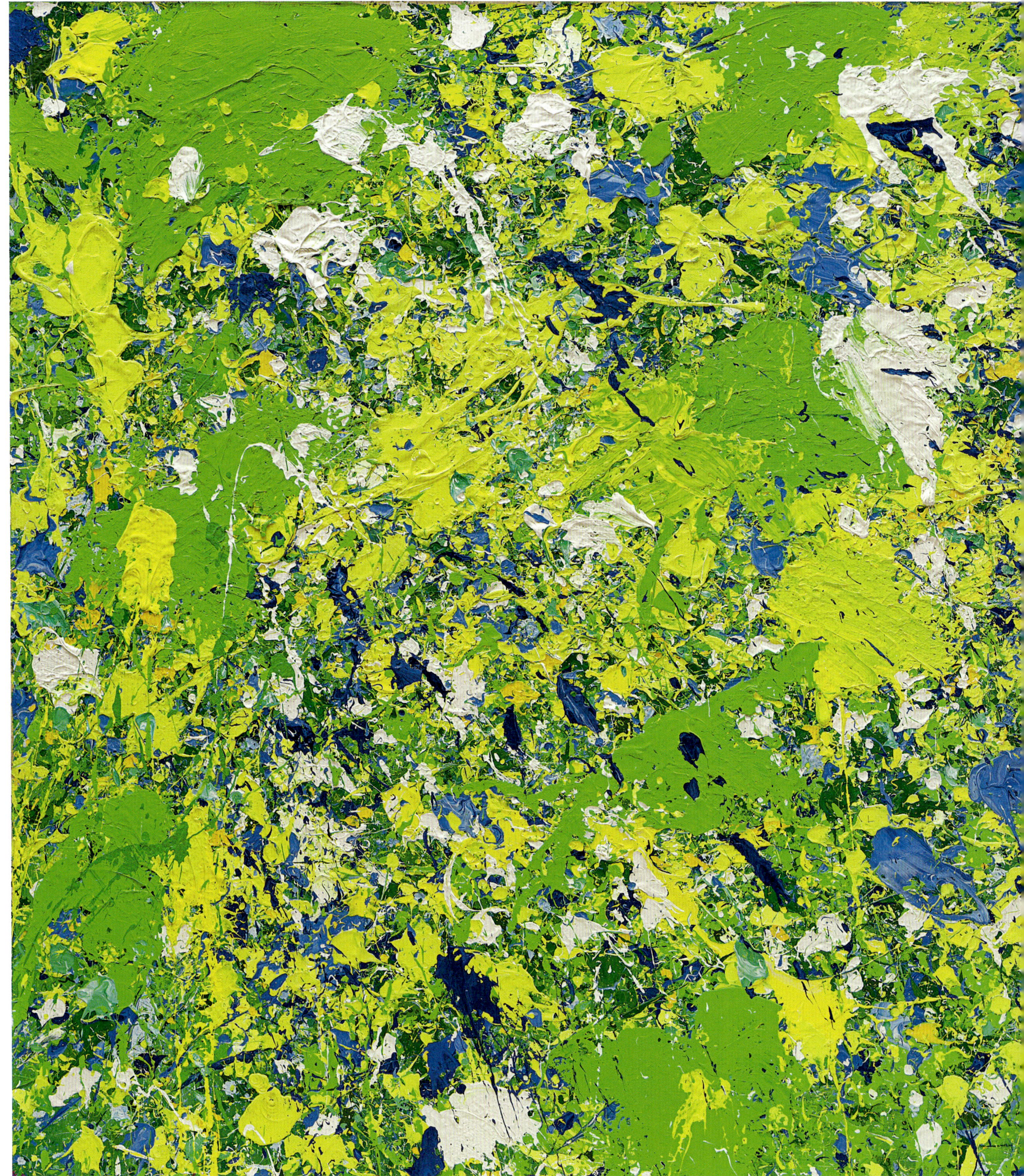

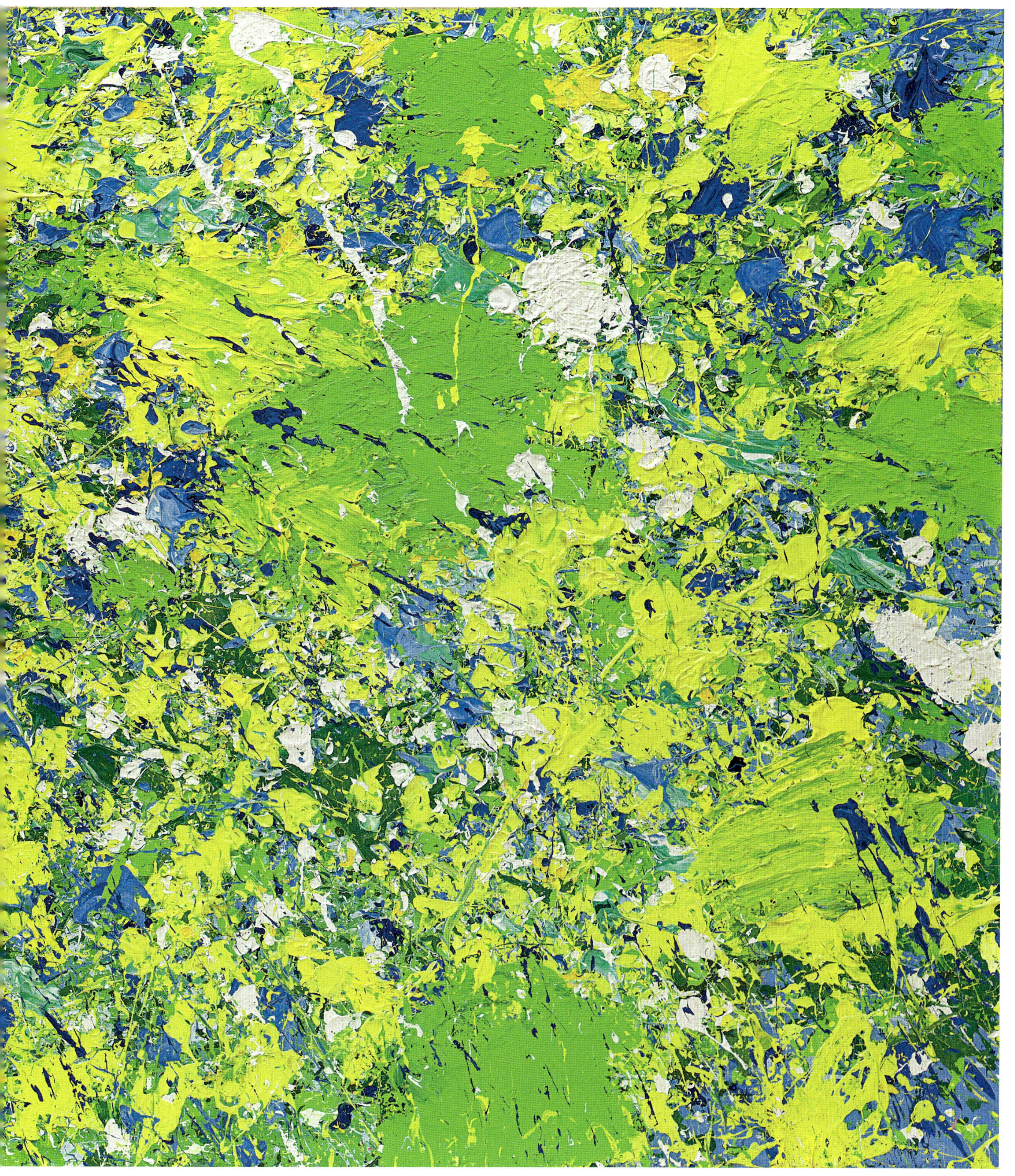

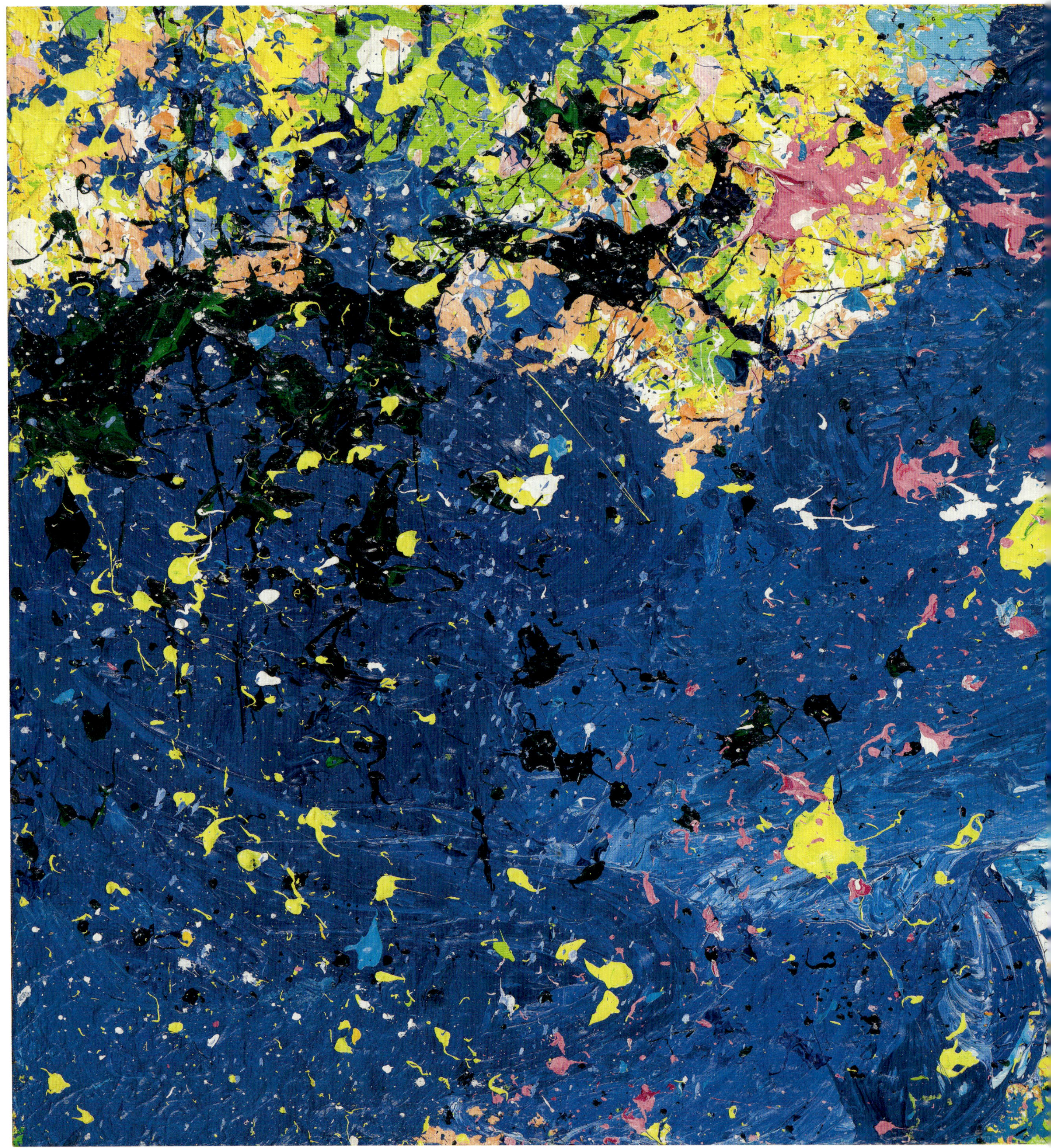

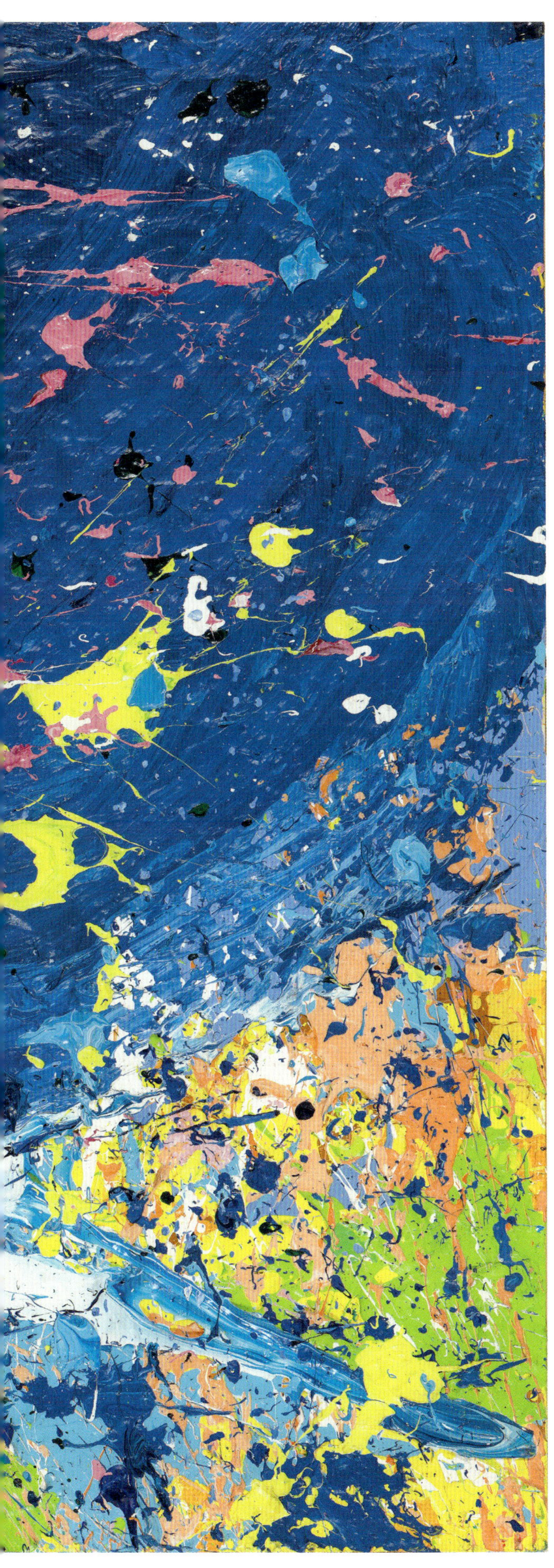

I Take off my Pants Facing Sunset, 1969
Acrylic on canvas
40.2 × 51.9 in. / 102 × 132 cm

Following pages
Ting's paint brushes

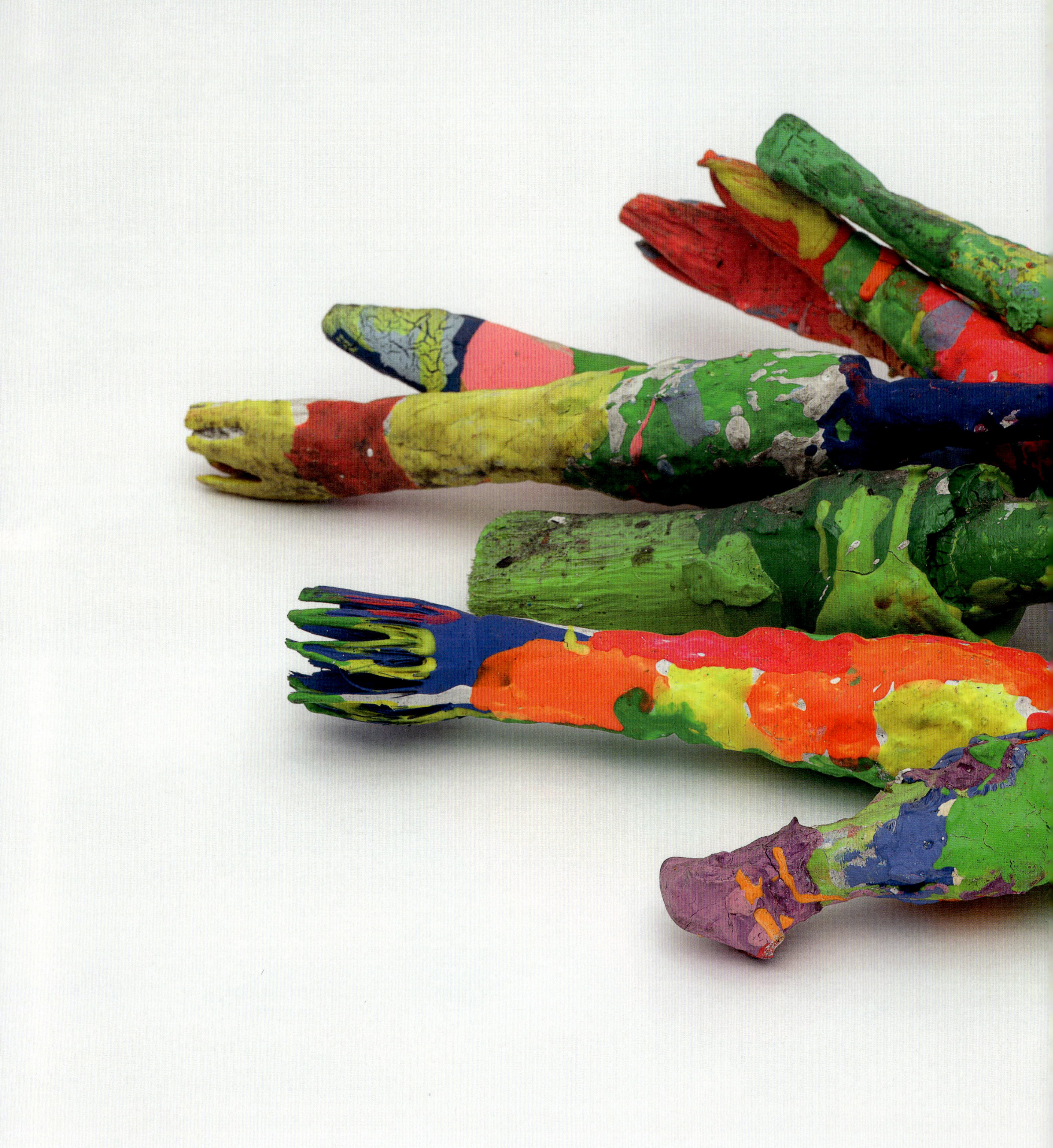

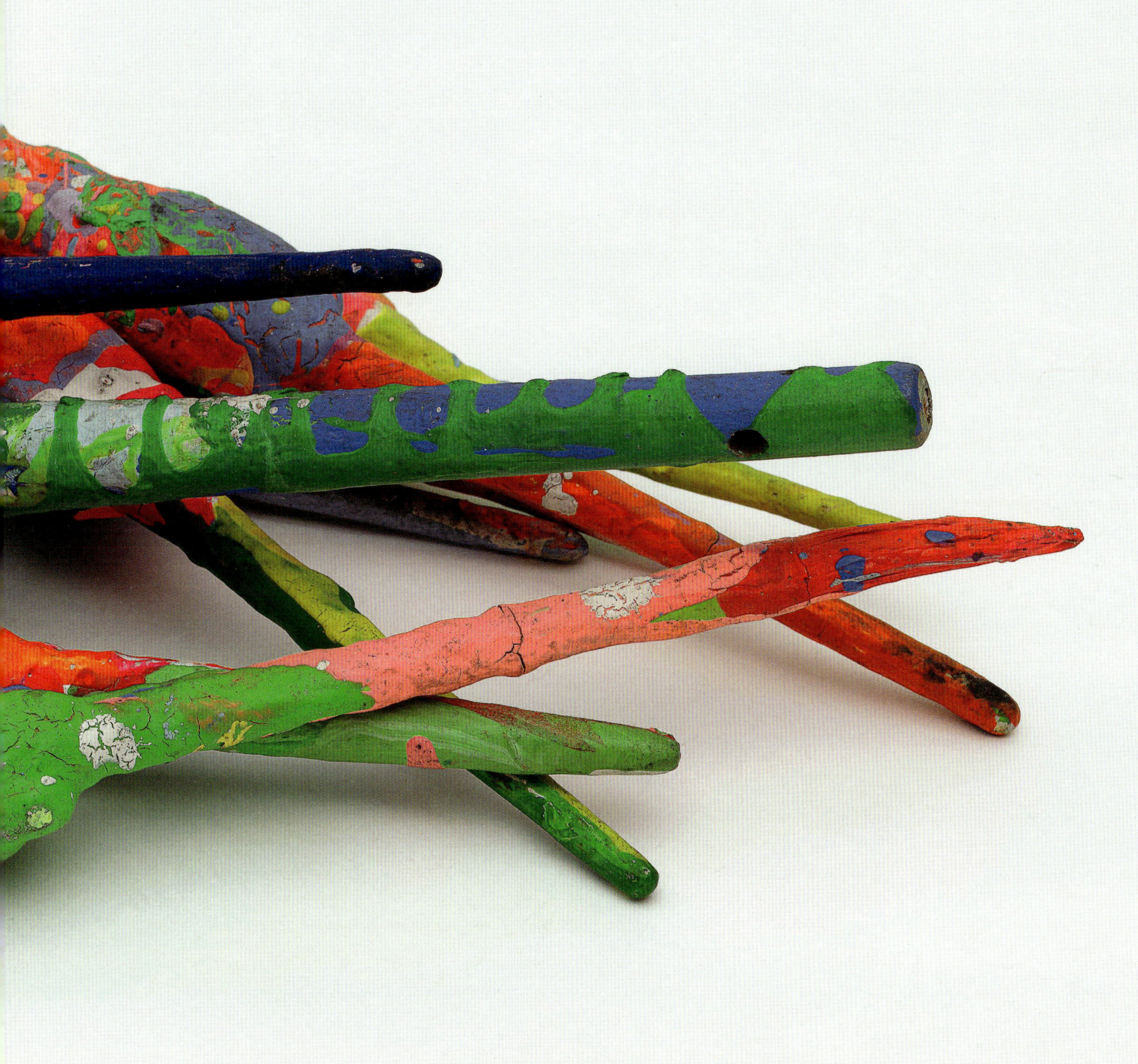

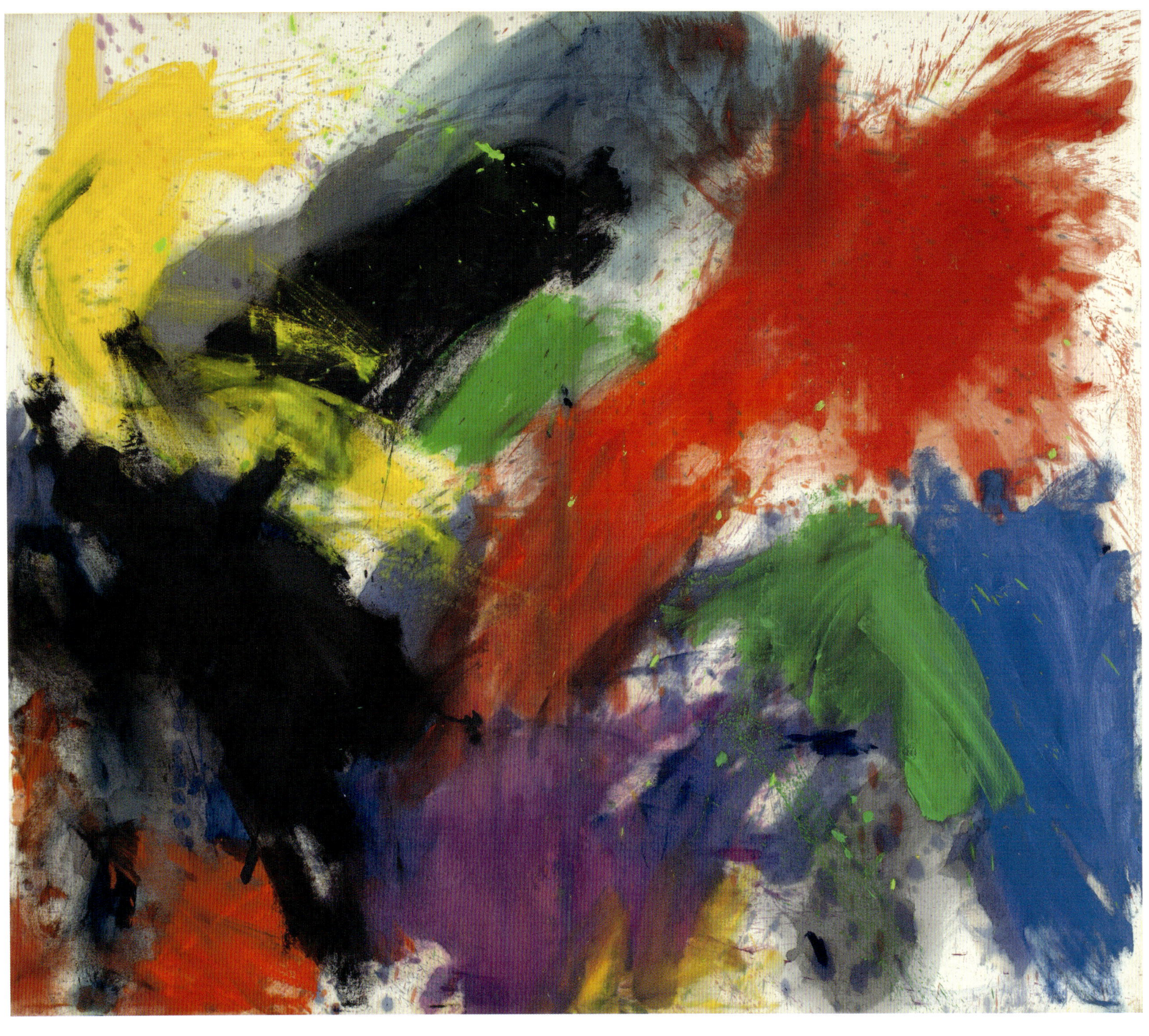

Lightning Strike (Blikseminslag), 1962
Oil on canvas
39.6 × 63.2 in. / 100.5 × 160.5 cm
Collection Stedelijk Museum, Amsterdam

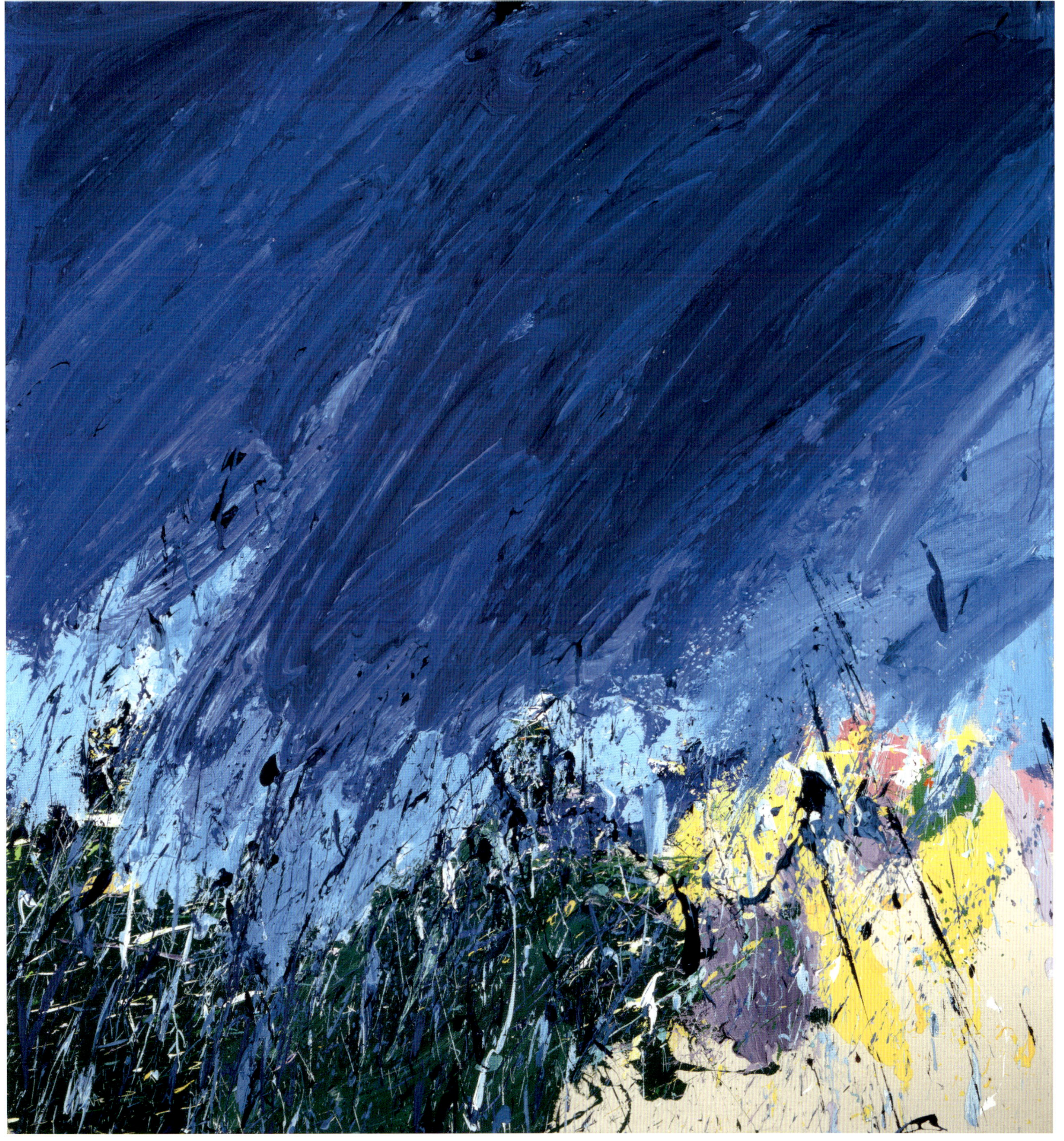

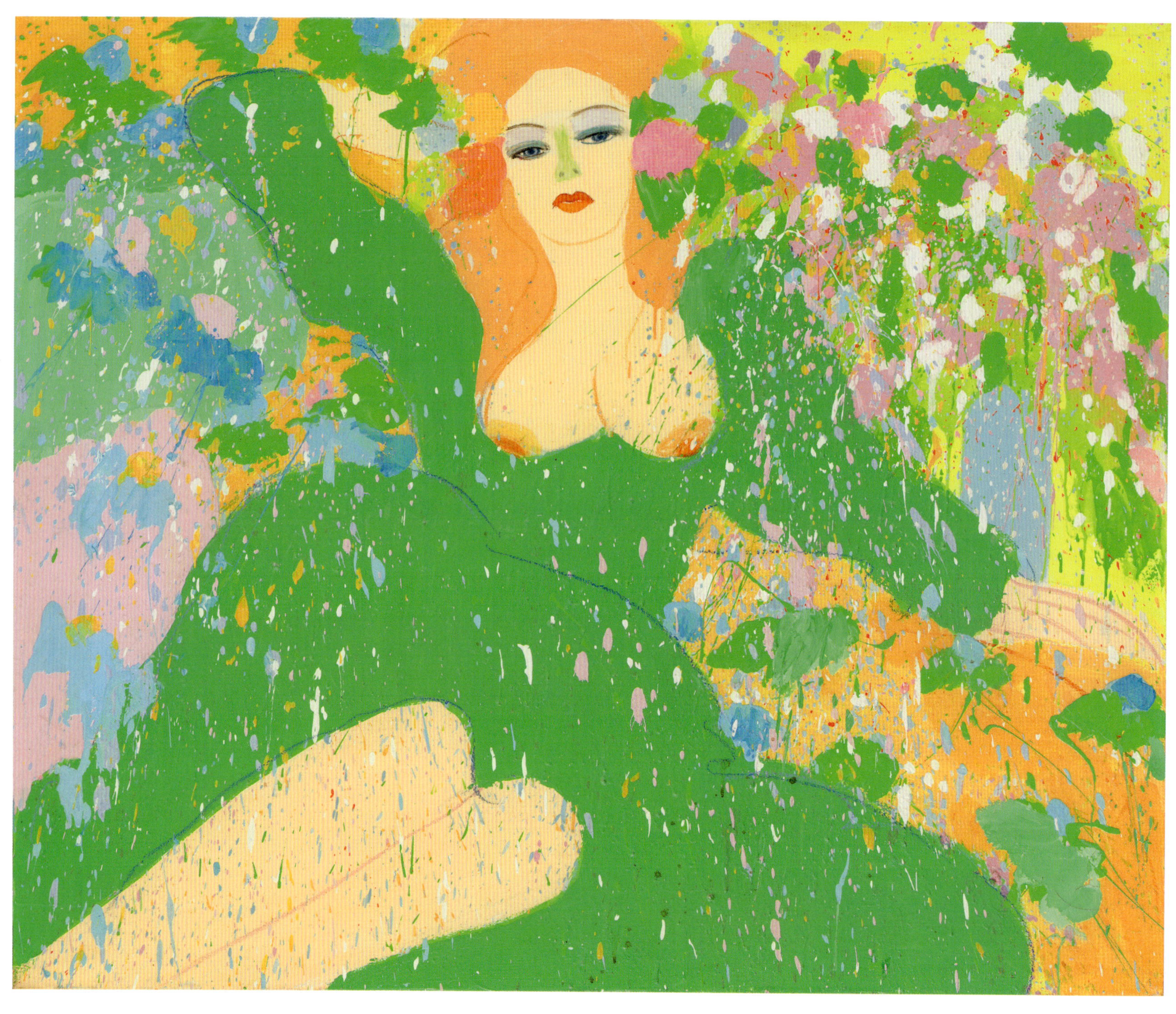

*Love Me With Your Heart
That I Want*, 1975
Acrylic on canvas
55 × 64 in. / 139.7 × 162.6 cm

98

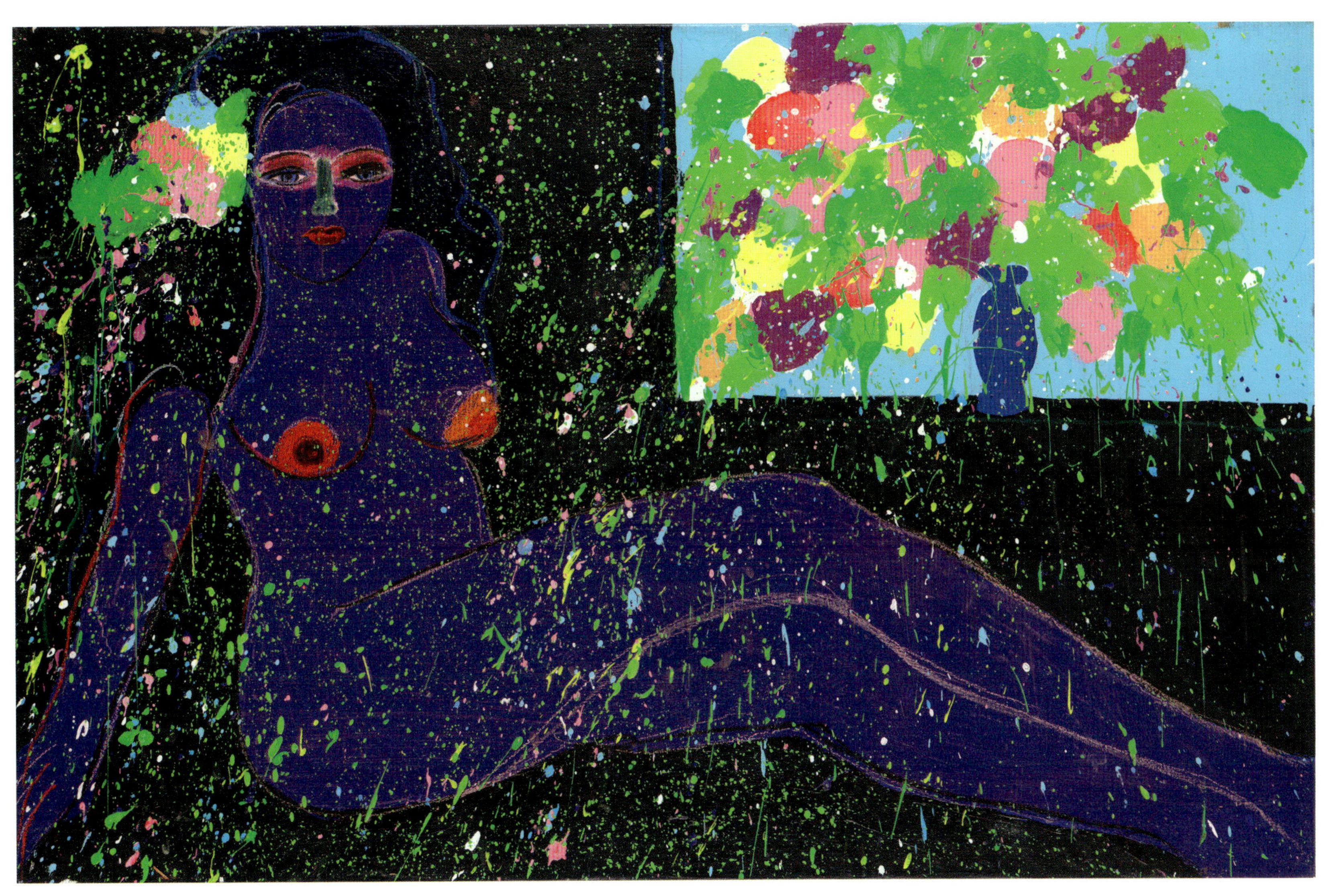

Do You Like Moonlight?, 1977
Acrylic on canvas
40 × 60 in. / 101.6 × 152.4 cm
Private Collection, New York

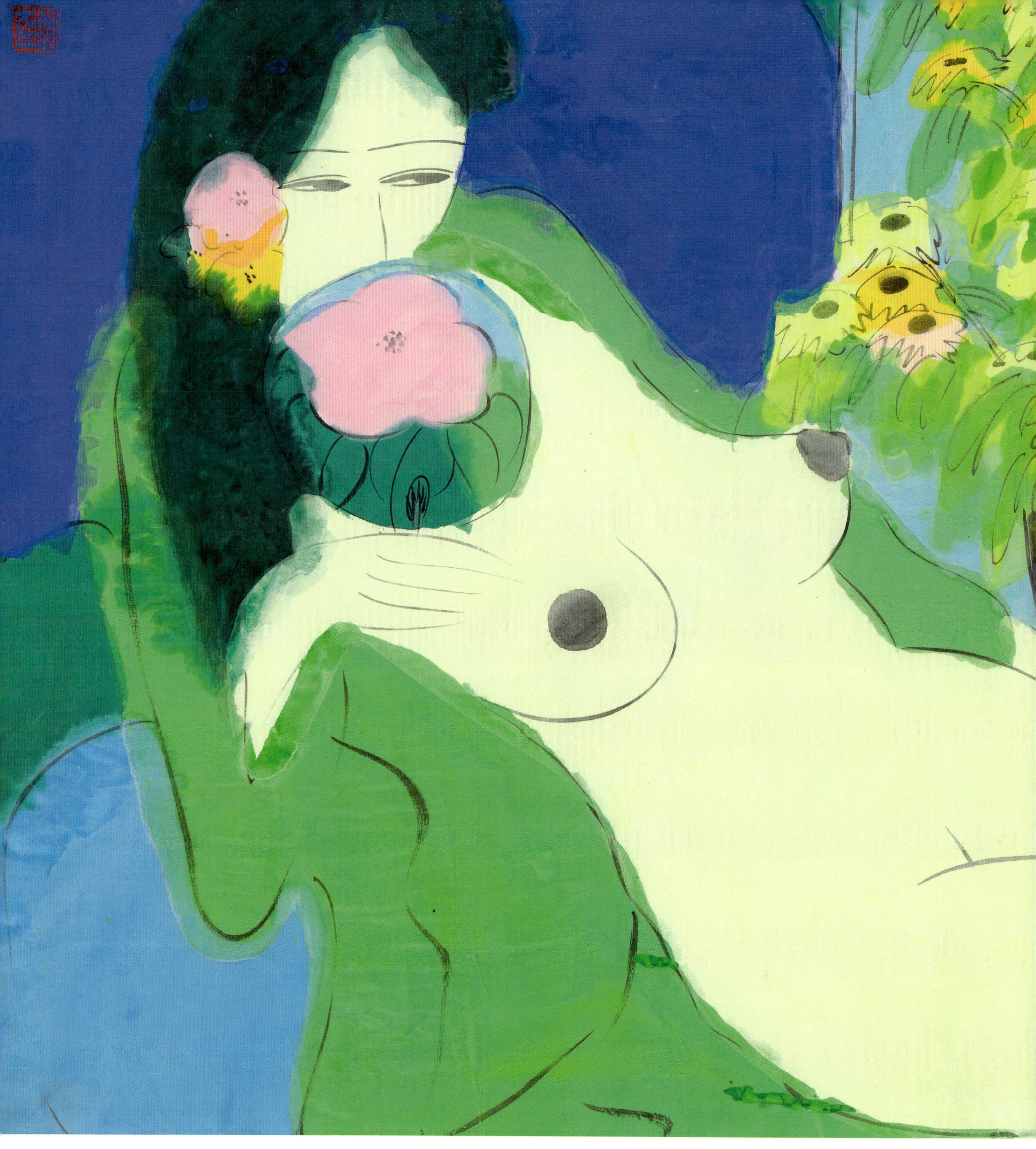

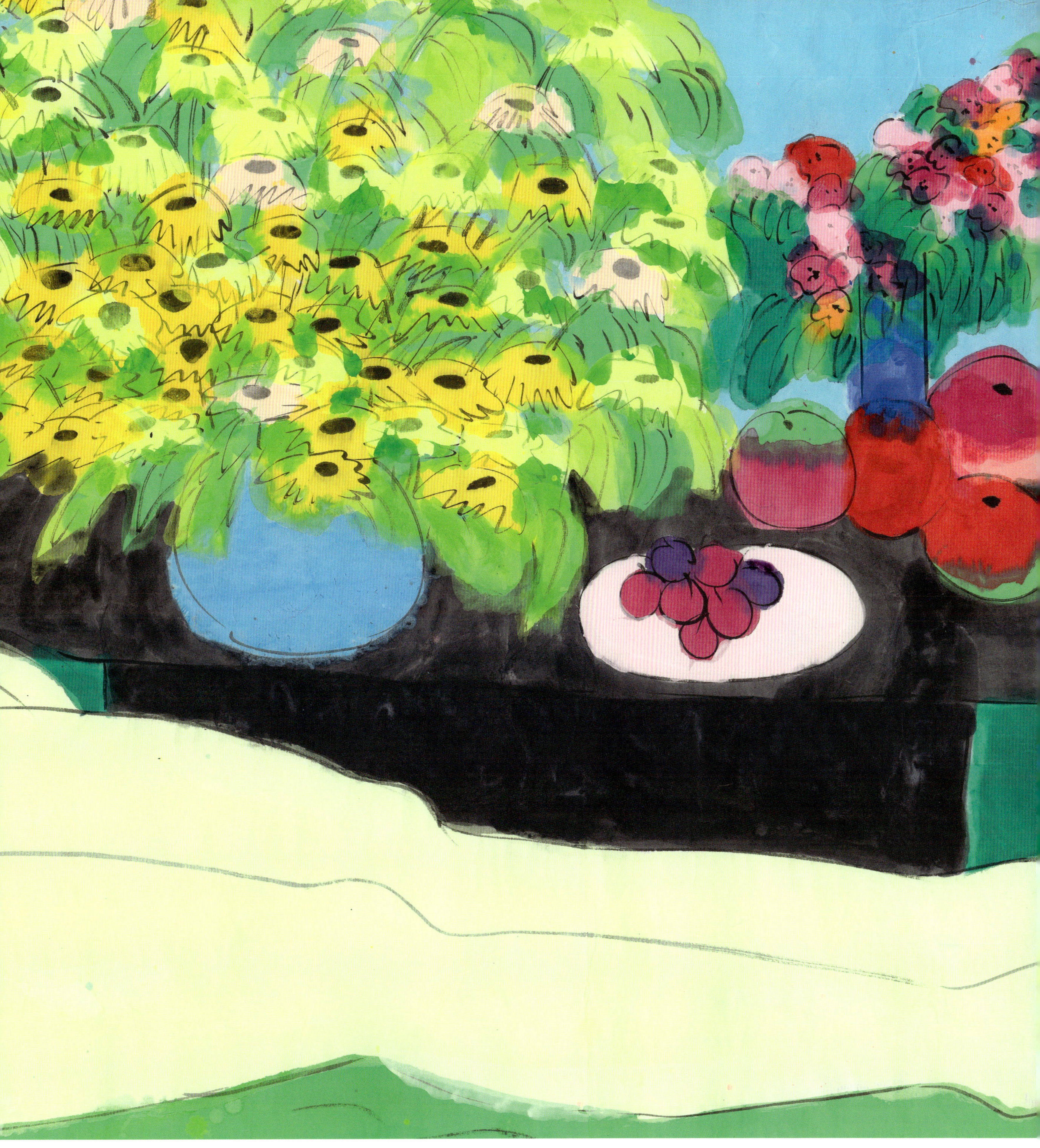

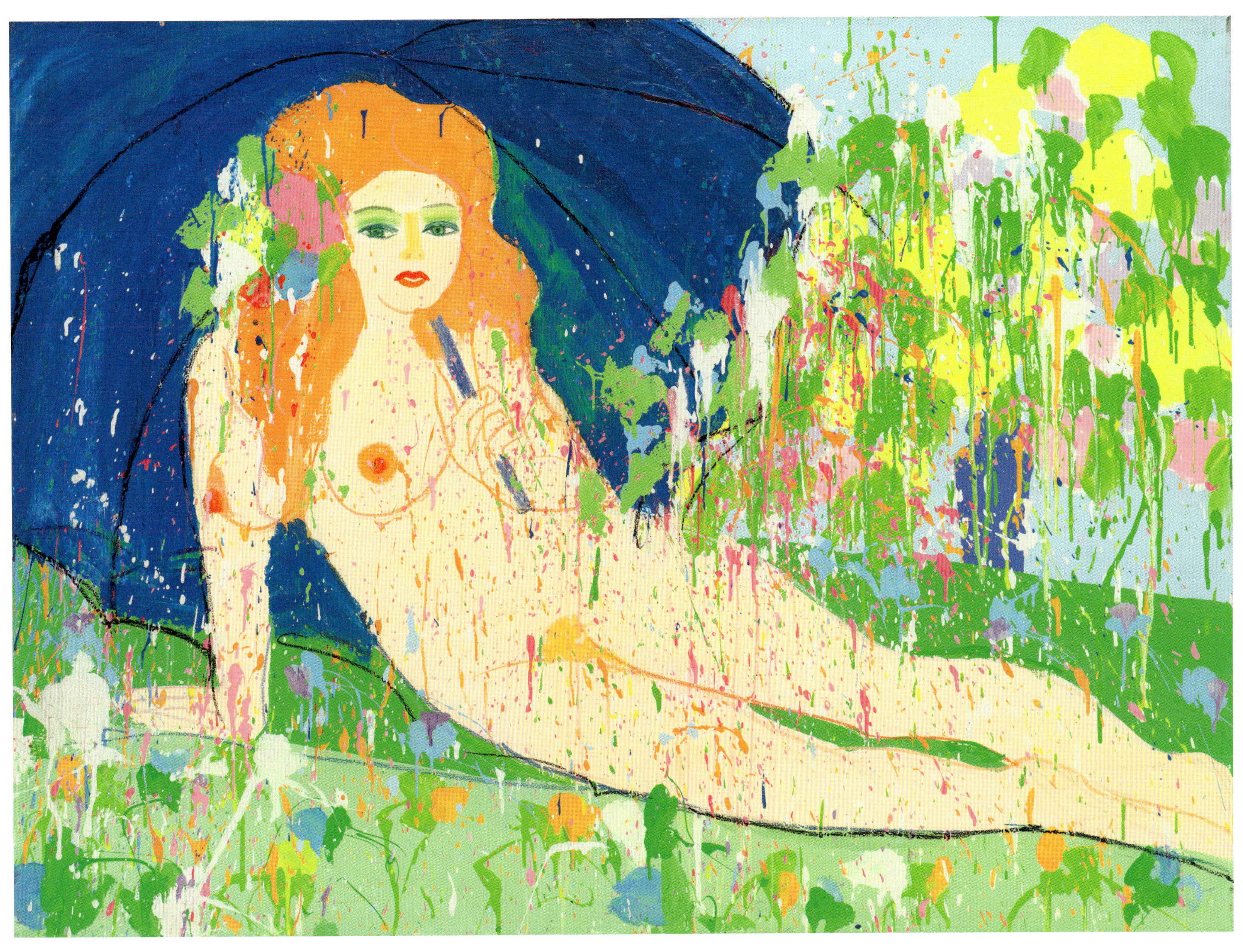

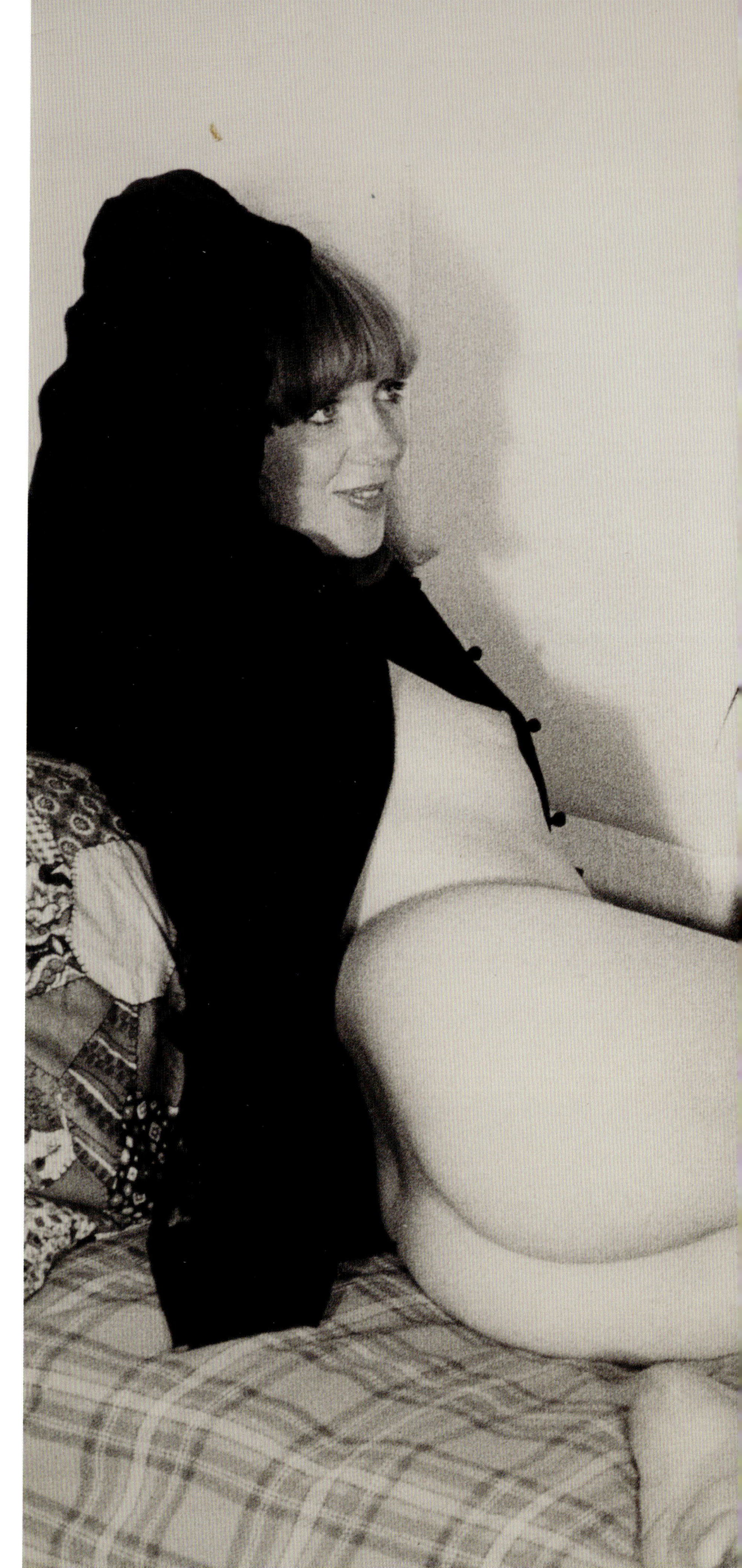

Walasse Ting and model at West 25th
Street studio, New York, early 1970s

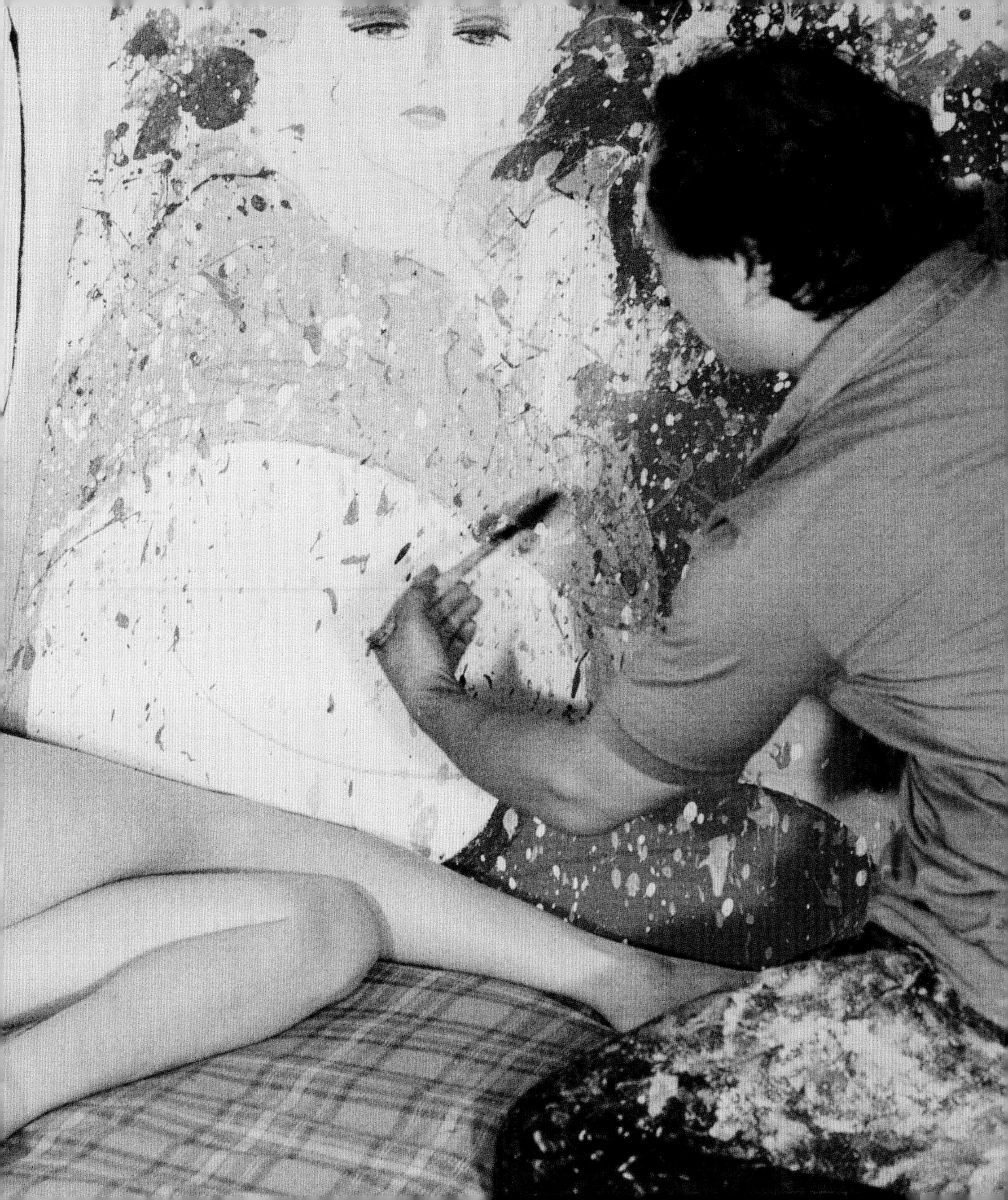

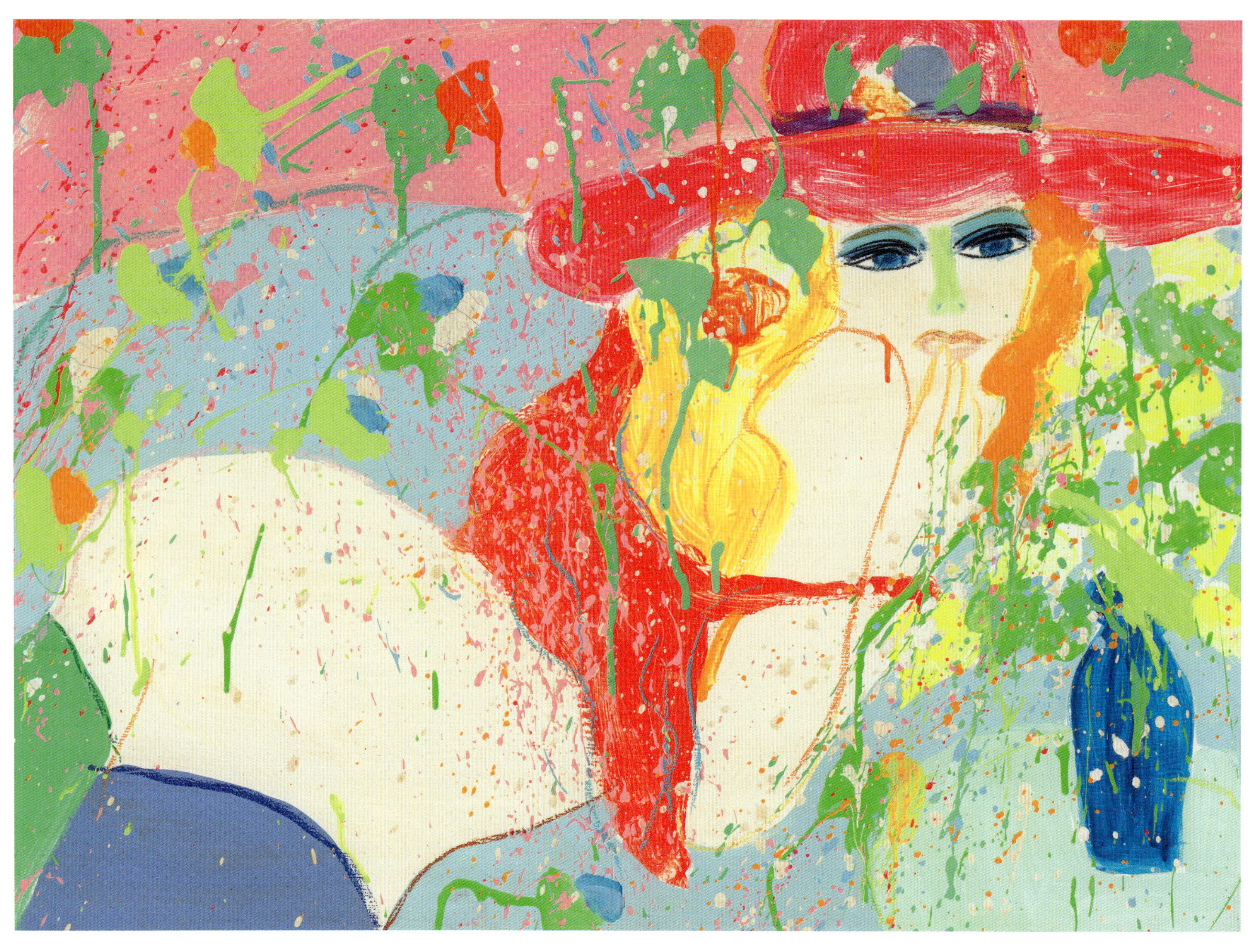

American Beauty, 1974
Acrylic on canvas
24 × 32 in. / 61 × 81.3 cm
Collection of Phyllis Lipton

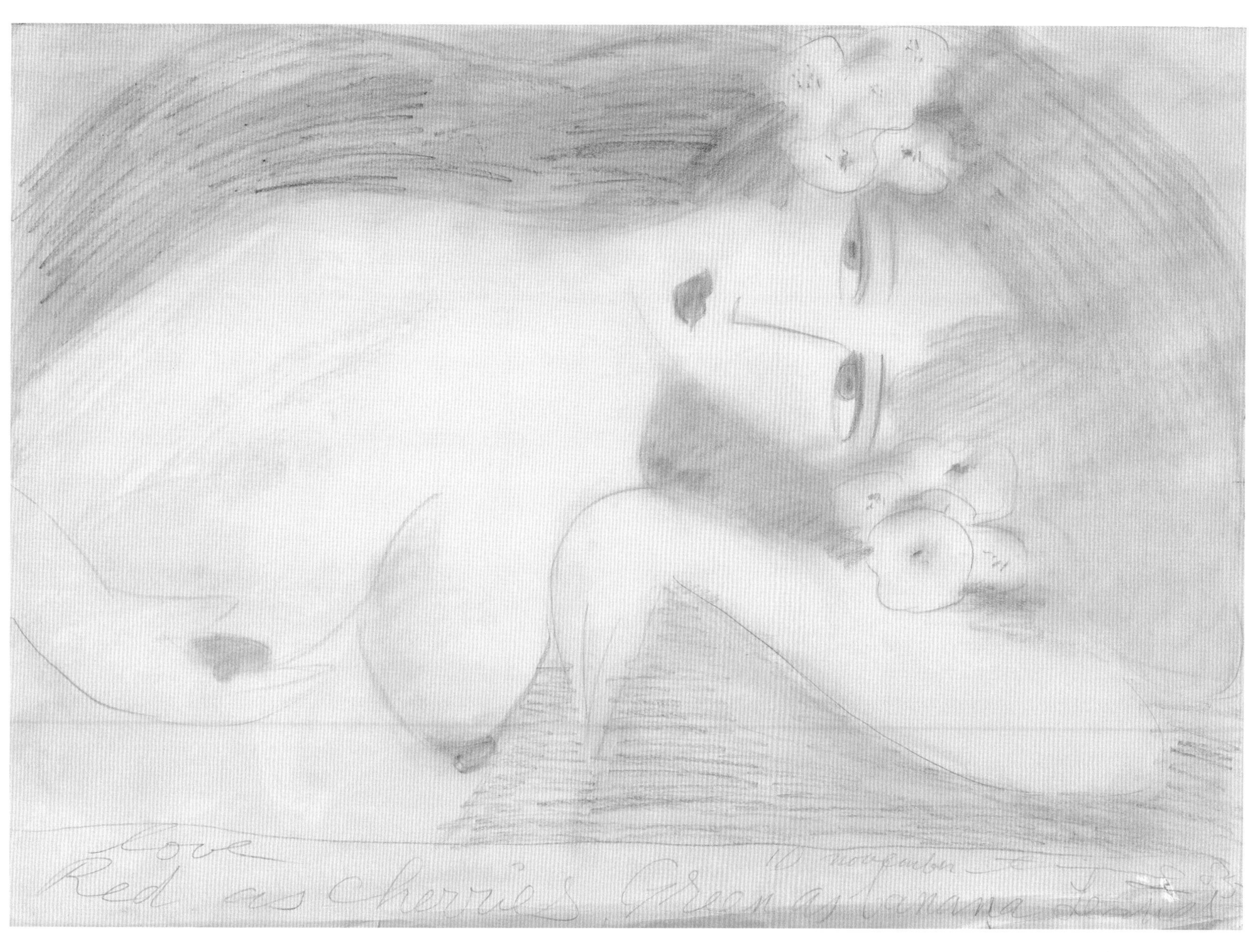

Love as Red as Cherries,
Green as Banana Leaves, 1985
Graphite on Arches paper
22.7 × 27.5 in. / 57.6 × 69.8 cm
Private Collection, New York

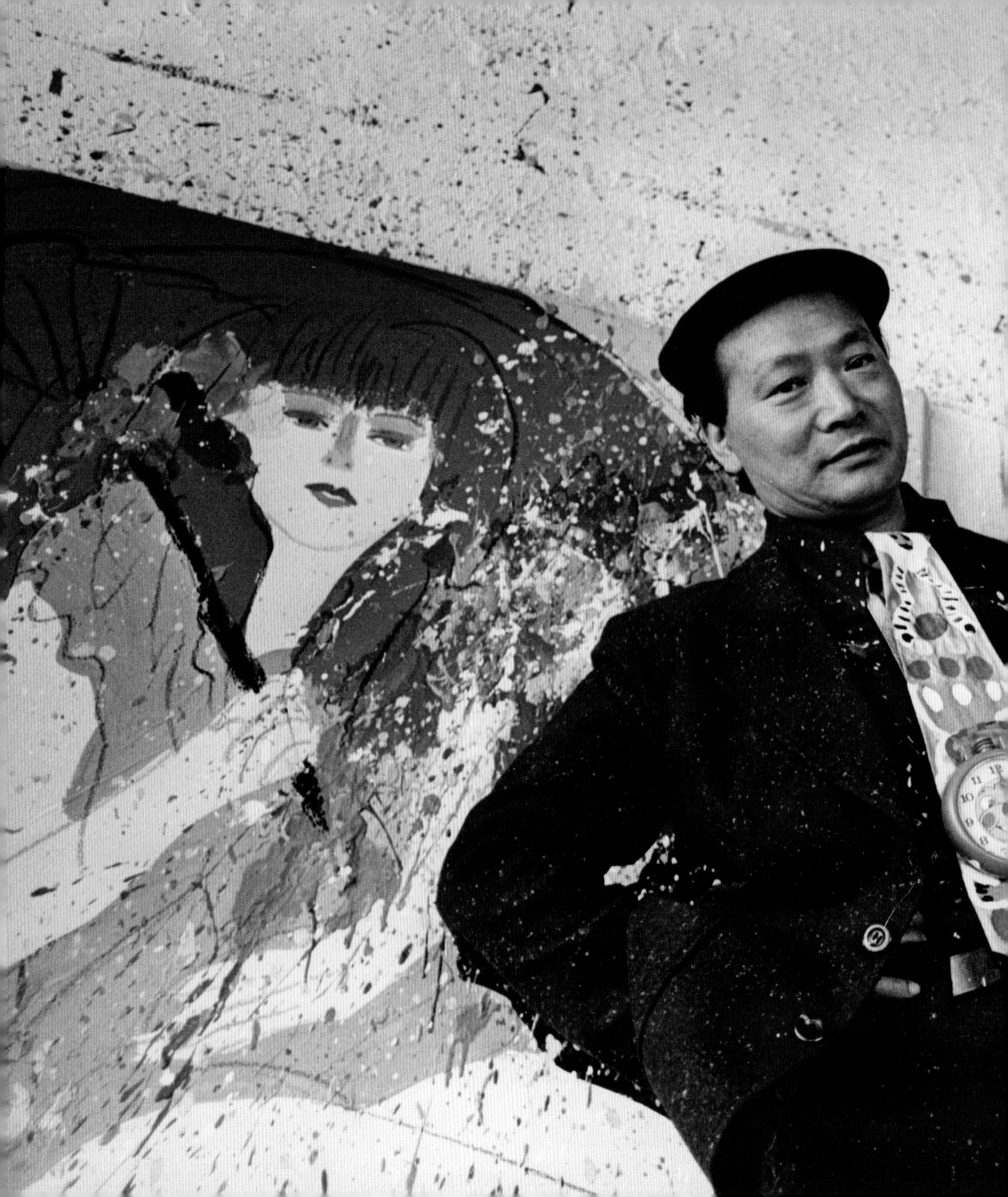

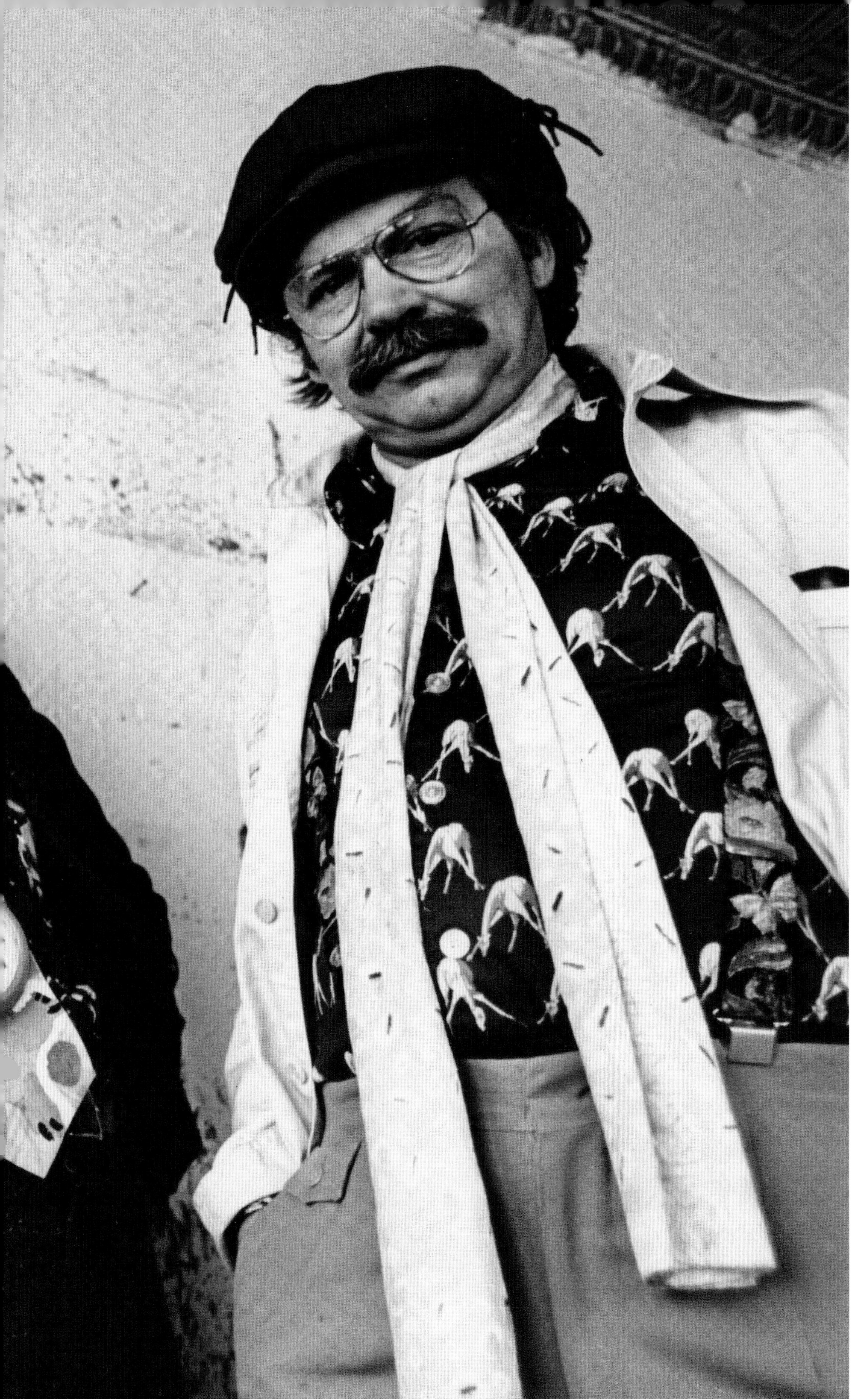

Walasse Ting and Karel Appel, early 1970s
Walasse Ting studio, New York

Following pages
Miss World, 1975
Acrylic on canvas
90 × 150 in. / 229 × 381 cm

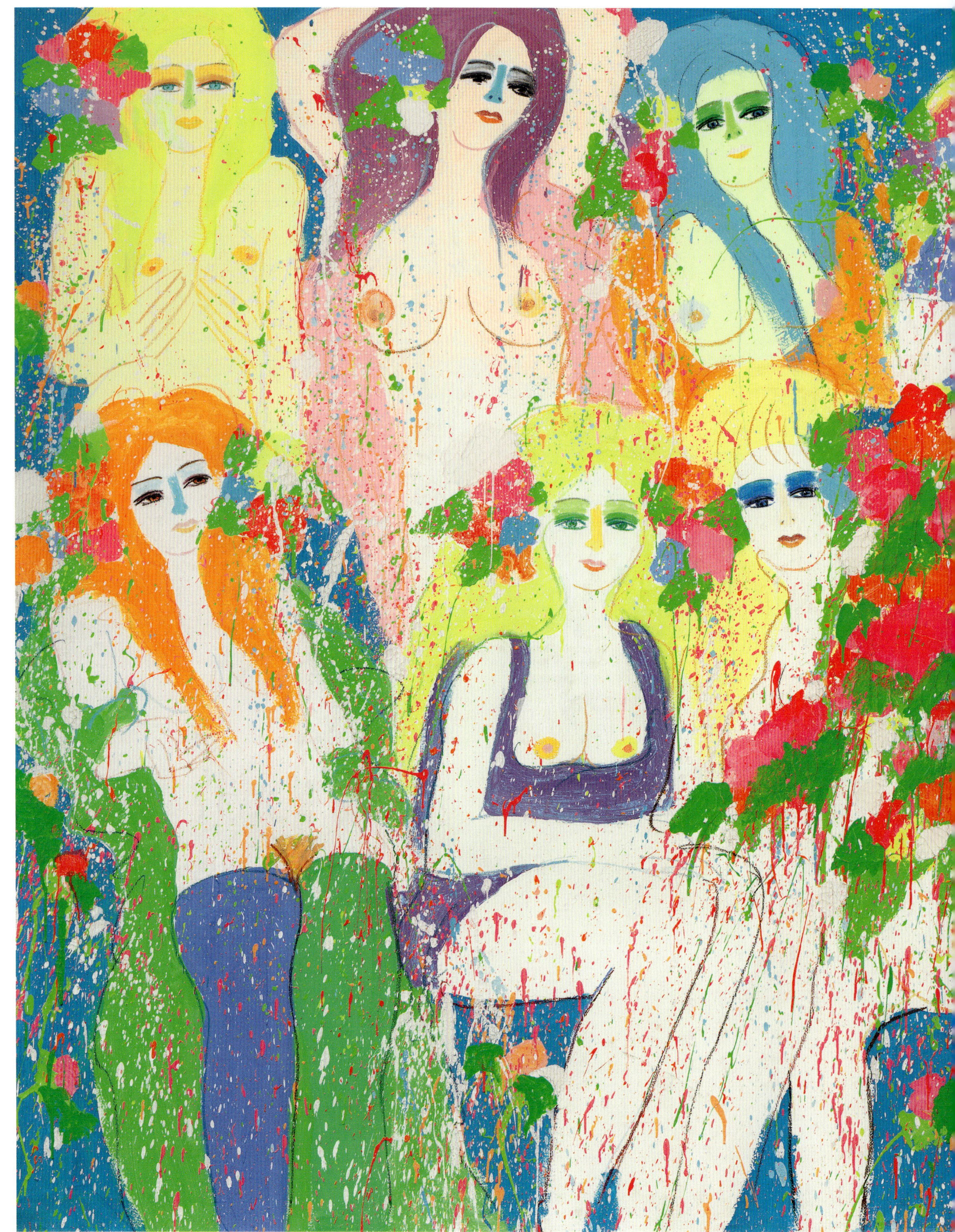

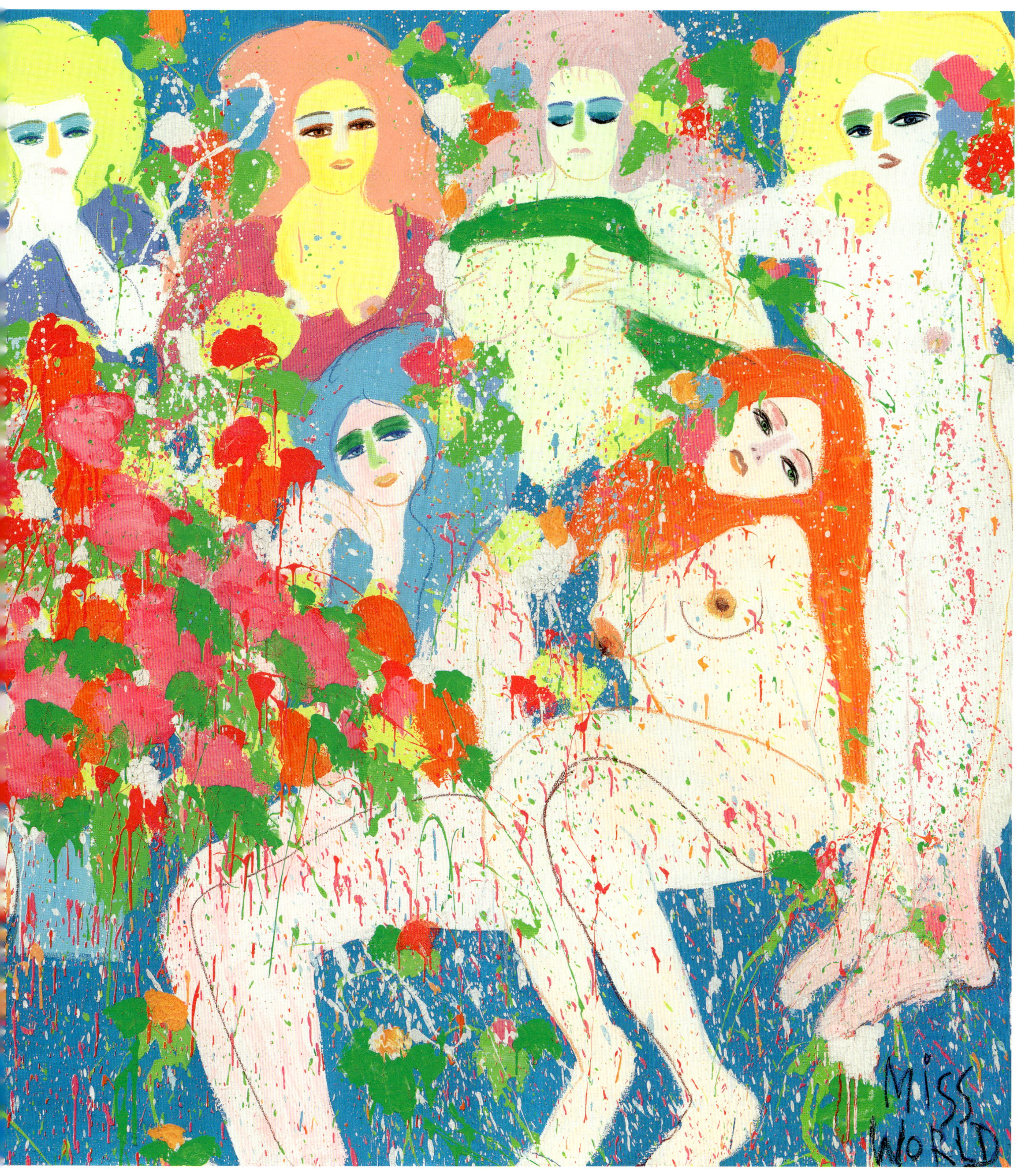

MISS
WORLD

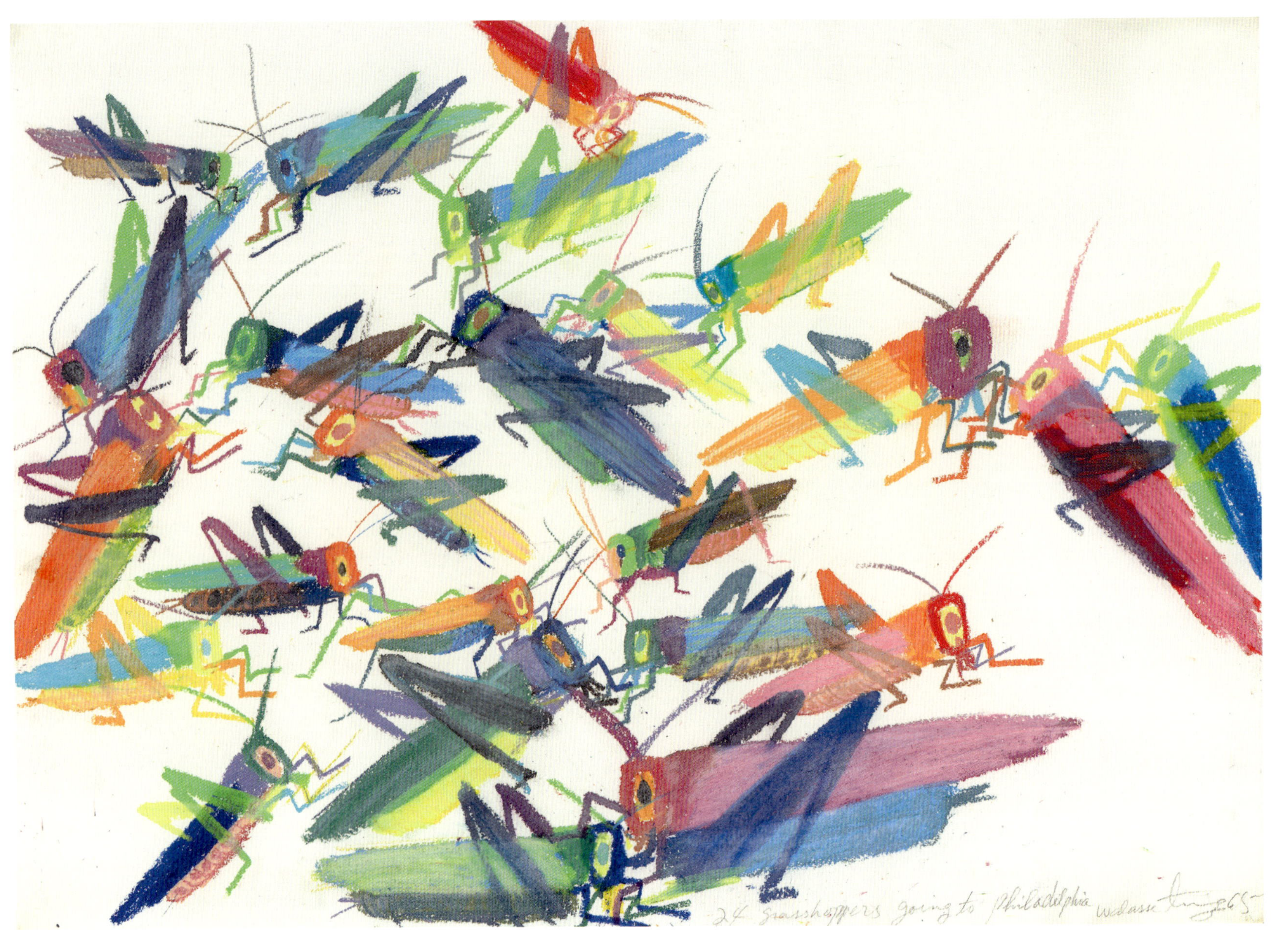

*24 Grasshoppers Going
to Philadelphia*, 1965
Color crayon on paper
22.5 × 36 in. / 57.2 × 91.4 cm

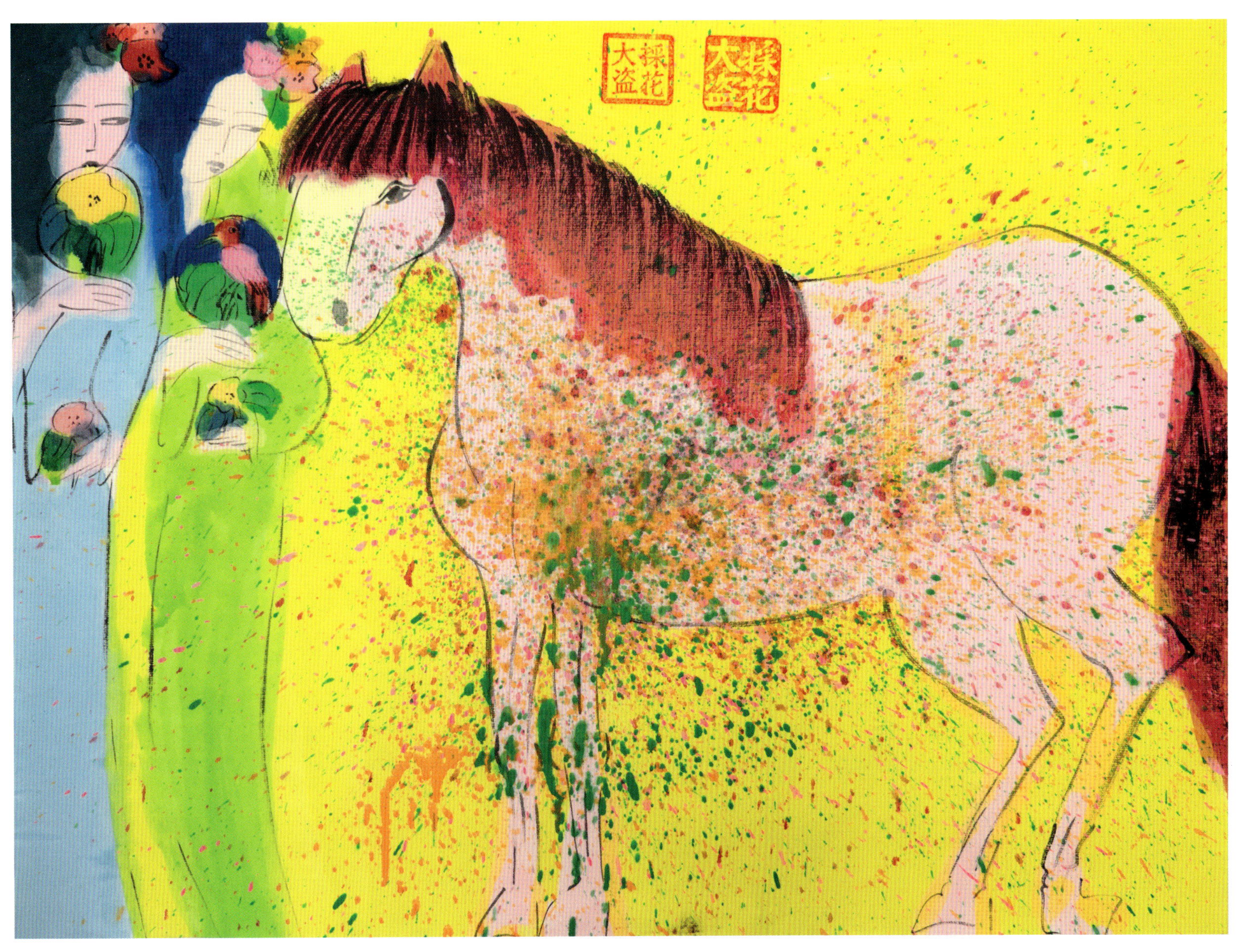

*Untitled (Women with Paint Splattered
Horse)*, early mid-1980s
Chinese ink and acrylic on rice paper
18 × 23 in. / 45.8 × 59.6 cm
Private Collection

Following pages
Ting's paint bowls and hake brushes

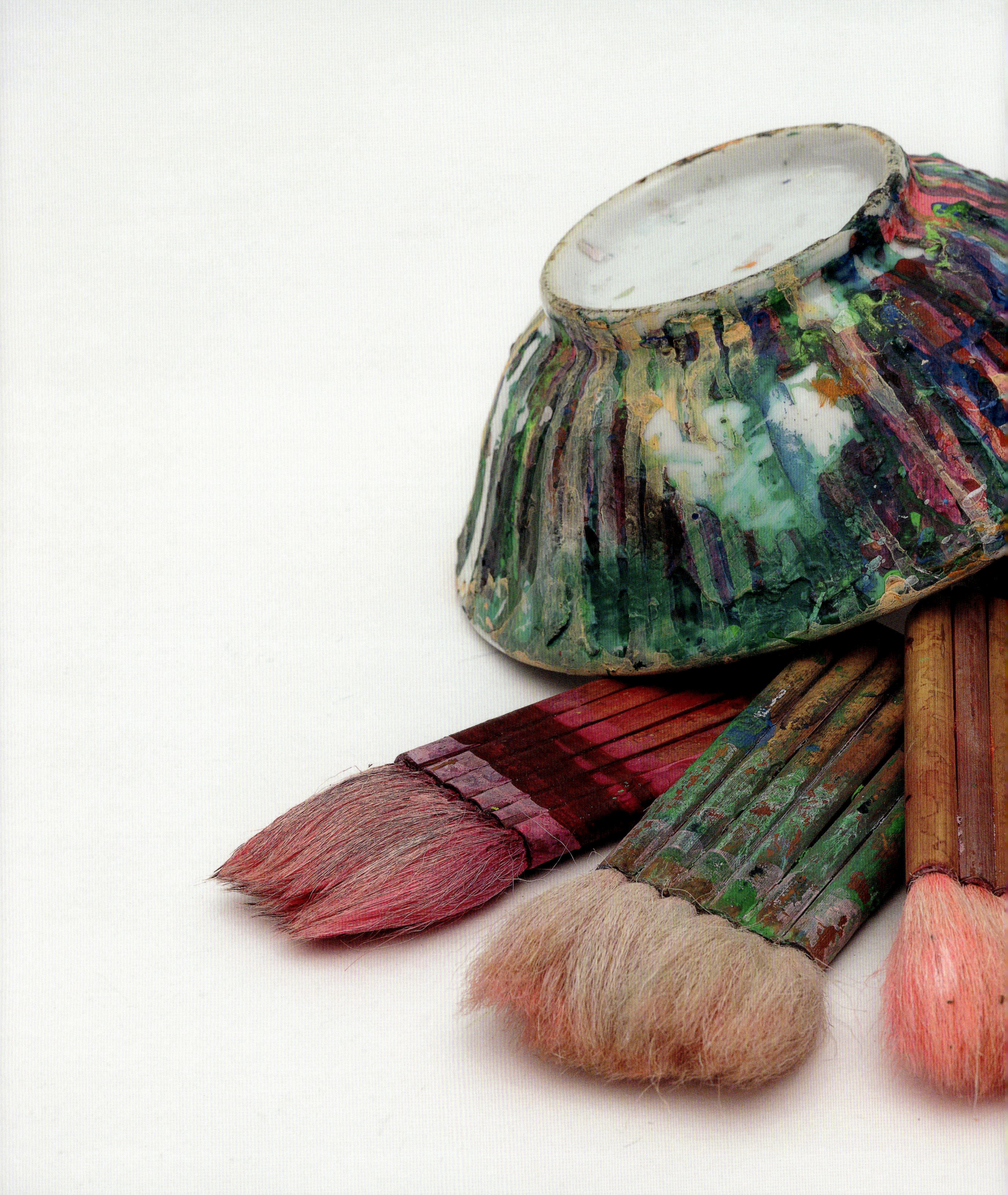

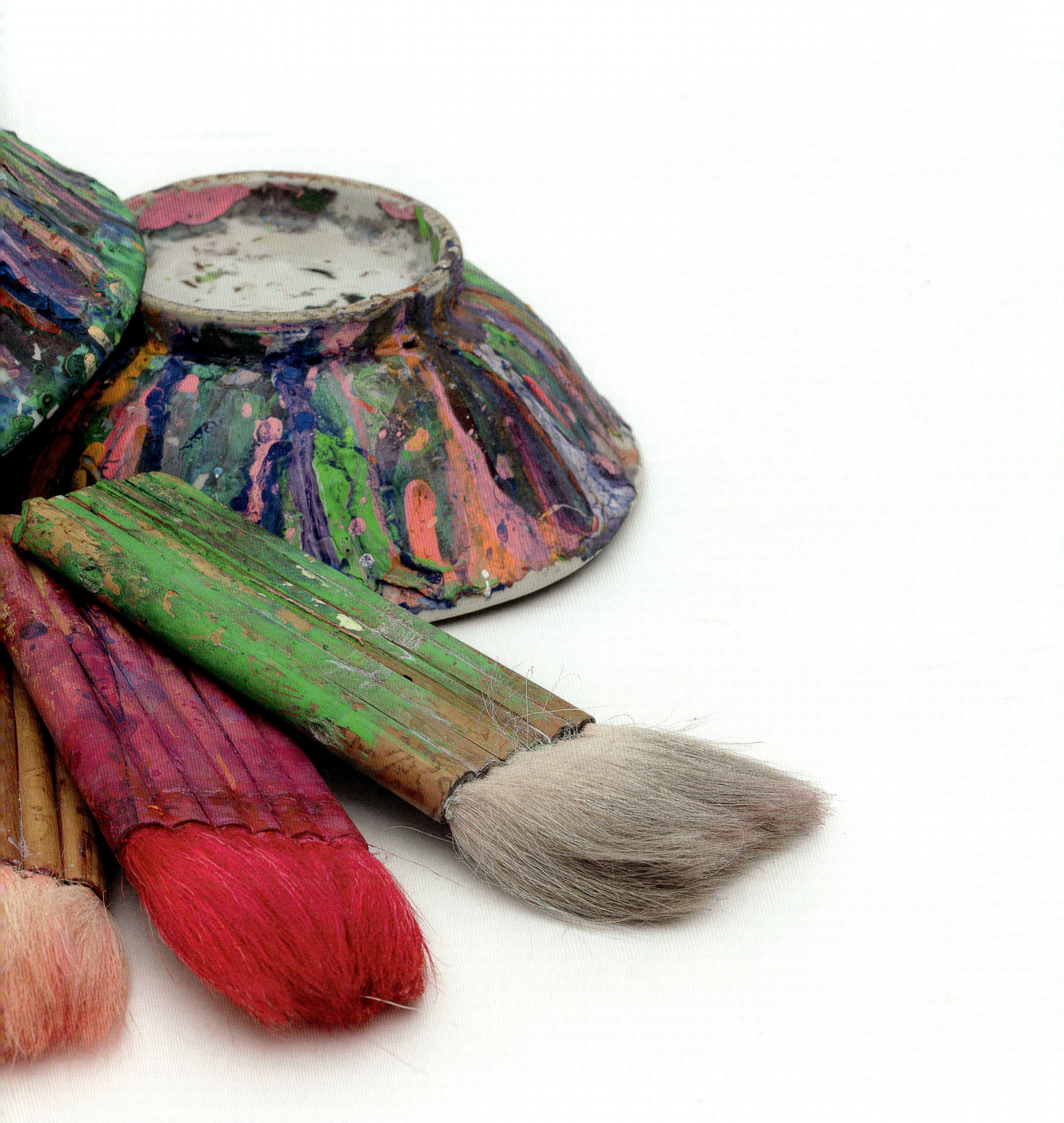

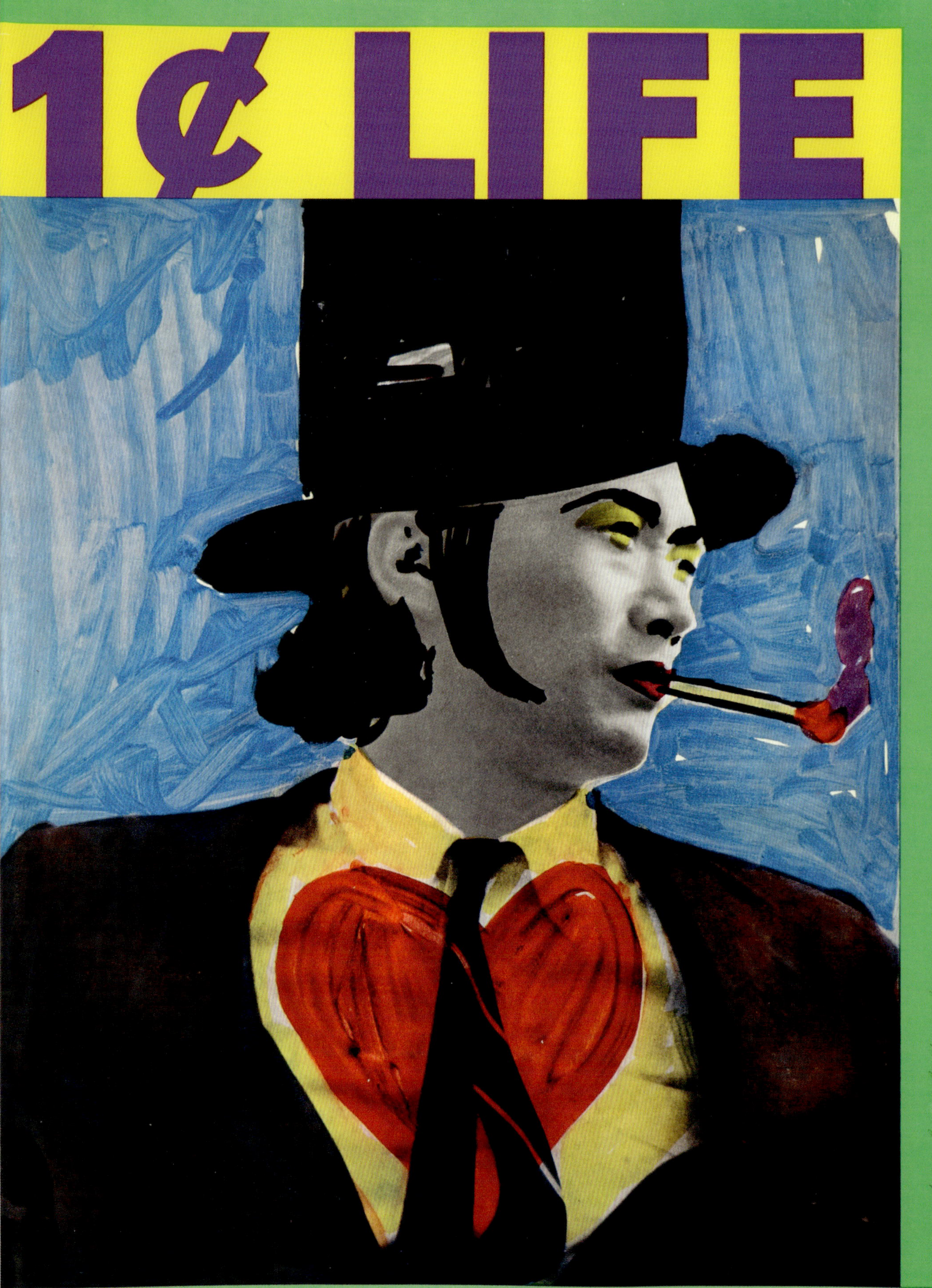

1¢ LIFE
cover design by machteld appel

Walasse Ting: How to See the World with Warmer Eyes

Xiao (Amanda) Ju

Reading Walasse Ting's books is an abundant experience. There is a lot to take in. Born in Wuxi, China and raised in the art worlds of Hong Kong, Paris, New York, then Amsterdam, Ting was unabashedly puckish, exuberantly absurd, and dauntingly prolific. There is a metonymy of forms both in the poems and images that surround them. The 1964 book *1¢ Life*, for instance, has 61 poems by Ting and 62 original lithographs by a league of collaborators and friends: Alan Davie, Alfred Jensen, Sam Francis, Walasse Ting, James Rosenquist, Pierre Alechinsky, Kimber Smith, Alfred Leslie, Antonio Saura, Kiki O.K. [Kiki Kogelnik], Asger Jorn, Robert Indiana, Jean-Paul Riopelle, Karel Appel, Tom Wesselmann, Bram van Velde, Joan Mitchell, Allan Kaprow, Andy Warhol, Robert Rauschenberg, K.R.H. Sonderborg, Roy Lichtenstein, Öyvind Fahlström, Reinhoud d'Haese, Claes Oldenburg, Jim Dine, Mel Ramos, and Enrico Baj.

One gets the sense that Ting's words and these contributor's images bounce off each other, promiscuously, transformatively, exploring the erotics and sociality of an *artist book*. Yet the collaboration is not just with the proper "artists" around him, Ting's poems hold a particular mode of togetherness with the world he inhabited. They are composed of the pulsating rhythms of the city (its material forms and social reality), told via whispers to the prostitutes and shouts at private property, stories of orgasms and neurosis, acts of killing and flagellation.

1¢ Life, 1964
Illustrated book with sixty-two lithographs and reproductions
Contributing artists: Pierre Alechinsky, Karel Appel, Enrico Baj, Reinhoud d'Haese, Alan Davie, Jim Dine, Öyvind Fahlström, Sam Francis, Robert Indiana, Alfred Jensen, Asger Jorn, Allan Kaprow, Kiki O.K. [Kiki Kogelnik], Alfred Leslie, Roy Lichtenstein, Joan Mitchell, Claes Oldenburg, Mel Ramos, Robert Rauschenberg, Jean-Paul Riopelle, James Rosenquist, Antonio Saura, Kimber Smith, K.R.H. Sonderborg, Walasse Ting, Bram van Velde, Andy Warhol, Tom Wesselmann.
Editor: Sam Francis.
Publisher: Eberhard W. Kornfeld, Bern, Switzerland, Printer: Maurice Beaudet

fig. 1. *1¢ Life* party, Atelier Beaudet, Paris, 1964
Top left: Walasse Ting and Sam Francis, bottom left: Pierre Alechinsky, Walasse Ting and guest

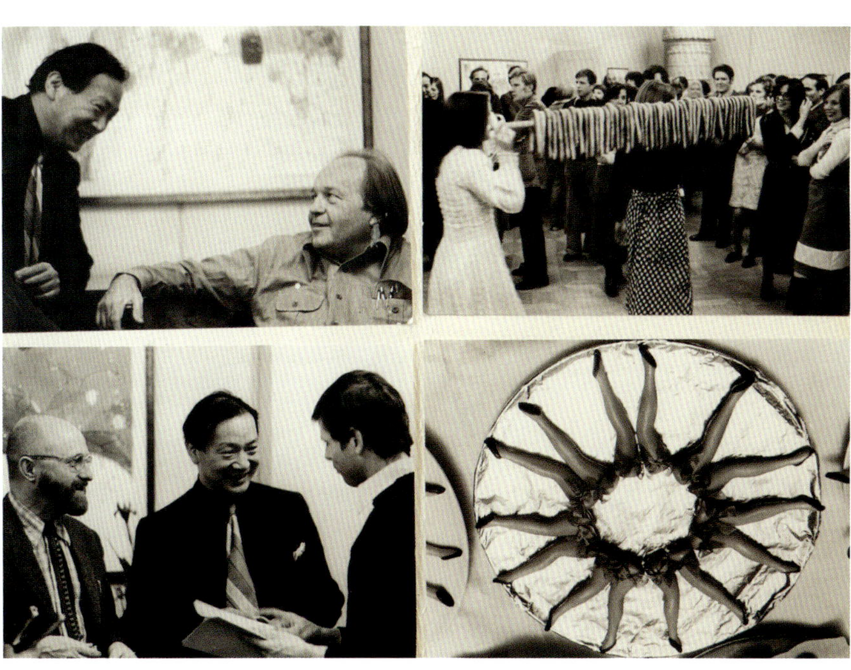

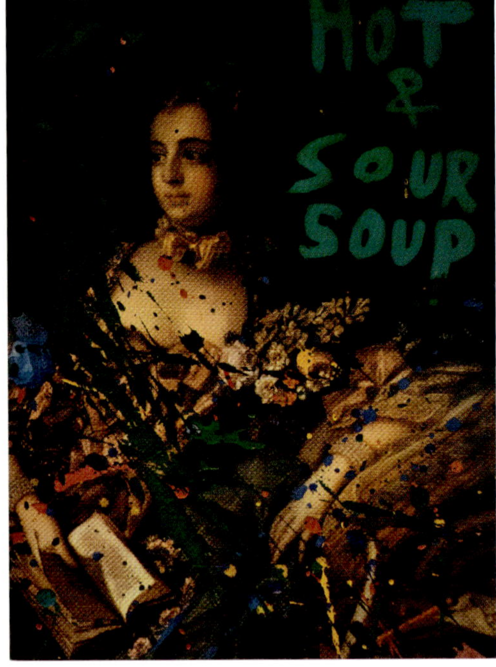

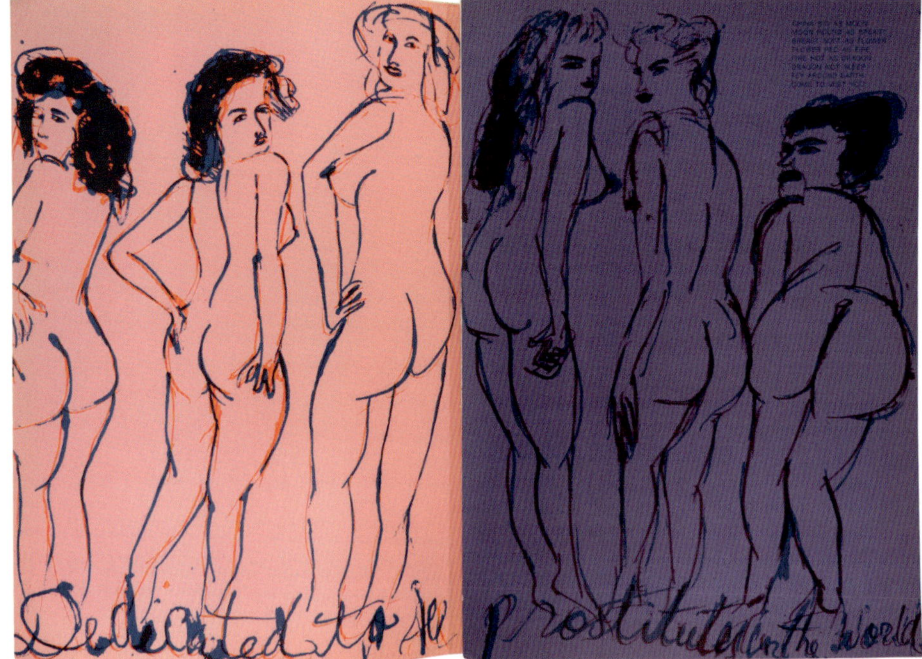

fig. 2. Walasse Ting, "Modification by
Walasse Ting on *Madame de Pompadour*
by François Boucher," *Hot and Sour Soup*
(Los Angeles and Copenhagen: The Sam
Francis Foundation and Bjørn Rosengreen
Printing, 1969), cover

fig. 3. Walasse Ting, "China big as moon,"
Hot and Sour Soup (Los Angeles and
Copenhagen: The Sam Francis
Foundation and Bjørn Rosengreen
Printing, 1969), 2–3

The 1969 book *Hot and Sour Soup* opens with the line "dedicated to all
prostitutes in the world". Six naked women posing from their back fill up the pages
from head to bottom. Spreading across the open leaves, they address us with
swinging hips, puckered lips, and saucy smiles. A tiny poem tucked into the upper
right corner reads:

CHINA BIG AS MOON
MOON ROUND AS BREAST
BREAST SOFT AS FLOWER
FLOWER RED AS FIRE
FIRE HOT AS DRAGON
DRAGON NOT SLEEP
FLY AROUND EARTH
COME TO VISIT YOU

For anyone who knows the work and world of Walasse Ting, the sociality and
conviviality tumbling through this chain of metaphors is a recurring resource and
model. If China feels big, he imagines that feeling as big as the moon, the moon
supple as breast, breast becoming flower. Flower saturated by its blazing color
becomes fire, fire conjures dragon, dragon defying the sleeping plot, travels
around the earth, and come to visit YOU. This is Ting's world, where if he sees a
brilliant, blooming dahlia, he becomes one, and nature's immodest abundance of
form heralds his own.

Today I wear a yellow shirt
I feel myself become a butterfly;
My life like waterlily
My love like dahlia
My painting like peony

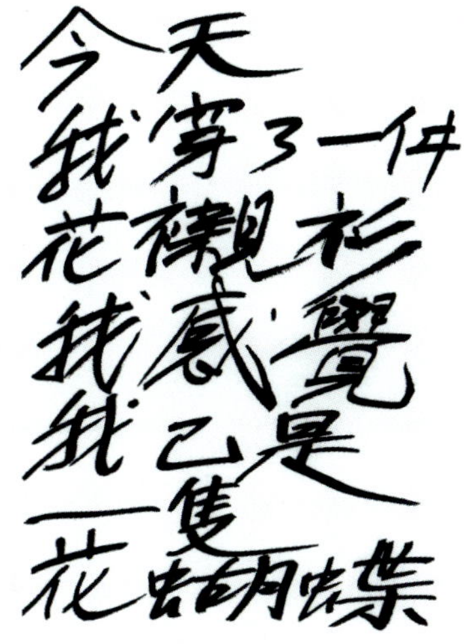

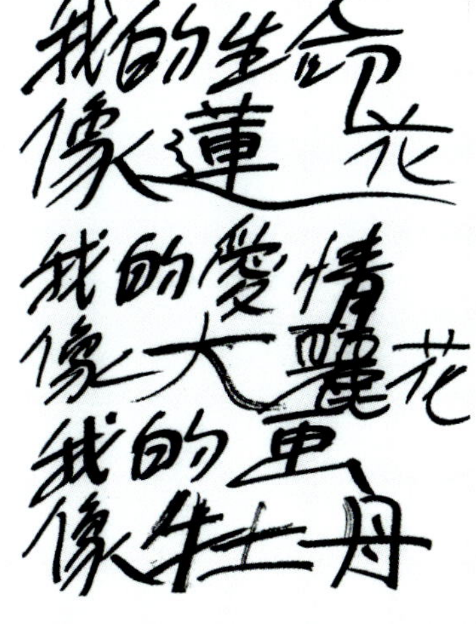

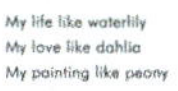

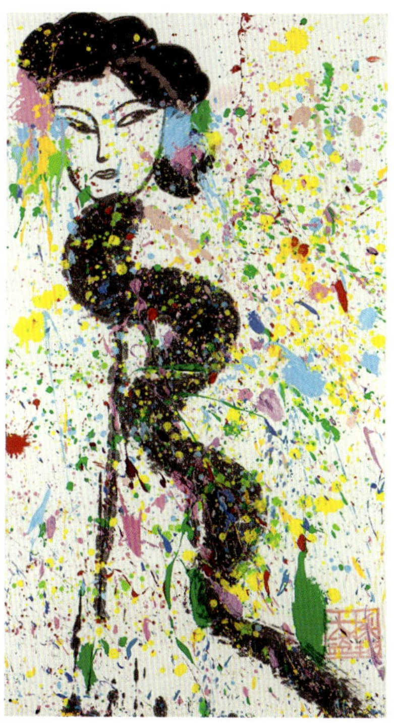

fig. 5. Walasse Ting
Beauté, 1970
Ink and colors on paper
69.8 × 37 in. / 177.3 × 94.1 cm
Courtesy of Musée Cernuschi, Asian Arts Museum of Paris

[1] "牡丹花下死, 做鬼也風流。採花大盜戲筆, 龍牛狎客" Inscription accompanying the painting *Beauté* (仕女), 1970.

By 1969, Ting had lived in Paris and New York, published three artist books, translated a volume of classical Chinese poetry, and held multiple solo gallery exhibitions in Europe and the U.S. In a year's time, he would take on the persona of "The Flower Thief," partially modeled after the Ming Dynasty poet and painter Tang Yin (唐寅) (1470–1524). The use of a poetic persona is often encountered in classical Chinese poetry, in which the author speaks through the voice of another person (or more frequently types of person). These personas are often conventional figures such as the palace lady waiting for her absent lover or the musician missing the perfect listener. The indeterminacy of the Chinese poetic language means that the personal pronoun is often absent, making it easy for the poet to take on a different voice, thus offering the poem a rich and ambiguous possibility. The irreverent charm of Tang Yin as "The Flower Thief" came largely from posthumous fictions based on the poet's life; they include stories of the talented literati courting a prostitute who endured a turbulent life. Ting "The Flower Thief" writes in character that, "If I should die beneath peony flowers, I will still be charming as a ghost. Along the brush of the Flower Thief, customer of pleasure houses."[1] "The Flower Thief" is thus a seducer of women. The indeterminate poetic subject allows him to adore women's beauty while purloining their sex. This carnal metaphor reverberates in Ting's poems. Recall the opening pages of *Hot and Sour Soup*: "BREAST SOFT AS FLOWER/ FLOWER RED AS FIRE."

Yet during this period, Ting also wrote extensive letters to his brothers in China in a confessional voice that was distinct from his otherwise artworld persona as a deliberate dandy, a stylist of prose, poetry, painting, and clothes:

I now know that mother has been laid to rest after the letter I received on April 3rd. I didn't cry or feel hard while reading your letter: instead, I have a feeling that mother has been here, sitting with me.

It's without any sound, but it's so much more than real that I can feel it truly happened. Sometimes I remember I am still a part of mother just like a tree; just like little Mia is part of me. Moreover I will love Mia as much as I love mother. Unlike stultified minds, I read Tang [618–906 A.D.] and Song [960–1127 A.D.] poetry a lot. It seems like I could have long conversation with these poets throughout the night to reflect and understand modern day situations such as: Why was there a revolution to overthrow the emperor? Why did Mao expel Chiang Kai-shek out of China? Those who care about nothing but money never see anything true. (Ancient poets like Li Bai (李白), Du Fu (杜甫) and Bai Juyi (白居易) could find truths in life and nature).[2] April 1971

Truth is to be found in life, we are told, and to see truth with the capacious eye of a poet, Ting enlisted literary and affective resources that ranged widely and freely over vast expanses of time and space—from freedom found in a pared-down pidgin English to dialogues with classical Chinese poets, and to the modernist project of remodeling ancient literature that connected Ting with Taiwanese poets such as Lo Fu (洛夫) (1928–2018) and Guan Guan (管管) (1929–2021) and Taiwan's New Poetry Movement.[3] Quoting the American critic J.D. Frodsham, Lo Fu compared the structural freedom of Ting's words to unitary bricks, "Unrestricted by grammatical voice, parts of speech, and style, his words pile on like bricks composing a wall. They are at once structurally sound and compositionally free."[4] Living in between languages and cultures can be alienating. Yet instead of seeing a world of impoverished relations and isolated objects, Ting seems to have done his best to create affiliations that invite capacious forms of affection and recognition. Such an effort runs through the accumulative structure of his poetry and prose.

fig. 6. Walasse Ting, "33 ways to open," *Hot and Sour Soup* (Los Angeles and Copenhagen: The Sam Francis Foundation and Bjørn Rosengreen Printing, 1969), 11

[2] Walasse Ting, "Walasse Ting Family Letters – 2," in *Walasse Ting: Red Mouth Series 1 - 1973–1977 - Acrylic and Oil Pastel on Western Paper* (Shanghai: Longmen Art Projects, 2012), 19–21, 19.

[3] In 1975, Walasse Ting held his first solo show in Taiwan at the National Museum of History, marking his first visit to Taiwan. It was during this trip that Ting met poets associated with the journal *The Epoch Poetry Quarterly* and officially joined the group. The New Poetry Movement in Taiwan began in the 1930s. Like the New Poetry Movement in China led by Hu Shi (胡適) (1891–1962), the call for modern poetry in Taiwan embodied iconoclasm, aspirations to modernity, and a new, vernacular orientation of poetry. Early influences include Japanese modernism, the New Literature Movement in mainland China, and Surrealism. The poetry group Epoch (Chuangshiji - 创世纪) was founded in 1954, notably by Lo Fu. Lo Fu was interested in the particularity of Chinese language and in preservation of its heritage. Strongly influenced by French Surrealism, poets associated with *Epoch* saw expressions via image as one of the central conceits of poetic form. See also Cédric Laurent, "Walasse Ting: Text and Image, Painting and Poetry," in *Walasse Ting: The Flower Thief* (Paris: Paris Musées, 2017), 85–92, 88.

[4] Lo Fu, "Walasse Ting's Painting and Poem," *The Epoch Poetry Quarterly*, April 1975, 40.

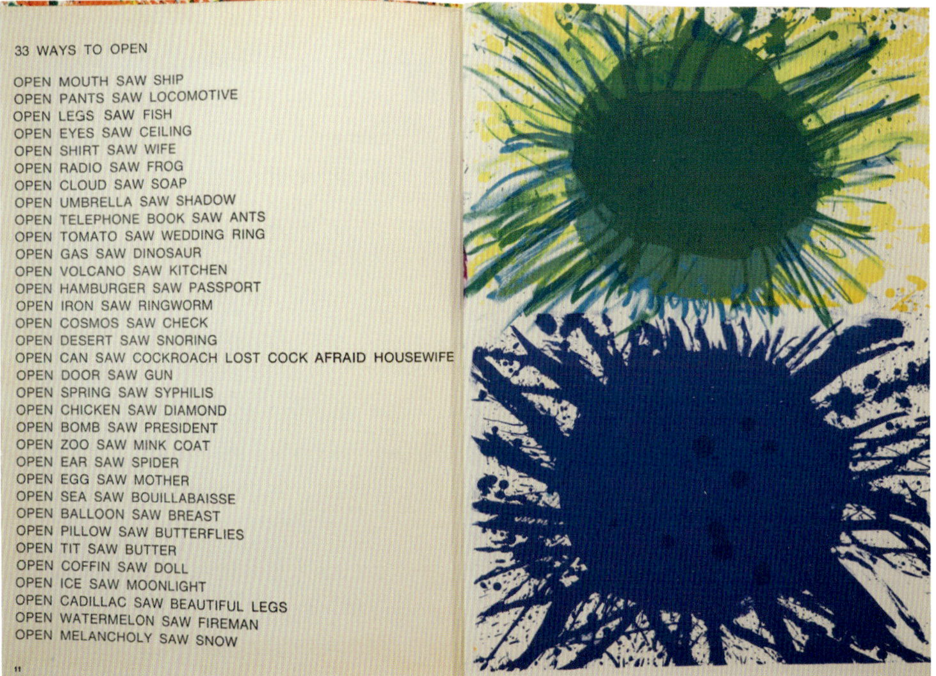

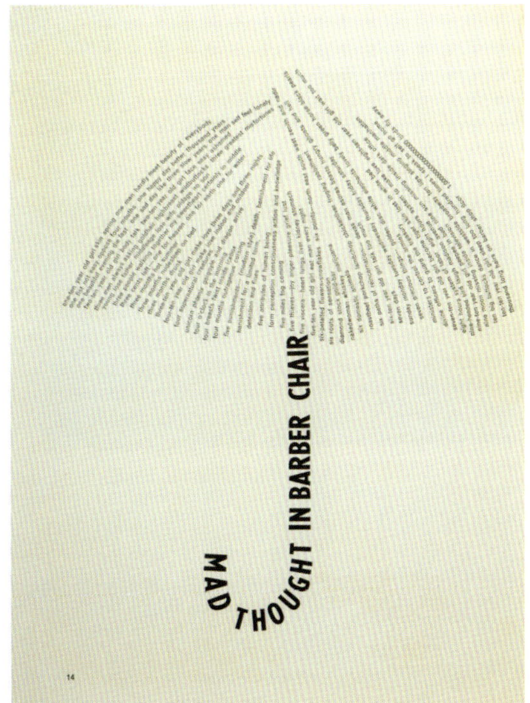

In 1973, the Taiwanese writer and photographer Ruan Yizhong (阮义忠)
conducted an extensive set of interviews with Ting. When asked what makes
a good painting and a good poem, Ting answered with the following poesis:

> [A] good painting and a good poem cannot be made with a cold eye…
> What I want to share is…when you look at the sky, you imagine yourself
> being the sky; cloud will fly on your belly; when you look at mountains,
> you imagine yourself being mountains; tigers and deer will skip under
> your armpits; when you see the ocean, you become the ocean; whale,
> tiger grouper, yellow croaker, and goldfish will swim in your mouth; when
> you see a tree, you are a tree, shooting up from the ground; cherries,
> plums, and lychees are falling from your arms. How do transformations
> happen? Think of the cloud and rain in the sky, they split and join, join
> and split. Splitting is expressive, to divide oneself into a thousand
> pieces; joining is absorbent, folding-in to form a network. Everything
> around you—the sun, the moon, the blade of grass on the pavement
> and the drops of dew, the dog pee, and the osmanthus—they all split
> and join like matches made in heaven. Yet we don't notice them, as if
> they have nothing to be recognized.[5]

If good painting and good poetry cannot be made by a cold eye, what follows is a
Tingian exercise on how to see the world with warmer eyes. Ting's primary method
for pursuing such a project was an inventive way to draw out similarities in different
objects by imagining oneself as those objects, letting their shape, color, and
ecosystem be the forces that compose you. The cultural critic Walter Benjamin
called this "gift for seeing similarity," our mimetic faculty, which for him is "a
rudiment of the once powerful compulsion to become similar and to behave
mimetically."[6] A good example can be observed in child's play. The child's mimetic

[5] Ruan Yizhong, "Interviewing Walasse
Ting," *The Epoch Poetry Quarterly*, 164,
September 2010, 119.
[6] Walter Benjamin, "On the Mimetic Faculty,"
in *Walter Benjamin: Selected Writings*, vol. 2,
ed. Howard Eiland and Michael W. Jennings,
trans. Edmund Jephcott et al. (Cambridge,
MA: Harvard University Press, 2003),
720–22. 720. For an inspiring read of Andy
Warhol's pursuit of "liking things," see
Jonathan Flatley, *Like Andy Warhol* (Chicago:
The University of Chicago press, 2017).

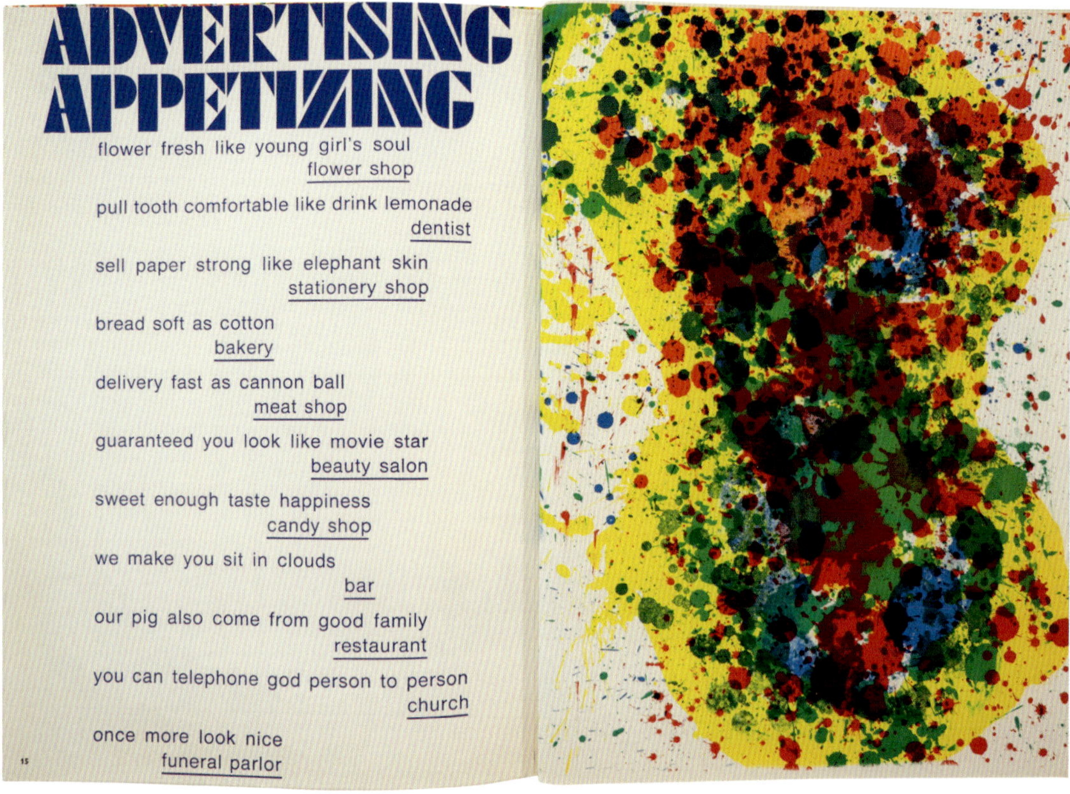
ADVERTISING APPETIZING
flower fresh like young girl's soul
flower shop
pull tooth comfortable like drink lemonade
dentist
sell paper strong like elephant skin
stationery shop
bread soft as cotton
bakery
delivery fast as cannon ball
meat shop
guaranteed you look like movie star
beauty salon
sweet enough taste happiness
candy shop
we make you sit in clouds
bar
our pig also come from good family
restaurant
you can telephone god person to person
church
once more look nice
funeral parlor
15

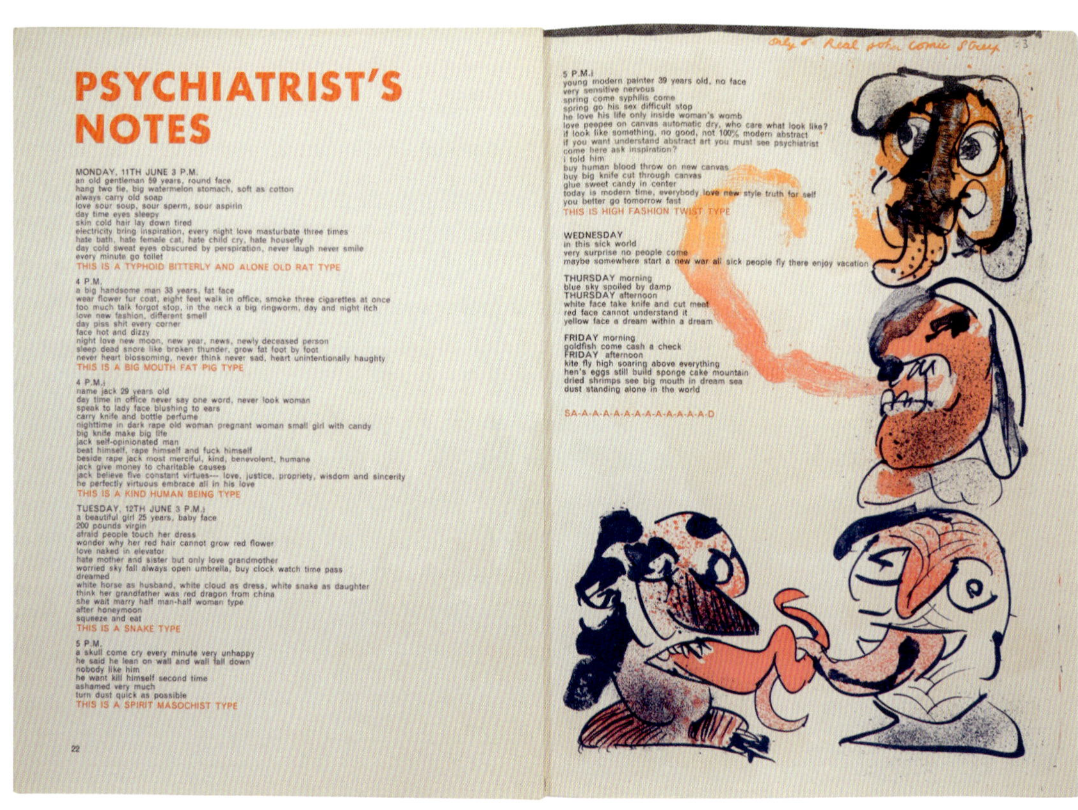
PSYCHIATRIST'S NOTES

MONDAY, 11TH JUNE 3 P.M.
an old gentleman 59 years, round face
hang two tie, big watermelon stomach, soft as cotton
always carry old soap
love sour soup, sour sperm, sour aspirin
day time eyes sleepy
skin cold hair lay down tired
electricity bring inspiration, every night love masturbate three times
hate bath, hate female cat, hate child cry, hate housefly
day cold sweat eyes obscured by perspiration, never laugh never smile
every minute go toilet
THIS IS A TYPHOID BITTERLY AND ALONE OLD RAT TYPE

4 P.M.
a big handsome man 33 years, fat face
wear flower fur coat, eight feet walk in office, smoke three cigarettes at once
too much talk forgot stop, in the neck a big ringworm, day and night itch
love new fashion, different smell
day piss shit every corner
face hot and dizzy
night love new moon, new year, news, newly deceased person
sleep dead snore like broken thunder, grow fat foot by foot
never heart blossoming, never think never sad, heart unintentionally haughty
THIS IS A BIG MOUTH FAT PIG TYPE

4 P.M.
name jack 29 years old
day time in office never say one word, never look woman
speak to lady face blushing to ears
carry knife and bottle perfume
nighttime in dark rape old woman pregnant woman small girl with candy
big knife make big life
jack self-opinionated man
beat himself, rape himself and fuck himself
beside rape jack most merciful, kind, benevolent, humane
jack give money to charitable causes
jack believe five constant virtues— love, justice, propriety, wisdom and sincerity
he perfectly virtuous embrace all in his love
THIS IS A KIND HUMAN BEING TYPE

TUESDAY, 12TH JUNE 3 P.M.
a beautiful girl 25 years, baby face
200 pounds virgin
afraid people touch her dress
wonder why her red hair cannot grow red flower
love naked in elevator
hate mother and sister but only love grandmother
worried sky fall always open umbrella, buy clock watch time pass
dreamed
white horse as husband, white cloud as dress, white snake as daughter
think her grandfather was red dragon from china
she wait marry half man-half woman type
after honeymoon
squeeze and eat
THIS IS A SNAKE TYPE

5 P.M.
a skull come cry every minute very unhappy
he said he lean on wall and wall fall down
nobody like him
he want kill himself second time
ashamed very much
turn dust quick as possible
THIS IS A SPIRIT MASOCHIST TYPE

22

5 P.M.
young modern painter 39 years old, no face
very sensitive nervous
spring come syphilis come
spring go his sex difficult stop
he love his life only inside woman's womb
love peepee on canvas automatic dry, who care what look like?
if look like something, no good, not 100% modern abstract
if you want understand abstract art you must see psychiatrist
come here ask inspiration?
i told him
buy human blood throw on new canvas
buy big knife cut through canvas
glue sweet candy in center
today is modern time, everybody love new style truth for self
you better go tomorrow fast
THIS IS HIGH FASHION TWIST TYPE

WEDNESDAY
in this sick world
very surprise no people come
maybe somewhere start a new war all sick people fly there enjoy vacation

THURSDAY morning
blue sky spoiled by damp
THURSDAY afternoon
white face take knife and cut meat
red face cannot understand it
yellow face a dream within a dream

FRIDAY morning
goldfish come cash a check
FRIDAY afternoon
kite fly high soaring above everything
hen's eggs still build sponge cake mountain
dried shrimps see big mouth in dream sea
dust standing alone in the world

SA-A-A-A-A-A-A-A-A-A-A-D

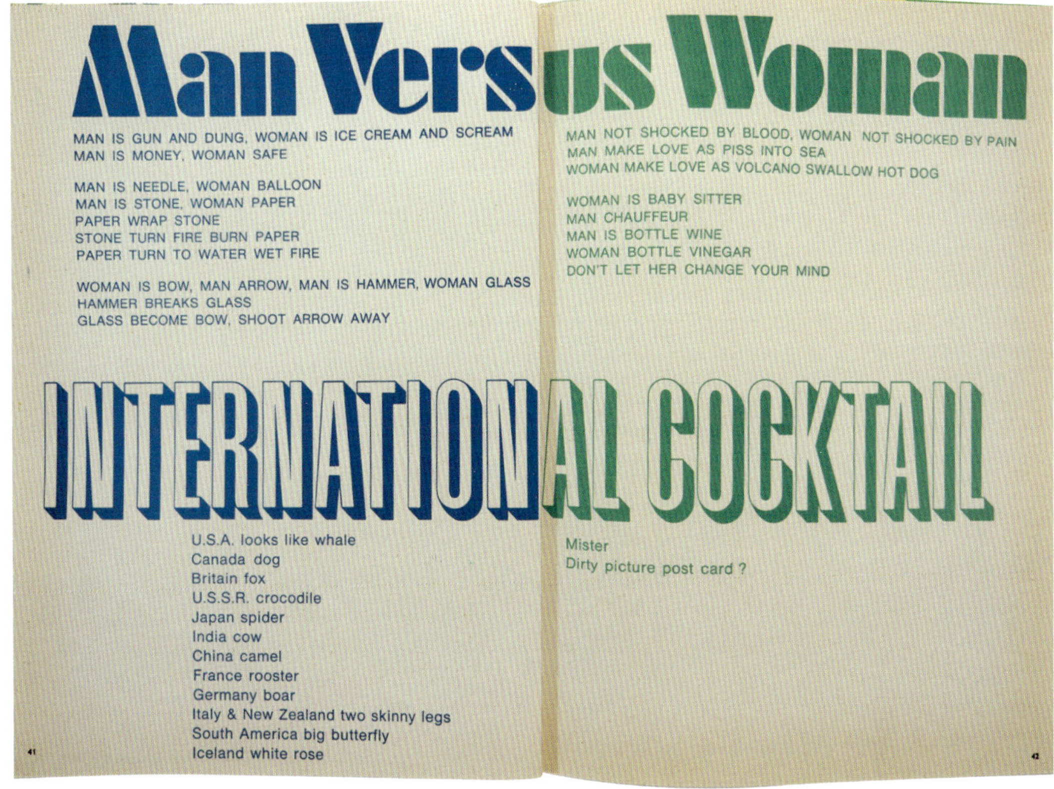

behavior is by no means limited to what one person can imitate in another. Rather, children play, "at being not only a shopkeeper or teacher, but also a windmill and a train."[7] This compulsion to be alike is thus not only a "representational category" pertaining to a particular relationship with a specific object. Rather, and vitally, it is a "*relational* practice—a process, comportment, or activity of 'producing similarities' (such as astrology, dance, and play)"—that allows us to relate and connect to the world.[8] Perhaps it is precisely in a world of migration, translation, and difference that Ting finds great pleasure in illuminating resemblance. The practice of seeing and liking, of personifying and recognizing, are habitual inclinations that can be cultivated and encouraged. However, Ting's more ambitious attempt still is initiating his audience into this world of belonging and becoming. If the poem at the beginning of *Hot and Sour Soup* is dedicated to the world's prostitutes and addressed to YOU, can you imagine yourself being looped into this orbit of the moon and breast and flower, and finding it abundant? Would this world become all the more attractive because you can imagine your own participation in it?

This togetherness with the world cannot, however, be equated with a blissful ignorance. What we find in Ting's poems is not just the magical correspondences that allow us to think more like trees, the ocean, and the sky. There are outlines of the modern institution, those orders from without that transformed man's mimetic faculty and made us ever less capacious. Donning a particular sensibility of pop culture, Ting's poems point us to the language of advertisement, psychiatry, gender, and the nation state. In their prescription of pleasure, identity, and cure, these institutions also consolidated borders, engrained prohibitions, and identified pathologies. To write a good poem is thus to write promiscuously, to traverse the social fabric like the migrant, the queer, the affectionate, the comedic, and the Marxist. Such an ethos of artmaking supports "a greater variety of forms of affectional and sexual relationships, a proliferation of variously organized friendships

[7] Benjamin, "On the Mimetic Faculty," 720.
[8] Miriam Hansen, *Cinema and Experience: Siegfried Kracauer, Walter Benjamin, and Theodor W. Adorno* (Berkeley: University of California Press, 2012), 147.

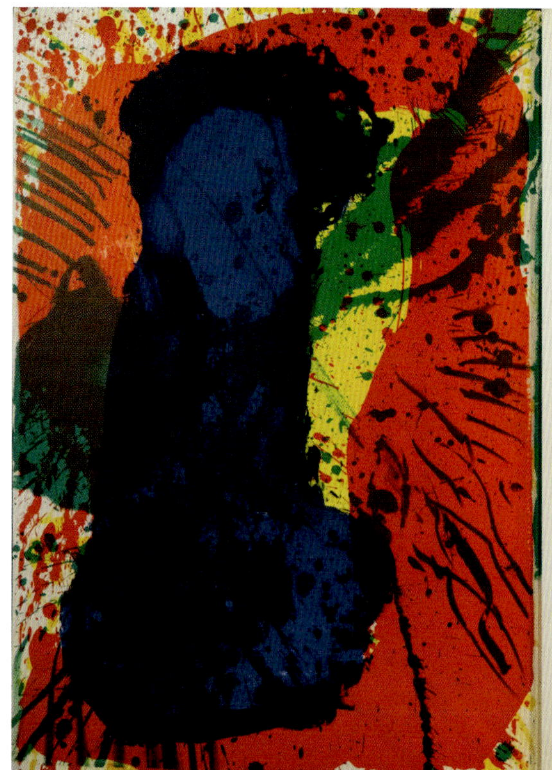

fig. 11. Walasse Ting, "Narrow Heaven," *Hot and Sour Soup* (Los Angeles and Copenhagen: The Sam Francis Foundation and Bjørn Rosengreen Printing, 1969), 4

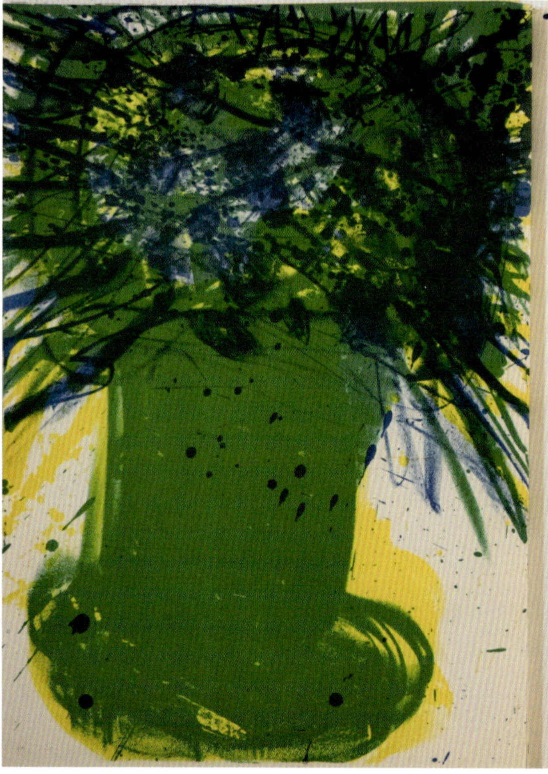

fig. 12. Walasse Ting, "Modern Man," *Hot and Sour Soup* (Los Angeles and Copenhagen: The Sam Francis Foundation and Bjørn Rosengreen Printing, 1969) 48

and community relationships, which made for a great many options for obtaining pleasure and forming human connection and intimacy."[9]

To write good poetry is thus to protest against the *Narrow Heaven* of ideological fault lines. It is to be against the inhibition that "passengers not permitted to stay between Communist & Capitalist Line." As you read against this *Narrow Heaven*, remember to not curb your desire to laugh:

> No hugging No necking No kissing No chicken
> No puffing No laughing No giggling
> No dancing No joking No smoking
> No drinking king size or baby size
> No discount No onion soup No Palmolive soap
> No stand up No sit down No lying down
> No sex No Marx No lox
> No pork chop No lamb chop No steak No mistake
> No spitting No walking No looking No thinking
> No talking No shitting No fucking
> NO NO NO NO
> No kidding $25 fine or 10 days in jail

Against the Narrow Heaven, good poetry will begin to draw the outline of a different man. He would still be marked by modernity's incongruous histories, yet as we see those histories in fuller, transnational conjectures, we are also invited by the poet to configure the modern man otherwise:

> Modern Man
> Head Communist
> Pocket Capitalist
> Stomach Fascist
> Penis Imperialist
> Tits Cubist
> Mouth Animalist
> Nose Surrealist
> Fuck Nudist
> Buttocks Anarchist
> Skin Abstract Expressionist
> Love Impressionist
> Dance Socialist
> Blood Pianist
> Shit Super Realist

This is far from a portrait of a good man, someone who makes good decisions, has clear boundaries, is politically invested, has compassion, holds care, and all the while not engaging in behaviors that are self-effacing. Here listed are also bodily pursuits that we aren't to do, much less fetishize. Yet, in them is a frank willingness to confront the aggressive *and* sexual histories of Modern Man, and finally to confront them without the veneer of rationalization.[10] Here then, reunited with our irreverent side, we might also begin to see the world with warmer eyes.

[9] Here I am quoting the cultural critic Douglas Crimp from his discussion of the ethos of gay liberation regarding the expansion of affectional possibility. See Tina Takemoto, "The Melancholia of AIDS: Interview with Douglas Crimp," *Art Journal*, 62, no. 4, Winter 2003, 80–90, 86.

[10] Finding ways to navigate our pleasures and desires require real attempts to test the boundaries that we live under. As the psychoanalyst and writer Jamieson Webster wrote, "the promised image of goodness skirts pleasures that—for obscure reasons—you aren't sure you can want." These reasons are obscure, and they are historically complex; they are structured by institutions such as education, marriage, sexual identity, and health that make desire compulsory and "free will" a tricky term to employ. Even though desire often feels compulsory, testing these boundaries take time and care. I think Ting's poetry and art invite us to approach the crossing of those lines freely, responsibly, and that opening up to the world might help us feel a little bit more at home with our desires. See Jamieson Webster. "I Don't Need to Be a 'Good Person.' Neither Do You," *The New York Times*, August 25, 2023. https://www.nytimes.com/2023/08/25/opinion/desires-good-person.html.

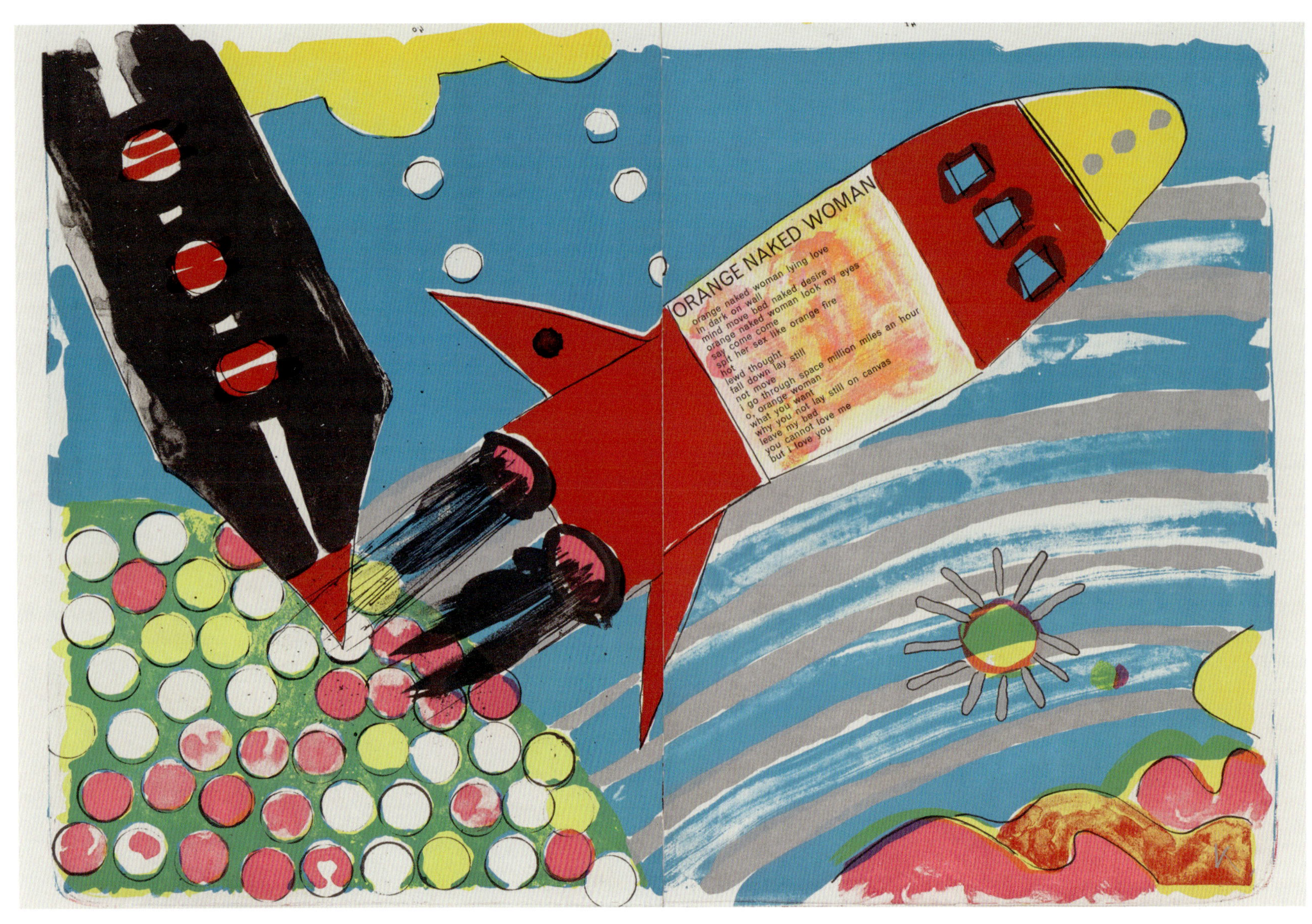

Kiki O.K. [Kiki Kogelnik]
Orange Naked Woman (double page
in-text plate, pages 40 and 41),
from *1¢ Life*, 1964
Color lithograph
16 1/8 × 22 13/16 in. / 40.3 × 56 cm
© 1964 Kiki Kogelnik Foundation.
All rights reserved

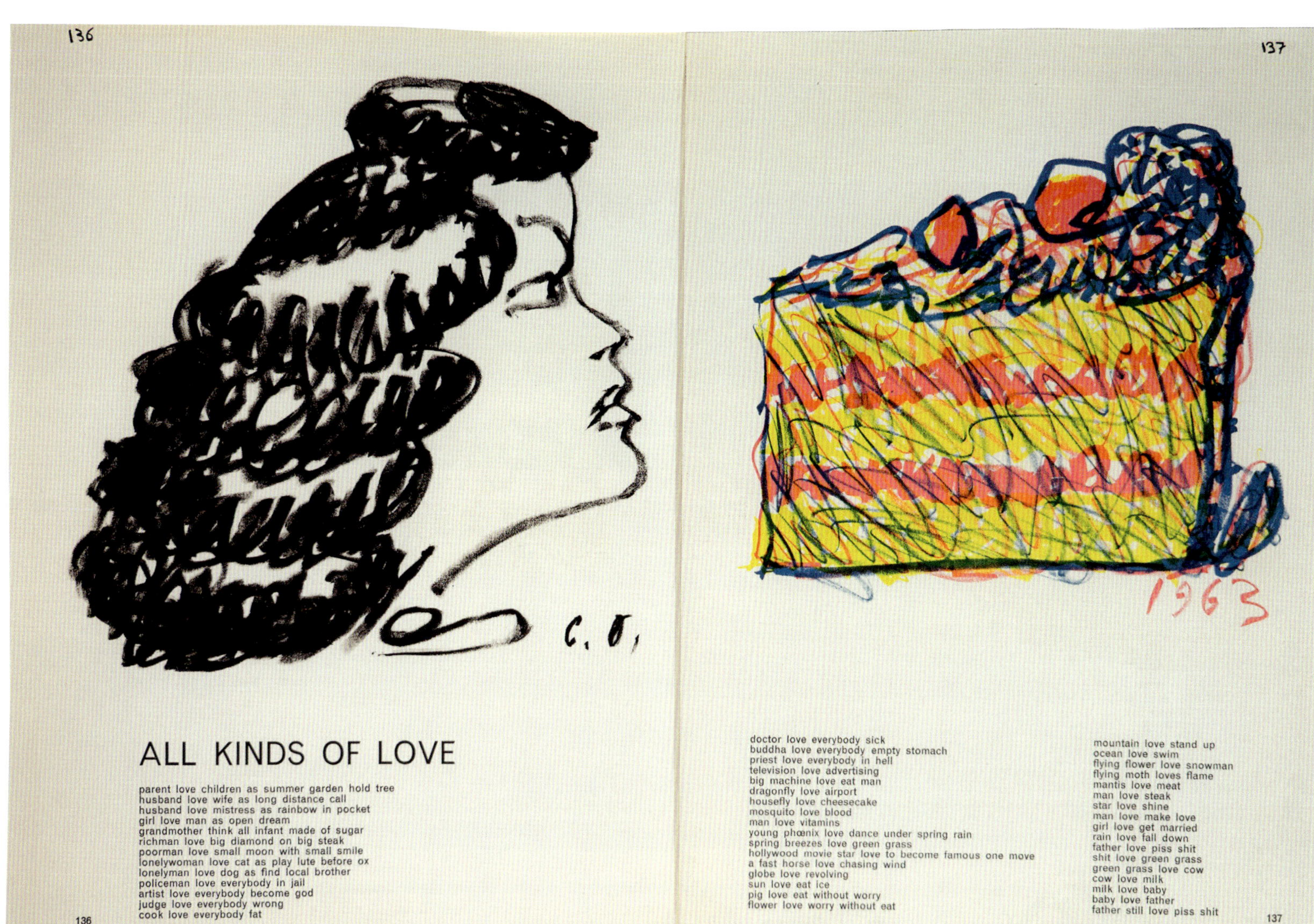

ALL KINDS OF LOVE

parent love children as summer garden hold tree
husband love wife as long distance call
husband love mistress as rainbow in pocket
girl love man as open dream
grandmother think all infant made of sugar
richman love big diamond on big steak
poorman love small moon with small smile
lonelywoman love cat as play lute before ox
lonelyman love dog as find local brother
policeman love everybody in jail
artist love everybody become god
judge love everybody wrong
cook love everybody fat

doctor love everybody sick
buddha love everybody empty stomach
priest love everybody in hell
television love advertising
big machine love eat man
dragonfly love airport
housefly love cheesecake
mosquito love blood
man love vitamins
young phœnix love dance under spring rain
spring breezes love green grass
hollywood movie star love to become famous one move
a fast horse love chasing wind
globe love revolving
sun love eat ice
pig love eat without worry
flower love worry without eat

mountain love stand up
ocean love swim
flying flower love snowman
flying moth loves flame
mantis love meat
man love steak
star love shine
man love make love
girl love get married
rain love fall down
father love piss shit
shit love green grass
green grass love cow
cow love milk
milk love baby
baby love father
father still love piss shit

Claes Oldenburg
Untitled (All Kinds of Love) (double page
in-text plate, pages 136 and 137),
from *1¢ Life*, 1964
Color lithograph
16 1/8 × 22 13/16 in. / 41 × 58 cm
Courtesy the Oldenburg van Bruggen
Foundation

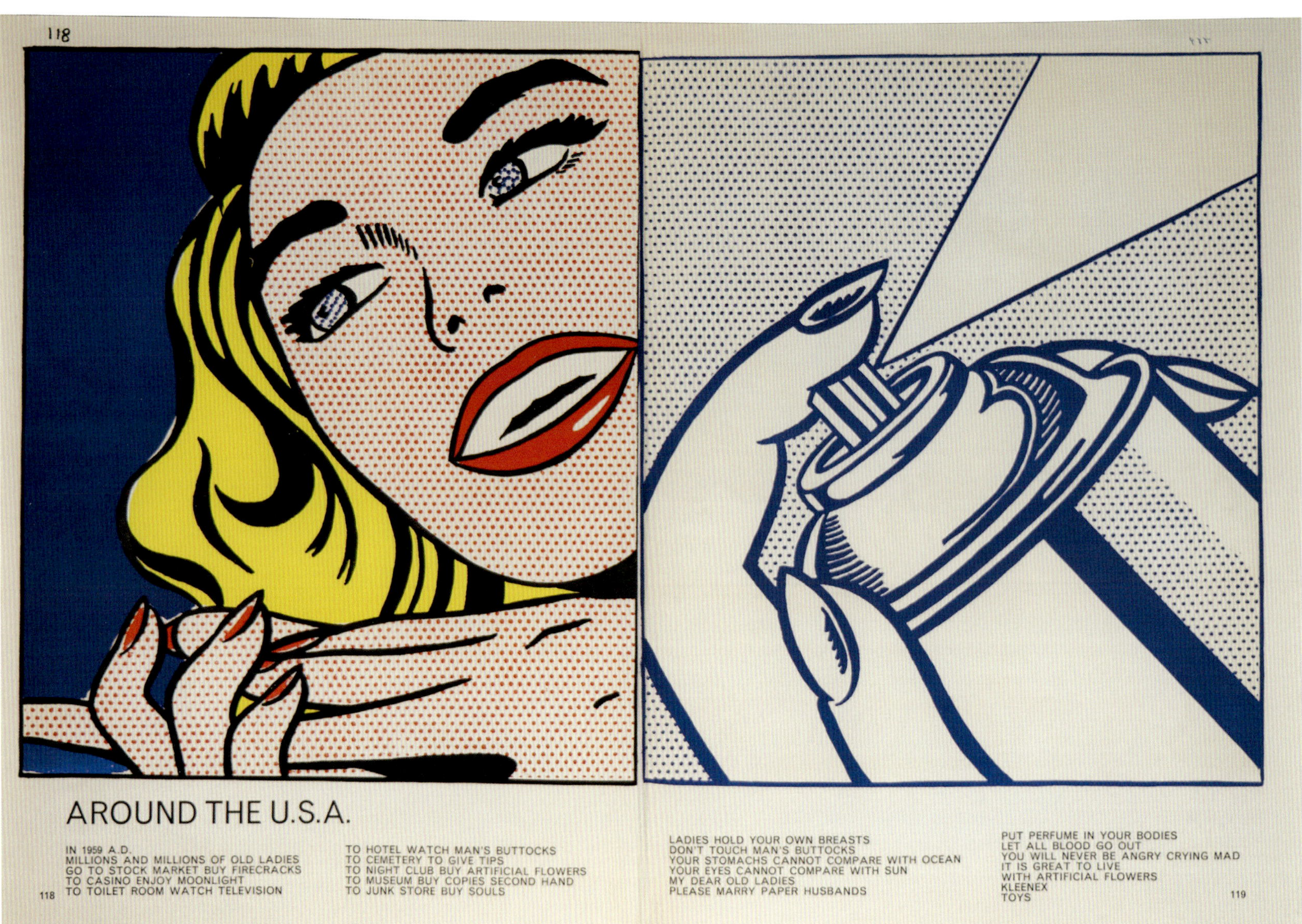

Roy Lichtenstein
Around the U.S.A. (double page
headpiece, pages 118 and 119)
from *1¢ Life*, 1963, published 1964
Color lithograph
16 1/8 × 22 13/16 in. / 41 × 58 cm
Estate of Roy Lichtenstein

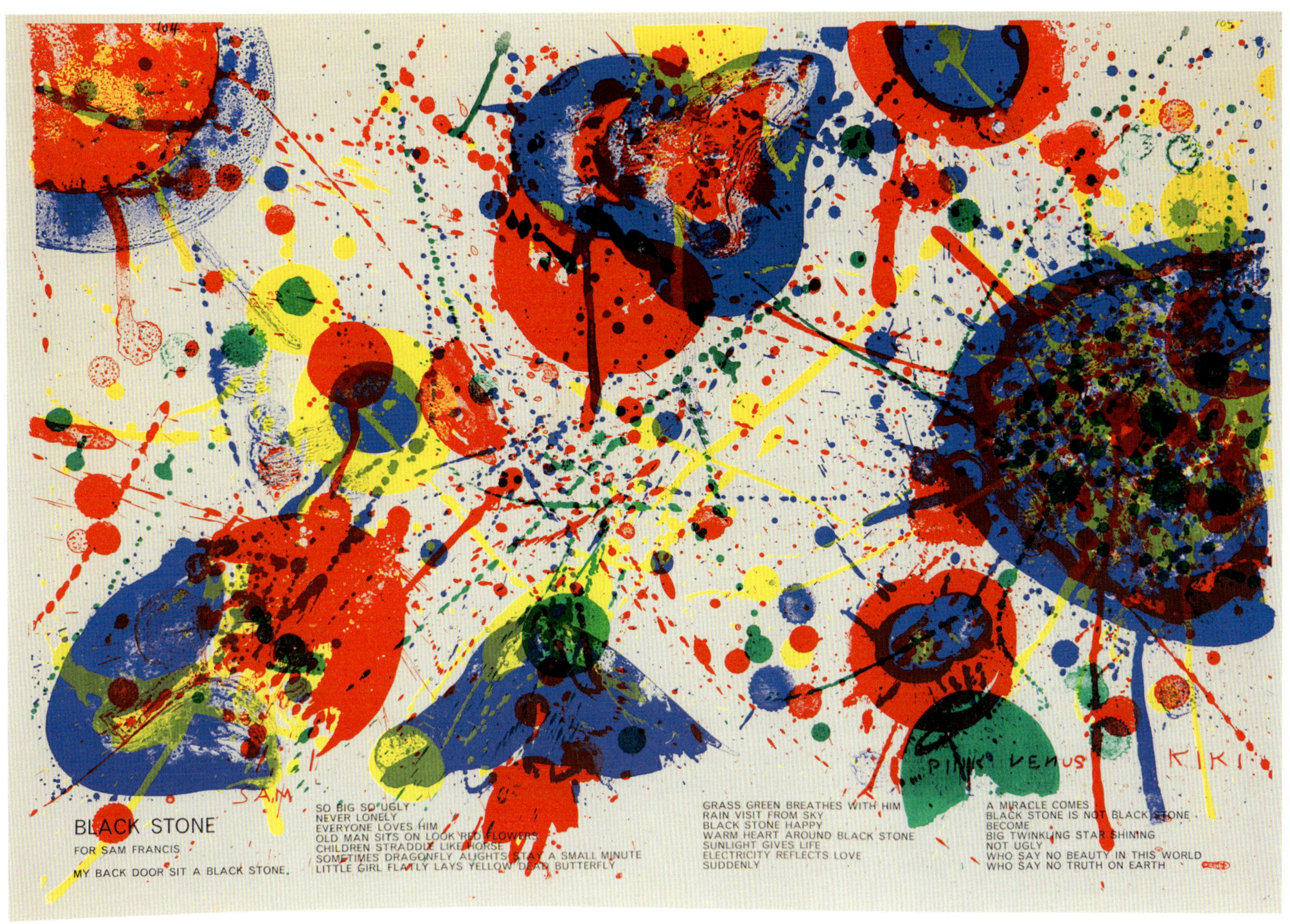

Sam Francis
Pink Venus Kiki (double page headpiece, pages 104 and 105) from *1¢ Life*, 1964
Color lithograph
16 1/8 × 22 13/16 in. / 41 × 58 cm
Artwork © 2023 Sam Francis Foundation, California/ Artists Rights Society (ARS), New York

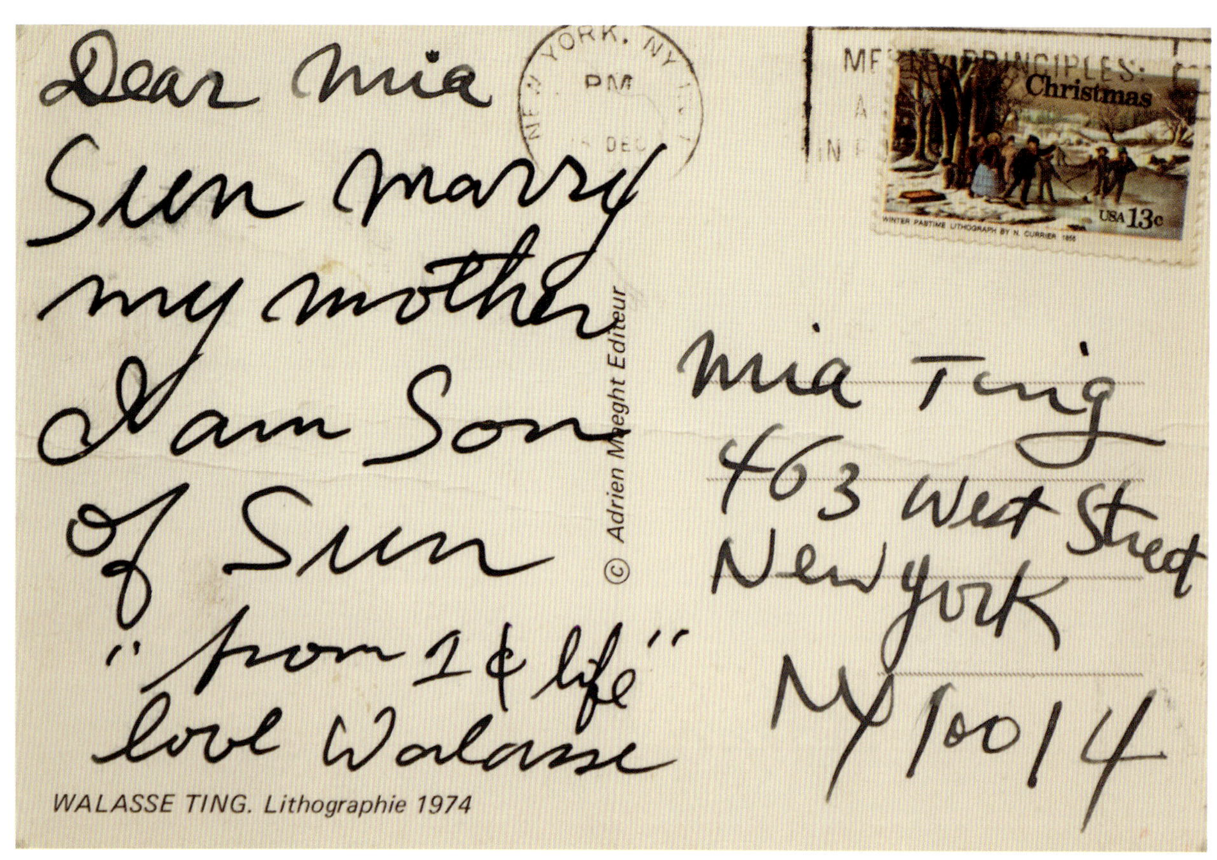

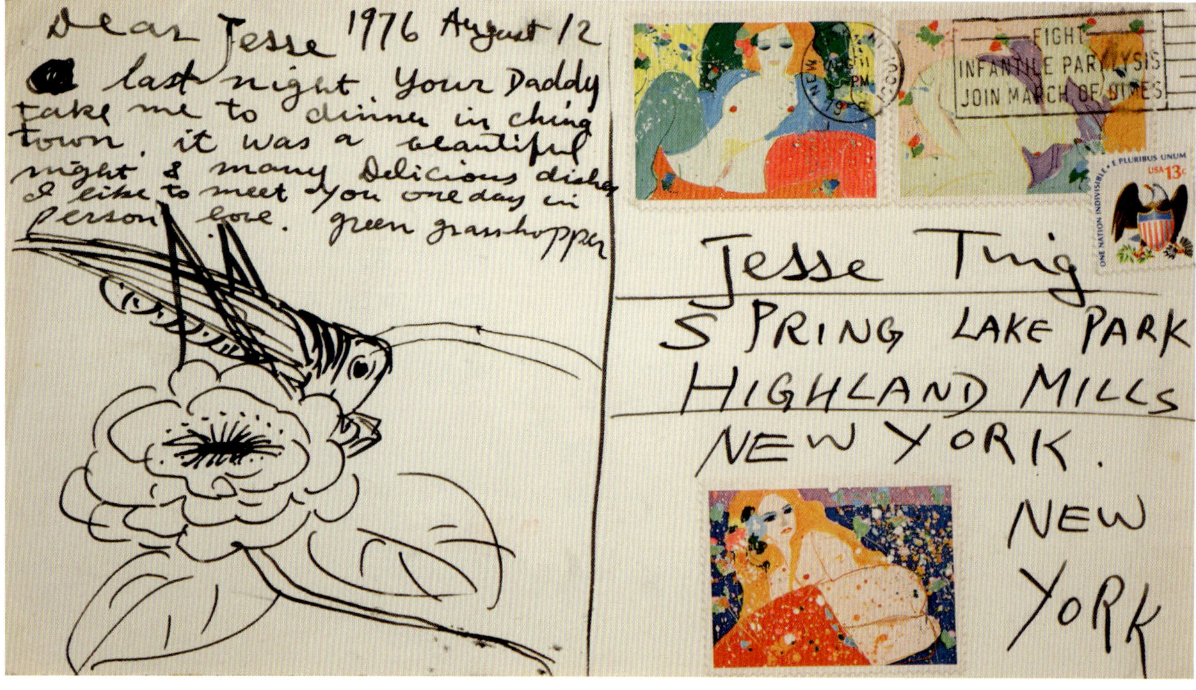

Postcard to Mia Ting from Walasse Ting
signed "I am Son of Sun from '1¢ life',"
c. 1974

Postcard to Jesse Ting from Walasse Ting
signed "green grasshopper,"
August 12, 1976

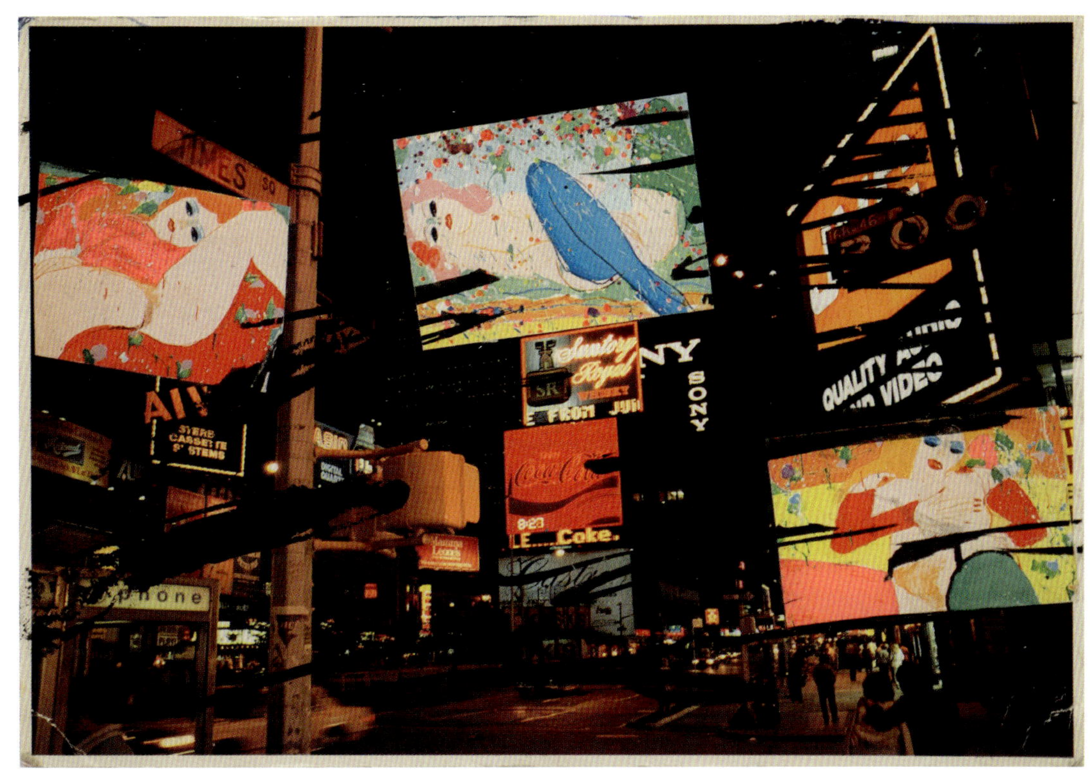

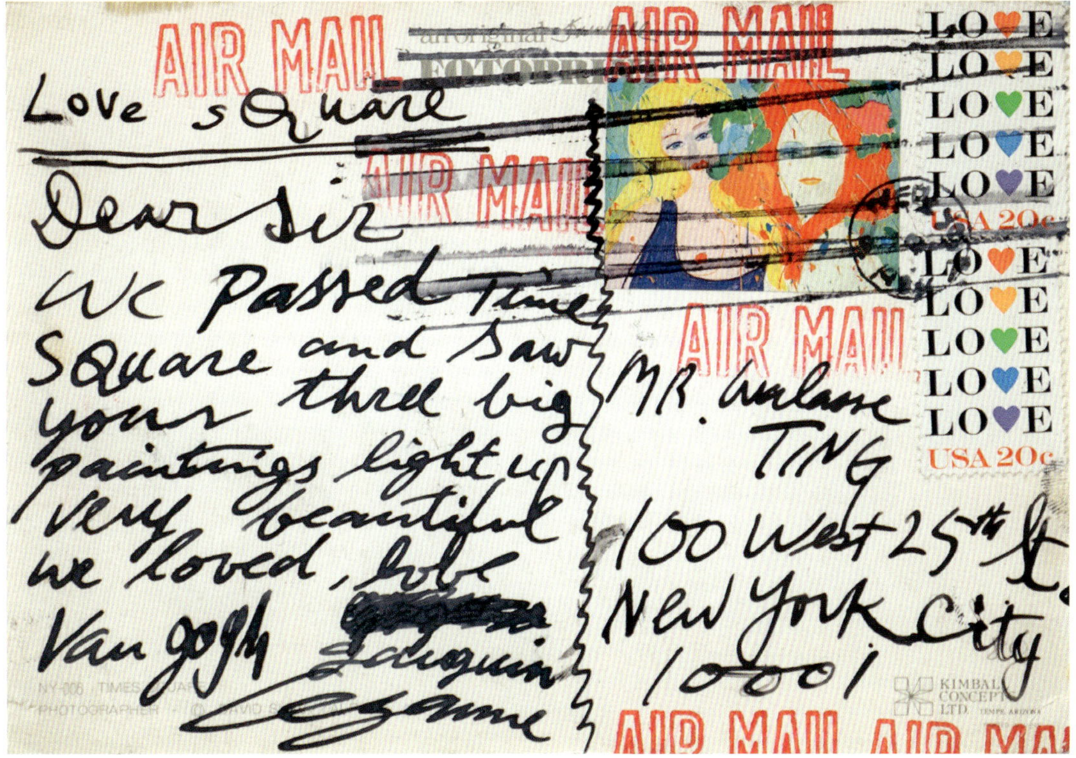

Walasse Ting modified postcard, 1984
(recto)

Postcard to Walasse Ting from Walasse
Ting signed "Van Gogh, Gauguin
and Cezanne," 1984 (verso)

Plates

Section Three

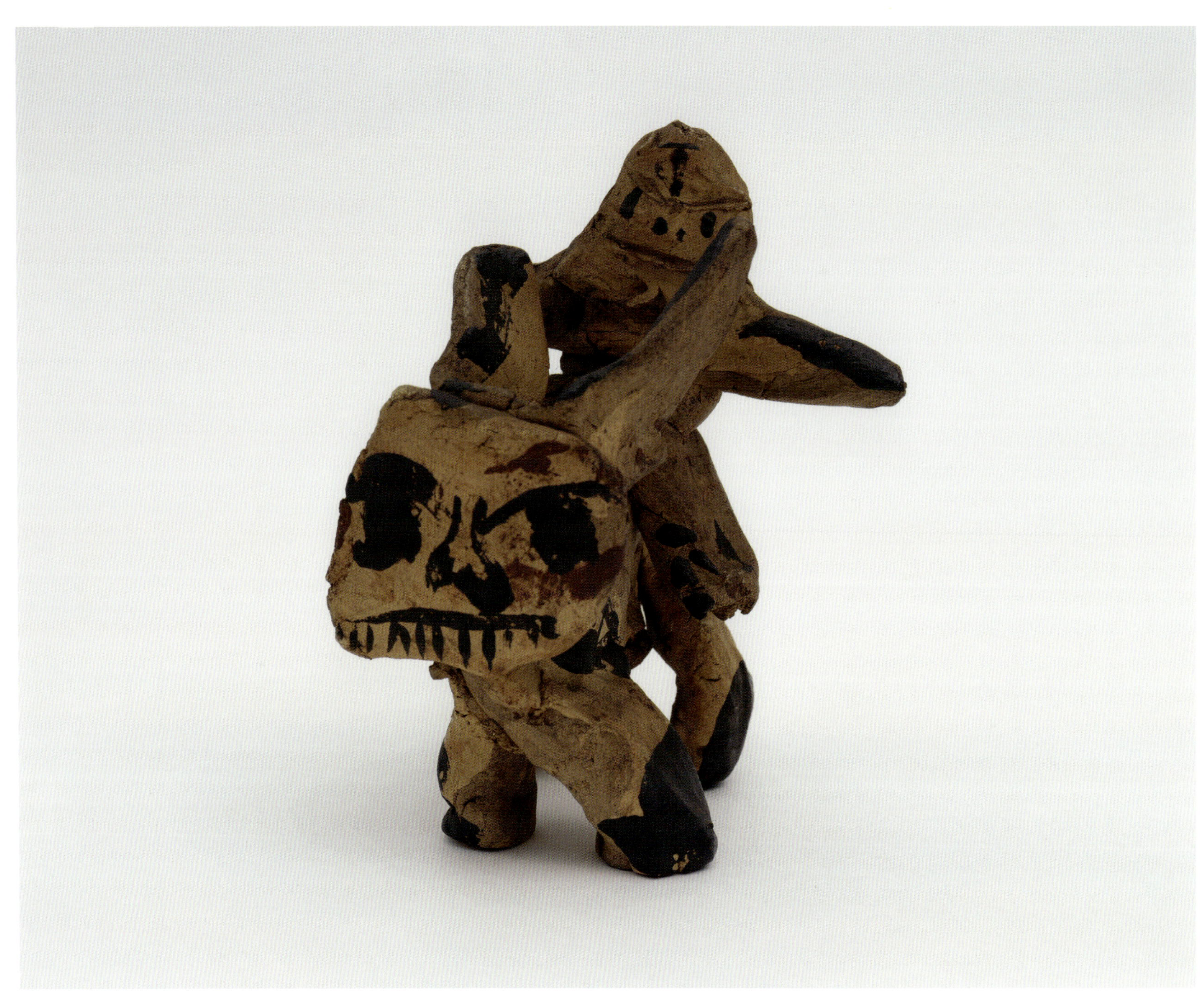

Untitled (Figure on Donkey), 1957
Terracotta clay
6 × 5 × 5 in. / 15.2 × 12.7 × 12.7 cm
Private Collection

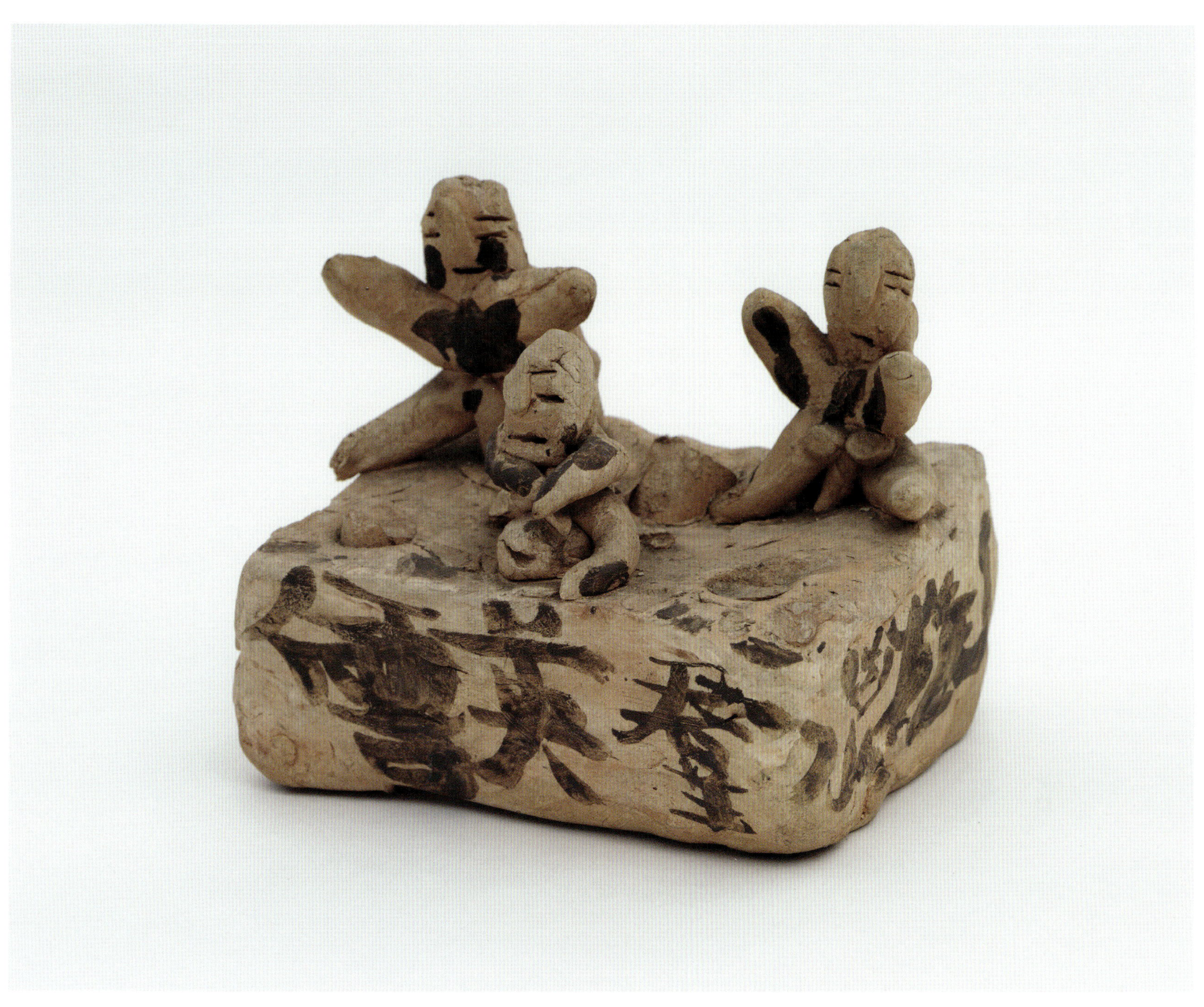

Untitled (Hero Gathering), 1957
Terracotta clay
6 × 6.2 × 6 in. / 15.2 × 15.8 × 15.2 cm
Private Collection

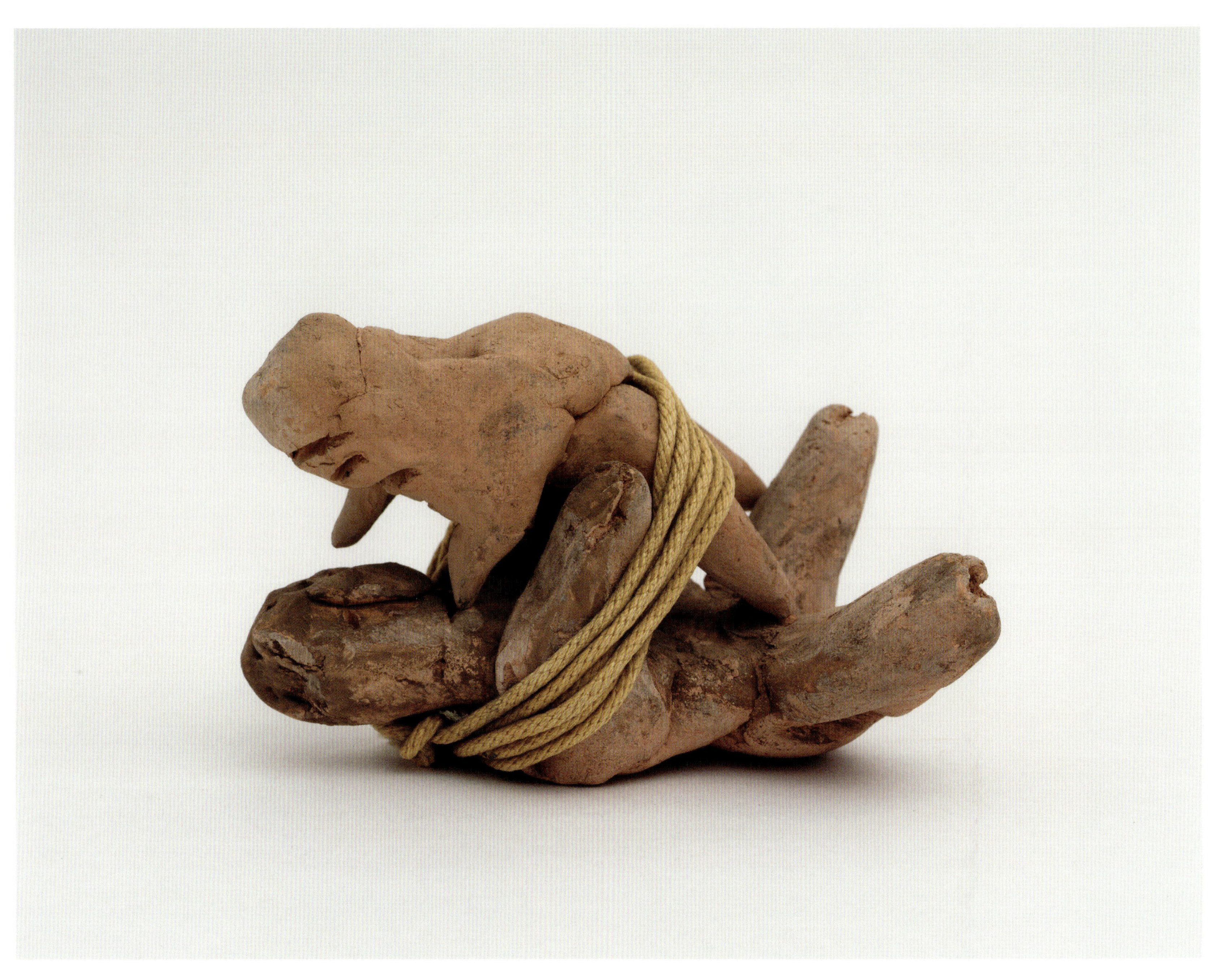

Untitled (Couple Bound), 1957
Terracotta clay
3 × 5.2 × 4 in. / 7.6 × 13.3 × 10.1 cm
Private Collection

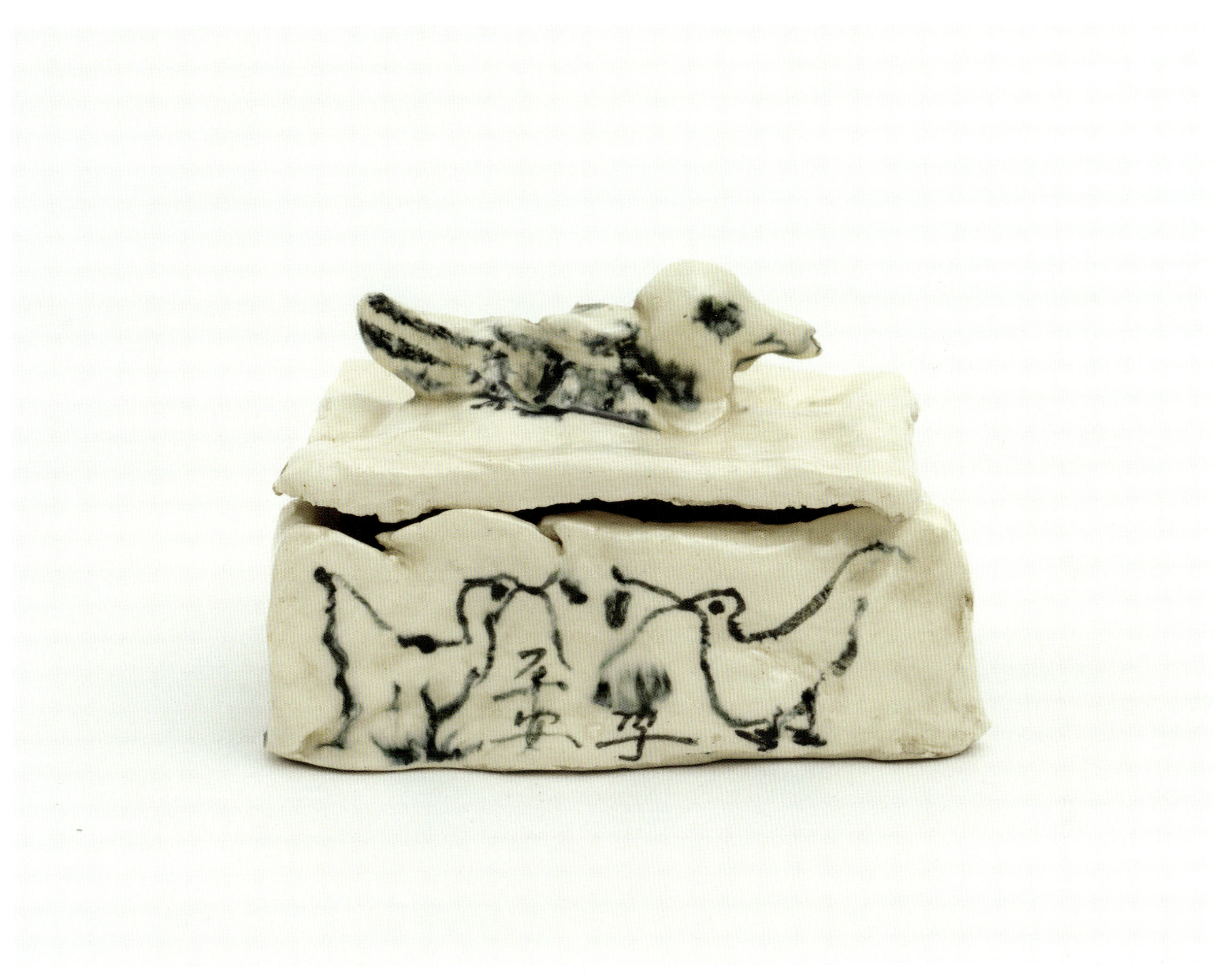

Untitled (Double Happiness Box), 1957
Underglazed stoneware
3 × 4 × 3 in. / 7.6 × 10.1 × 7.6 cm
Private Collection

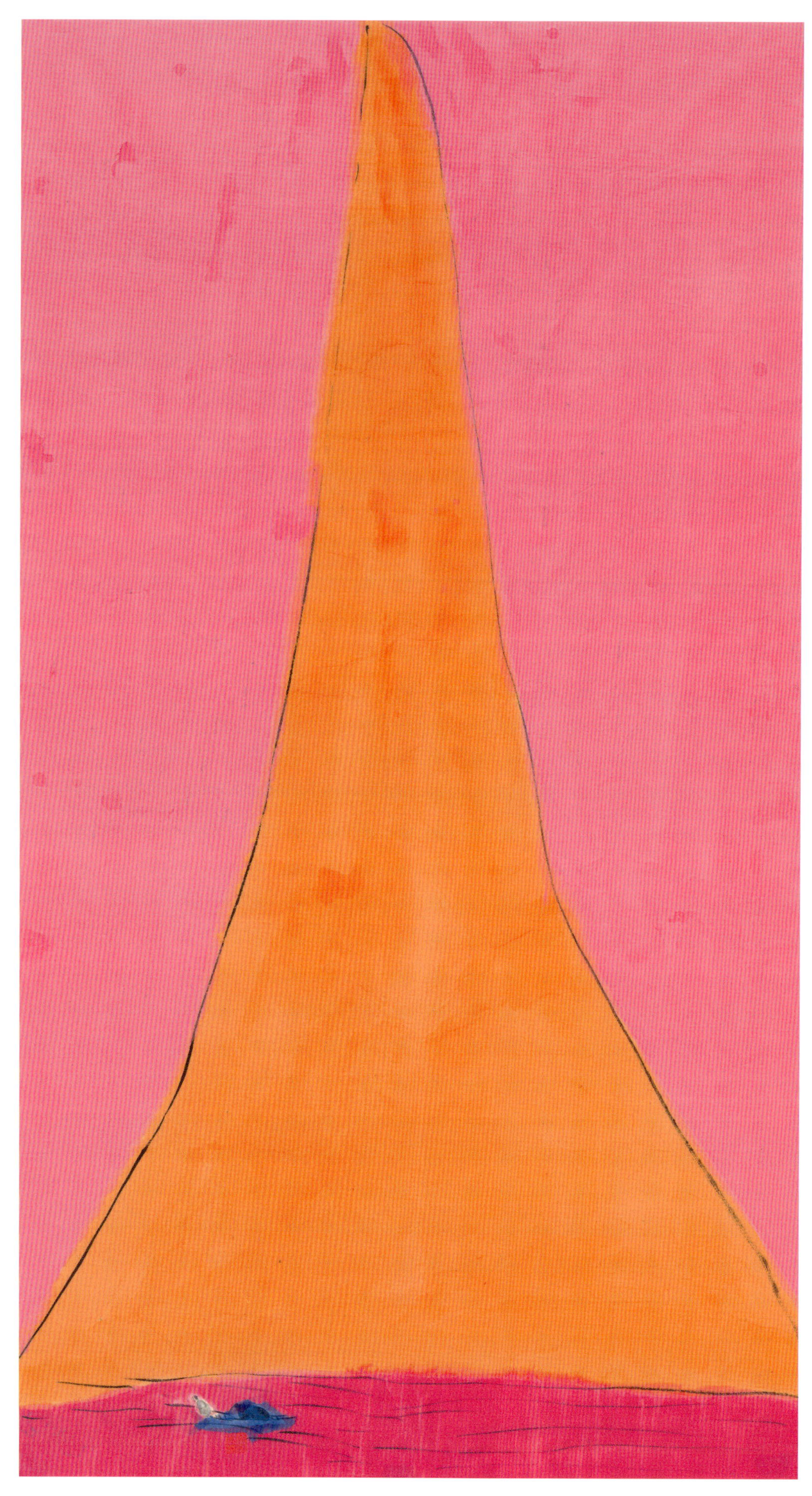

Untitled, mid-1980s
Acrylic and Chinese ink on rice paper
70 × 38 in. / 177.8 × 96.5 cm
Private Collection, Hong Kong

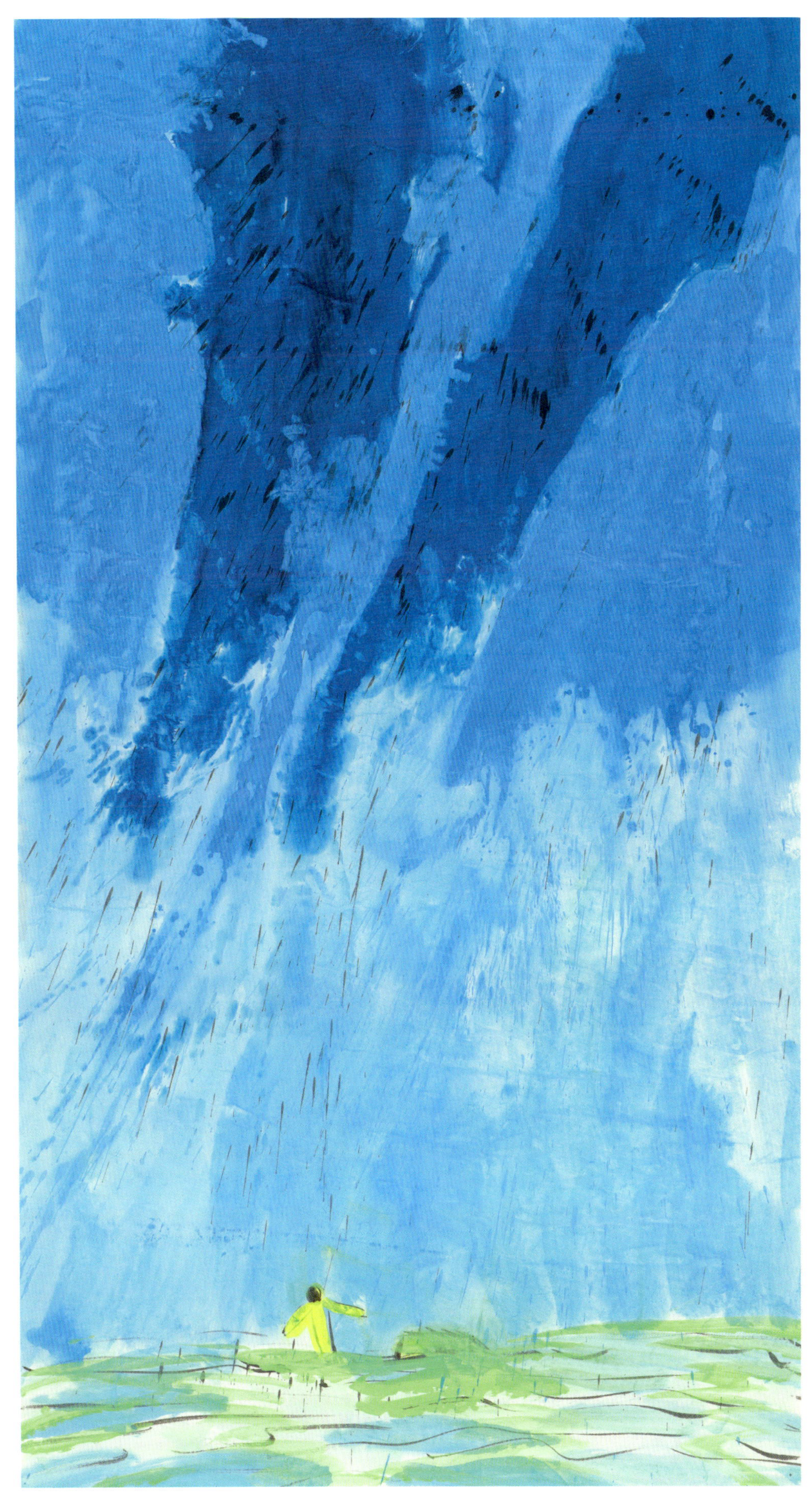

Untitled, early 1990s
Acrylic and Chinese ink on rice paper
70.5 × 37.5 in. / 179.1 × 95.3 cm

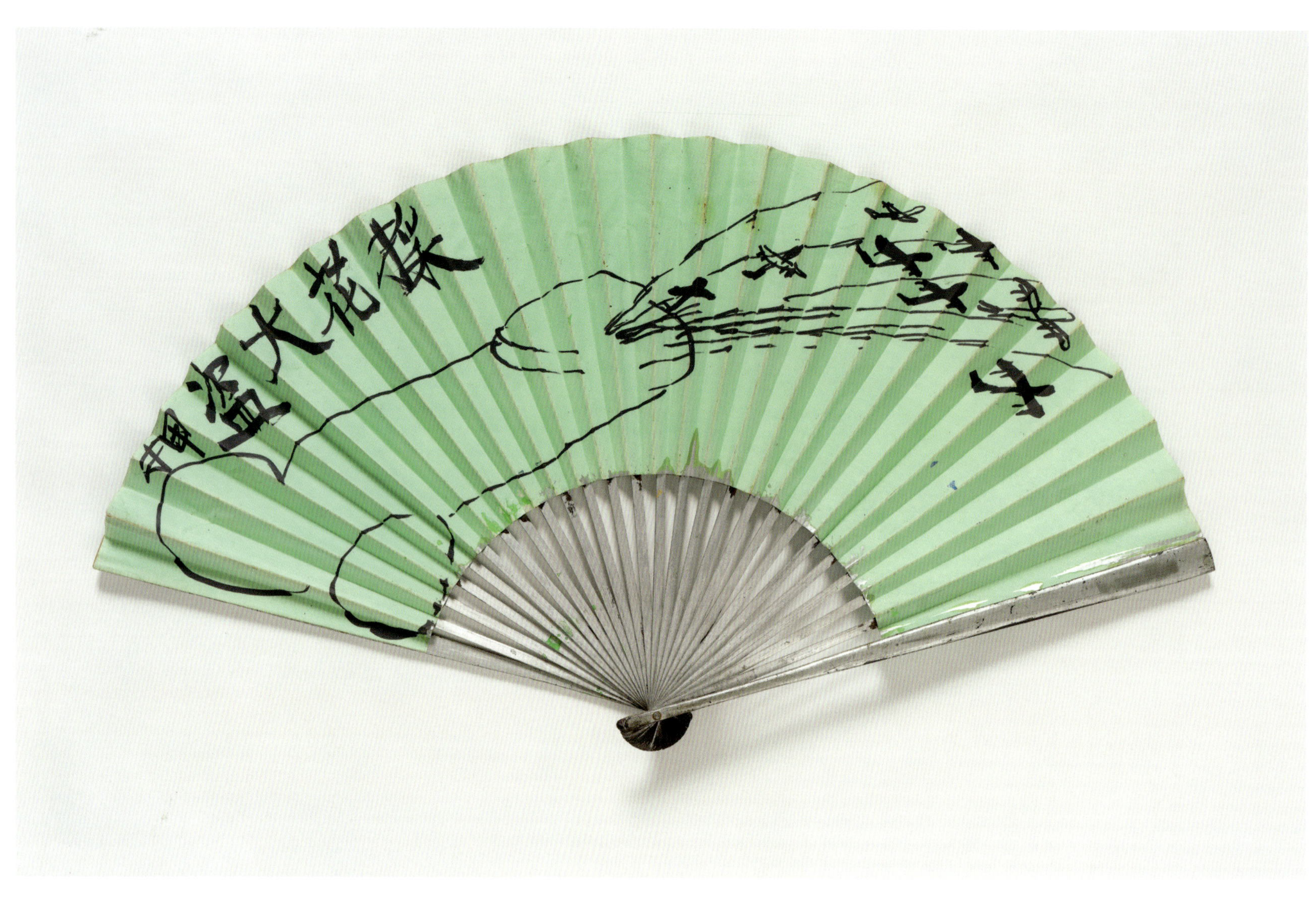

Zheshan (折扇) folding fan
modified by Ting, n.d.

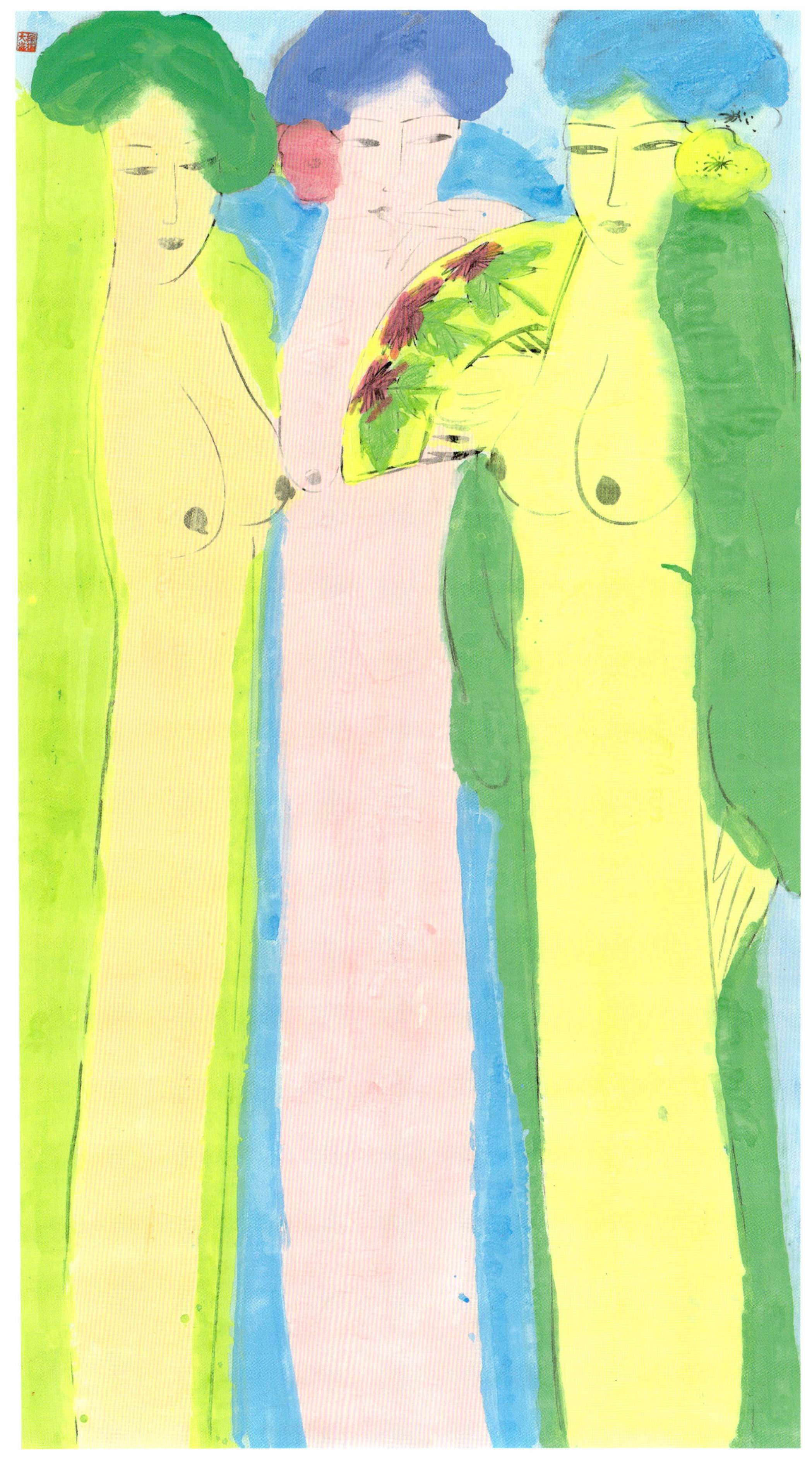

Untitled, late 1970s–early 1980s
Acrylic and Chinese ink on rice paper
70 × 38 in. / 177.8 × 96.5 cm
Private Collection, Amsterdam

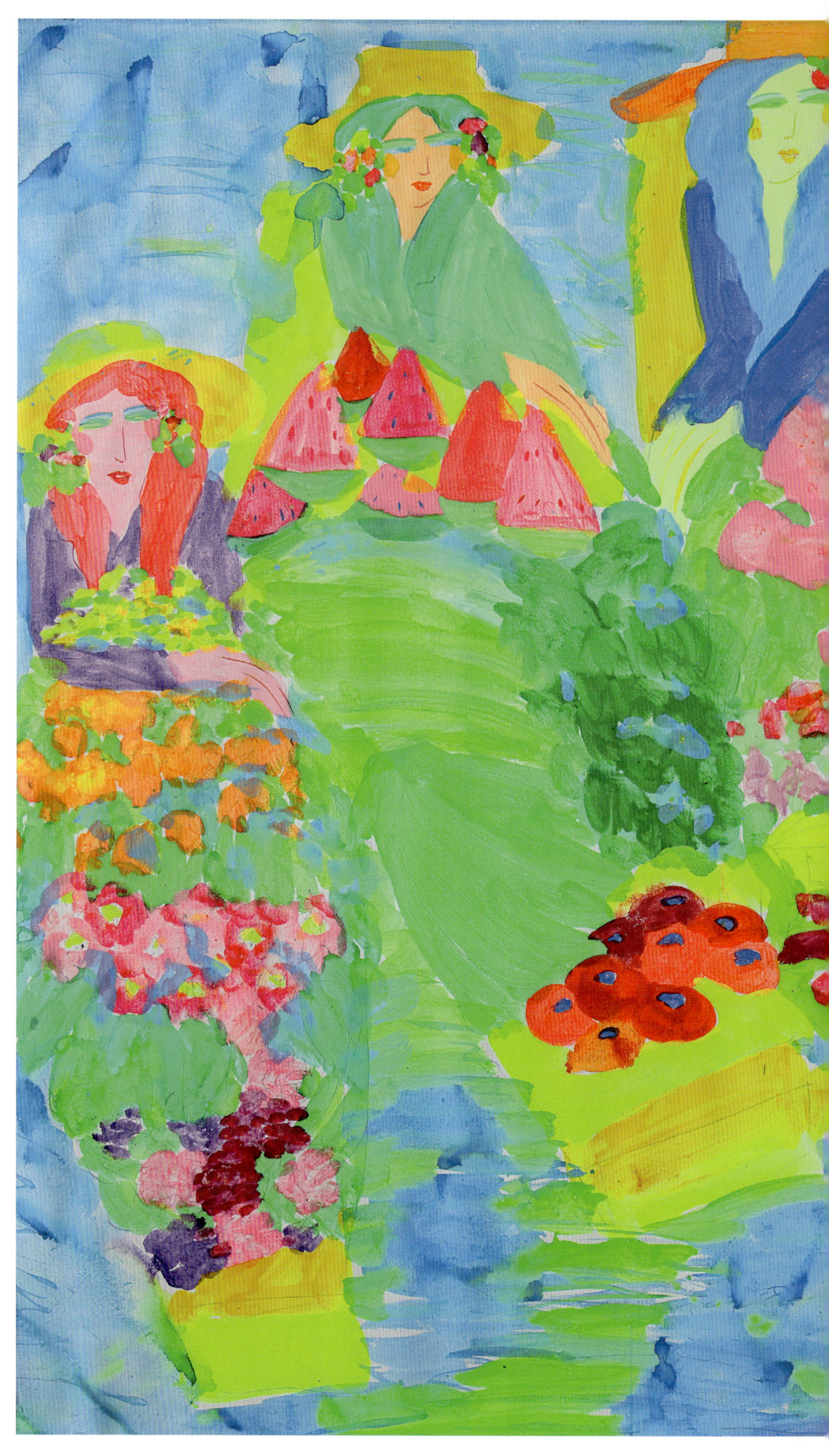

Floating Market, 1994
Acrylic on canvas
85.8 × 133.1 in. / 218 × 338 cm
Private Collection, Shanghai

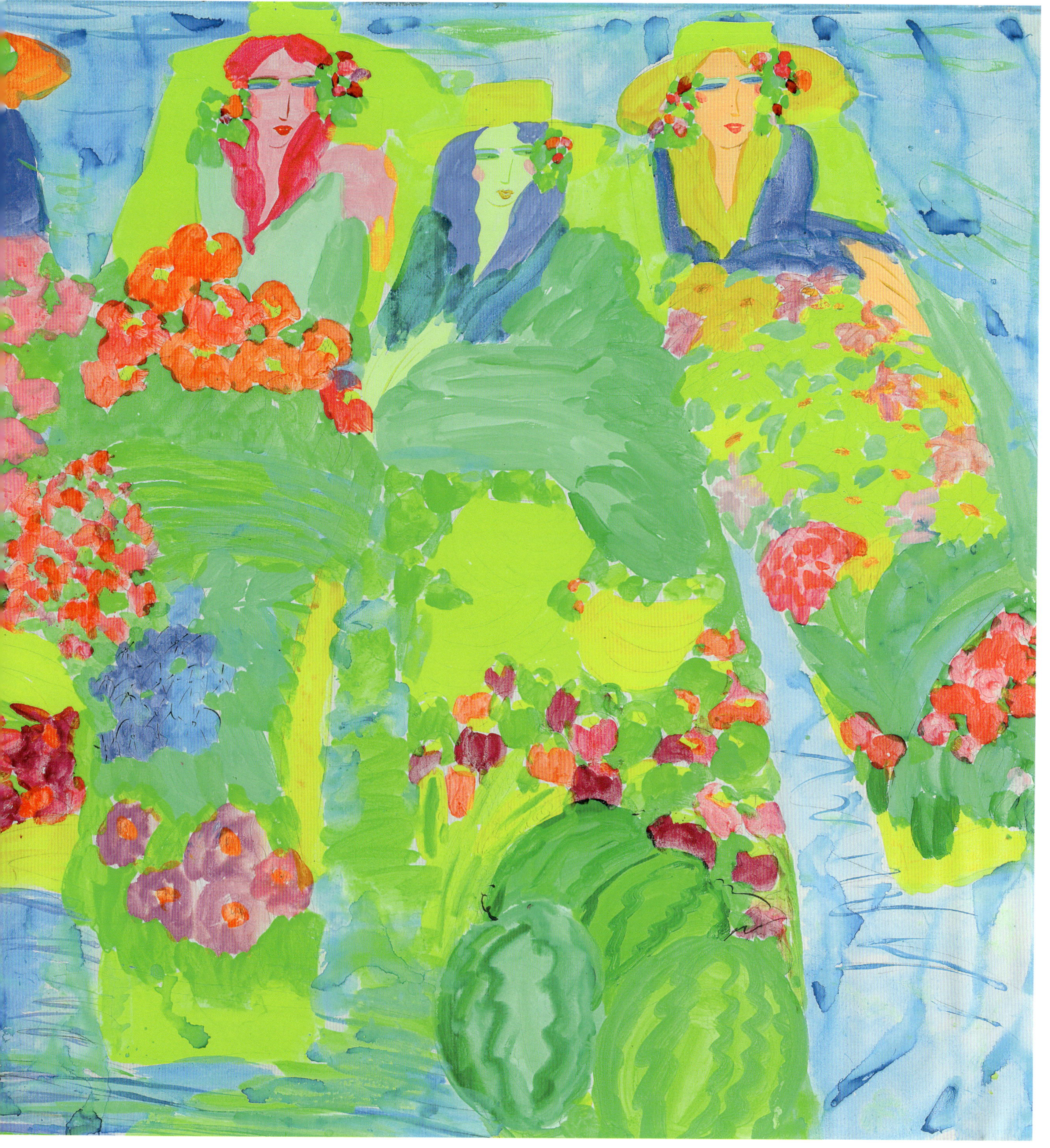

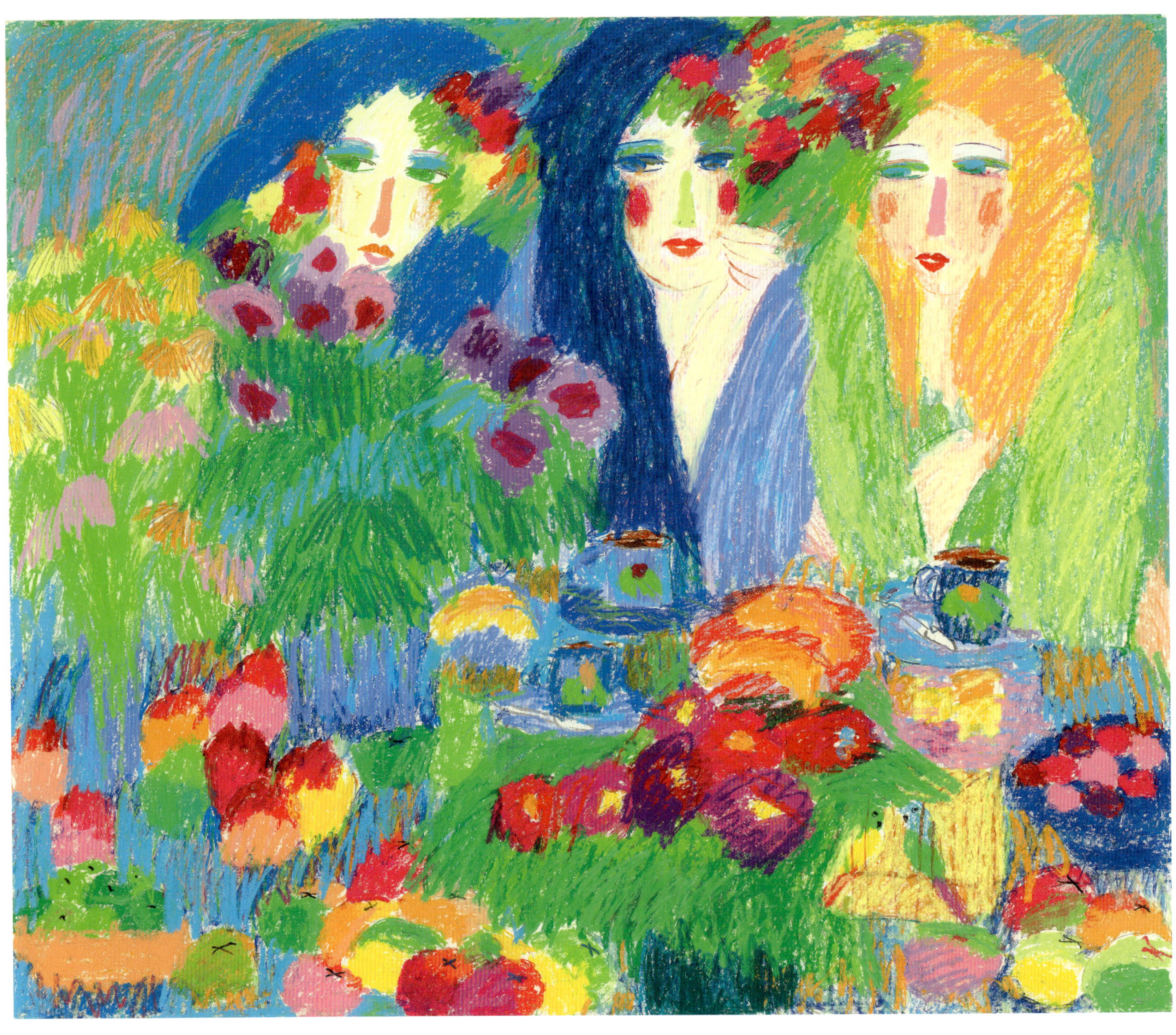

Afternoon Tea, 1985
Pastel on Arches paper
52.5 × 60 in. / 133.4 × 152.4 cm
Private Collection, Amsterdam

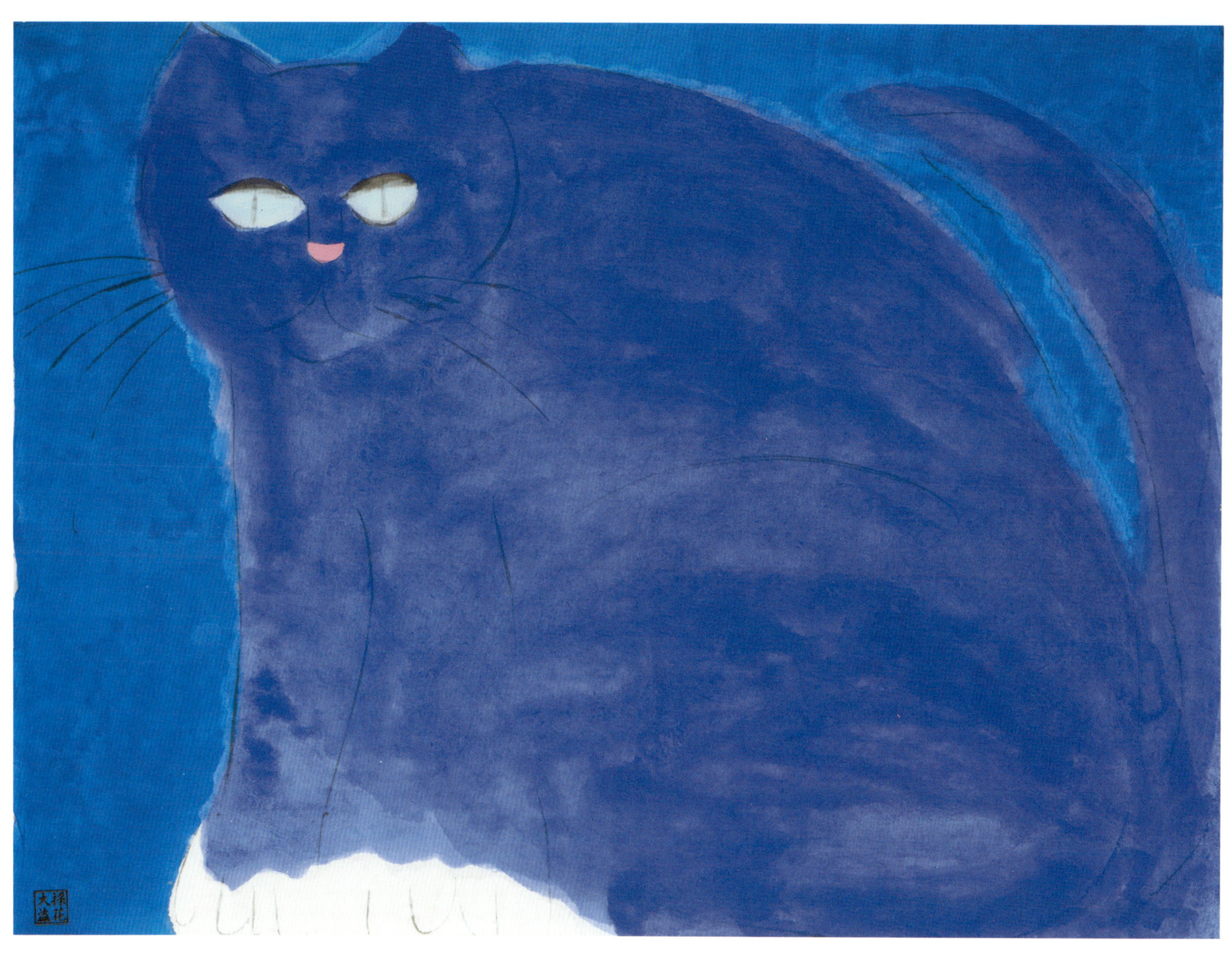

Untitled (Chat bleu - Blue Cat), late 1990s
Acrylic and Chinese ink on rice paper
29 × 38 in. / 73.7 × 96.5 cm
Private Collection, Amsterdam

146

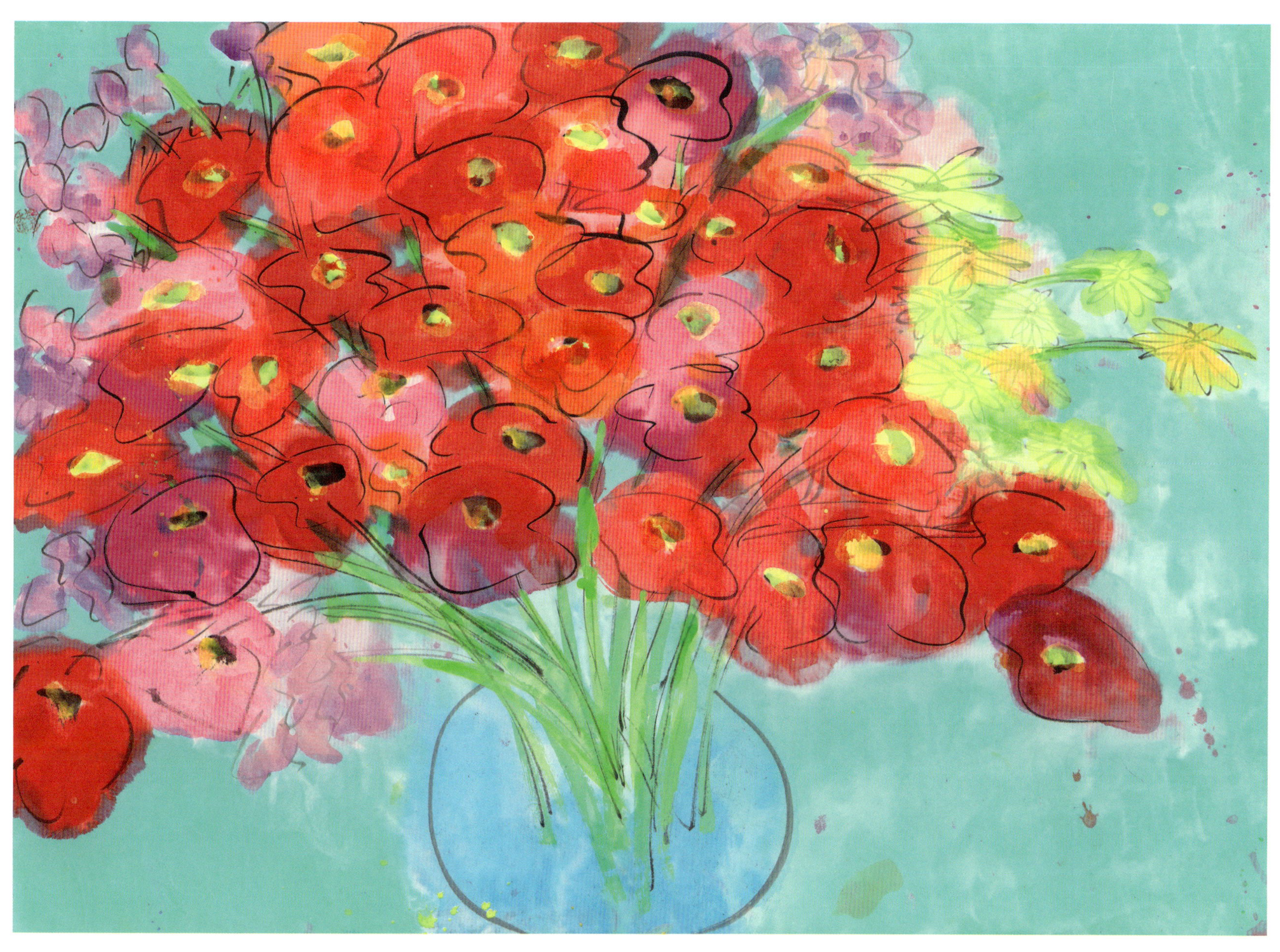

Untitled (Fleurs d'été - Summer Flowers),
late 1980s–early 1990s
Acrylic and Chinese ink on mounted
rice paper
27.5 × 38 in. / 69.9 × 96.5 cm

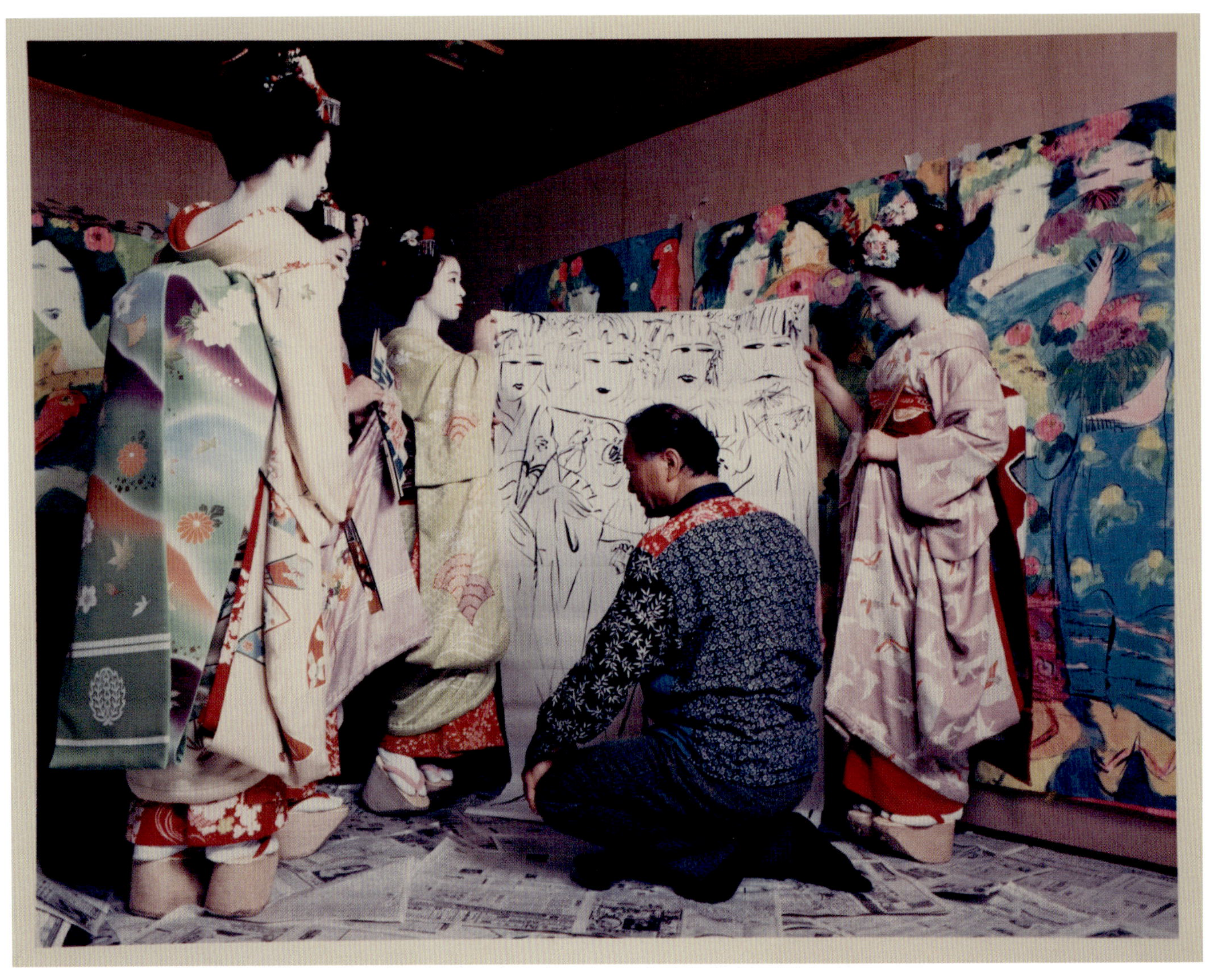

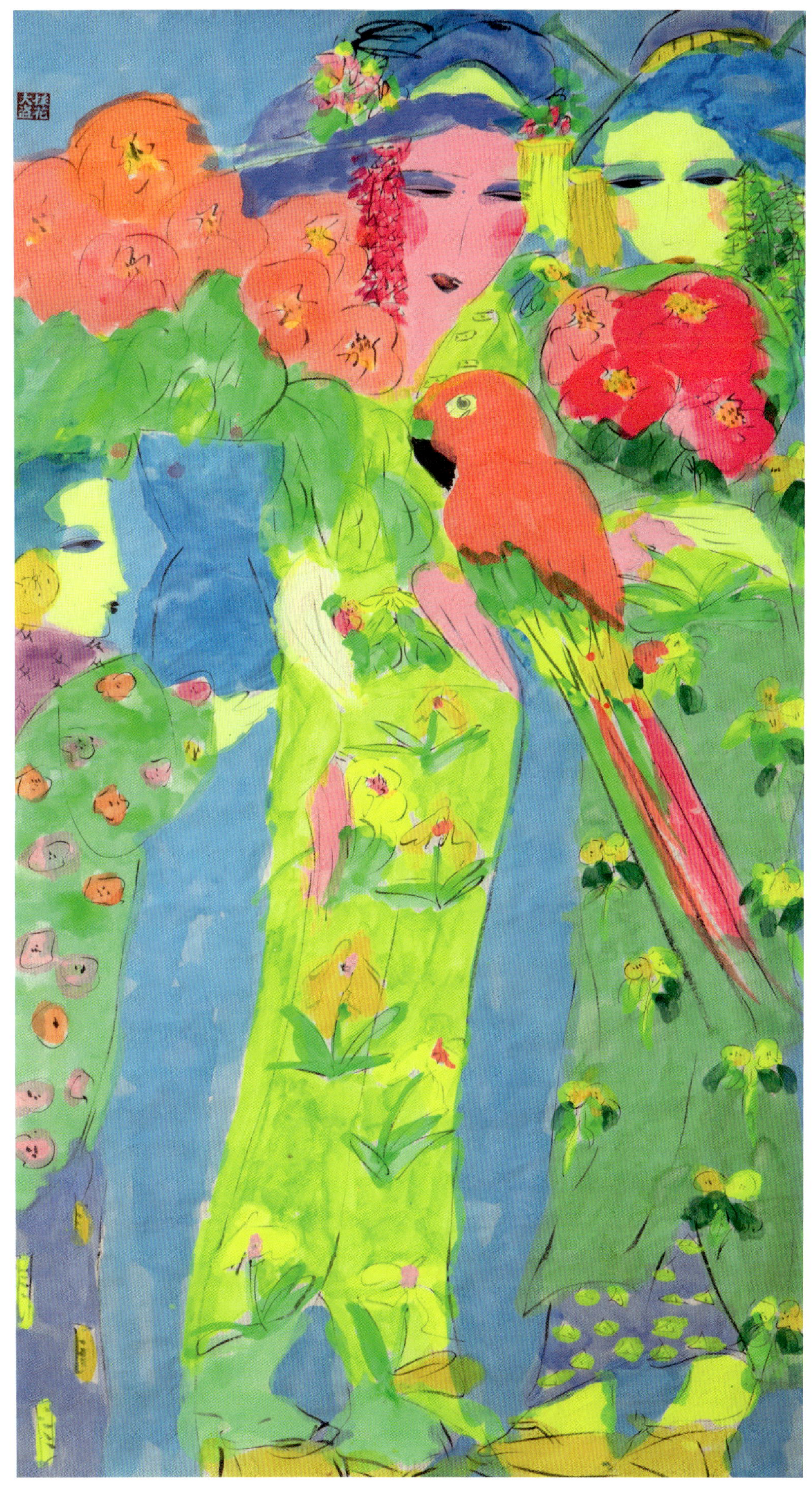

Untitled, late 1990s
Acrylic and Chinese ink on rice paper
70 × 38 in. / 177.8 × 96.5 cm
Private Collection, Amsterdam

Untitled (Butterflies), late 1980s
Acrylic and Chinese ink on rice paper
23 ¾ × 34 ½ in. / 60.3 × 87.6 cm

Following pages
Cherry Blossom, early 1990s
Acrylic and Chinese ink on rice paper
47.3 × 55.1 in. / 120 × 140 cm
Private Collection, Amsterdam

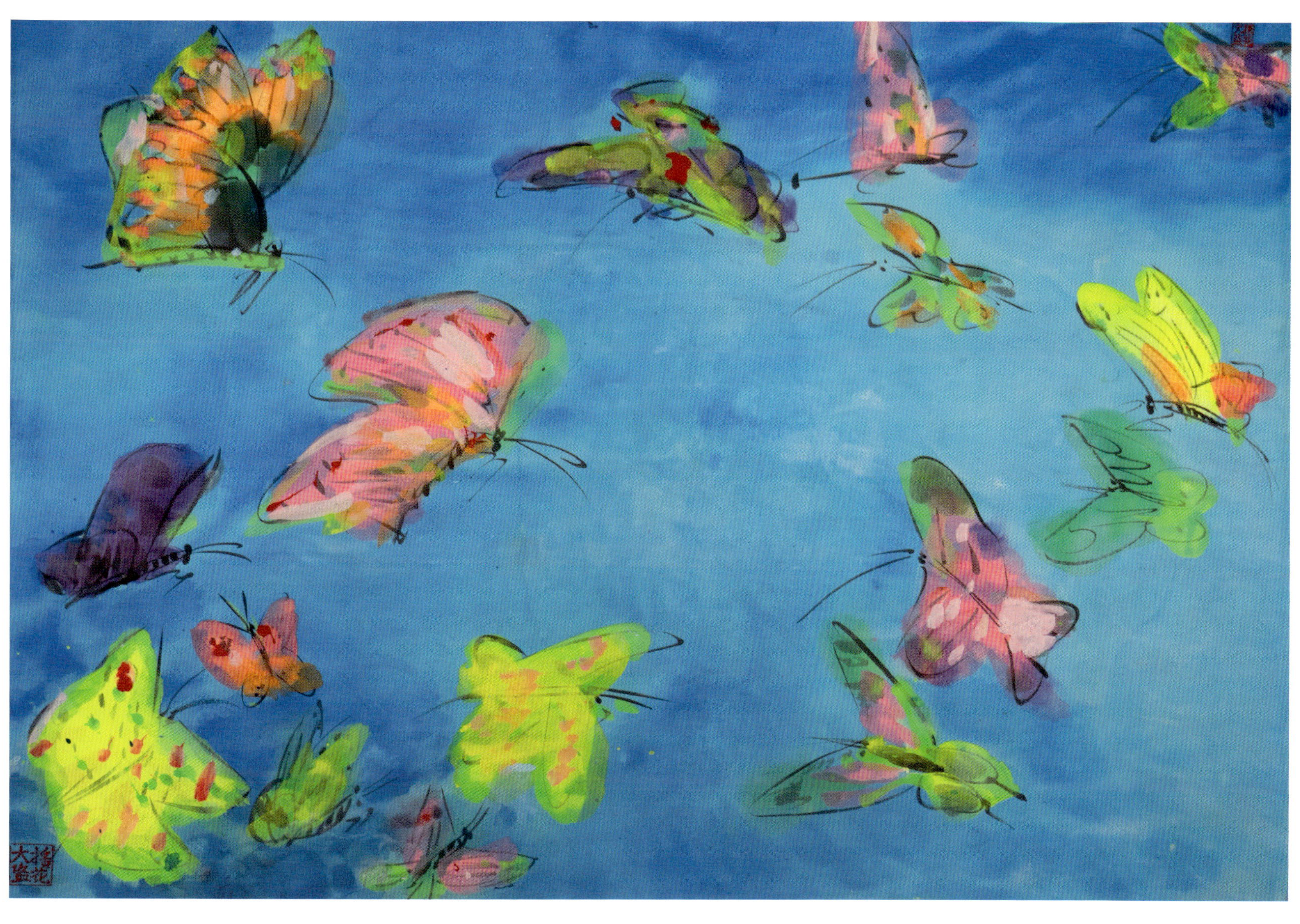

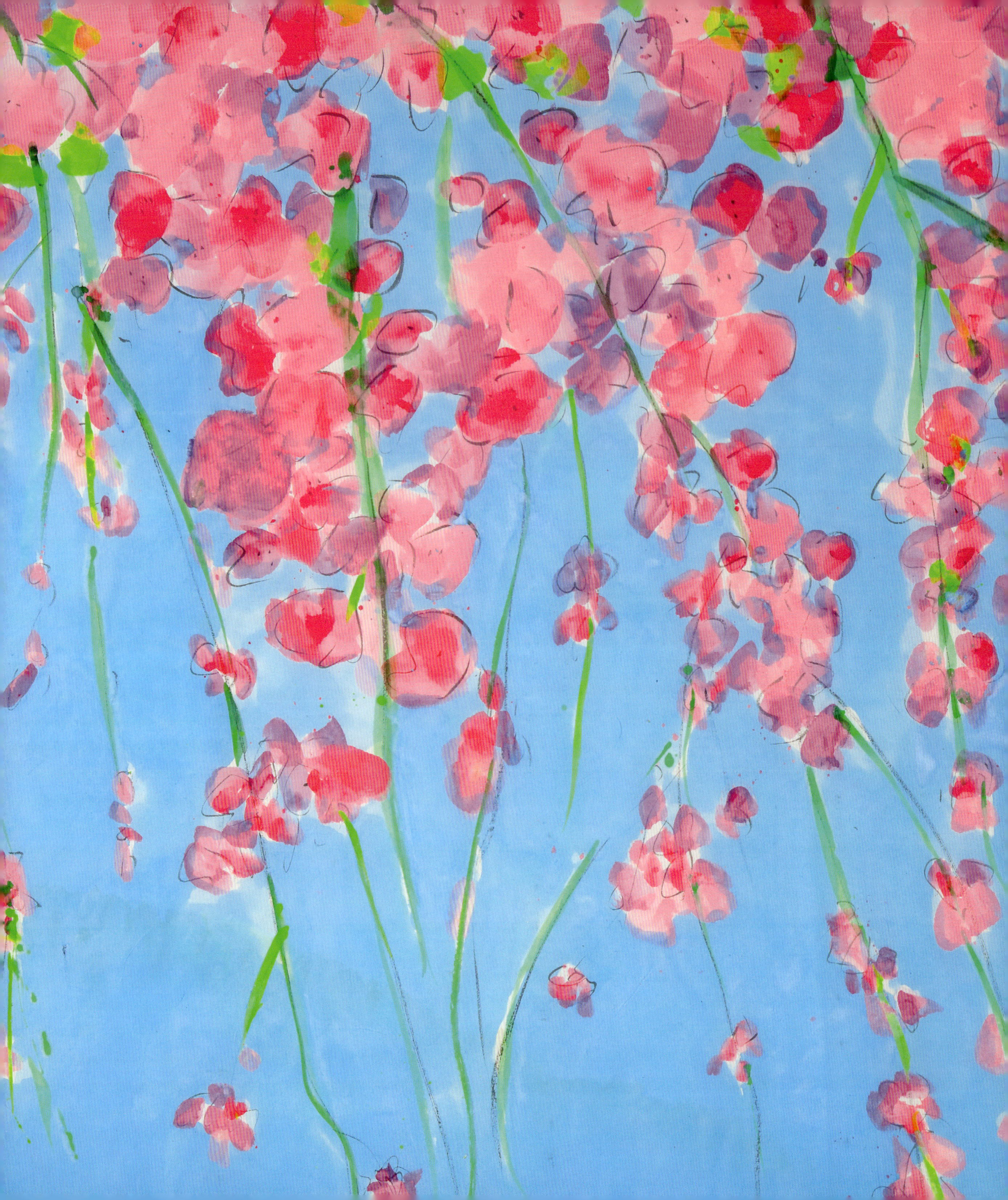

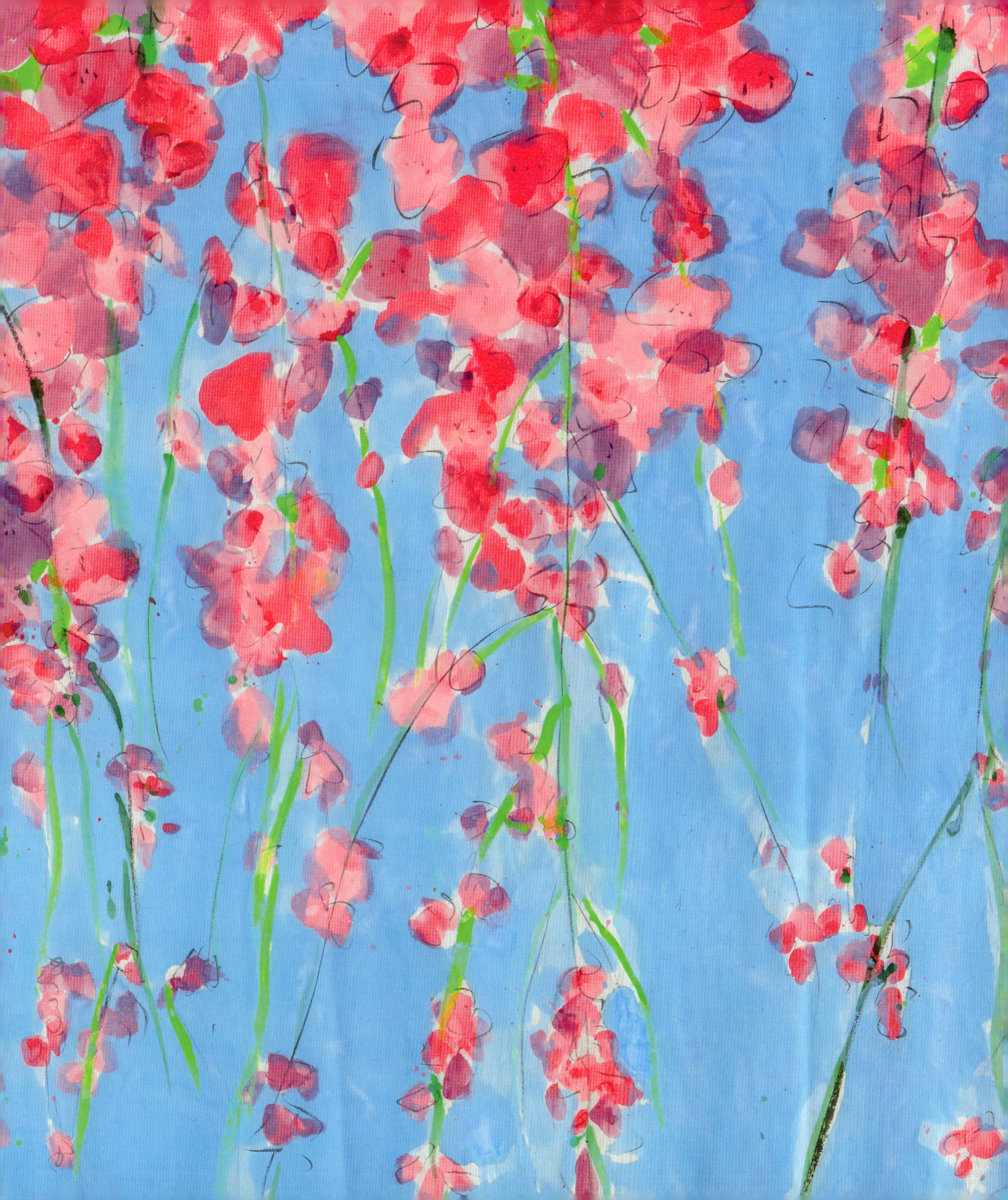

Pierre Alechinsky, extrait de
Roue libre, Skira 1971

En automne 1954, j'observe à Paris Walasse Ting dans sa piaule du quartier chinois, passage Raguinot ; il est accroupi devant son papier. Je suis les mouvements du pinceau, la vitesse. Très important les variations de la vitesse d'un trait. Accélération, freinage. Immobilisation. La tache inamovible légère, la tache inamovible lourde. Les blancs, tous les gris, le noir. Lenteur et fulgurance. Ting hésite, puis tout à coup la solution, la chute du chat sur ses pattes. Dernière figure gracieuse au-delà du papier.

Cet automne encore, à New York, dans l'atelier de Ting. Un large bol à la main (large pour faciliter au pinceau l'accès à la réserve de couleur) je me penche sur le papier, posé au sol, maintenu par quatre plombs d'imprimerie. Je me vide. Les lignes ont pris les formes d'une gueule ouverte tirant la langue, d'un dos rond, d'une queue battant le fond jaunâtre. Un dragon loin du volcan. L'air circule, passe par les détroits des traits interrompus.

– Si manque l'air, si lignes bloquées, impossible bouger la tête, déclare Ting. Peintre chinois toujours ouvrir les lignes. Respirer. Si lignes pas ouvertes, image mourir.

Se pencher ? Plus qu'une attitude physique, un conditionnement mental. Le peintre à l'occidentale se tient debout, droit. Escrimeur, il combat, monte à la toile, recule pour juger de la touche. Souvent, en raison de l'automatisme de cette reculade, au lieu de poursuivre le trait ou la forme ou la couleur ou l'image ou l'idée ou le tout à la fois, il n'y revient pas. Il dérive, hésite, pèse les pour et les contre, réfléchit trop. Ainsi, sans vraiment se l'avouer (maintenant il met de l'ordre dans l'atelier, taille un bout de crayon, déplace des objets, chavire), maintes fois opte-t-il pour contre. L'œil sur un, deux, trois, quatre travaux d'hier, comme sur ses barreaux le prisonnier, tête vide, il nettoie, gratte, trie. Le cuisinier redevient gâte-sauce. Rétrogradation. Rien qu'un pas et c'est joué. Foncer à nouveau ? Autre affaire ! Toutes les raisons de douter l'assiégeront une fois de plus. Est-ce le moment ? Dois-je développer ceci – pense-t-il – plutôt que cela ? Est-ce bien ? Mieux comme ça ? Etc. De même devant la toile vierge. De même ? Pire ! Au contraire, si cette surface gît à ses pieds, à la bonne heure ! Il peut croire qu'il la domine, la dominera. Il se courbe vers elle, passive qui semble l'attendre. La pesanteur est pour lui, avec lui. Se relever ? Effort pénible, plus pénible que, debout, le repli. Ting :

– Quand l'idée est au bout du pinceau, pas la peine aller jusqu'au bout de l'idée.

Et pourtant il ne s'arrête pas toujours. Il peint parfois couche sur couche. Couleur sur couleur. Tache sur tache. « Ce n'est pas tableau qui compte – explique-t-il – ni image après, c'est pendant, c'est peindre. »

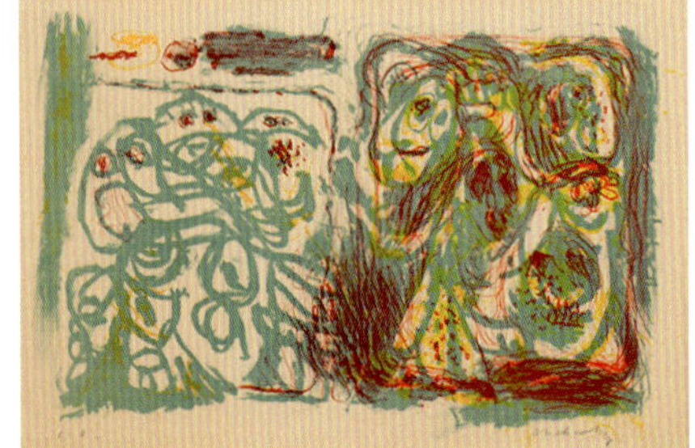

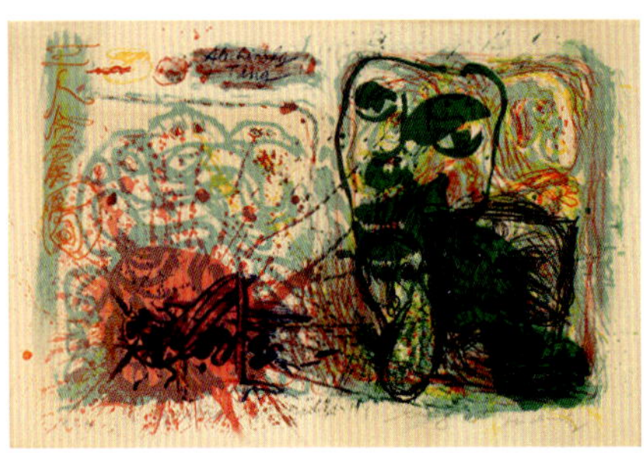

figs. 1–2. Walasse Ting, Pierre Alechinsky
Aleching (1er état), (2eme état), 1963
Color lithograph
14 × 21 in. / 35.5 × 53.3 cm (each)
NSU Art Museum Fort Lauderdale,
Cobra Collection, gift of Golda
and Meyer Marks

Pierre Alechinsky, extract from
Free Wheel, Skira 1971

In the fall of 1954, I observe Walasse Ting in his Chinatown spot in Paris, Passage Raguinot; he crouches before his paper. I follow the movements of the brush, the speed. Very important, the variations in the speed of a line. Speeding up, slowing down. Stopping still. The light unbudgeable blob, the heavy unbudgeable blob. The whites, all the greys, the black. Slowness and lightning speed. Ting hesitates, then in a flash the solution, the cat falling onto its feet. Last graceful figure extending beyond the paper.

Fall still, in New York, in Ting's studio.

A wide bowl in my hand (wide so that the brush has easy access to the reserve of color), I lean over the paper, placed on the floor, held in position by four printer's leads. I empty myself. The lines have taken the shapes of an open mouth sticking out its tongue, a round back, a tail thrashing against the yellowish background. A dragon far from the volcano. The air circulates, passes through the straits formed by the broken lines.

– If lack air, if lines blocked, impossible to move head, declares Ting. Chinese painter always open lines. Breathe. If lines not open, image die.

Lean? More than a physical attitude, a mental conditioning. The Western-style painter stands erect. A fencer, he engages, lunges towards the canvas, steps back to assess his brushstrokes. Often, because of this reflex of stepping back, instead of continuing the line or the form or the color or the image or the idea or everything at the same time, he does not come back to it. He wanders, hesitates, weighs up the pros and cons, thinks too much. Thus, without really admitting it to himself (now he tidies up the studio, sharpens a pencil stub, re-arranges objects, flounders), again and again he is ruled by the cons. His eyes on one, two, three, four of yesterday's paintings, like a prisoner gazing at his bars, his head empty, he cleans, scrapes, sorts. The cook goes back to being a kitchen boy. A downgrade. No more than a step and the die is cast. Launch into it again? A further engagement! He will be besieged once again by all the reasons for doubting. Is it the right moment? Should I develop this—he thinks—rather than that? Is it alright like this? Better like that? Etc. The same thing in front of the blank canvas. The same thing? Worse! But if, on the contrary, the surface to be painted lies at his feet, then well and good, he is able to think that he dominates it, that he will dominate it. He bends down towards it, passively seeming to wait for him. Gravity is on his side. Get up again? That would involve a painful effort, more painful than that required to move back when standing. Ting:

When the idea is on the tip of your brush, no need to follow the idea through.

And yet he doesn't always stop there. He sometimes paints layer upon layer. Color upon color. Blob upon blob. What counts, he explains, is not picture, not image after, but during, what counts is painting.

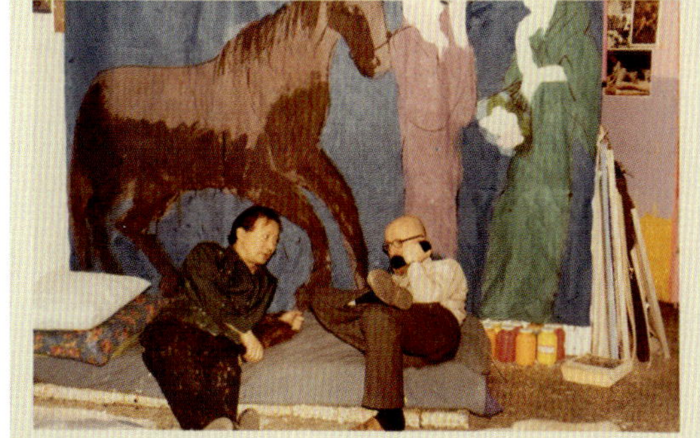

fig. 3. Ting in his New York studio with Alechinsky, 1978

(Translation by Michael Fineberg)

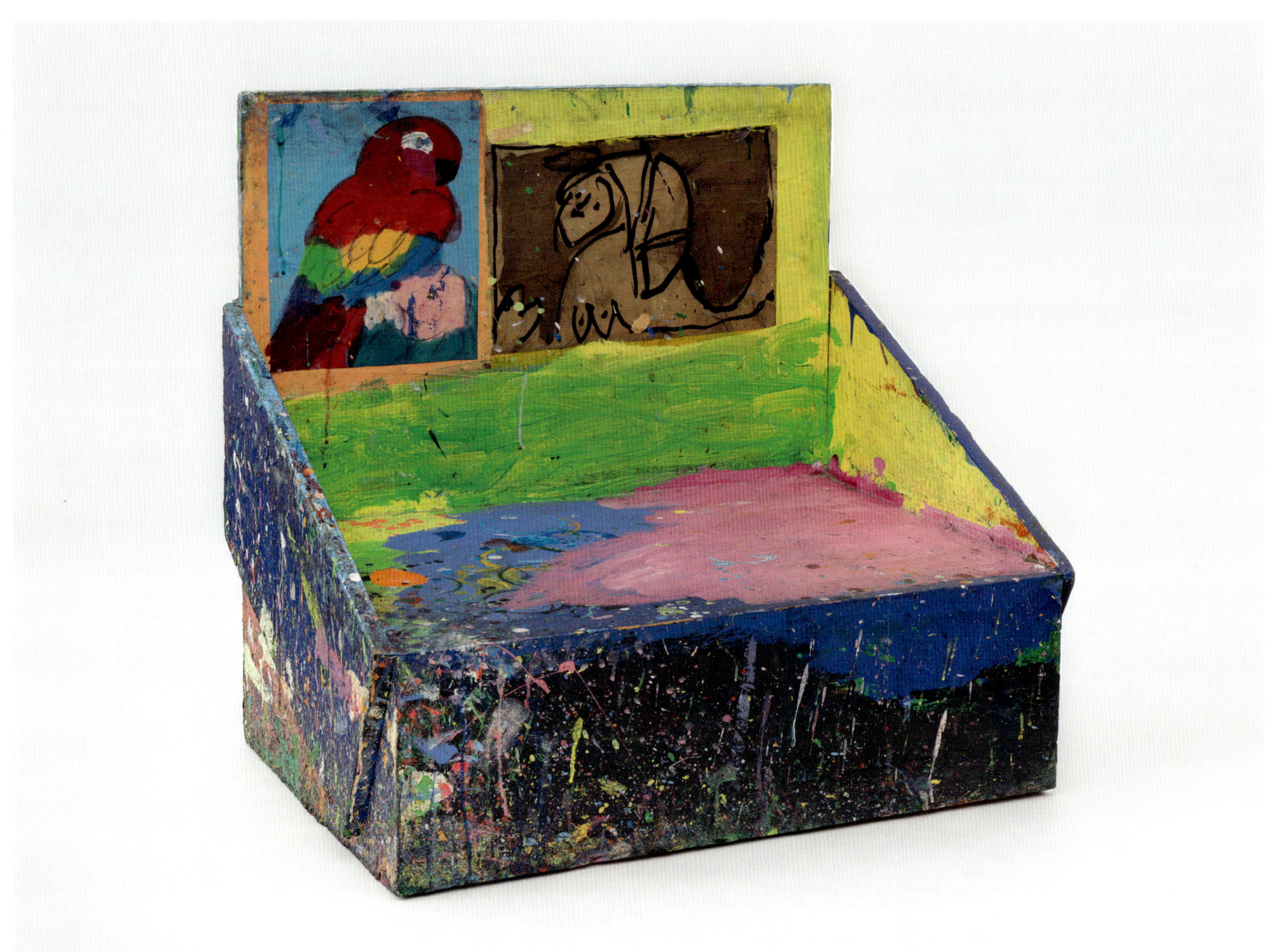

fig. 4. *Seat A*, built and decorated by
Walasse Ting, ink by Pierre Alechinsky, n.d.

Right
fig. 5. Ting in the mirror, wall ink by
Alechinsky. Ting's New York studio,
c. 1970

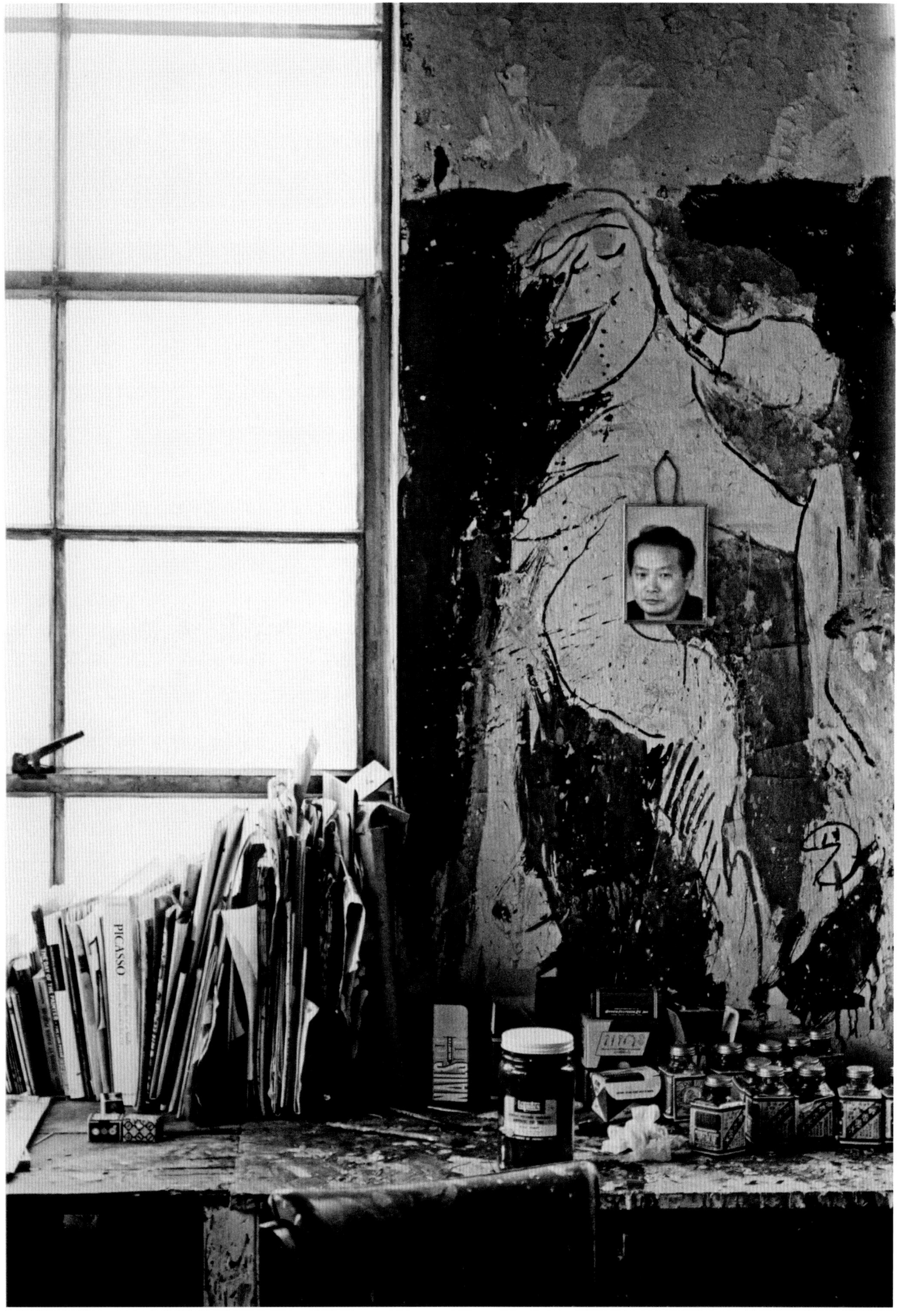

Exhibition Checklist

All works by Walasse Ting,
courtesy of The Estate of Walasse
Ting, unless otherwise noted.

Baby Girl, 1953
Oil on canvas
25 × 21 in. / 63.5 × 53.3 cm
p. 79

Pekin Opera, 1955
Chinese ink and oil on paper mounted
on canvas
35.1 × 39.8 in. / 89 × 101 cm
p. 67

Untitled (Manet), 1956
Oil pastel on paper
8.5 × 11 in. / 21.6 × 27.94 cm (each)
p. 50

Untitled, 1956
Oil pastel on paper
8.5 × 11 in. / 21.6 × 27.9 cm
not reproduced

Untitled (Figure on Donkey), 1957
Terracotta clay
6 × 5 × 5 in. / 15.2 × 12.7 × 12.7 cm
Private Collection
p. 134

Untitled (Hero Gathering), 1957
Terracotta clay
6 × 6.2 × 6 in. / 15.2 × 15.8 × 15.2 cm
Private Collection
p. 135

Untitled (Couple Bound), 1957
Terracotta clay
3 × 5.2 × 4 in. / 7.6 × 13.3 × 10.1 cm
Private Collection
p. 136

Untitled (Double Happiness Box), 1957
Underglazed stoneware
3 × 4 × 3 in. / 7.6 × 10.1 × 7.6 cm
Private Collection
p. 137

Untitled, 1957
Oil pastel on paper
11 × 12 in. / 27.9 × 30.5 cm
not reproduced

Untitled, 1957
Oil pastel on paper
11 × 12 in. / 27.9 × 30.5 cm
not reproduced

My Memory is Too Much, 1958
Oil on canvas
53.4 × 70.3 in. / 135.5 × 178.8 cm
p. 83

My Blue Mood, 1959
Acrylic and oil pastel on paper
12.5 × 17.5 in. / 31.8 × 44.5 cm
p. 78

Fire, 1959
Oil on unprimed canvas
88 × 72 in. / 223.5 × 182.8 cm
Guy and Nora Barron Family
p. 84

Chinese City, 1959
Oil on canvas
90.5 × 70.8 in. / 230 × 180 cm
p. 85

Three Tang Era Women, 1960s
Acrylic and Chinese ink mounted
on black silk and bamboo scroll
65 × 47 in. / 165.1 × 119.4 cm
p. 76

Walasse Ting, Pierre Alechinsky
Aleching, 1961
Gouache and crayon on paper
22.1 × 29.5 in. / 56 × 75 cm
Museum Jorn, Silkeborg
p. 68

Walasse Ting, Pierre Alechinsky
Divorce Lent, 1962
Oil on canvas
31.5 × 39.4 in. / 80 × 100 cm
Museum Jorn, Silkeborg
p. 71

No Fuck S.V.P, 1962
Oil on canvas
48 × 60 in. / 121.9 × 152.4 cm
p. 80

My Sweetheart Thinks too Much, 1962
Oil on canvas
59.8 × 32.3 in. / 152 × 82 cm
Collection Stedelijk Museum, Amsterdam
Donated by the artist to Willem Sandberg on
the occasion of his retirement as director of the
Stedelijk Museum in Amsterdam (the so-called
Sandberg collection)
p. 81

Lightning Strike (Blikseminslag), 1962
Oil on canvas
39.6 × 63.2 in. / 100.5 × 160.5 cm
Collection Stedelijk Museum, Amsterdam
p. 94

Walasse Ting, Asger Jorn
Spring Garden for Asger, 1963
Acrylic on found oil painting on canvas
25.5 × 39.5 in. / 64.7 × 100.3 cm
p. 72

Walasse Ting, Pierre Alechinsky
Aleching (1er état), (2eme état), 1963
Color lithograph
14 × 21 in. / 35.5 × 53.3 cm (each)
NSU Art Museum Fort Lauderdale, Cobra
Collection, gift of Golda and Meyer Marks
p. 154

1¢ Life, 1964
Illustrated book with sixty-two lithographs
and reproductions
Contributing artists: Pierre Alechinsky, Karel
Appel, Enrico Baj, Reinhoud d'Haese, Alan Davie,
Jim Dine, Öyvind Fahlström, Sam Francis,
Robert Indiana, Alfred Jensen, Asger Jorn, Allan
Kaprow, Kiki O.K.[Kiki Kogelnik], Alfred Leslie,
Roy Lichtenstein, Joan Mitchell, Claes Oldenburg,
Mel Ramos, Robert Rauschenberg, Jean-Paul
Riopelle, James Rosenquist, Antonio Saura,
Kimber Smith, K.R.H. Sonderborg, Walasse Ting,
Bram van Velde, Andy Warhol, Tom Wesselmann.
Editor: Sam Francis
Publisher: Eberhard W. Kornfeld, Bern,
Switzerland, Printer: Maurice Beaudet
p. 116

24 Grasshoppers Going to Philadelphia, 1965
Color crayon on paper
22.5 × 36 in. / 57.2 × 91.4 cm
p. 112

La Naissance de Vénus (The Birth of Venus), 1966
Acrylic on canvas
72.1 × 90.6 in. / 183 × 230 cm
Pierre Alechinsky Archives
p. 55

Walasse Ting, Asger Jorn
Come to Me Give to Me Baby, 1968
Acrylic on found oil painting on canvas
11 × 16 in. / 27.9 × 40.6 cm
p. 73

Looking for a Bee, 1968
Acrylic on canvas
80 × 140.3 in. / 203.2 × 356.2 cm
Solomon R. Guggenheim Museum, New York
Gift of David Kluger, 1975, 69.1890
pp. 88–89

Karel Appel
Portret (Portrait) of Walasse Ting, 1969
Acrylic on canvas
53 × 63 in. / 134.6 × 160 cm
p. 47

Walasse Ting, Pierre Alechinsky
Untitled, 1969
Etching and aquatint on paper
19.6 × 25.8 in. / 50.5 × 65.4 cm
NSU Art Museum Fort Lauderdale, Cobra
Collection, gift of Golda and Meyer Marks
p. 70

I Take off my Pants Facing Sunset, 1969
Acrylic on canvas
40.2 × 51.9 in. / 102 × 132 cm
pp. 90–91

Walasse Ting, Pierre Alechinsky, Asger Jorn
Jorn's grave?, 1970–1993
Acrylic on paper mounted on canvas
25.2 × 37 in. / 64 × 94 cm
Museum Jorn, Silkeborg
pp. 74–75

Whistling All Night, 1971
Acrylic on canvas
70 × 90 in. / 177.8 × 228.6 cm
Private Collection, New York
p. 54

Fresh Green Leaves, 1972
Oil on canvas
40.4 × 60.4 in. / 102.6 × 153.4 cm
Private Collection
p. 86

Raindrops on My Eyes, 1974
Acrylic on canvas
59 × 90.1 in. / 149.9 × 228.9 cm
p. 103

American Beauty, 1974
Acrylic on canvas
24 × 32 in. / 61 × 81.3 cm
Collection of Phyllis Lipton
p. 106

Love Me With Your Heart That I Want, 1975
Acrylic on canvas
55 × 64 in. / 139.7 × 162.6 cm
p. 98

Miss World, 1975
Acrylic on canvas
90 × 150 in. / 229 × 381 cm
pp. 110–111

Do You Like Moonlight?, 1977
Acrylic on canvas
40 × 60 in. / 101.6 × 152.4 cm
Private Collection, New York
p. 99

Untitled, late 1970s–early 1980s
Acrylic and Chinese ink on rice paper
70 × 38 in. / 177.8 × 96.5 cm (each)
pp. 20–23

Untitled, late 1970s–early 1980s
Acrylic and Chinese ink on rice paper
70 × 38 in. / 177.8 × 96.5 cm
Private Collection, Amsterdam
p. 141

Untitled, early 1980s
Acrylic and Chinese ink on rice paper
mounted on canvas
25 × 45 in. / 63.5 × 114.3 cm
Collection Marlène Brody
p. 27

Untitled, early 1980s
Acrylic and Chinese ink on rice paper
70 × 38 in. / 177.8 × 96.5 cm
Private Collection, Hong Kong
p. 31

Untitled, early 1980s
Acrylic and Chinese ink on rice paper
70 × 38 in. / 177.8 × 96.5 cm
Private Collection, Amsterdam
p. 36

The Red Horse, early 1980s
Acrylic and Chinese ink on rice paper
mounted on canvas
38 × 69 in. / 96.5 × 175.2 cm
Collection Marlène Brody
p. 77

Untitled, early 1980s
Acrylic and Chinese ink on paper
38 × 70 in. / 96.5 × 177.8 cm
Private Collection, New York
pp. 100–101

Untitled (Women with Paint Splattered Horse), early mid-1980s
Chinese ink and acrylic on rice paper
18 × 23 in. / 45.8 × 59.6 cm
Private Collection
p. 113

Untitled, mid-1980s
Acrylic and Chinese ink on rice paper
38 × 70 in. / 96.5 × 177.8 cm
Private Collection, Amsterdam
pp. 32–33

Untitled, mid-1980s
Acrylic and Chinese ink on rice paper
14 × 19 in. / 35.5 × 48.2 cm
Private Collection, New York
p. 34

Untitled, mid-1980s
Acrylic and Chinese ink on rice paper
27.5 × 38 in. / 69.9 × 96.5 cm
Private Collection, Shanghai
p. 35

Untitled, mid-1980s
Acrylic and Chinese ink on rice paper
70 × 38 in. / 177.8 × 96.5 cm
Private Collection, Hong Kong
p. 138

My World, 1985
Acrylic and Chinese ink on rice paper
mounted on canvas
16 × 23 in. / 40.6 × 58.4 cm
pp. 38–39

It is Warm Today, 1985
Acrylic on canvas
28 × 42 in. / 71.1 × 106.7 cm
Private Collection
p. 87

Love as Red as Cherries, Green as Banana Leaves, 1985
Graphite on Arches paper
22.7 × 27.5 in./ 57.6 × 69.8 cm
Private Collection, New York
p. 107

Afternoon Tea, 1985
Pastel on Arches paper
52.5 × 60 in. / 133.4 × 152.4 cm
Private Collection, Amsterdam
p. 144

Untitled, late 1980s–early 1990s
Acrylic and Chinese ink on rice paper
38 × 70 in. / 96.5 × 177.8 cm
Private Collection, New York
pp. 28–29

Untitled, late 1980s–early 1990s
Acrylic and Chinese ink on rice paper
70.5 × 37.5 in. / 179.1 × 95.3 cm
Private Collection, New York
p. 37

Untitled (Fleurs d'été - Summer Flowers), late 1980s–early 1990s
Acrylic and Chinese ink on mounted rice paper
27.5 × 38 in. / 69.9 × 96.5 cm
p. 147

Pink Room, 1993
Acrylic on canvas
59.1 × 98.4 in. / 150 × 250 cm
p. 46

Floating Market, 1994
Acrylic on canvas
85.8 × 133.1 in. / 218 × 338 cm
Private Collection, Shanghai
pp. 142–143

Untitled, early 1990s
Acrylic and Chinese ink on rice paper
70.5 × 37.5 in. / 179.1 × 95.3 cm
p. 139

Cherry Blossom, early 1990s
Acrylic and Chinese ink on rice paper
47.3 × 55.1 in. / 120 × 140 cm
Private Collection, Amsterdam
pp. 152–153

Green Peacock, January 16, 1995
Acrylic and Chinese ink on rice paper
48.1 × 85.1 in. / 122 × 216 cm
Private Collection, Amsterdam
pp. 24–25

Untitled, mid-1990s
Acrylic and Chinese ink on rices paper
11.8 × 17 in. / 29.8 × 43.2 cm
Private Collection, New York
p. 30

Untitled (Chat bleu - Blue Cat), late 1990s
Acrylic and Chinese ink on rice paper
29 × 38 in. / 73.7 × 96.5 cm
Private Collection, Amsterdam
p. 146

Untitled, late 1990s
Acrylic and Chinese ink on rice paper
70 × 38 in. / 177.8 × 96.5 cm
Private Collection, Amsterdam
p. 149

Pink Flamingo, August 10, 1997
Acrylic on canvas
83.3 × 393 in. / 212 × 1000 cm
Private Collection, Amsterdam
pp. 6–7

Walasse Ting, Pierre Alechinsky
Aleching, n.d.
Watercolor on paper
11.8 × 12.3 in. / 29.8 × 31.3 cm (each)
Museum Jorn, Silkeborg.
p. 69

Pumpkin and Eight Grasshoppers, c. late 1950s
Chinese ink and oil on rice paper mounted
on silk scroll
not reproduced

Walasse Ting, Pierre Alechinsky
Sun, c. late 1950s–early 1960s
Acrylic on found burlap
not reproduced

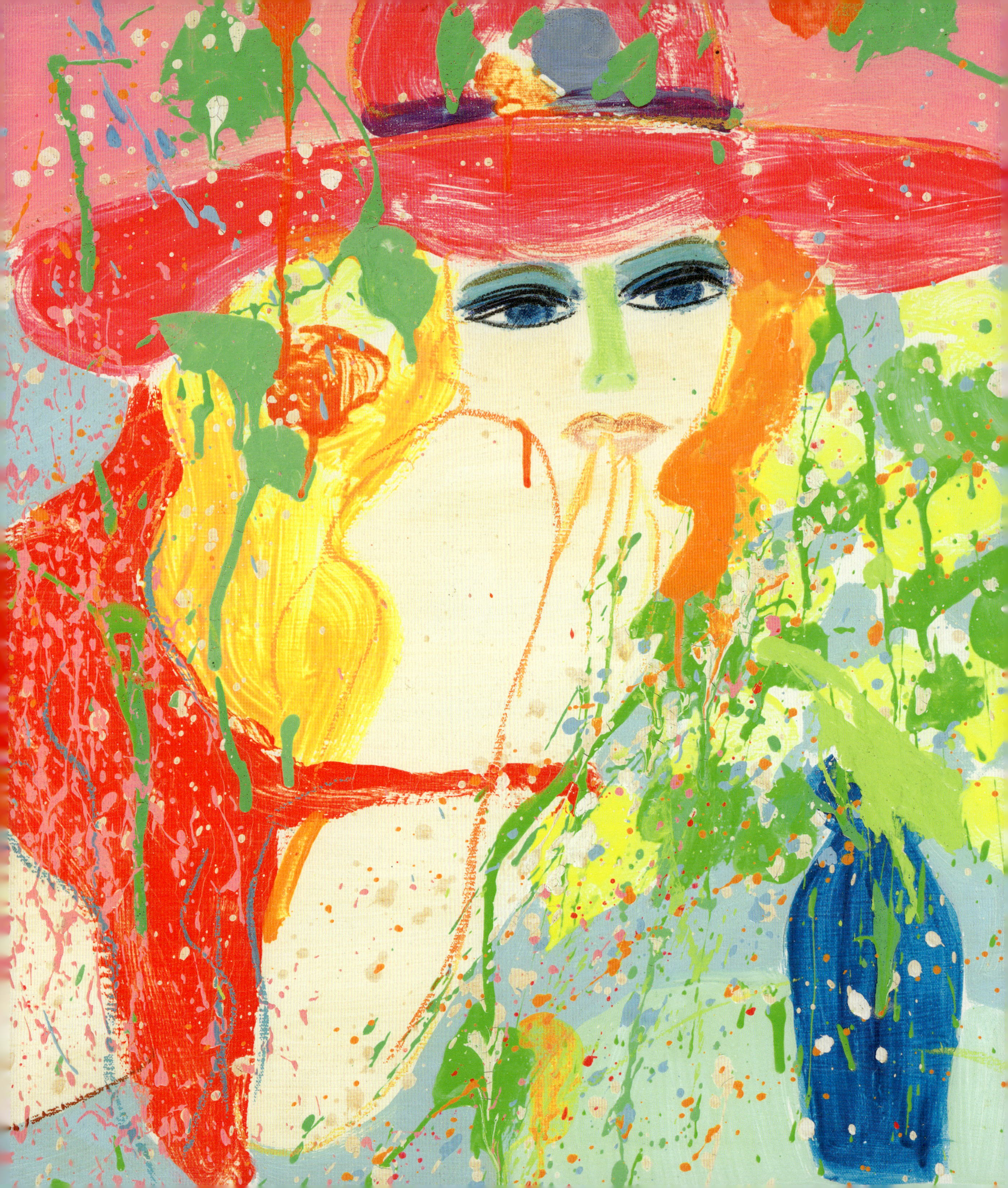

Walasse Ting Exhibition History

SOLO EXHIBITIONS

1952
• *Walasse Ting: Modern Paintings of Eastern & Western Styles*, Hotel Cecil, Hong Kong.
1954
• *Walasse Ting*, Studio Paul Facchetti, Paris, France.
1956
• *Walasse Ting*, Galerie Taptoe, Brussels, Belgium.
1957
• *Walasse Ting: Paintings*, Galerie Chalette, New York NY.
1959
• *Paintings by Walasse Ting*, Martha Jackson Gallery, New York NY.
1960
• *TING*, Martha Jackson Gallery, New York NY.
• *TING*, Galerie Espace, Amsterdam, Netherlands.
• *Walasse Ting*, Galerie Birch, Copenhagen, Denmark.
1961
• *Solo Exhibition by Walasse Ting*, Galerie Rive Gauche, Paris, France.
• *Walasse Ting: Öbilder*, Galerie Van de Loo, Munich, Germany.
• *My Shit and My Love: 10 Poems*, Galerie Smith, Brussels, Belgium.
1962
• *Walasse Ting*, Galerie St. Stephan, Vienna, Austria.
1963
• *3 X TING (TING very Chinese, TING very abstract, TING very (but very) figurative*, Lefebre Gallery, New York NY.
• *TING*, Galerie Birch, Copenhagen, Denmark.
1965
Walasse Ting: Lithographs done in Tamarind, Carriage House Art Gallery, Cambridge MA.
Walasse Ting: Ink Scrolls, Lefebre Gallery, New York NY.
1966
• *Walasse Ting: Recent Oils*, Lefebre Gallery, New York NY.
1967
• *Walasse Ting*, J.L. Hudson Gallery, Detroit MI.
• *Walasse Ting*, Lefebre Gallery, New York NY.
1968
• *Walasse Ting: Recent Paintings*, Lefebre Gallery, New York NY.
• *Walasse Ting*, Galerie de France, Paris, France.
1969
• *Walasse Ting: Recent Paintings*, Lefebre Gallery, New York NY.
1970
• *Walasse Ting: New Paintings*, Lefebre Gallery, New York NY.
• *Walasse Ting*, Galerie Birch, Copenhagen, Denmark.

• *Walasse Ting*, Esther Bear Gallery, Santa Barbara CA.
1971
• *Walasse Ting: Green Banana*, Lefebre Gallery, New York NY.
1972
• *Walasse Ting*, Galerie Birch, Copenhagen, Denmark.
1973
• *Walasse Ting*, Galerie Birch, Copenhagen, Denmark.
• *Walasse Ting: New Paintings*, Lefebre Gallery, New York NY.
1974
• *Walasse Ting*, Galerie Minami, Tokyo, Japan.
• *Walasse Ting: Nude Exhibition*, Galerie Adrian Maeght, Paris, France.
1975
• *Walasse Ting: Exhibition of Recent Lithographs*, National Museum of History, Taipei, Taiwan.
• *Walasse Ting*, Galerie Birch, Copenhagen, Denmark.
• *Walasse Ting*, Galerie Nord, Randers, Denmark.
• *Walasse Ting: The Ting Girls, New York 1973-74*, Galerie Kornfeld, Bern, Switzerland.
1977
• *Walasse Ting: Paintings and Lithographs*, Galerie Adrian Maeght, Paris, France.
• *Walasse Ting*, Galleria Grafica Club, Milan, Italy.
• *Walasse Ting: Miss USA*, Calligrammes Gallery, Ottawa, Canada.
1978
• *Walasse Ting: Paintings*, Lefebre Gallery, New York NY.
• *TING*, Lens Fine Art, Antwerp, Belgium.
• *Walasse Ting*, Galerie Aele, Madrid, Spain.
1979
• *Walasse Ting*, Galerie Nouvelles Images, The Hague, Netherlands.
• *Walasse Ting: Recent Paintings*, Lefebre Gallery, New York NY.
1980
• *Walasse Ting: Recent Paintings, Very Chinese*, Lefebre Gallery, New York NY.
• *Walasse Ting*, Galerie Birch, Copenhagen, Denmark.
1981
• *Walasse Ting*, National Gallery of Art, Reykjavik, Iceland.
• *Walasse Ting*, Galerie Birch, Copenhagen, Denmark.
1982
• *Walasse Ting: Acrylic Paintings on Chinese Paper*, Lefebre Gallery, New York NY.
1983
• *Walasse Ting*, Galerie Dessers, Hasselt, Belgium.
• *Walasse Ting*, Galerie Nouvelles Images, La Hague, France.

• *Walasse Ting*, Gallery Koppelmann, Leverkusen, Germany.
• *Walasse Ting*, Lens Fine Art, Antwerp, Belgium.
• *Walasse Ting*, Galerie Grafica Club, Milan, Italy.
• *Walasse Ting*, Galerie Birch, Copenhagen, Denmark.
• *Walasse Ting*, Galerie Moderne, Silkeborg, Denmark.
1984
• *Walasse Ting*, Galerie Huset, Copenhagen, Denmark.
• *Walasse Ting: Still Lifes*, Lefebre Gallery, New York NY.
• *WALASSE TING: Rice Paper Paintings*, Lung Men Art Gallery, Taipei, Taiwan.
• *LADÁNYI COLLAGES: GREETING LADÁNYI by WALASSE TING*, Matignon Gallery, New York NY.
• *Walasse Ting*, Avant-Garde Art Center, Taichung, Taiwan.
• *Walasse Ting*, Lung Chiang Art Gallery, Kaohsuing, Taipei, Taiwan.
• *Walasse Ting*, Galerie BBL, Antwerp, Belgium.
• *Walasse Ting*, Galeria 2RC, Rome and Milan, Italy.
1985
• *Walasse Ting*, Galerie La Hune, Paris, France.
• *Walasse Ting*, Galerie Asbaek, Copenhagen, Denmark.
• *Walasse Ting*, Art Unlimited, Amsterdam, Netherlands.
• *Walasse Ting*, Arti et Amicitiae, Amsterdam, Netherlands.
1986
• *Walasse Ting*, Alisan Fine Arts, Hong Kong.
• *Walasse Ting*, Galerie Nouvelles Images, The Hague, Netherlands.
• *Walasse Ting*, P Gallery, Hamburg, Germany.
• *Walasse Ting*, Galleria del Manifesto, Verona, Italy.
• *Walasse Ting*, Galerie Dessers Hasselt, Hasselt, Belgium.
• *Walasse Ting*, Kunstforum, Ghent, Belgium.
1987
• *Walasse Ting*, Taipei Fine Art Museum, Taipei, Taiwan.
• *Walasse Ting*, Galerie Asbaek, Copenhagen, Denmark.
• *Walasse Ting*, Gallery Esperanza, Montreal, Quebec.
• *Walasse Ting*, Elfin Art Gallery, Los Angeles CA.
• *Walasse Ting*, Ars Mundi, Hanover, Germany.
• *Walasse Ting*, Galerie l'Orangerie, Geneva, Switzerland.
1988
• *Walasse Ting · Works on Paper*, Lung Men Art Gallery, Taipei, Taiwan.
• *Walasse Ting*, Galerie Alcolea, Barcelona, Spain.
• *Walasse Ting*, Galerie Alcolea, Madrid, Spain.
• *Walasse Ting*, Galerie Guy Pieters, Knokke, Belgium.
• *Walasse Ting*, Galerie Asbaek, Horsens, Denmark.
• *Walasse Ting*, Galeria Torres Clary, Reus, Spain.
• *Walasse Ting*, Lineart, Ghent, Belgium.
1989
• *Walasse Ting*, American Club, Hong Kong.
• *Walasse Ting*, Lens Fine Art, Antwerp, Belgium.
• *Walasse Ting*, American Prints, Valencia, Spain.
• *Walasse Ting*, Galerie Lucy Weill-Seligmann, Paris, France.
• *Walasse Ting*, Galerie Ostermaln, Stockholm, Sweden.
• *Walasse Ting*, Galerie Scandinavia, Gothenburg, Sweden.
1990
• *Walasse Ting*, Galerie Alcolea, Madrid, Spain.
• *Walasse Ting*, Galerie Moustache, Osaka, Japan.
• *Walasse Ting*, Galerie l'Orangerie, St. Paul-de-Vence, France.
• *Walasse Ting*, Lineart, Ghent, Belgium.
• *Walasse Ting*, Galleria 2RC, Milan, Italy.
• *Walasse Ting*, Galeria de Arte, Almansil, Portugal.
• *Walasse Ting: Recent Works on Rice Paper*, Louis Stern Galleries, Beverly Hills CA.
1991
• *The Enchanting World of Walasse Ting*, Alisan Fine Arts, Hong Kong.
• *Walasse Ting*, Sala Nonell, Barcelona, Spain.
• *Walasse Ting*, Galerie Acolea, Madrid, Spain.
• *Walasse Ting*, Il Monte Ischia Gallery, Naples, Italy.
• *Walasse Ting*, Arthouse Gallery, Copenhagen, Denmark.
1992
• *Wind, Flower, Snow, Moon, Women-Women, Walasse Ting Exhibition*, Lung Men Art Gallery, Taipei, Taiwan.
• *Walasse Ting*, Alisan Fine Arts, Hong Kong.
• *Walasse Ting*, Galerie Acolea, Madrid, Spain.
• *Walasse Ting*, Lineart, Ghent, Belgium.
1993
• *The Magical World of Walasse Ting*, Alisan Fine Art, Hong Kong.
• *Flower Theft's World of Black & White, Walasse Ink Painting Exhibition*, Lung Men Art Gallery, Taipei, Taiwan.
• *Walasse Ting*, Apollo Gallery, Taipei, Taiwan.
• *Walasse Ting*, Avant-Garde Art Center, Taipei, Taiwan.
• *Walasse Ting*, Hong Kong Art Centre, Hong Kong.
• *Walasse Ting*, P Gallery, Hamburg, Germany.
• *Expo Walasse Ting*, Galerie Luc Pieters, Knokke-Heist, Belgium.
• *Walasse Ting*, Galerie de l'Orangerie, St. Paul-de-Vence, France.
1994
• *Encountering Flower Red & Willow Green, Walasse Ting Exhibition*, Lung Men Art Gallery, Taipei, Taiwan.
• *Walasse Ting*, Kunstforum, Ghent, Belgium.
• *Walasse Ting*, P. Gallery, Hamburg, Germany.
• *Walasse Ting*, Tresors, Singapore.
1995
• *Walasse Ting*, Gallerie Guy Pieters, Knokke-Heist, Belgium.
• *Walasse Ting*, Alisan Fine Arts, Hong Kong.
1996
• *Walasse Ting*, Wetterling Teo Gallery, Singapore.
• *Walasse Ting*, Galerie Delaive, Amsterdam, Netherlands.
• *Walasse Ting*, Alisan Fine Arts, Hong Kong.
1997
• *Walasse Ting: A Very Hot Day*, Shanghai Art Museum, Shanghai, China.
• *Walasse Ting*, Alisan Fine Arts, Hong Kong.
1998
• *Walasse Ting: His Utopian World*, Alisan Fine Arts, Hong Kong.
1999
• *Walasse Ting*, The Catto Gallery, London, England.

2000

• *Walasse Ting*, Scheringa Museum voor Realisme, Spanbroek, Netherlands.

2001

• *The Black and White World of Walasse Ting*, Alisan Fine Arts, Hong Kong.

• *Walasse Ting, Romancing Garden, Ink Paintings of Flower & Birds*, Lung Men Art Gallery, Taipei, Taiwan.

• *Walasse Ting*, The Catto Gallery, London, England.

2002

• *The Sizzling Palette of Walasse Ting: Celebrating the Year of the Horse*, Alisan Fine Arts, Hong Kong.

• *Spring Drink, Flower Giggling*, Yibo Gallery, Shanghai, China.

2008

• *Walasse Ting 10th Exhibition*, Alisan Fine Arts, Hong Kong.

2009

• *Walasse Ting*, The Catto Gallery, London, England.

2010

• *From Heroic Expression to Resplendent Color: Walasse Ting Retrospective Exhibition*, Taipei Fine Arts Museum, Taipei, Taiwan.

• *The Floral Journey - The Artistic Memoir of Walasse Ting*, /SOKA Art Center, Taipei, Taiwan.

• *I Love Flowers - All My Life*, Hong Kong Arts Centre, the Pao Galleries, Hong Kong.

• *Amazing Feelings*, New Millennium Gallery, Beijing, China

2011

• *Walasse Ting: To Love to Fresh: Exhibition of Walasse Ting Works from the 1980s & 1990s*, Longmen Art Projects, Hwa's Gallery, Shanghai, China.

• *The Floral Journey-The Artistic Memoir of Walasse Ting*, Soka Art Center, Beijing, China.

2012

• *Walasse Ting: RED MOUTH series*, Longmen Art Projects, Shanghai, China.

2013

• *Walasse Ting: Blue Sky in My Heart*, Longmen Art Projects, Shanghai, China.

2014

A book like hundred flower garden: Walasse Ting's 1¢ Life, de Young Museum, Fine Arts Museum of San Francisco, San Francisco CA (traveling exhibition).

2015

• *Forget Lovesick, Admire Wind & Moon: Walasse Ting's Mountains, Water, Flower & Birds*, Longmen Art Projects, Shanghai, China.

2016

• *Walasse Ting: le voleur des fleurs (Walasse Ting: The Flower Thief)*, Musée Cernuschi, Paris, France.

2017

• *Walasse Ting: Symphony of Colours*, Alisan Fine Arts, Hong Kong.

2018

• *Walasse Ting: The Amsterdam Years*, Museum Jan, Amstelveen, Netherlands.

• *Walasse Ting: The Flower Thief All Landscapes, Thousand Mountains Long Journey*, Longmen Art Projects, Shanghai, China.

2022

• *Walasse Ting*, The Catto Gallery, London, England.

2023

• *Walasse Ting: Parrot Jungle*, NSU Art Museum Fort Lauderdale, Fort Lauderdale FL.

SELECTED TWO PERSON AND GROUP EXHIBITIONS

1955

• Hansa Gallery, *6 Exemplary Paintings and 1 Sculpture*, New York NY.

1956

• *Alechinsky, Appel, Baj, Jorn, Rein et Roel d'Haese, Ting, Wickaert et Dotremont avec Cobra*, Galerie Taptoe, Brussels, Belgium.

1957

• Mi Chou Gallery, Inc., New York NY.

1958

• *Fifth International Biennial of Contemporary Color Lithography*, The Cincinnati Art Museum, Cincinnati OH.

1960

• *New Forms - New Media*, Martha Jackson Gallery, New York NY.

1961

• *The 1961 Pittsburgh International Exhibition of Contemporary Painting and Sculpture*, Museum of Art, Carnegie Institute, Pittsburgh PA.

• *Arte e contemplazione*, Palazzo Grassi, Venice, Italy.

1962

• *Art Since 1950*, Seattle World's Fair, Seattle WA.

1963

• *Reinhoud, Alechinsky & Ting - Solo de sculpture et divertissement arrangé pour peinture à quatre mains*, Galerie de France, Paris, France.

• *Parisiens with an Accent*, Lefebre Gallery, New York NY.

• *À deux pinceaux: Alechinsky & Walasse Ting*, Birch Gallery, Copenhagen, Denmark.

1964

• *Salon de Mai*, Musée d'Art Moderne de la Ville de Paris, Paris, France.

• *The 1964 Pittsburgh International Exhibition of Contemporary Painting and Sculpture*, Museum of Art, Carnegie Institute, Pittsburgh PA.

• *Contemporary Painters and Sculptors as Printmakers*, Museum of Modern Art, New York NY.

1965

• *Salon de Mai*, Musée d'Art Moderne de la Ville de Paris, Paris, France.

1966

• *Salon de Mai*, Musée d'Art Moderne de la Ville de Paris, Paris, France.

1967

• *Salon de Mai*, Musée d'Art Moderne de la Ville de Paris, Paris, France.

• *The 1967 Pittsburgh International Exhibition of Contemporary Painting and Sculpture*, Museum of Art, Carnegie Institute, Pittsburgh PA.

1968

• *Salon de Mai*, Musée d'Art Moderne de la Ville de Paris, Paris, France.

1970

• *The 1970 Pittsburgh International Exhibition of Contemporary Painting and Sculpture*, Museum of Art, Carnegie Institute, Pittsburgh PA.

1972

• *Fresh Air School: Exhibition of Paintings - Sam Francis, Joan Mitchell and Walasse Ting*, Museum of Art, Carnegie Institute, Pittsburgh PA (traveling exhibition).

1974
• *Selected Works by Alechinsky, Antes, Bossier, Corneille, Hartung, Jorn, Reinhoud, Seugi, Sonderborg, Ting*, Lefebre Gallery, New York NY.
• *Livres et estampes: Alechinsky, Atlan and Dotremont, Courtin, Saura, Ting and Bram van Velde*, Achille Weber Gallery, Paris, France.
1975
• *35th Western New York Exhibition*, Albright-Knox Art Gallery, Buffalo NY.
1977
Prints: Pierre Alechinsky, Karel Appel & Walasse Ting, Juliette Halioua Gallery, New York NY.
1982
• *9 & 9*, Hubert Winter Gallery, Vienna, Austria.
• *20/20: Twenty Artists/Twenty Galleries*, Terry Dintenfass and Grace Borgenicht Galleries, New York NY.
1984
• *Selections from the Permanent Collection: Prints and Illustrated Books*, Museum of Modern Art, New York NY.
1985
• *HSIAO CHIN-WALASSE TING*, Taipei Fine Arts, Taipei, Taiwan.
• The Three Musketeers from New York - *Walasse Ting. Hilo Chen, Dennis Huang*, Longmen Art Projects, Shanghai, China.
• *New Editions from 2 RC: Alechinsky, Graves, Sam Francis, Ting*, Wirtz Gallery, San Francisco CA.
1988
• *Bonnard to Kiefer: 20th-Century Artist-Illustrated Books from the Bareiss Collection*, Toledo Museum of Art, Toledo OH.
1990
• *Een Tijdbeeld Van Appel tot Warhol*, Delaive Gallery, Amsterdam, Netherlands.
1993
• *Neither East Nor West: Seven Contemporary New York Artists*, Taipei Gallery, New York NY.
1994
• *A Century of Artists Books*, Museum of Modern Art, New York NY.
1997
• *Asian Traditions/Modern Expressions: Asian-American Artists and Abstraction 1945-1970*, Jane Voorhees Zimmerli Art Museum, Rutgers University and Taipei Gallery, New Brunswick NJ and New York NY (traveling exhibition).
1999
• *Pop Impressions Europe/USA: Prints and Multiples from the Museum of Modern Art*, Museum of Modern Art, New York NY.
• *Dubuffet to de Kooning: Expressionist Prints from Europe and America*, Museum of Modern Art, New York NY.
• *Spring Beyond the Cultural Revolution, Paintings from 1966-1976*, Longmen Art Projects, Shanghai, China.
2000
• *Graphic Art: Drawings and Sculptures*, Kunstkabinett, Regensburg, Germany.
2001
• *Corps à corps*, Centre de la gravure et de l'image imprimée, La Louvière, France.
• *The Stamp of Impulse: Abstract Impressionist Prints*, Worcester Art Museum, Worcester MA.

2003
• *Pierre Alechinsky / Satie en miroir et autres pièces à quatre mains*, Galerie Nationale de Jeu de Paume, Paris, France.
2004
• *Rhapsody in Color: Abstract Art from the Permanent Collection*, Southern Alleghenies Museum of Art, Pittsburgh-Johnstown PA.
2006
• *1¢ Life exhibition: 1964 portfolio exhibition*, Woodward Gallery, New York NY.
• *Sam Francis and Walasse Ting: Friends*, Galerie Delaive, Amsterdam, Netherlands.
• *Accrochage*, Kunstkabinett, Regensburg, Germany.
2014
• *Reset Chinese Contemporary Art*, Soka Art Center, Beijing, China.
• *Summer Lovin', Selections from the Collection*, Taubman Museum of Art, Roanoke VA.
2015
• *The Avant-Garde Won't Give Up: Cobra and Its Legacy*, Blum & Poe, Los Angeles CA.
2016
• *Zao Wou-ki*, Musée Cernuschi, Paris, France.
2017
• *Cat Love. Nine lives in the arts*, Kunsthal Rotterdam, Rotterdam, Netherlands.
• *Off the Shelf: Modern & Contemporary Artists' Books*, Baltimore Museum of Art, Baltimore MD.
2019
• *Centripetal / Centrifugal: Asian American Art*, Allen Memorial Art Museum, Oberlin College, Oberlin OH.
2020
• *1¢ Life*, Bechtler Museum of Modern Art, Charlotte NC.
2021
• *Celebrating a Friendship: Walasse Ting & Sam Francis*, Alisan Fine Arts, Hong Kong.
• *Hard Copies: Prints Done The Old-fashioned Way*, Galerie Simon Blais, Montreal, Quebec, Canada.
• *Transgression throughout the Volatile World*, Asia Art Center, Taipei, Taiwan.
• *Ink City*, Tai Kwun, Central Hong Kong, Hong Kong. *Individuals, Networks, Expressions*, South Galleries, M+, Hong Kong.
• *Art and Writing: Gao Xingjian, Gu Gan, Walasse Ting, Wang Tiande, Wang Dongling*, Southside Saturday, Alisan Fine Arts-Aberdeen, Hong Kong.
• *NOT A Fashion Store!*, Hong Kong Museum of Art, Hong Kong.
2022
• *Confrontation: Keith Haring & Pierre Alechinsky*, NSU Art Museum Fort Lauderdale, Fort Lauderdale FL.
• *Eye of Cobra*, NSU Art Museum Fort Lauderdale, Fort Lauderdale FL.
• *A Book Like Hundred Flower Garden: Walasse Ting's 1¢ Life*, University of Arizona Museum of Art, Tucson AZ.
• *Ink in Motion: A History of Chinese Painting in the 20th Century*, Musée Cernuschi, Paris, France.
• *Being*, Zhi Art Museum, Chengdu, China.
• *Contemporary Chinese Art, Asian Art in London*, Alisan Fine Arts, Cromwell Place, London, England
• *Dead Lecturer/Distant Relative*, Wallach Art Gallery, Columbia University, New York NY.

AWARDS

1964
• Tamarind Fellowship Artist, Los Angeles CA.
1970
• John Simon Guggenheim Memorial Foundation
Fellowship, New York NY.

MUSEUM COLLECTIONS

Ashmolean Museum, University of Oxford,
Oxford, England.
Buffalo AKG Art Museum, Buffalo NY.
Carnegie Museum of Art, Pittsburgh PA.
Detroit Institute of Arts, Detroit MI.
Guggenheim Museum, New York NY.
Hong Kong Museum of Art, Hong Kong.
The Israel Museum, Jerusalem, Israel.
M+ Museum, Hong Kong.
Metropolitan Museum of Art, New York NY.
Musée Cernuschi, Paris, France.
Museum Jorn, Silkeborg, Denmark.
Museum of Modern Art, New York NY.
Norton Simon Museum, Pasadena CA.
Randers Kunstmuseum, Jutland, Denmark.
Santa Barbara Museum of Art, Santa Barbara CA.
Shanghai Art Museum, Shanghai, China.
Stedelijk Museum, Amsterdam, Netherlands.
Taipei Fine Art Museum, Taipei, Taiwan.

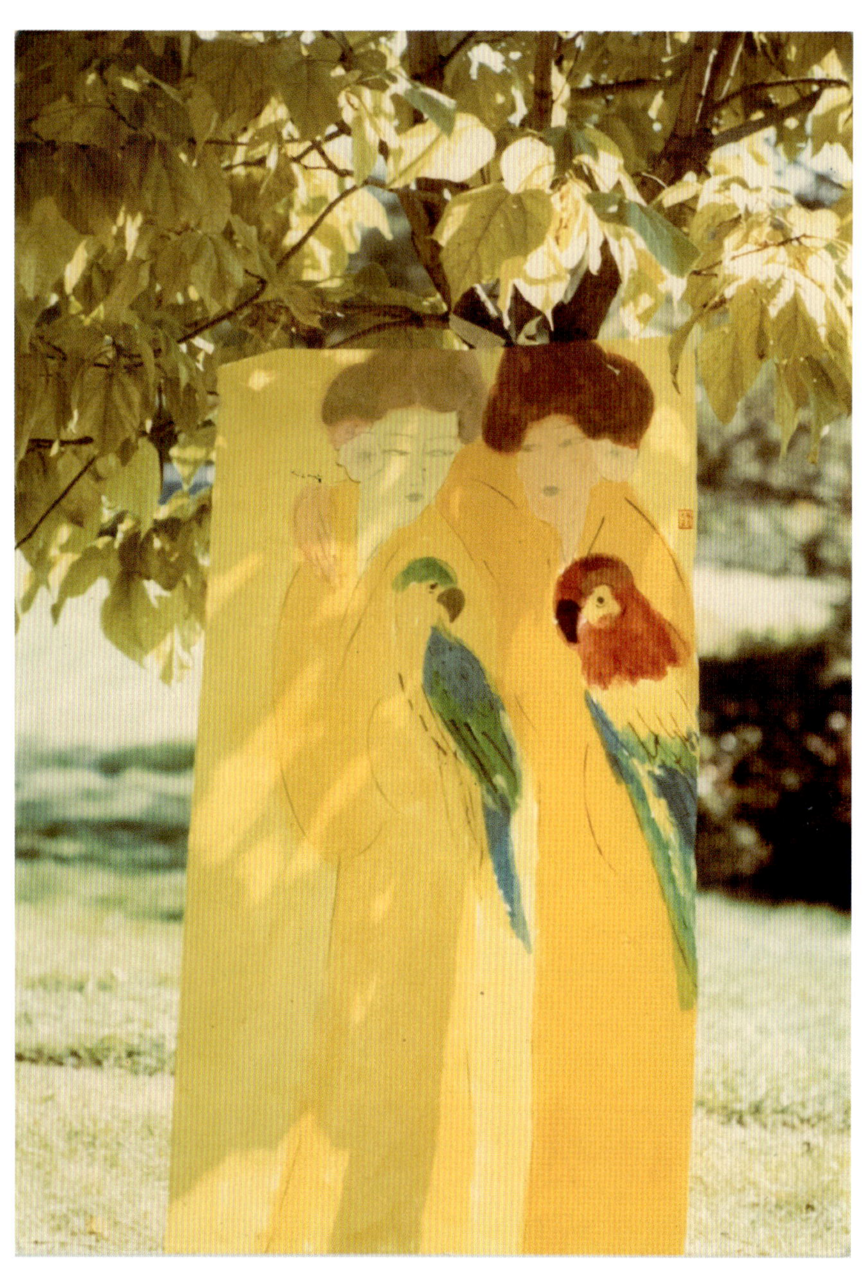

Walasse Ting Bibliography

**ARTIST BOOKS AND WRITINGS
BY WALASSE TING**

• Ting, Walasse, *My Shit and My Love
10 Poems* (Paris: Maurice Baeudet & Georges
Girar, 1961).
• Ting, Walasse, *1¢ Life* (Bern: Sam Francis
and E.W. Kornfeld, 1964).
• Ting, Walasse, "Near 1¢ Life," *Art News*, vol. 65,
no. 3, May 1966, 38, 67–68.
• Ting, Walasse, *Chinese Moonlight: 63 poems
by 33 poets* (New York: Wittenborn & Co, 1967).
• Ting, Walasse, *Hot and Sour Soup* (California:
Sam Francis Foundation, 1969).
• Jorn, Asger and Walasse Ting, *La Flûte de
Jade / Jadefløjten / The Jade Flute* (St. Gallen:
Erker Verlag, 1970).
• Ting, Walasse, *Green Banana* (New York and
Copenhagen: Lefebre Gallery and Rosengreen
Litografi, 1971).
• *Fresh Air School: Sam Francis, Joan Mitchell,
Walasse Ting* (exh. cat.) (Pittsburgh: Carnegie
Museum of Art, 1972).
• Ting, Walasse, *Red Mouth* (Hong Kong: Toppan
Printing Co., 1977).
• Ting, Walasse, *Rice Paper Paintings* (Paris: Yves
Rivière, 1984).
• Ting, Walasse, *Jolies Dames* (Paris: Yves Rivière,
1988).
• Ting, Walasse, *Blue Sky* (Amsterdam: Art
Unlimited, 1993).
• Ting, Walasse, *Walasse Ting: A Very Hot Day*
(Shanghai: Shanghai Art Museum, 1997).

MONOGRAPHS

• King, Alice (foreword), *The Black and White
World of Walasse Ting* (Hong Kong: Alisan Fine
Arts, 2001).
• Chaoying, Wu (ed.), *From Heroic Expression
to Resplendent Color: Walasse Ting
Retrospective Exhibition* (Taipei: Taipei Fine
Arts Museum, 2010).
• Ting, Walasse, *Walasse Ting: 1980s & 1990s*
(Shanghai: Longmen Art Projects, 2011).
• Ting, Walasse, *Walasse Ting: Red Mouth
Series 1 - 1973–1977 - Acrylic and Oil Pastel
on Western Paper* (Shanghai: Longmen Art
Projects, 2012).
• Ting, Walasse, *Walasse Ting: Red Mouth
Series 2 - 1973–1977 - Acrylic and Oil Pastel
on Western Paper* (Shanghai: Longmen Art
Projects, 2012).
• Ting, Walasse, *Walasse Ting: Forget Lovesick
Admire Wind & Moon* (Shanghai: Longmen Art
Projects, 2015).
• Lefebvre, Éric and Maël Bellec (eds.), *Walasse
Ting: le voleur de fleurs* (Paris: Paris Musées,
2016). English translation: Lefebvre, Éric and Maël
Bellec (eds.), *Walasse Ting: The Flower Thief*
(Paris: Paris Musées, 2016).
• Ting, Walasse, *Walasse Ting: All Landscapes
Thousand Mountains Long Journey* (Shanghai:
Longmen Art Projects, 2018).
• Wolens, Ariella (ed.), *Walasse Ting: Parrot
Jungle* (Milan: Skira editore, 2023).

SELECTED ARTICLES AND PERIODICALS

• "MODERN MUSEUM TO SHOW NEW ART,"
The New York Times, March 10, 1957, 77.
• Ashton, Dore, "Group Show and Paintings
by Ting," *The New York Times*, March 13,
1957, 24.
• "Berserik en Ting," *De Telegraaf*, November 10,
1960, 9.
• Page, A.F., "An Action Painting," *Bulletin of the
Detroit Institute of Arts*, vol. 40, no. 1, 1960, 12–13.
• "Lefebre Gallery," *Art Gallery Review*, January
18, 1963.
• [Adlow, Dorothy], "Three Views of Ting Talent at
Lefebre," *Christian Science Monitor*, January 19,
1963.
• Adlow, Dorothy, "Understanding Oriental
Art," *Christian Science Monitor*, January 19, 1963.
• Levy, Judy, "In The Galleries," *West Side
News*, January 31, 1963.
• Dotremont, Christian, "Peintures à quatre mains,"
Art International 7, no. 9, December 5, 1963, 40.
• S., J., "Walasse Ting's Ink Scrolls," *Artist's Proof*,
Issue 8., vol V, no. 2, 1965.
• Canaday, John, "Philly, Pop, Ting, Etc.,"
The New York Times, July 18, 1965, 21.
• "Reviews and Previews: Walasse Ting," *Art
News*, vol. 64, no. 8, December 1965, 12.
• [Gruen, John], "Walasse Ting," *New York Herald
Tribune*, December 11, 1965.
• Gruen, John, "Walasse Ting," *World Journal
Tribune*, December 30, 1966.
• Canaday, John, "Nivola and Ting Have Gallery
Exhibitions," *The New York Times*, December 31,
1966, 35.
• Dolbin, Benedict F., "Walasse Ting," *Aufbau*,
January 27, 1967, 17.
• Daniell, Rosemary, "Ancient Verse: Pure Images
Saved from Old China," *The New York Times
Book Review*, 1967.
• Keneas, Alexander, "Chinese Painter-Poet Fuses
2 Cultures," *The New York Times*, November 26,
1967, 68.
• "Walasse Ting: 'Recent Paintings'," *Aufbau*,
February 9, 1968, 19.
• Willard, Charlotte, "In the Art Galleries: Walasse
Ting," *New York Post*, February 17, 1968.
• B., A., "Reviews and Previews/Walasse Ting."
Art News, vol. 67, no. 1, March 1968, 24.

Photo of Walasse Ting rice paper painting,
Two Yellow Girls with Parrots, 1980
at Spring Lake Park, Highland Mills,
New York, 1980

• Merwin, W.S., "Into English," *The New York Times*, March 17, 1968, 6.
• Canaday, John, "Art: Results of a Foreign Study Program," *The New York Times*, September 27, 1969, 27.
• Glueck, Grace, "Open Season. New York Gallery Notes," *Art in America*, vol. 57, no. 5, Sept/Oct. 1969, 117.
• Dolbin, Benedict F., "Walasse Ting: neueste Gemälde," *Aufbau*, October 3, 1969, 22.
• Frank, Suzanne, "Hot and Sour Soup," *Arts Magazine*, May 1970.
• Lefebre, John, "Lefebre," *Special Edition Arts Magazine*, April 1971, 46.
• R., J.H., "Die Farbenromantik von Walasse Ting," *Aufbau*, November 5, 1971, 14.
• Canaday, John, "Art: Ting and Boghosian in Other Exhibitions," *The New York Times*, November 6, 1971, 27.
• Frank, Peter, "Art New York: Around the Galleries – Walasse Ting," *Columbia Daily Spectator*, vol. CXVI, no. 25, November 8, 1971, 7–8.
• C[ampbell], L[awrence], "Reviews and Previews: Walasse Ting," *Art News*, December 1971.
• Brown, Gordon, "Wallasse [*sic*] Ting," *Arts Magazine*, vol. 46, Issue 3, December 1971 – January 1972.
• Fu, Lo, "Walasse Ting's Painting and Poem," *The Epoch Quarterly*, 40, April 1975.
• Smythe, Robert, "Eros and eggs: sensual painting goes to Market," *The Citizen, Ottawa*, December 9, 1977, 49.
• "The Magnificent Obsession, Or, Good Nudes for Art Lovers: Playboy's Roving Eye," *Playboy*, November 1978, 310–311.
• Alechinsky, Pierre, "Quelques Notes sur Walasse Ting, Peintre Obligé," *Art International*, 22, no. 7, November-December 1978.
• Downey, Peter and Jeff Lewis, "Walasse Ting on Painting, Artists, Prostitutes, Love and Life," *The Real World*, Summer 1979, Issue 12, 22–25.
• "Scroll Painter Ting: Scrawling Success," *New York Sunday News*, January 3, 1980, 16.
• Helfer, Judith, "Neue Malereien von Walasse Ting," *Aufbau*, May 11, 1984, 16.
• Mingqiu, Feng, "The Flower Picker Walasse Ting," *PhotoArt*, Issue 79, October 1987, 34.
• Quint, Ingrid Gouda, "Walasse Ting: Straalverliefd op de Nederlandse vrouw," *Panorama*, January 1989, 40–43.
• "Walasse Ting Solo Exhibition: The Flower Thief," *New Phase Art News*, Issue 11, April 1993, cover, 4–5.
• Adams, Clinton, "East Coast, West Coast Tamarind Lithography Workshop and the American Print Establishment," *Print Quarterly*, 14, no. 3, 1997, 252–83.
• Finlay, Victoria, "Brushes with beauty," *Weekend Entertainment, South China Morning Post*, June 6, 1997, cover, 3.
• Wong, Nancy, "Shock Culture," *Esquire HK*, September 1997, cover, 12–14.
• Yi Ru, Dai, "Interview with Walasse Ting," *Xinmin Evening News*, November 17, 1997, 25.
• Millichap, John, "Against the Tide," *Asian Art News*, January/February 1999. 62.
• You Fang, Cao, "EAT. ART. SEX." *Elegance Magazine*, 2000, 99–101.
• "Walasse Ting en zijn vrouwen in Spanbroek," *Noordhollands Dagblad*, July 10, 2000, D21.
• McHugh, Fionnuala, "The Interview," *Post Magazine*, May 6, 2001, 4–5.
• Wakeford, Leslie K., "Partnerships in Print: Avant-Garde Periodical Design," *Art Institute of Chicago Museum Studies*, 34, no. 2, 2008, 52–94.
• Kramer, Danielle N., "One Cent Life," *Art Institute of Chicago Museum Studies*, 34, no. 2, 2008, 56–58, 94.
• Epoch Quarterly, Editorial Board, "Walasse Ting Memorial Special," *Epoch Poetry Quarterly*, Issue 164, September 2010, 105–132.
• Yizhong, Ruan, "Interviewing Walasse Ting," *The Epoch Quarterly*, Issue 164, September 2010, 119.
• Frazier, David, "A Neon Legacy," *Taipei Times*, December 8, 2010, 14.
• Collection Curators, The Kenneth E. Tyler, "Remembering Walasse Ting," *National Gallery Australia*, August 28, 2013. https://nga.gov.au/stories-ideas/remembering-walasse-ting/"Walasse Ting: Graveur de la couleur," *Arts & Métiers du Livre*, no. 295, March-April 2013, 48–55.
• Stromberg, Matt, "ArtRX LA," *Hyperallergic*, December 22, 2015. https://hyperallergic.com/263589/artrx-la-74/Lechable, Camille, "Découverte Walasse Ting: Un peintre chinois à Paris," *L'Œil* #694, October 2016, cover, 60–65.
• Yau, John, "No Point of View Is the Best View of All: Artists Working Between 1952-65, Many of Whom Are Forgotten," *Hyperallergic*, January 15, 2017. https://hyperallergic.com/351444/no-point-of-view-is-the-best-view-of-all-artists-working-between-1952-1965-many-of-whom-are-forgotten
• Lefebvre, Éric, Hélène Chollet, Maël Bellec and Anne Fort, "Activités Du Musée Cernuschi." *Arts Asiatiques*, 72, 2017, 127–44.
• Yau, John, "12 Revelatory Exhibitions from 2017," *Hyperallergic*, December 31, 2017. https://hyperallergic.com/419429/12-revelatory-exhibitions-from-2017/Heyward, Anna, "Book Corner: One-Cent Life," *Gagosian Quarterly*, Spring 2017, 166–167.
• Seed, John, "DEAR Big SAM: The Letters of Walasse Ting to Sam Francis Tell the Story of Their Friendship Over Time," *Arts of Asia*, September-October, 2018, 84–93.

SELECTED BOOKS AND CATALOGUES

• Jackson, Martha, *New Forms – New Media I* (New York: Martha Jackson Gallery, 1960).
• Dorfles, Gillo (ed.), *Arte e contemplazione* (Venice: Centro internazionale delle arti e del costume, 1961).
• Department of Fine Arts, Carnegie Institute, *The 1961 Pittsburgh International Exhibition of Contemporary and Painting and Sculpture* (Pittsburgh: Carnegie Institute Press, 1962).
• Michelson, Annette, *Parisiens with an Accent* (New York: Lefebre Gallery, 1963).
• Earls-Solari, Bonnie, *The 1964 Pittsburgh International Exhibition of Contemporary Painting and Sculpture* (Pittsburgh: Carnegie Institute, 1964).
• Johnson, Una E., *Drawings of the Masters: 20th Century Drawings Part II: 1940 to the Present* (Plainview: Shorewood Publishers Inc., 1964).

• Alechinsky, Pierre, *Le test du titre: 6 planches et 61 titreurs d'élite* (Paris: Eric Losfeld, 1967).

• Museum of Art, Carnegie Institute, *Pittsburgh International Exhibition of Contemporary Painting and Sculpture – 1967* (Pittsburgh: Carnegie Institute, 1967).

• Alechinsky, Pierre, *Titres et pains perdus* (Paris: Denoël, 1968).

• Alechinsky, Pierre, *Le musée de poche* (Paris: Musée de poche, 1971).

• Alechinsky, Pierre, *Roue Libre: Les sentiers de la création* (Genève: Albert Skira, 1971).

• Munsterberg, Hugo, *The Arts of China* (Vermont and Tokyo: Tuttle Publishing, 1972).

• Alechinsky, Pierre, *Les estampes de 1946 a 1972* (Paris: Yves Riviere, 1973).

• Ragon, Michel and Michel Seuphor, *L'art abstrait: 1945/1970* (Paris: Maeght Editeur, 1974).

• Selz, Peter, *Sam Francis* (New York: Harry N. Abrams, 1975).

• Atkins, Guy, *Asger Jorn: The Crucial Years: 1954–1964* (London: Lund Humphries Publishers Ltd, 1977).

• Alechinsky, Pierre, *Alechinsky: Paintings and Writings* (Pittsburgh: Museum of Art Carnegie Institute, 1978).

• Büchler, Marianne, *Das Schubladenmuseum - The Museum of Drawers - Le Musée en Tiroirs* (Zürich: Kunsthaus Zürich, 1978).

• Jouve, Anne and Adrien Maeght (eds.), *Les foulards de maeght: Impression de Lyon* (Lyon: Musée des Tissus et des Arts Décoratifs, 1984).

• Ruiping, Su (ed.), *Overseas Chinese Artists Exhibition / Haiwai Yishujia Zhuanji* (Taipei: Taipei Fine Arts Museum, 1984).

• Feldman, Frayda and Jörg Schellmann (eds.), *Andy Warhol Prints* (New York: Abbeville Press, 1985).

• Su Fu, Martha and Chen Houei-Kuen, *A Retrospective Exhibition of Contemporary Chinese Art* (Taipei: Taipei Fine Arts Museum, 1986).

• Anbinder, Paul (ed.), *Albright-Knox Art Gallery: The Painting and Sculpture Collection: Acquisitions Since 1972* (New York: Hudson Hills Press, Inc., 1987).

• Gibson, Michael Francis and Pierre Alechinsky, *Pierre Alechinsky: Margin and Center* (New York: Solomon R Guggenheim Museum, 1987).

• Alechinsky, Pierre, *Walasse Ting, peintre obligé* (Saint-Clément-de-Rivière: Fata Morgana, 1988).

• Alechinsky, Pierre and Michel Sicard (eds.), *Extraits pour traits* (Paris: Galilée, 1989).

• Hagenberg, Roland (ed.), *Dupe of Being* (New York: Lafayette, 1989).

• Alechinsky, Pierre, *Blauchon et ricochets* (Paris: Gallimard, 1994).

• Alechinsky, Pierre, *Remarques marginals* (Paris: Gallimard, 1994).

• Alechinsky, Pierre, *Travaux à deux ou trois* (Paris: Éditions Galilée, 1994).

• Castleman, Riva, *A Century of Artists Books* (New York: The Museum of Modern Art, 1994).

• Wechsler, Jeffery (ed.), *Asian Traditions/Modern Expressions: Asian American Artists and Abstraction 1945-1970* (New York: Harry N. Abrams, 1997).

• Wolf, Reva, *Andy Warhol, Poetry, and Gossip in the 1960s* (Chicago: University of Chicago Press, 1997).

• Bonnefoy, François and Sarah Clément, *Alechinsky* (Paris: Galerie Nationale du Jeu de Paume, 1998).

• Westgeet, Helen, *Zen in the Fifties: Interaction in Art Between East and West* (London: Reaktion Books, 1998).

• Jacobsen, Karen (ed.), *Radical Past: Contemporary Art & Music in Pasadena, 1960-1974* (Pasadena: Armory Center for the Arts and Art Center College, 1999).

• Alechinsky, Pierre, *Alechinsky* (Valencia: IVAM, Instituto Valenciano de Arte Moderno, 2000).

• Action, David, *The Stamp of Impulse: Abstract Expressionist Prints* (Worchester: Worcester Art Museum, 2001).

• Alechinsky, Pierre, *Des deux mains: Traits et portraits* (Paris: Mercure de France, 2004).

• Bourguignon, Katherine, *American Artists' Books in Europe, 1960-2000* (Giverny: Musée d'Art Americain, 2004).

• Chicha, Céline and Marie-Françoise Quignar (eds.), *Les Impressions de Pierre Alechinsky* (Paris: Bibliothèque nationale de France, 2005).

• Alechinsky, Pierre, *Alechinsky Les Affiches* (Lausanne: Ides et Calendes, 2007).

• De Groof, Piet, *Le général situationniste* (Paris: Allia, 2007).

• Abadie, Daniel, Hélène Cixous and Pierre Alechinsky, *Alechinsky: Les ateliers du midi* (Paris: Musée Granet, 2010).

• Couvreur, Aurélie, *Asger Jorn: un artiste libre* (Lausanne: La Bibliothèque des Arts / Fondation de l'Hermitage, 2012).

• Dervaux, Isabelle, *Dan Flavin: Drawing* (New York and Munich: The Morgan Library & Museum and Hirmer Verlag GmbH, 2012).

• Zhaoling, Fang, *Vigorous and Fresh Chinese Ink Painting* (Hong Kong: Aliasan Fine Arts, 2012).

• Shan, Zhang (ed.), *Chinese Ink Painting in America* (Hangzhou: China Academy of Fine Art Press, 2013).

• Mulroney, Lucy, *Reading Andy Warhol: Author Illustrator Publisher* (Berlin: Hatje Cantz Verlag, 2014).

• Alechinsky, Pierre, *ALECHINSKY N 225* (Paris: Connaissance des arts, 2014).

• Kurczynski, Karen and Karen Friis (eds.), *Expo Jorn: Art is a Festival!* (Silkeborg: Museum Jorn, 2014).

• Lefebvre, Éric, *Paris. Chinese Painting: Legacy of the 20th Century Chinese Masters* (Hong Kong: Hong Kong Museum of Art, 2014).

• Weiguang, Lin and Zhang Yan (eds.), *Shanghai/ Paris: Modern Art of China* (Shanghai: Shanghai Fine Arts Publishing, 2014).

• King, Daphne (ed.), *Alisan Fine Arts: Thirty-Five Years* (Hong Kong: Alisan Fine Arts Limited, 2016).

• Coppel, Stephen, Catherine Daunt and Susan Tallman (eds.), *The American Dream: Pop to the Present* (London: Thames & Hudson and the British Museum, 2017).

• Gingeras, Alison M. (ed.), *The Avant-Garde Won't Give Up: Cobra and its Legacy* (Los Angeles: Blum & Poe, 2017).

• Morell, Lars, *The Art of Asger Jorn* (Aarhus: Aarhaus University Press, 2017).

• Stokvis, Willemijn, *Cobra: A History of a European Avant-Garde Movement: 1948-1951* (Rotterdam: Nai010, 2017).
• Cazé, Sophie, Yann Hendgen, Éric Lefebvre and Françoise Marquet-Zao (eds.), *Zao Wou-Ki collectionneur: L'homme des deux rive* (Paris: Flammarion, 2017).
• Selz, Gabrielle, *Light on Fire: The Art and Life of Sam Francis* (Berkeley: University of California Press, 2021).
• Lefebvre, Éric and Maël Bellec (eds.), *L'encre en mouvement: Une histoire de la peinture chinoise au XXe siècle* (Paris: Paris Musées, 2022).

MISCELLANY AND EPHEMERA

• Alechinsky, Pierre, *Walasse Ting* (Brussels: Galerie Taptoe, 1956).
• Weng, Wango, *Walasse Ting. Paintings* (New York: Galerie Chalette, 1957).
• Ting, Walasse, *Walasse Ting* (New York: Martha Jackson Gallery, 1959).
• Ting, Walasse, *Walasse Ting: Ölbilder* (Munich: Galerie van der Loo, 1961).
• Ting, Walasse, *3 x Ting* (New York: Lefebre Gallery, 1965).
• Alechinsky, Pierre, "Ting's Studio, New York (projections de Ting)," *Les Poquettes volantes*, vol. 14, 1967.
• Ting, Walasse, *Walasse Ting: Recent Paintings* (New York: Lefebre Gallery, 1969).
• Ting, Walasse, *Ting* (New York: Lefebre Gallery, 1971).
• Alechinsky, Pierre, *Walasse Ting: nude exhibition* (Paris: Galerie Adrien Maeght, 1974).
• Ting, Walasse, *The Ting Girls: New York 1973–74* (Bern: Kornfeld und Klipstein, 1975).
• Alechinsky, Pierre, *Ting* (Antwerp: Lens Fine Art, 1978).
• Alechinsky, Pierre, *Walasse Ting: Recent Paintings. Very Chinese* (New York: Lefebre Gallery, 1980).

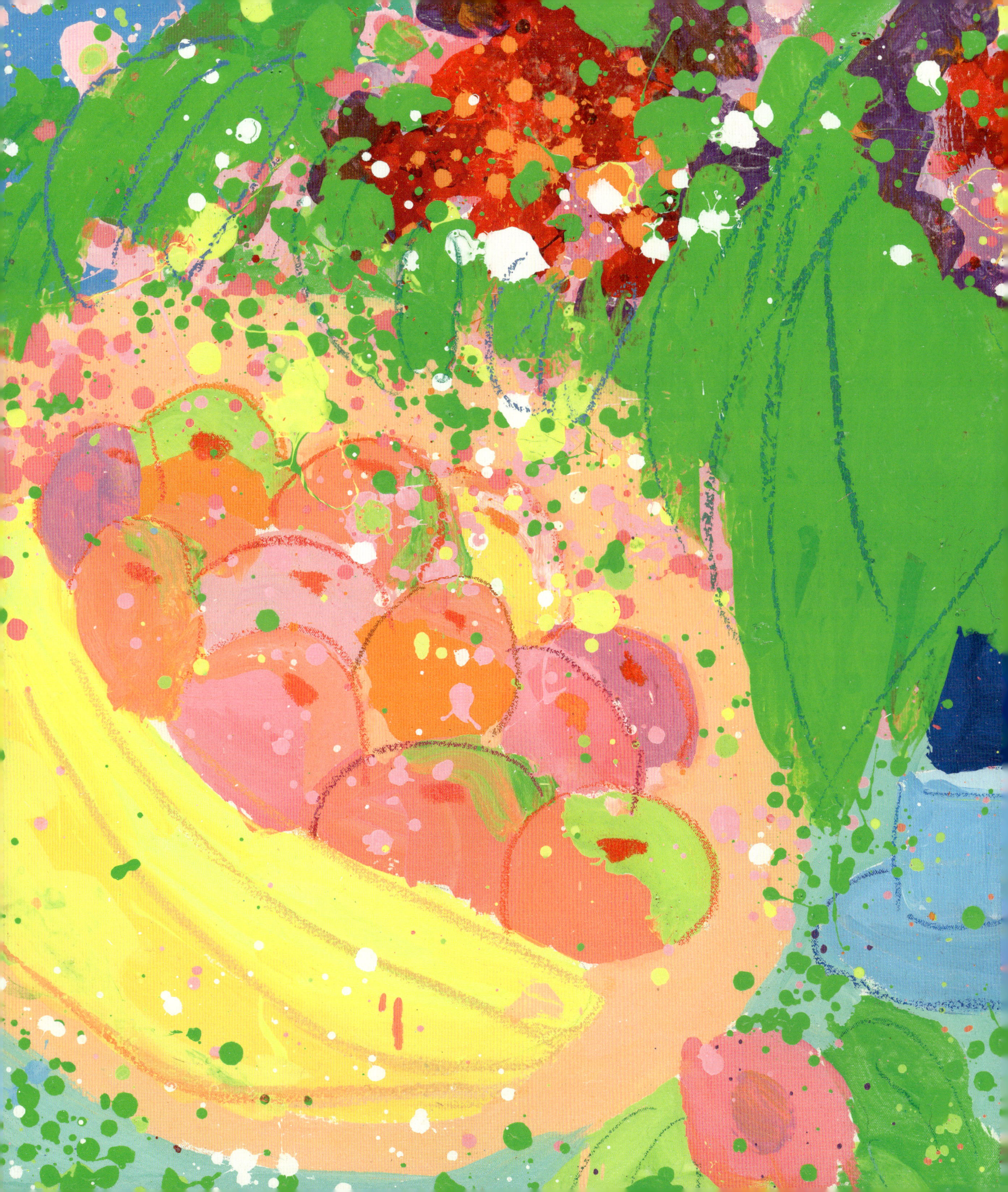

Upon joining NSU Art Museum Fort Lauderdale in early 2021, I submerged myself in the Museum's Golda and Meyer Marks Cobra Collection, home to works by Walasse Ting and a Cobra universe. I thank Stephen Marks and Linda Nathan Marks, and their partners Joan Marks and Berenice Fisher, for their continued stewardship of their parents' monumental legacy, and all they have done to make our exhibitions, research and care of this collection possible.

Thank you to our Director and Chief Curator Bonnie Clearwater, who granted me the life-changing experience of engaging with this historic collection and contributing to our institution. I am grateful for the opportunity and for her prescient recognition of this much needed reconsideration of Walasse Ting. I extend my sincere thanks to Nancy Bryant and Jerry Taylor, whose gracious endowment has made it possible for me to be here.

I am unable to express the extent of my gratitude to Mia and Jesse Ting. Spending time in their world has been nothing but joy. I have felt the abundant generosity of their father in all they have shared with me. Their support has been unparalleled, and I profoundly appreciate their allowing me to wholly engage in their father's life and work. I also thank Alexandra Stonehill, for graciously giving her time and support to this endeavor.

When I began my work with the Museum's Cobra Collection, the first thing I wanted to do was go straight to the source and seek out the group's last living member: Pierre Alechinsky. Engaging with Alechinsky has been a privilege, and I am honored to have worked with him on a 2022 exhibition of his art in conversation with that of Keith Haring, and to be able to continue our conversations in the making of this Ting retrospective. It was my study of Alechinsky that originally led me to Walasse Ting; it was the one name kept cropping up throughout my research. It was Ting who introduced Alechinsky to the "corporeal way of painting," encouraged him to travel to Japan to observe the master calligraphers, taught him his signature *marouflage* technique and for 40 years, worked side-by-side with Ting on their animated "four handed paintings." As I dug through the archive of Alechinsky's gallerist, John Lefebre, I again saw more and more of Ting, and was subsequently baffled to learn that he had never had a solo museum exhibition in the U.S. I did not have to spend much time with the work for it to become abundantly clear that this was in dire need of correction. This project would not have happened without the guidance of Pierre Alechinsky and the encouragement of Marion Lefebre, Marlène Brody and Kristen Accola. Their support has been invaluable.

From its inception, this project has been fostered by the work of my colleagues across the museum, nothing would be possible without their dedicated efforts. Thank you to Jordyn Newsome for being a great collaborator and the most effective organizer I have ever encountered.

I thank Rebecca Vaughn and Caroline McNabb for their extreme diligence and patience in caring for Ting's treasures. Thank you to David Guidi for his many hours spent documenting the contents of this book, to Chuck Ross for always being a helping hand, and to our art handling team: Oliver Loaiza, Chris Byrd, Marcos Cherlo, Anthony Costa, Vincent Miranda, Aven Schnitzius, Edward Oh and Geoff Vick, for their endless hard work and magic-making in turning our exhibition hopes into reality. I thank Tristan Trivett, Leila Murray, Charlotte Carter and Cathie Conn for their research and keen eye for detail in putting together the many checklists, citings and reconfigurations of myriad material within this book. Thank you to Xiao (Amanda) Ju for her enlivened contribution to this book, to Jeffrey Sturges for his dedicated work documenting the Ting estate, and to Todd Bradway for his eagle eye. I am grateful to John Robinson for being so accommodating with our many visits to Ting's trove. Thank you to Daphne King Yao and Pansy Chiu of Alisan Fine Arts, along with Lily Lee and Jeffrey Lee of Longmen Art Projects, for their guidance across Ting's terrain. I extend my appreciation to Lesley Ma for her counsel and support of this project. To the Skira team, thank you for nurturing this project and putting together this beautiful publication.

An enormous thank you goes to the sponsors and donors who recognized the importance of this project and committed to making this show happen. To those who wish to remain anonymous, your generosity is remarkable. Thank you to Nora and Guy Barron (for so many reasons), Eric Barron and Wenise Wong, Marlène Brody, the Funding Arts Broward Foundation, Marion Lefebre and Robert S. Pynoos, Stephen and Joan Marks, Linda Nathan Marks and Berenice Fisher, Caroline Cruise and David Stonehill, Judith Stonehill, Dorothy Lichtenstein and the Imperfect Family Foundation, and to Debra Burchett-Lere, Beth Ann Whittaker-Williams, John Seed and The Sam Francis Foundation; I am deeply grateful. Thank you to the individuals and institutions who graciously loaned their invaluable artworks to this exhibition. I give heartfelt thanks once again to our private lenders, to Guy and Nora Barron, Marlène Brody, Anette Birch, and to Tracey Bashkoff, Katherine Brinson and David Horowitz of the Guggenheim Museum; Lucas Haberkorn at Museum Jorn; and Rein Wolfs and Sarah-Jane Stockings of the Stedelijk Museum.

Thank you to my parents, Roberta and Gary Wolens, my brothers Fred, Zachary and Jared, for a lifetime of encouragement and to my friends who have been a constant source of compassion. I am indebted to Alison Gingeras for opening up this world to me. And a monumental thank you to Adam Rife for his support, both intellectual and emotional, that has kept me afloat.

This project is dedicated to the memory of Walasse and Natalie Ting.

Ariella Wolens

Cover
Untitled, mid-1980s
Acrylic and Chinese ink on rice paper
38 × 70 in. / 96.5 × 177.8 cm
Private Collection, Amsterdam

Front endpaper
Walasse Ting's studio copy of *Parrot Jungle*
brochure front and back cover, 1980s.
Courtesy of Debra Mumaw
and the Scherr Family

Back endpaper
Flamingos at Parrot Jungle, interior image
from Walasse Ting's studio copy of *Parrot
Jungle* brochure, 1980s
Courtesy of Debra Mumaw
and the Scherr Family

Art director
Luigi Fiore

Design
Anna Cattaneo

Editorial coordination
Emma Cavazzini

Copy editing
Filomena Moscatelli

Layout
Barbara Galotta

First published in Italy in 2023 by
Skira editore S.p.A.
Palazzo Casati Stampa
via Torino 61
20123 Milano
Italy

All works by Walasse Ting © 2023 Walasse
Ting / Artists Rights Society (ARS), New York
© 2023 NSU Art Museum Fort Lauderdale
© 2023 The authors for their texts
© 2023 Skira editore, Milano
© 2023 Pierre Alechinsky / Artists Rights
Society (ARS), New York / ADAGP, Paris
© 2023 Karel Appel Foundation / Artists
Rights Society (ARS), New York / c/o
Pictoright Amsterdam
© 2023 Donation Jorn, Silkeborg / Artists
Rights Society (ARS), New York / VISDA
© 1964 Kiki Kogelnik Foundation. All rights
reserved
Artwork © 2023 Sam Francis Foundation,
California/ Artists Rights Society (ARS),
New York
© Estate of Roy Lichtenstein
© 2022 Succession H. Matisse / Artists Rights
Society (ARS), New York
© Claes Oldenburg and Coosje van
Bruggen / Courtesy the Oldenburg van
Bruggen Foundation
Courtesy Pierre Alechinsky Archives
Carnegie Museum of Art
Courtesy Alisan Fine Arts
© ESQUIRE Chinese edition
Collection Fotomuseum Antwerpen
Sam Francis Papers, Getty Research Institute,
Los Angeles
Courtesy of the Lefebre Gallery Archives
Courtesy Deborah Mumaw
The Palace Museum, Beijing, China

All rights reserved under international
copyright conventions.
No part of this book may be reproduced or
utilized in any form or by any means,
electronic or mechanical, including
photocopying, recording, or any information
storage and retrieval system, without
permission in writing
from the publisher.

Printed and bound in Italy. First edition

ISBN: 978-88-572-5135-6

Distributed in USA, Canada, Central
& South America by ARTBOOK | D.A.P.
75 Broad Street Suite 630, New York,
NY 10004, USA.
Distributed elsewhere in the world
by Thames and Hudson Ltd.
181A High Holborn, London WC1V 7QX,
United Kingdom

www.skira.net

Photographic Credits
All works and illustrations courtesy
of the Estate of Walasse Ting unless
noted otherwise.

Pierre Alechinsky: p. 8
Zachary Balber: pp. 27, 77
Nico Delaive: p. 148
Suzi Embo: fig. 1 p. 117
Aaron Farley: p. 84
David Guidi: front endpaper, back endpaper,
fig. 11 p. 48, figs. 23 and 24 p. 58, pp. 79, 113,
116, figs. 2 and 3 p. 118, fig. 6 p. 120, fig. 7
p. 121, fig. 8 p. 122, fig. 10 p. 123, figs. 11
and 12 p. 124, pp. 126–131, 149, 151
Eddie Jim: p. 60
John Lefebre: fig. 5 p. 157
David Regen: p. 86
Angelika Rinnhofer: p. 70, figs. 1 and 2 p. 154
Michiel Elsevier Stokmans: pp. 6–7, 24–25,
fig. 8 p. 46, pp. 67, 152–153
Jeffrey Sturges: cover, pp. 20–23, 28–39,
fig. 9 p. 47, figs. 13 and 14 p. 50, fig. 17 p. 54,
pp. 73, 76, 78, 80, 83, 85, 87, pp. 90–93,
98-101, 103, 106, 107, 110–112, 114–115,
134–141, 146–147, fig. 4 p. 156
Jesse Ting: fig. 4 p. 16
Mia Ting: fig. 22 p. 58
Natalie Ting: figs.1 and 2 p. 15, fig. 7 p. 17,
fig. 10 p. 47
Walasse Ting: fig. 3 p. 15, figs. 5 and 6 p. 16,
fig. 16 p. 53, p. 168
Joshua White: p. 72

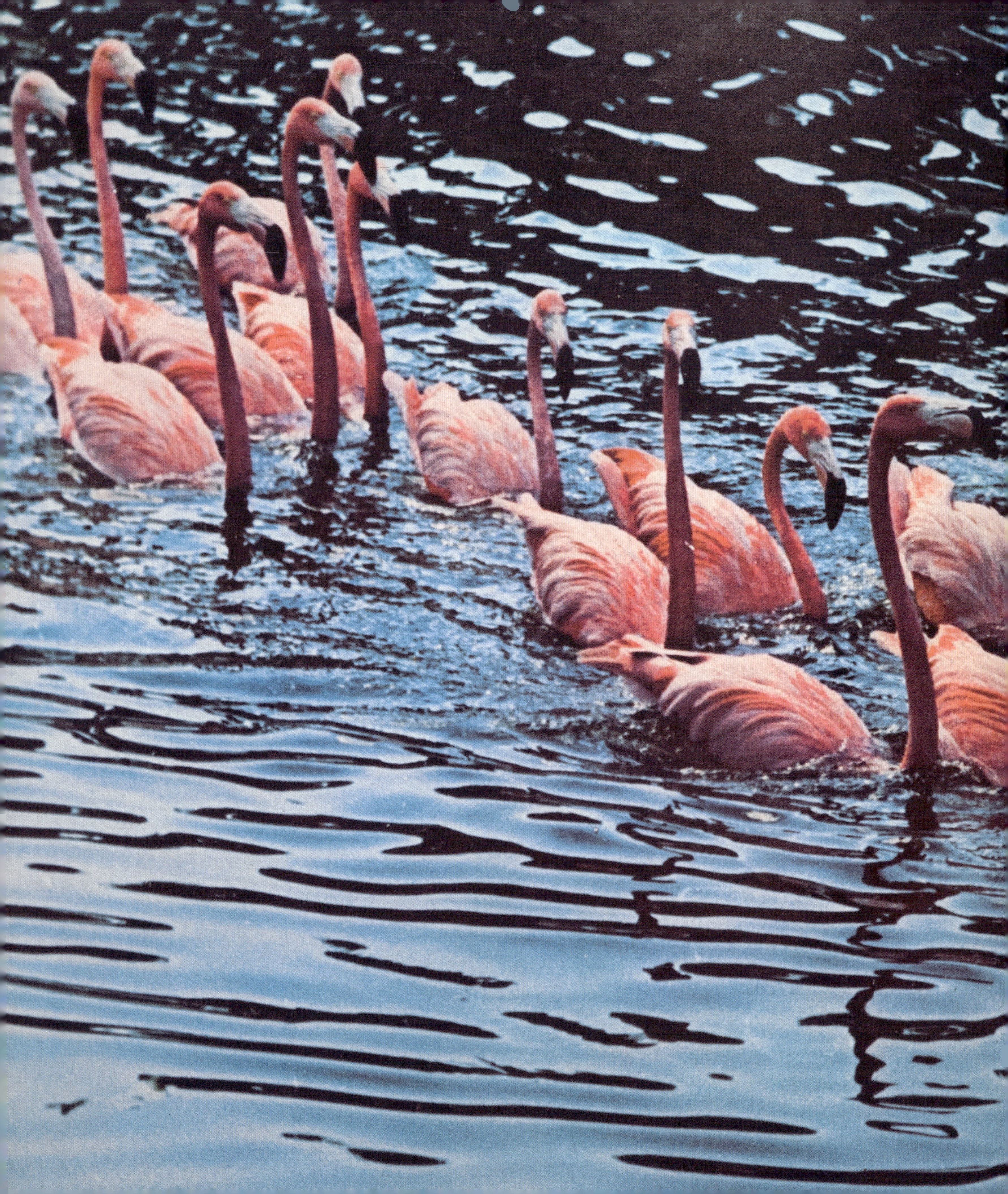